Theory and History in the Human and Social Sciences

Series Editor
Jaan Valsiner, 133 Essex Drive, Chapel Hill, NC, USA

Theory and History in the Human and Social Sciences fills the gap in the existing coverage of links between new theoretical advancements in the social and human sciences and their historical roots. Making that linkage is crucial for interdisciplinary synthesis across the disciplines of psychology, anthropology, sociology, history, semiotics, and the political sciences. In contemporary human sciences of the 21st century, there exists increasing differentiation between neurosciences and all other sciences that are aimed at making sense of complex social, psychological, and political processes. This series serves the purpose of (1) coordinating such efforts across the borders of existing human and social sciences, (2) providing an arena for possible inter-disciplinary theoretical synthesis, (3) bringing to the attention of our contemporary scientific community innovative ideas that have been lost in the dustbin of history for no good reason, and (4) providing an arena for international communication between social and human scientists across the world.

Marc Antoine Campill • Natalie Jancosek
Teppei Tsuchimoto
Editors

New Paths in Trajectory Equifinality Modelling

Unity Through Individuality

Springer

Editors
Marc Antoine Campill
Department of Humanities, Philosophical and Training
University of Salerno
Fisciano, Italy

Natalie Jancosek
Senior Researcher
Fondazione Jaan Valsiner: University for the Future
Salerno, Italy

Teppei Tsuchimoto
Eminent Associate Professor
Research Organization of Open Innovation & Collaboration
Ritsumeikan University
Kyoto, Japan

ISSN 2523-8663 ISSN 2523-8671 (electronic)
Theory and History in the Human and Social Sciences
ISBN 978-3-032-25854-0 ISBN 978-3-032-25855-7 (eBook)
https://doi.org/10.1007/978-3-032-25855-7

This Springer imprint is published by the registered company Springer Nature Switzerland AG
The registered company address is: Gewerbestrasse 11, 6330 Cham, Switzerland

To those who face the complexity of the world...
To those who play in the garden between reality and imagination...
To those who struggle to grasp the brilliance of a life...
To those who savor the fragrance of TEA (but not the tea).
To all curious minds, who seek knowledge…
To all knowers, who are losing themselves in thoughts…
To all brilliant thinkers, with an open mind…
To all open-minded, who explore beyond the familiar.
To those who do not choose to blindly believe in facts and knowledge...
To those who do not stagnate in arrogance and ignorance...
To those who strive to grow beyond what is believed to be impossible...
We hope that in here you will find the inspiration for novelty.

Preface

The Trajectory Equifinality Approach (TEA) has a birthday. It was on the day when the symposium *"Cultural Psychology and Various Aspects of Human Relationships"* was held at Ritsumeikan University. On that occasion, I came up with the idea of applying the concept of *equifinality in development* (Valsiner, 2001; Fig. 3.4; p. 62) to the analysis of my own data. The date was January 25, 2004. At the invitation of Jaan Valsiner, I participated in a symposium at the 28th International Congress of Psychology (ICP), held in Beijing in August of that year, where I presented the Trajectory Equifinality Model (TEM) together with two of my students (Sato et al., 2004).

At the core of the Trajectory Equifinality Model (TEM) lies a simple yet powerful idea: to treat the equifinality point (EFP) as a research question and to trace the multiple possible pathways that lead toward it. This foundational concept was further developed through collaborative efforts following its initial presentation. The article by Valsiner and Sato (2006), as well as the theses written by my graduate and undergraduate students at the time—Yuko Yasuda, Ayae Kido, and Saori Takada—helped refine the theoretical structure of the model. One such development was the concept of the *Polarized Equifinality Point (Polarized EFP)*. Strictly speaking, this notion slightly deviates from the original definition of equifinality, which simply refers to the existence of multiple routes toward a common endpoint. However, by incorporating the possibility of *not* reaching the equifinality point—introducing unrealized goals as a dimension—the model evolved into a two-dimensional representation of life trajectories.

During the subsequent development of TEM, some of Jaan Valsiner's ideas were also integrated into the framework. A notable example is the concept of the *Promoter Sign* (Valsiner, 2004). Inspired by the role of promoter genes in genetics, this notion was conceived as a sign that facilitates the emergence of new I-positions within the dialogical self. It is neither a stimulus that directly triggers reactions nor a force that compels action; rather, it is a semiotic device that promotes future-oriented activity through imaginative anticipation. The term "sign" here refers not to a structuralist or semiotic symbol in the traditional sense, but to a Vygotskian sign—a tool embedded in human psychological development. In this way, the Promoter Sign clarifies the temporal function of signs for human beings by bringing the dimension of time explicitly into the Vygotskian perspective.

By incorporating additional frameworks such as the Three-Layer Model of Genesis (TLMG) and Historically Structured Inviting (HSI), the broader umbrella of the Trajectory Equifinality Approach (TEA) was gradually established. While the acronym "TEA" may evoke the image of a beverage, its very status as a common noun has the unexpected advantage of preventing trademark registration, thus preserving its open and academic character. It now seems increasingly plausible that, in the near future, the term *Japanese TEA* will no longer be associated with a drink, but rather be recognized internationally—indeed, transnationally—as a distinctive and evolving mode of qualitative inquiry.

In the field of (developmental) psychology, there have been few methodologies that allow us to depict life trajectories without abstracting away the dimension of time. The conceptual breakthrough underlying the Trajectory Equifinality Approach (TEA) may well be described as a "Columbus's egg" moment—an idea that seems simple in hindsight, yet had not been realized before. TEA has significantly enriched the landscape of qualitative methodology, not only by expanding its conceptual repertoire but also by deepening its application across a wide range of disciplines. In Japan, TEA has secured its place as a leading qualitative research methodology. More than 300 scholars have gathered under the umbrella of the TEA and the Society for Qualitative Inquiry, engaging in ongoing collaborative inquiry. The model resonates with the Japanese cultural inclination to liken life to the flow of a river—a metaphor deeply rooted in the national psyche.Yet, its influence is by no means confined to Japan. Through the scholarly networks developed by Jaan Valsiner, TEA has gained traction in several European countries and in Brazil, among other regions. It is a true source of happiness to know that so many like-minded colleagues are working together around the world. Increasingly, researchers from abroad are also coming to Japan to study and receive guidance in this approach.

It gives me great pleasure that this volume is being edited and published in English by three scholars from the younger generation: Dr. Tsuchimoto from Japan, and Campill and Jancosek from Europe. With a shared aim of bridging empirical research on TEA conducted in Japan and its theoretical applications in Europe, the editors have assembled a collection that not only presents new methodological developments within TEA, but also explores its potential applications in previously unexplored fields. Until now, the only comprehensive English-language volume on TEA has been the 2016 book (Sato, T. et al., 2016). For that reason alone, this new publication represents a significant contribution to the growing body of international TEA scholarship.

As with many new ideas, the development of TEA was not without its challenges. Along the way, we occasionally encountered misunderstandings—even reactions bordering on ridicule. Such responses, however, have now become little more than anecdotes we can laugh about. For a brief account of this trajectory, see Sato, T. et al. (2021). Among the editors of this volume, Dr. Tsuchimoto has distinguished himself as a rising scholar by proposing Auto-TEM, an innovative method that integrates the Trajectory Equifinality Model with autoethnography, thereby opening new horizons for TEA. As this development illustrates, TEA remains an evolving framework. It is my sincere hope that this book will inspire readers from various backgrounds and contribute to the continued growth and refinement of TEA.

Osaka, Japan Tatsuya Sato

References

Sato, T., Mori, N., & Valsiner, J. (2016). *Making of the future: The Trajectory Equifinality Approach in cultural psychology*. Information Age Publishing.

Sato, T., Tsuchimoto, T., Yasuda, Y., Kido, A. (2021). Jaan Valsiner in Japan: The Trajectory Equifinality Approach (TEA). In B. Wagoner, B. A. Christensen, C. Demuth (Eds.) *Culture as process*. Springer. https://doi.org/10.1007/978-3-030-77892-7_39

Sato, T., Yasuda, Y., & Kido, A. (2004, August 12). *Historically structured sampling (HSS) model: A contribution from cultural psychology*. The 28th International Congress of Psychology (Oral Presentation at the Symposium), Beijing, China.

Valsiner, J. (2001). *Comparative study of human cultural development*. Infancia y Aprendizaje.

Valsiner, J. (2004, July 12). *The Promoter Sign: Developmental transformation within the structure of Dialogical Self*. Paper presented at the Biennial Meeting of the International Society for the Study of Behavioural Development (ISSBD), Gent (Symposium Developmental aspects of the dialogical self Hubert Hermans, Convener).

Valsiner, J., & Sato, T. (2006). Historically Structured Sampling (HSS): How can psychology's methodology become tuned in to the reality of the historical nature of cultural psychology? In J. Straub, C. Kölbl, D. Weidemann, & B. Zielke (Eds.) *Pursuit of meaning. Advances in cultural and cross-cultural psychology* (pp. 215–251). Transcript Verlag. Accessed November 13, 2025, from http://www.psy.ritsumei.ac.jp/~satot/TEA/valsiner_Sato_HSS_2006.pdf

Short Story

Ayaka's TEA party

The basics of the **t**rajectory **e**quifinality **a**pproach

あやかのティーパーティ

複線径路等至性アプローチの基本

Storyboard by ***Campilli Marc Antoine*** and ***Teppei Tsuchimoto***
Translation into Japanese by ***Teppei Tsuchimoto***
Illustration by ***Campili Marc Antoine***

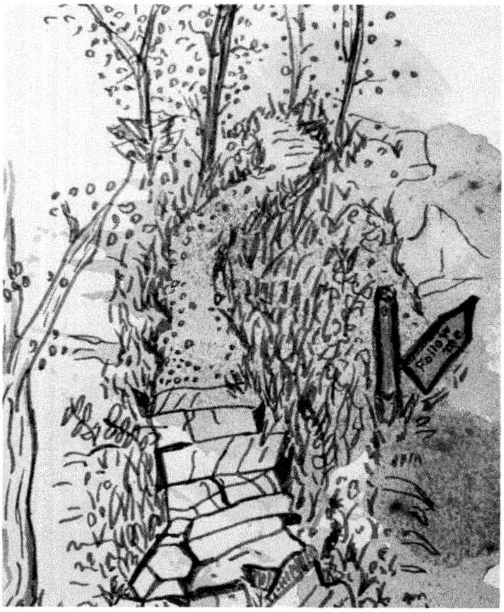

Today we are having Tea with Ayaka.

Let’s go!

今日はあやかとのティーパーティ。

さあ出発**!**

<u>Ayaka</u> "Welcome to my tea party!"
<u>Guest</u> "Ohh it looks beautiful! We have all kinds of Tea: Black Tea, Green Tea, Herbal Tea… But What is that?"

Ayaka's Dad brought a Paper sheet. What is written on it?

<u>Dad</u> "Trajectory equifinality approach"
<u>Guest</u> "Ohh that is strange Tea!"
<u>Guest</u> "Ayaka, can you explain to us what that TEA is?"

<u>あやか</u> 「私のティーパーティへようこそ!」
<u>お客さん</u> 「わあ、とっても素敵!ここにはたくさんのお茶があるよ。紅茶に緑茶に、ハーブティー!…… ところで、これは何?」

そこにあやかのパパが、一切れの紙を持ってきました。何が書かれているのでしょう?

<u>パパ</u> 「複線径路等至性アプローチ(略して、TEA)」
<u>お客さん</u> 「わあ、不思議なティーだね!」
<u>お客さん</u> 「あやか、みんなに、このティーについて教えてくれるかい?」

Ayaka “Yesterday Mom and Dad played with me. Mom told me to play a Giraffe and I started to crawl and transform into a Giraffe ‘Like this.’”
Guest “So, Trajectory in TEA means becoming a Giraffe?”
Dad “Sometimes… But it is more the expectation of how something will happen!”
Ayaka “Like I saw a Giraffe in a zoo. It was huge. I wanted to be a giraffe, so I tried to be tall. I saw the giraffe in my mind. Then I tried to move like it.
Dad “And like Mom asking you to play a Giraffe?”
Ayaka “Yes”

あやか 「私がパパとママと昨日遊んだとき、ママが、キリンさんになって!って言ったんだ。だから私は、キリンさんに変身したの。こんなふうに!」
お客さん 「つまり、キリンさんになることが、ティーの径路ってこと?」
パパ 「そうかもね……でも、何かが起こるかも知れない、っていう期待の方が大事だよ!」
あやか 「私が動物園でキリンさんを見たときみたいにね。キリンさんは大きかったし、キリンさんになりたかったから、わたしも大きくなろうとしたの。心の中にキリンさんがいたんだよ。それで、キリンさんみたいに動いたの。」
パパ 「ママに、『キリンさんになって!』って言われたときのことだね。」
あやか 「うん。」

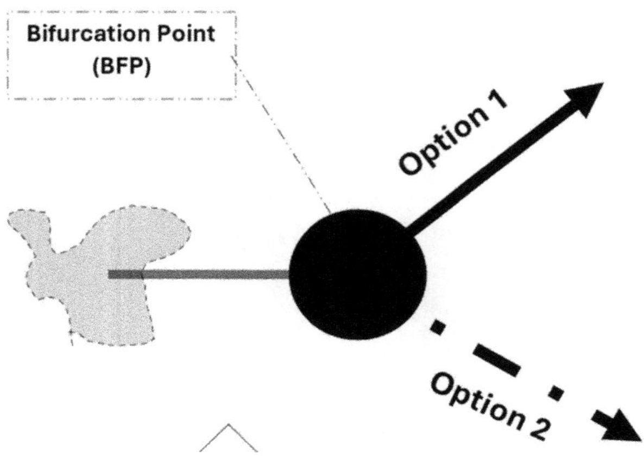

<u>Guest</u> "But What happens, if we have more choices?"
<u>Ayaka</u> "That is a great Question! What happens then, Dad?"
<u>Dad</u> "Well, we call this the Bifurcation point (BFP)"
<u>Guest</u> "And what would that look like?"
<u>Ayaka</u> "Hmm"

<u>お客さん</u> 「じゃあ、もし、もっと沢山の選択肢があれば、何が起こるの?」
<u>あやか</u> 「いい質問だね!何が起こるの、パパ?」
<u>パパ</u> 「、これは分岐点(BFP)と呼ばれているんだ」
<u>お客さん</u> 「それってどんな感じ?」
<u>あやか</u> 「ええとね。」

<u>Dad</u> "Well, yesterday Ayaka was not only a giraffe, but she also played a lion. What do you think did she become afterward?"
<u>Guest</u> "Maybe an elephant?"
<u>Ayaka</u> *"I saw one in the Zoo!"*
<u>Dad</u> "We could believe it, but no. Ayaka decided to give me a shell."

パパ 「そうだ、あやかは昨日、キリンさんだけじゃなくてライオンさんにもなっていたね。そのあとは何になったと思う?」
お客さん 「ゾウさんかな?」
あやか 「動物園でみたよ!」
パパ 「そうかもしれないけど、違ったね。パパに貝殻をくれたんだ。」

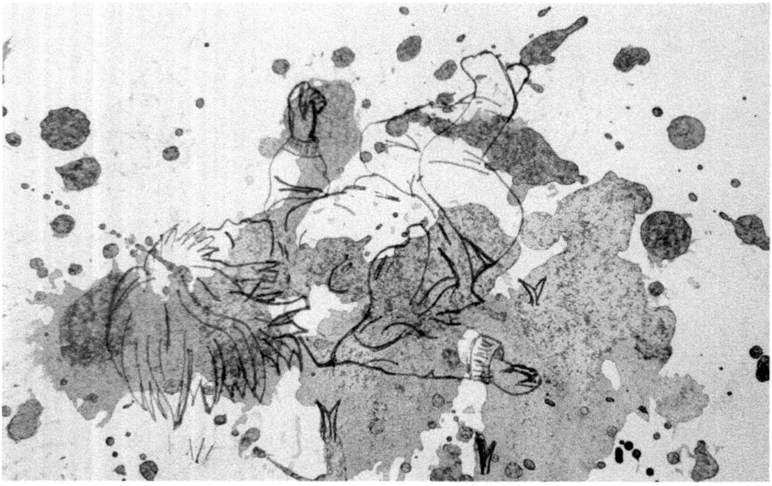

Ayaka "And this means Beef Pie?"
Dad "BFP. It means that in one moment we have more than one possibility to play."
Guest "We can decide how we like to play?"
Dad "Yes. We imagine the past and the future to find ideas. So, also how we could play."

あやか 「つまりそれがビーフパイ?」
パパ 「BFP。一度にひとつだけじゃなくて、いろんなのものになれるってこと」
お客さん 「私たちが、どうなりたいか決められるってこと?」
パパ 「そうそう。私たちは、なにかを考えるとき、過去や未来を想像するんだ。何になりたいかを考えるときにもね。」

Guest “But I expected Ayaka to be an elephant! I would never come up with her playing with shells?”
Ayaka “That is a good observation!”
Dad “Ayaka! Why did you give me a shell?”
Ayaka “Well in the last movie, a girl gave a shell to a friend. I liked that!”

お客さん 「でも、あやかはゾウになると思ってた!貝殻で遊ぶなんて思いもしなかったよ?」
あやか 「たしかに!」
パパ 「あやか!どうしてパパに貝殻をくれたの?」
あやか 「えっとね、前に見た映画で、女の子がお友達に貝殻をあげていたの。わたし、それが大好きだったの。」

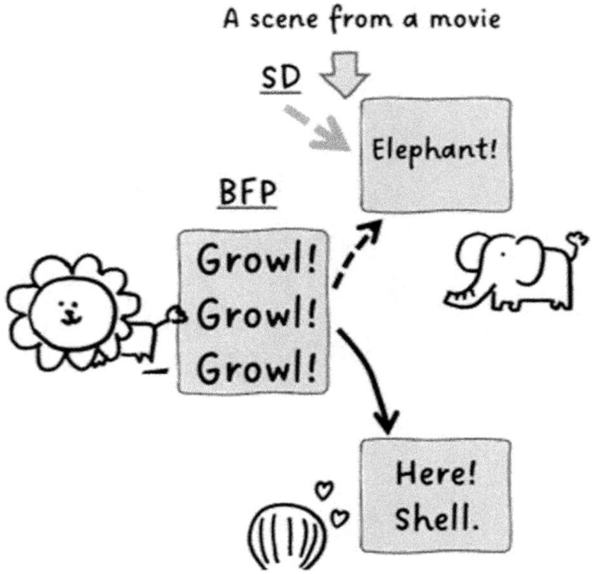

Dad "I see. What we see here is that Ayaka experienced a Social Direction (SD). Maybe Ayaka acted following the expectations of the movie. Considering the movie as part of her environment (society). The movie offered her an, by the environment (society) expected idea of what she could do."

Guest "And the Zoo?"

パパ 「そうか、あやかは、このとき社会的方向づけ(SD)を経験したんだね。きっとあやかは、映画のやっているのと同じように貝殻を渡したんだろうね。映画は、あやかにとっての環境(社会)だからね。つまり、映画は、環境(社会)によって期待された、『あやかが何ができるのか』の考えを提供しているね。」

お客さん 「動物園は?」

Dad	"The Zoo is a little bit different. We have been with Ayaka in the Zoo, and she liked giraffes and lions a lot. If Dad and Mum hadn't taken Ayaka to the zoo, she might never have met this kind of animals.
Ayaka	"Got it! It is called Social Guidance."
Dad	"Yes, and at the same time, it is also a …"
Ayaka	"SD!"

パパ	「動物園は少し違っているね。この前、あやかと一緒に動物園に行ったとき、あやかはキリンさんやライオンさんが大好きになったんだ。でも、パパとママがあやかを動物園に連れて行かなければ、キリンさんやライオンさんには会えなかったかもしれないね。」
あやか	「わかった!それはSGだね!」
パパ	「そう、だけどSGでもあるし.....」
あやか	「SDでもあるんだ!」

Guest	"Ohh, that is difficult!"
Dad	"Yes, but we are at the end and soon we will have cake!"
All	"Yeah!!"
Dad	"Cake sounds great?"
Ayaka	"Of course. It is tasty and yummy!"

お客さん	「ああ、これって難しいね!」
パパ	「そうだね、でももうおしまい。もうすぐケーキが食べられるよ!」
みんな	「やった!!」
パパ	「あやかはケーキ好き?」
あやか	「もちろん。とってもおいしいよ!」

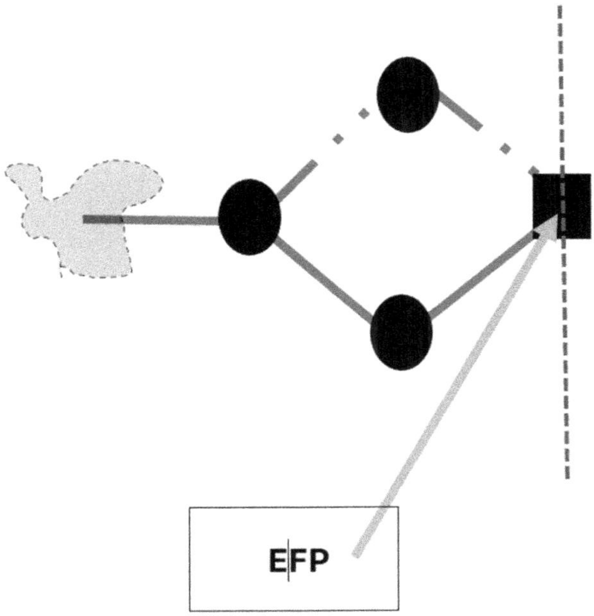

<u>Dad</u> "Well, and this is what we call an Equifinality point (EFP)."
<u>All</u> "A treat we all have been waiting for!"
<u>Dad</u> "Yes, and the goal we have been working towards! Having fun, all together."

<u>パパ</u> 「そして、これは等至点(EFP)っていうんだ。」
<u>みんな</u> 「ずっと待ってたごちそうだ!」
<u>パパ</u> 「そう、そして私たちが目指してきたゴール!みんなで、楽しむこと。」

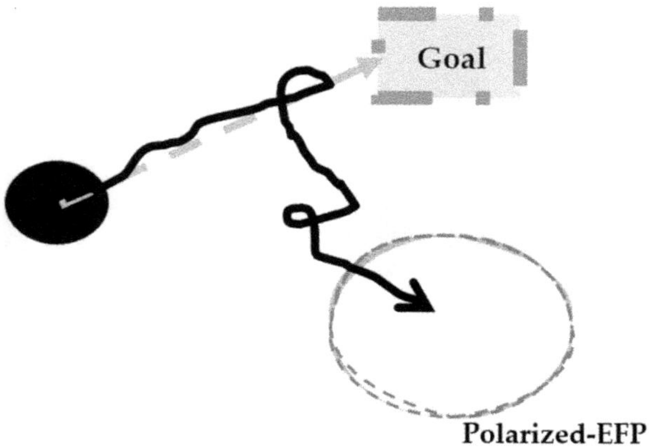

…… ***Something our friends do not need to know on such a funny day is the Polarized-EFP! It represents the moments when we move away from our initial goal. Like leaving the tea table and starting to explore with the others.***

…… こんな楽しい日には、お友達には「両極化された等至点」のことは内緒にしておいてくださいね!これは、最初に目指していたことから離れてしまうことを表しています。例えば、ティーテーブルをほったらかしで、他のお友達と探検に出かけてしまうような。

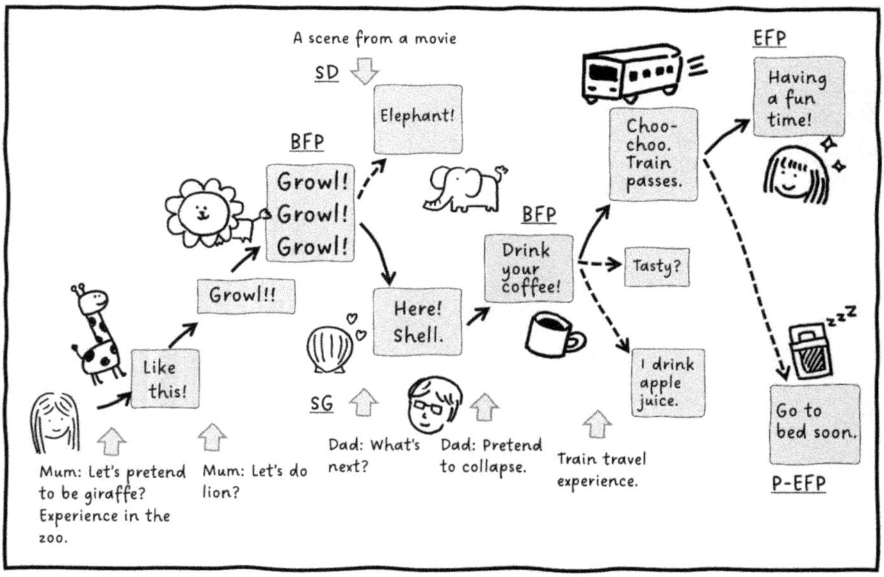

Guest “Hey, wait what is on the other side of Ayaka’s dad’s paper sheet?”
Ayaka “Let’s have a look!”
Dad “This is a TEM a model of yesterday in TEA-style!”
Ayaka “OHH WOW…”

お客さん 「ねえ、待って。あやかのパパの紙の裏には何が描いてあるの?」
あやか 「見てみよう!」
パパ 「これは昨日の出来事をTEM図にしたものだよ!」
あやか 「わあ、すごいね……」

It's your turn:

やってみよう:

Guest “That is so cool! You can collect a lot of nice memories of a day. And also, for those who have played with me, I can imagine ‘what if this had happened’ or ‘what might have happened’!
Guest “Let’s do a TEM by ourselves!”

It’s your turn:

お客さん 「とってもいいね!今日のすてきな思い出をたくさん集めることができるね。それに、一緒に遊んでくれた人のために、『もしこうだったら』ってことや、『こうだったかもしれない』ってことを想像することもできる!」
お客さん 「私たちもTEMを描いてみよう!」

やってみよう:

It’s your turn:

やってみよう：

Dad “That was TEA-time with Ayaka.”
Ayaka “I hope you enjoyed the TEA.”

Take one last sip and on we go.
See you soon.

パパ 「あやかとのティータイムはこれでおしまい。」
あやか 「TEAを楽しんでもらえたでしょうか?」

最後に一口飲んで、さあ出発。
またね。

Contents

The Outbreaking Self from Arts into TEA

Conclusion

Contributors

Dany Boulanger Université du Québec en Outaouais, Outaouais, Canada

Marc Antoine Campill Department of Humanities, Philosophical and Training, University of Salerno, Fisciano, Italy

Rebecca Moura de Almeida Ferreira Carvalho PUC-Campinas Investigates the potential of comics and animations within the field of Psychology, São Paulo, Brazil

Anna Fedorova Sigmund Freud PrivatUniversity, Vienna, Austria

Enno von Fircks Jaan Valsiner Resesarch Foundation, Salerno, Italy

Misato Fukuyama Graduate School of Human Science, Ritsumeikan University, Osaka, Japan

Lisa-Marie Geberth Divine Savior Hospital, Vienna, Austria

Tomoo Hidaka Department of Hygiene and Preventive Medicine, Fukushima Medical University, Fukushima, Japan

Natalie Jancosek Fondazione Jaan Valsiner: University for the Future, Salerno, Italy

Taeko Kamikawa Soka University, Tokyo, Japan

Mami Kanzaki Kyoto University of Education, Kyoto, Japan

Nozomi Kato Fukuyama City University, Hiroshima, Japan

Tamiyo Koyama Graduate School of Human Science, Ritsumeikan University/ Japan Society for the Promotion of Science (JSPS), Osaka, Japan

Kenichi Kubota Kansai University, Suita, Japan

Namrataa Mamgai Department of Human Development and Childhood Studies, Lady Irwin College, University of Delhi, Delhi, India

Giuseppina Marsico University of Salerno, Fisciano, Italy

Taiyo Miyashita The Japan Research Institute, Limited/Ritsumeikan University, Osaka, Japan

Akiyo Nakamoto Konan Women's University, Hyogo, Japan

Fuminori Nakatsubo Hiroshima University, Hiroshima, Japan

Akinobu Nameda Shizuoka University, Shizuoka, Japan

Punya Pillai Department of Human Development and Childhood Studies, Lady Irwin College, University of Delhi, Delhi, India

Sebastian Resch EmPath – Centre for Health and Quality of Life, Vienna, Austria

Tatsuya Sato Ritsumeikan University, Osaka, Japan

Crisleane de Araújo Silva Federal University of Bahia, Salvador, Brazil

Vera Lucia Trevisan de Souza Stricto Sensu Graduate Program in Psychology, Pontifical Catholic University of Campinas (PUC-Campinas), São Paulo, Brazil

Aniko Szeko Sigmund Freud University Vienna, Vienna, Austria

Chihiro Tanaka Teikyo University, Tokyo, Japan

Teppei Tsuchimoto Research Organization of Open Innovation & Collaboration, Ritsumeikan University, Kyoto, Japan

Mila Tuli Institute of Home Economics, University of Delhi, Delhi, India

Megha Verma Department of Human Development and Childhood Studies, Lady Irwin College, University of Delhi, Delhi, India

Xiaohong Zhang Kansai University, Suita, Japan

Introduction

It's TEA-Time: Expressing Incomparable Unity Through Individuality

Marc Antoine Campill, Natalie Jancosek, and Teppei Tsuchimoto

A Brief Introduction to TEA/TEM

The Trajectory Equifinality Approach (TEA), by Jaan Valsiner and Tatsuya Sato, represents a central milestone for cultural psychology and for any related scientific discipline or approach. The potential of this approach is border-crossing, as it assesses individual life courses and thus opens up the space for the consideration of individuality rather than restricting itself to the urge of generalisation. Knowledge, just like the knowledge-carriers and knowledge-surfacers, is unique and dynamic—and through the TEA it has obtained the opportunity to unfold within it. The knowledge constructed within the cultural psychology of dynamic semiosis covers two important termini, the *Trajectory Equifinality Approach* and *Trajectory Equifinality Modelling*.

M. A. Campill (✉)
Department of Humanities, Philosophical and Training, University of Salerno, Fisciano, Italy

N. Jancosek
Senior Researcher, Fondazione Jaan Valsiner: University for the Future, Salerno, Italy

T. Tsuchimoto
Eminent Associate Professor, Research Organization of Open Innovation & Collaboration, Ritsumeikan University, Kyoto, Japan

M. A. Campill et al. (eds.), *New Paths in Trajectory Equifinality Modelling*, Theory and History in the Human and Social Sciences,
https://doi.org/10.1007/978-3-032-25855-7_1

Trajectory Equifinality Approach

Trajectory Equifinality Approach (TEA; Sato, 2017) consists of three components, namely, Trajectory Equifinality Modelling (TEM),[1] Three Layers Model of Genesis (TLMG), and Historically Structured Inviting (HSI). TEM is a method that describes the life trajectories of the developing subject within the flow of irreversible time. TLMG is a model that considers the self in three layers, namely, action, sign, and value, whereas HSI is a method of inviting research participants based on a personal history of the subject.

The critical concepts of TEA are *multilinearity* and *equifinality*, where the natural and traditional social sciences consider the object of the study a closed system. In this system, researchers assume the absence of interaction or exchange between the system and the outside world (environment). Therefore, the relationship between the initial (cause) and final (effect) conditions is determined in a linear manner, which is similar to classical mechanics in physics. In contrast, *open systems* promise interaction and exchange between the system and the outside world. In TEA, people, who are the system that constructs life trajectories, are regarded as an open system. In other words, the leading assumption is that life trajectories are not in causal relationships. For example, an unclear decision-making at a given life moment does not immediately lead to failure in life. A mode of reasoning that linearly relates life experiences (here, unclear decisions and subsequent life failures) is inadequate for understanding human development. The life trajectory of an open system is considered *multilinear* (Valsiner, 2000) with the possibility of taking various trajectories during interaction with the world.

Furthermore, the concept of *equifinality* is crucial to open systems. This concept indicates that people may reach a similar state from different initial conditions and different trajectories over time (Valsiner & Sato, 2006). Two points should be underscored here. First, the developmental view in TEA is fundamentally *epigenetic*. That is, in the Bergsonian's *irreversible time*, there is no repetition of the *same* experience, but only *similar* experiences. In other words, we believe that creativity can be discovered in the "repetitive" experiences. Here, time means *Kairos* time, as Paul Tillich calls it—i.e., subjective, existential, experiencing time. This is one *epistemological creative restriction* that seeks to grasp "time" in the life course. Second, the life course we focus on is assumed to be guided by culture or society. That is, in contrast to Waddington's epigenetic landscape (Waddington, 1957), we assume that rather than an infinite variety of future possibilities, their actualisation is in relation to social, cultural, and historical guidance. Thus, the idea suggests that even if a certain form of power interrupts the life trajectory of a person, such a person can still reach the goal (equifinality point; EFP) using different paths. Therefore, instead of focusing on the causes that influence the results experienced by people (e.g.,

[1] Note that TEM was an acronym for 'Trajectory Equifinality Model' when it was proposed. However, this has now become an abbreviation for 'Trajectory Equifinality Modelling'. This is in recognition of the dynamic and interactive aspects of the process of creating models (TEM diagrams) with others.

being enrolled in college or got married), TEA focuses on the actual or possible trajectories that are available to reach such a condition.

Trajectory Equifinality Modelling

TEM is explained in this section as it is the central method in TEA. In Japan, TEM is being developed as a methodological rather than theoretical model to enable trans-disciplinary dialogue. Indeed, beyond the discipline of psychology from which TEM originated, it has been applied to empirical research in childcare, nursing, language education, disability studies, management, and other fields. With the methodological development of TEM, scholars have proposed various conceptual tools for describing life trajectories. Two concepts of particular importance—the *equifinality point* (EFP) and the *bifurcation point* (BFP)—are briefly described here. EFP refers to a specific history experienced by the participant (e.g., entering college and getting married). In other words, initial interest of the researcher tentatively characterises the experiences of the participants. BFP is essential for TEM, because this concept implicates that life trajectory is non-linear. The BFP occurs when the trajectory branches and signs emerge; I-position dialogs occur (Hermans & Konopka, 2010); and imagination is triggered (Zittoun & Gillespie, 2015). The relationship between these concepts can be drawn as follows.

TEM has a feature in which it can depict life trajectory within the *actual-possible* (vertical axis) and the irreversible time dimension (horizontal axis). It shows the development of individuals towards future goals and how the trajectory moves forward with socio-cultural guidance. This guidance creates the BFP tension (Fig. 1). In TEM it is possible to analyse and describe personal experiences, assuming that they are related to socio-cultural aspects.

Notably, the arrows in the TEM do not represent spatialised, measurable time or direction. Instead, they make us aware of the theoretical assumption of irreversible

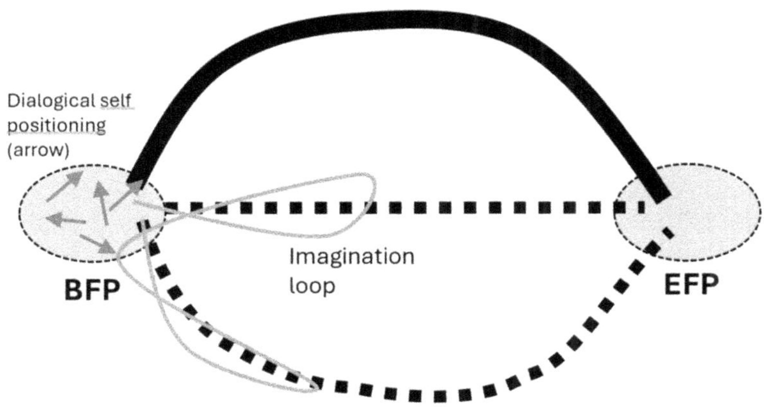

Fig. 1 Diagram of BFP-EFP relationship

time when we describe the TEM diagram. Therefore, it is essential to understand the qualitative time (rather than chronological time) that an individual experiences when making a particular decision.

Dividing the life stories (or histories) into periods from the narrator's perspective is also sometimes a part of the TEM analysis. These periods deepen the qualitative time in the life trajectory of the individual. By dividing the life trajectory into periods based on the transition point for the individual, this enables the analysis to consider developmental and clinical support from the perspective of the person and analytical expansions that focus on specific periods (Yasuda, 2015). These divisions also make it possible to visualise the minimum developmental units over the life course.

TEA as the Origin of Understanding for Contemporary Research and Practice

The TEA approach is celebrating its increasing popularity, especially within life course development research, psychological therapy, and phenomenology of individual experiences. Perhaps another aspect, which contributes to the growing presence of this approach, is the possibility to unfold and express multiple perspectives within individual Trajectory Equifinality Models. Thus, it is most probably only a matter of time until the TEA shall reach new dimensions and lead to a shattering of our fundamental understandings of social sciences and cultural phenomena overall.

There are multiple options for viewing and studying the individual within a society on scientific bases; some approaches highlight individuality and the uniqueness of each story; other ones respect the group and generalise individual experiences into the experiences of many. The TEA emphasises the individuals' experiences and life courses as central elements of the psychological understanding of individual lives within cultures and societies. These are understood as unique, even though the events occurring in individual lives might seem similar. The focus is not strictly directed towards the events but much more on the personal and emotional experiences that accompanied these events and that resulted in a personal change or inner dialogue leading towards a dynamic development within the individual.

The position and viewpoint of each person represent individual perceptions of any given situation, which is why it is possible to obtain unique experiences even in the case of a shared event. The different perceptions result from an interplay of the past, present moment, and a future towards which the present moment is directed (Campill, 2021; Valsiner, 2006, 2009). Just like that, each individual has their own past experiences that range from very pleasant, often recalled memories to experiences that are disliked or ones the individual is indifferent to. Past experiences are well perceived if there is a given context to the palette of possible events. Thus, the cultural context becomes incredibly meaningful, especially if it is one of an important field or activity. The first contact with the given contextual field and first experiences in this area are crucial for establishing a relationship. The direction (e.g.

positivity, negativity, etc.) of these experiences conveys the future trajectories of the relationship between the individual and the life course pathway in time and space. Although the context can be shared by many individuals, each experience is perceived uniquely and embedded into the given person's identity based on the individual inner culture of each one.

The inner culture is the interplay of individual I-positions and counter-positions (Hermans & Konopka, 2010), which exist within each mind and form a complex matter called identity. The content of the identity is a sum of experiences and knowledge one continues to gain on a dynamic continuum. Because of this complex structure, it is possible for individuals to draw personal connections to other humans, things, or activities and thereby become creators of pathways and connections. Such a personal connection defines the base for relations and important events that structure individual existence.

The Trajectory Equifinality Model as a complex tool from cultural psychology allows for research approaches to understand and visualise the studied phenomena and to include the important element of time, which is frequently overlooked or neglected in other research fields. By those means, the understanding of personal pathways can be enhanced and elaborated to deeper and increasingly complex levels, going beyond the observable surface. The uniqueness embarks in the notion of social guidance and social direction, which are accompanied by internal dialogical processes.

The diversity and divergence of human life course trajectories open up the discussion of parallel structures which are present in individuals' minds whereby it is possible for a person to explore the idea of a multitude of personal elements interplaying. The proposition is that multiple trajectories, their alternatives, and continuities allow for individuality to emerge and for a series of social, dialectical, psychological, and cultural phenomena to be uncovered.

The perspectives through which the TEA/TEM shall be approached in this book are directed towards *theory, research,* and *practice*—meaningful and important areas of psychological analysis and applied use.

Exploring Opportunities for TEA/TEM in Theory, Research, and Practice

The Trajectory Equifinality Approach is of novel origin, showing meaningful potential to expand the borders of cultural research and of the understanding of the human mind, life course, and development. The possibilities of extension of TEA meanwhile reach the gates of most scientific domains concerning human living. The practical visualisation of this theoretical field, the TEM, has already established its confidence through the widespread use by researchers, mainly in Japan. Still, the possibilities of further exploring and using TEA/TEM remain open to all interested researchers and practitioners.

Trajectory Equifinality as a Base for Theoretical Development

Theoretical exploration and analysis set the meaningful basis for the exploration of new ideas and phenomena. TEA/TEM are valuable tools for such intentions as they allow for approaching theoretical topics in an in-depth manner, and thus dive far beyond the descriptive surface of such. As so far applied, the TEM is growing out of two central perspective layers in research; these two perspectives are a part of a spectrum-like field where both dimensions are in consideration, while one is at the given time in central focus, and the other one meanwhile explores the collective narrative. The idea is to elaborate the complexity of a phenomenological chain effect, which is often defined as the *experiencing* or *development* of human beings in their environment through their self-dynamics.[2] This is possible through exploring how meaning and meaningfulness arise within everyday things and activities, which then can lead to moving forward on the time continuum.

Through theoretical elaboration of the TEA/TEM, it is possible to address questions that explore personal moments of interest combined with decision-making. By the usage of personal experiences, it is possible to shape cumulative constructs that allow to explore the metaphysical and else purely hypothetical concept of "what-if". Examples are "Adolescents' mental health problems, teacher support, and school adaptation: A qualitative analysis based on the Trajectory Equifinality Model." (Amai, 2022). "This is the real *death-line* and I am still alive: A collaborative reflexivity about life trajectories" (Lehmann et al., 2020), "Equifinality approach to exploring the learning trajectories of language learners and teachers" (Aoyama & Yamamoto, 2021), "Existential Humanistic Leadership (EHL) as a Dialogical Process: Equality of the Non-equality in Organizations" (Fircks, 2020), "Self-regulated Learning from a Cultural Psychology Perspective: Shifting from Strategy to Process with the Trajectory Equifinality Approach" (Masaki, 2023), "Developmental Trajectory Patterns of Chinese Teachers Employing New Teaching Strategies with Thinking Tools" (Zhang et al., 2019), and "Career decision-making as dynamic semiosis: Autoethnographic trajectory equifinality modeling" (Tsuchimoto & Sato, 2024).

Exploring Research Potential Through the Trajectory Equifinality Approach

Once the theoretical analysis is extended to practical application in the given field of interest, researchers as well as their partners can profit from the use of the Trajectory Equifinality Approach. Visible advantages lie in the flexibility that occurs through the open approach of TEA. This opportunity can be particularly interesting for research in the field of psychology, but has the potential to go beyond the borders

[2] The theorem "self-dynamics" originates from the Dialogical Self Theory (James, Hermans) and explores internal multitude of positions which interact and co-exist in dynamic ways, which sets a base for individual development and consistency or change.

of this scientific discipline and to interest other fields as well. Taking into consideration that exploring phenomenological content in whatever scientific context underlies human fallibility and deepens researchers' daily notions of interest, the possibilities of the theoretical extension of TEA to applied research are nearly limitless.

Scientific research with the incorporation of TEA has the possibility to actively acknowledge the importance of the irreversible time continuum on which events of the human life course are happening. Within this continuity, the direction is always set forward on the timeline, without the possibility of return; however, it is within human nature to try to act against this force by compromising their future trajectories. Such actions create interesting phenomena, such as the idea of nostalgia, the urge to come back to certain places to evoke feelings and experiences from the past, or even change one's own future pathways based on past decisions. Further, the hierarchical relation between the positions of the researcher and research partners may be removed, as the role of the researcher shall not be interpretative, but much rather a dialogical supporting influence for the research partners. By this symbiosis, the research focus moves away from observational distortion towards the reception and understanding of the given individual experience.

The Potential and Use of Trajectory Equifinality in Practice

Besides theoretical exploration and applied research, TEA/TEM also finds its way in practical everyday use—such as sport, psychotherapy, coaching, etc. Dynamics which are captured within TEMs' reach from ordinary everyday life events all the way to unique experiences. The symbiosis of commonality and individuality undergoing the process of emergence with respect to the irreversible time axis has widespread opportunities of application. The communication of these situations or processes through an internal or external dialogue results in the identification of an individually suitable TEM which also offers the possibility of the analysis of alternative outcomes. This is particularly beneficial for clients of psychotherapy, coaching, or other acts of healing and self-development. In such a setting, alternative trajectories may be explored and possibly chosen, leading to a change in the given state or mood, e.g. a person suffering from depression who spent most of his days in bed chooses 1 day to get out of bed and thereby explores the possibility of a new pathway for his state. The practice of "hana-TEM" (art-based TEM using natural objects such as flowers and stones), which re-imagines TEM as an everyday healing practice, is creative in this context (Tsuchimoto et al., 2024).

Because of the emphasis on the irreversible timeline, TEMs make it possible to analyse past trajectories and their hypothetical alternatives from the present point of view. Hereby, individuals may return to some meaningful moments from the past and review them using a new perspective which aids in establishing a connection to the self and comprehending individual parts of identity.

Further, the idea of invisible trajectories, which happen in the present moment and result in decisions, is often visible in sports, learning processes, unexpected events, etc. An example could be an athlete who has made a mistake and thus chooses ad hoc an alternative strategy or pathway to compensate for the mistake and still reach the desired outcome of her athletic performance. This trajectory and its alternative may not be obvious to the observers in the exact moment when they are happening; the actor is, however, aware of them and may additionally reconnect to the experience ex post.

Connecting Trajectories of Japanese and European Approaches

This pioneering volume explores the multitude of uses and applications of the Trajectory Equifinality Approach together with Trajectory Equifinality Models. As already mentioned, the origin of this approach is in Japan, where it has grown in popularity over time. Today, an extraordinary community of researchers from multiple scientific fields recognises this approach and applies it to their research endeavours.

Because of its uniqueness and wide range of application possibilities, it is the aim of this volume to enhance the Trajectory Equifinality Approach and open doors for new additions and applications in diverse fields and regions. Most important to this project is the aim to encourage individuals to connect themselves and their endeavours to TEA and thus possibly explore new perspectives for their work. Through this, the possibility of supporting and expanding the meaningfulness of TEA in a multitude of sciences arises. However, the first step is, hopefully, inspiring individuals to give TEA a try and explore their own or others' pathways. This volume may be seen as an open invitation to such an exploration to creative researchers and curious readers.

References

Amai, K. (2022). Adolescents' mental health problems, teacher support, and school adaptation: A qualitative analysis based on the trajectory equifinality model. *International Journal of School & Educational Psychology, 10*(4), 510–526.

Aoyama, T., & Yamamoto, T. (2021). Equifinality approach to exploring the learning trajectories of language learners and teachers. In *Complexity perspectives on researching language learner and teacher psychology* (pp. 282–318).

Campill, M. A. (2021). Towards a wholistic model of identity: Why not a meadow? *Integrative Psychological and Behavioral Science, 55*(1), 112–127.

Fircks, E. F. (2020). Existential humanistic leadership (EHL) as a dialogical process: Equality of the non-equality in organizations. *Integrative Psychological and Behavioral Science, 54*, 719–741.

Hermans, H., & Konopka, A. (2010). *Dialogical self theory: Positioning and counter-positioning in a globalizing society*. Cambridge University Press.

Lehmann, O. V., Hansen, M., & Hurme, H. (2020). This is the real "death-line" AND I am still alive: A collaborative reflexivity about life trajectories. *Culture & Psychology, 26*(4), 819–836.

Masaki, F. (2023). Self-regulated learning from a cultural psychology perspective: Shifting from strategy to process with the trajectory equifinality approach. *Human Arenas*.

Sato, T. (2017). *Collected papers on trajectory equifinality approach*. Chitose Press.

Tsuchimoto, T., Kamikawa, T., Nakamoto, A., Kato, N., & Nakatsubo, F. (2024). 「hana-TEM: アートで描くわたしの径路」:TEAと質的探究学会第2回大会・研究交流委員会企画ワークショップ ('hana-TEM: Describing my trajectory through art': A workshop organized by the research exchange committee of the Japanese association of TEA for qualitative inquiry during the 2nd meeting.). *Qualitative Inquiry and Social Implementation, 1*, 66–77. https://www.ritsumei.ac.jp/file.jsp?id=613263 [in Japanese]

Tsuchimoto, T., & Sato, T. (2024). Career decision-making as dynamic semiosis: Autoethnographic trajectory equifinality modeling. *Culture & Psychology, 30*(1), 48–69.

Valsiner, J. (2000). *Culture and human development*. SAGE.

Valsiner, J. (2006). Dangerous curves in knowledge construction within psychology: Fragmentation of methodology. *Theory & Psychology, 16*(5), 597–612.

Valsiner, J. (2009). Cultural psychology today: Innovations and oversights. *Culture & Psychology, 15*(1), 5–39.

Valsiner, J., & Sato, T. (2006). Historically structured sampling (HSS): How can psychology's methodology become tuned in to the reality of the historical nature of cultural psychology? In J. Straub, C. Kölbl, D. Weidemann, & B. Zielke (Eds.), *Pursuit of meaning: Theoretical and methodological advances cultural and cross-cultural psychology* (pp. 215–252). Transcript.

Waddington, C. H. (1957). *The strategy of the genes*. Allen & Unwin.

Yasuda, Y. (2015). 画期をなすこと(making time divisions). In Y. Yasuda, A. Nameda, M. Fukuda, & T. Sato (Eds.), *TEA理論編: 複線径路等至性アプローチの基礎を学ぶ (TEA theory: Learning the basics of the trajectory equifinality approach)* (pp. 9–13). Shinyosha. [In Japanese].

Zhang, X., Kubota, K., Kubota, M., & Li, K. (2019). Developmental trajectory patterns of Chinese teachers employing new teaching strategies with thinking tools. *International Journal for Educational Media and Technology, 13*(1) https://ijemt.org/index.php/journal/article/view/192

Zittoun, T., & Gillespie, A. (2015). *Imagination in human and cultural development*. Routledge.

Exploring the New Umwelt with TEA

Linking the Semiosphere and the Concept of Umwelt in Trajectory Equifinality Approach

Taiyo Miyashita

The art and environment of a Blacksmith (by the author)

Introduction

We are humans, we create, use, and abandon signs. We are beings who live in various cultures and move across diverse cultural boundaries. This study examines the theoretical integration of two fundamental concepts—the semiosphere and umwelt—to expand the theoretical framework of the Trajectory Equifinality Approach (TEA) in cultural psychology. The semiosphere, proposed by Russian

T. Miyashita (✉)
The Japan Research Institute, Limited/Ritsumeikan University, Osaka, Japan

M. A. Campill et al. (eds.), *New Paths in Trajectory Equifinality Modelling*, Theory and History in the Human and Social Sciences,
https://doi.org/10.1007/978-3-032-25855-7_2

literary and cultural scholar Yuri Lotman, refers to the essential semiotic space necessary for signs to function and for communication to occur. Umwelt, a biological concept introduced by the Baltic German biologist Jakob von Uexküll, posits that all organisms inhabit species-specific perceptual worlds and function as subjects within these environments. Valsiner incorporated these concepts into semiotic cultural psychology, positioning them as the theoretical foundation for the "internalization-externalization process"—a key mechanism of cultural construction. Drawing upon Kalevi Kull's insight that "a semiosphere constitutes a set of interconnected umwelts," this paper explores how these concepts relate to and enhance our understanding of human development within TEA.

The primary aim of this paper is to clarify how the semiosphere and umwelt concepts connect to TEA and to introduce a third concept, liminality, as a theoretical bridge that elucidates how these two concepts are integrated within the TEA framework. By establishing the theoretical foundations of TEA's core concepts of "obligatory passage points" and "bifurcation points," this integration provides a comprehensive understanding of the interaction between signs and subjects in human developmental processes (that, for example, can be observed in the figure on the first page of the chapter by the forging of a sword, as well as the transitional processes between different semiospheres. This theoretical synthesis is expected to provide novel analytical perspectives on the increasingly complex processes of human development in contemporary society in which individuals navigate multiple semiospheres daily and experience frequent transitions through liminal states.

The Semiosphere and TEA

The "semiosphere" is a concept proposed by Russian literary and cultural scholar Yuri Lotman. This provides a perspective that captures the entire semiotic space in which signs function as integrated semiotic phenomena. Lotman explains the semiosphere as follows:

> the semiotic space necessary for the existence and functioning of languages, not the sum total of different languages; in a sense the semiosphere has a prior existence and is in constant interaction with languages [...] Outside the semiosphere there can be neither communication, nor language (Lotman, 1990, pp. 123–124).

Additionally, after stating that binarity and asymmetry are laws in semiotic systems, Lotman described the relationship between the semiosphere and culture as follows:

> The unit of semiosis, the smallest functioning mechanism, is not a separate language but the whole semiotic space of the culture in question. This is the space that we term the *semiosphere*. The semiosphere is the result and the condition for the development of culture (Lotman, 1990, p. 125).

From Lotman's definition, we can understand that the semiosphere is not merely a collection of signs but a "prerequisite" for signs to function. In other words, the semiosphere is an essential domain for meaning generation, where interactions between humans and signs occur; without this, semiotic communication cannot exist. The important point is that the existence of the semiosphere is essential for generating semiotic meaning. Suppose that a particular sign is not positioned within the corresponding semiosphere or is placed in a different semiosphere. In such cases, the sign does not generate its intended meaning or function.

Lotman (1990) cited the creation of heterogeneous and individual boundary characteristics as important features of the semiosphere. For Lotman, the boundary domain is the basic mechanism of semiotic differentiation, and defines the boundary of the semiosphere as a membrane-like permeable structure (Lotman, 1990). Lotman's conception of boundary domains is relative and arbitrary; how permeable and actual boundary domains are drawn depends on a series of cultural factors within the context of the semiosphere. Lotman (1990) also noted that contact between different semiospheres is constantly occurring and pointed out that all cultures begin by dividing the world into "our internal space" and "their external space."

Valsiner incorporates Lotman's concept of the semiosphere into his semiotic cultural psychology. Valsiner (2007) captured humans as transforming with culture and stated that culture is the adjustment of signs between humans and nature, rather than humans directly confronting nature through their physical bodies. He emphasized the importance of promotive signs, which incorporate time into the nature of signs. Promotive signs are "signs that have some function facing the future and lead from past states to something new." Humans inevitably face signs in the "now = present." Therefore, the present is distinguished from the past and future but simultaneously connects and bridges them. Signs act on humans in the present, and humans affected by signs always act in the future over time. Humans develop when they encounter signs within the semiosphere, sometimes through contact with other semiospheres. A culture was formed through this adjustment.

This semiosphere concept can be connected to the obligatory passage point in the TEA. The obligatory passage point was originally a geographical concept referring to point B, which had to be passed through to move from point A to another point. TEA is a framework that captures situations in which events or behavioral choices that one must experience inevitably appear in life paths or human development. Obligatory passage points include institutional, conventional, and resulting obligatory passage points. Institutional obligatory passage points include laws with legally binding forces and social or institutional constraints without vigorous enforcement (such as compulsory education). Conventional obligatory passage points are normative customs in society or specific groups that have been sustainably shared, and can be understood as the behavioral patterns of individuals (such as ceremonies). The resultant obligatory passage points are the inevitable consequences of certain events (such as changing residence following a disaster).

An obligatory passage point functions as such, because within a certain semiosphere, specific signs work as signs. Because signs function fully within the semiosphere, there is no fluctuation in people's behavior, and these points become obligatory passage points that must be passed through. In the TEA, which focuses on the semiotic process by which obligatory passage points transform into bifurcation points, attention is paid to the semiosphere as a prerequisite for transforming obligatory passage points into what they are. If we can more explicitly document how people generate new meanings through interactions with signs in the semiosphere using TEM diagrams, this will enrich the TEA.

The concepts of comprehensive systemic setting and semiotic protocols have been proposed to explain the process of interaction between people and their signs in the semiosphere (Miyashita et al., 2022). A comprehensive systemic setting refers to specific environments (places/situations) that repeatedly appear in a semiosphere and conceptualizes the environments necessary for signs to work as signs. A semiotic protocol refers to a bundle of actions required by the subjects in the semiosphere. When signs function fully in a comprehensive systemic setting, the behavioral sequence that people are typically expected to follow is a semiotic protocol. For example, in Japan, within the comprehensive systemic setting of the first business meeting, there is a semiotic protocol in which business cards are exchanged starting with the person with the highest rank.

To understand this concept, let us analyze "official drinking parties" in Japanese company organizations as a case study. Official drinking parties constitute a comprehensive systemic setting. Within this setting, the following structured behavioral patterns (semiotic protocols) were expected from the participants:

[Opening Stage]

1. At the beginning of a party, the highest-ranking person (usually the top-ranking individual) gives the toast.
2. The toast is implemented after drinks have been distributed to everyone.
3. No one may take a sip of their drink until the official toast has been made (therefore, if someone is late, people may start drinking under the pretense of "practicing" the toast).

[Progress Stage]

4. If someone joins late another toast may be performed.

[Closing Stage]

5. At the end of the party, an "appropriate person" different from the one who gave the toast gives the closing remarks.
6. Departure occurs in order of rank, with lower-ranking individuals not leaving until higher-ranking ones have left.

In the above example, the initial toast and final closing remarks are obligatory passages. Such protocols are only required in Japanese drinking parties, and people from overseas often feel uncomfortable participating. This discomfort arises from the discrepancy between the setting and protocol in the semiosphere and the recipient and often becomes a catalyst for research questions in semiotic cultural psychology. Since 2020, traditional drinking parties have decreased owing to the influence of COVID-19, whereas online drinking parties have become widespread, generating new settings and protocols.

When people can receive a comprehensive systemic setting and semiotic protocol in the semiosphere without discomfort, that is, when they can pass through obligatory passage points, they can walk through their lives without incidents. However, when people feel uncomfortable with comprehensive systemic settings and semiotic protocols, and experience conflicts in accepting them, bifurcation points emerge in their lives. TEA often focuses on bifurcation points.

The concept of the semiosphere has a dual significance within the TEA theoretical framework. First, it serves as an analytical concept for researchers to systematically articulate the complexity of the comprehensive systemic settings and semiotic protocols constituting their sociocultural fields of study. Second, and more essentially, the concept of the semiosphere provides a theoretical basis for the emergence of "obligatory passage points," a core concept in TEA. Obligatory passage points exist as "points that must be passed through" in life paths precisely because specific signs function in specific ways within a particular semiosphere.

When researchers conduct studies using TEA, focusing on the semiosphere and the comprehensive systemic settings and semiotic protocols that constitute it allows them to consciously engage in the adjustment process between the people and the signs they are researching.

Umwelt and TEA

Umwelt is a biological concept proposed by the Baltic German biologist Jakob von Uexküll, who posited that all animals live in species-specific perceptual worlds and function as subjects within them. von Uexküll (1970) stated that an organism's behavior is not a physical/bodily response to stimuli but exists because of the umwelt, and that universal time and space are perceived as unique time and space for animal subjects. Uexküll summarized the relationship between subject and object in the "functional cycle" (Funktionskreis) diagram in Fig. 1, stating that one subject is connected to the same or different objects through many functional cycles. As the first fundamental law of the umwelt theory, he claimed that even the most straightforward and complex animal subjects perfectly fit into their respective umwelts. Simple animals have simple umwelts, whereas complex animals have umwelts with rich and appropriate structures (von Uexküll, 1970).

Regarding this constructive process in which subjects and objects relate to each other, Uexküll used the example of ticks to provide an easily understandable explanation. According to Uexküll, certain ticks climb trees when they mature, cling to suitable branches, and wait for mammals to pass underneath for years. When a mammal passes by, it senses the odor of butyric acid and drops onto it. If they land successfully, they use their tactile senses to reach hairless skin and extract blood. This example demonstrates Uexküll's understanding of umwelt. From the infinitely complex world surrounding the tick, it selectively perceives only minimal stimuli (smell of butyric acid, temperature, and tactile features), ensuring certainty of the behavior necessary for survival. For Uexküll, this selectivity of perception is the essence of umwelt, where "certainty" is more important than "richness" of information (von Uexküll, 1970).

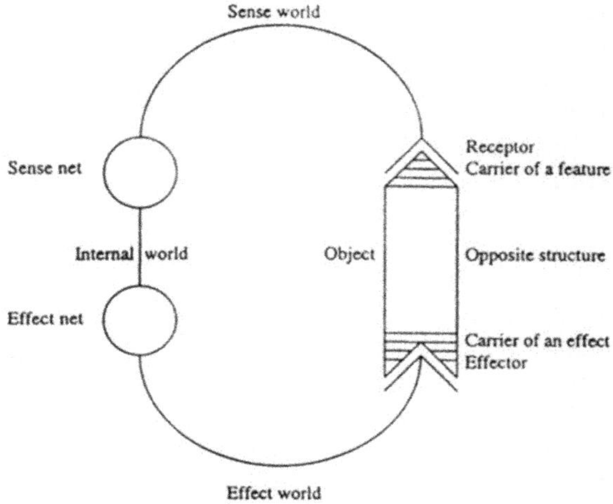

Fig. 1 Functional cycle diagram (Funktionskreis) (by von Uexküll, 1970)

Hoffmeyer (1993) stated that the key point of Uexküll's theory is that organisms are not passive entities moved by external forces, but create their own umwelts and thereby become part of the subject that creates nature itself. Hoffmeyer pointed out that the umwelt is how an organism opens its window into the surrounding world. An organism has a semiotic relationship with its surrounding ecosystem through its umwelt and becomes part of it.

While Uexküll, a biologist, mainly developed his umwelt theory by focusing on nonhuman organisms and their sensory perceptions, he also discussed human umwelt. However, when discussing human umwelts, following Vygotsky's classification, we must distinguish between lower (sensation, perception, etc.) and higher mental functions (voluntary attention, logical memory, conceptual thinking, etc.). Vygotsky believed that human-specific higher psychological processes always have an indirect character mediated by "tools." These "tools" are signs and language. In the "world of becoming," in which humans face the world around them, articulate the world, and live in interdependent relationships, the mediating element in this constructive process is a sign centered on language.

Kull (1998) further developed the umwelt concept, redefining it as "the semiotic world of an organism–the world an organism creates and lives in." According to Kull, the umwelt integrates all semiotic processes within an organism. Furthermore, he views semiotic systems simultaneously as "modelling systems," including biological and cultural systems (Kull, 2010; Magnus & Kull, 2012).

> All organisms participate in the construction of umwelten. Organisms participate in creating umwelten because this is generally a communication (including auto-communication) process that modifies and constructs umwelten. Building and modifying one's umwelt is simultaneously a communicative and modelling process. (Magnus & Kull, 2012)

Based on the Tartu-Moscow School of Semiotics, Magnus and Kull organized modelling systems as structural elements with analogical relationships to cognitive objects and their combinatorial rules. They pointed out that modelling systems provide a means for understanding the external world while simultaneously being significant sources of world formation. According to Kull, umwelt-making as modelling includes all construction, formation, and design that humans perform about the environment (not just "texts" in the narrow sense, but also clothing, tools, technology, architecture, landscapes), and he stated that culture is continuously created through such human umwelt-making (Magnus & Kull, 2012).

Jensen noted that humans are distinct from other animals when considering the umwelt. According to Jensen, different species live in different contexts, even within the same environment. However, the difference between most animals and humans is that humans are immature at birth (Jensen, 2020).

> There is however a very important difference between most animals and humans. When humans are born they are unfinished. So are some animals but they then finish their development in the way their genetic inheritance determine within narrow variations [...] Humans on the contrary can finish their development in very varied ways and this takes place in relation to the specific environment in which they develop. (Jensen, 2020)

Jensen thus emphasizes the importance of developing "personal contexts" as humans grow up in specific environments. In contrast, for most species, the contexts that they experience and deal with are largely genetically determined (Jensen, 2020).

Jensen states that "personal contexts" are established and developed throughout life. In this process, the environment influences one's personal umwelt. Conditions, possibilities, and challenges in the environment strengthen or hinder the construction of various aspects of the personal umwelt, and this process is reciprocal with people influencing the environment.

Jensen also stated that the core premise of cultural psychology is that humans actively engage with their experiences and create interpretations and meanings from them. When people experience something, they create meaning related to their personal context and act on the values and attitudes they possess (Jensen, 2020).

Jensen's personal context can be called the personal umwelt. The process by which this personal umwelt is created can be understood as a mutual adjustment process between the signs and people in the TEA. In TEA research, modelling the multilinear nature of research participants' life paths as TEM diagrams is equivalent to capturing the process by which their personal umwelts have been created.

Figure 2, Valsiner's (2014) diagram depicting the feedback of internalization and externalization, can be understood as illustrating how personal umwelts are created. It schematizes the constructive process (internalization/externalization) that interrelates with objects to build up the umwelt. Considering Valsiner's diagram expressing the relationship between person and environment as a mutually related constructive process, we can understand that individuals always actively create their personal umwelts while "articulating the world" through signs (language) in the constructive process with the environment.

In this sense, personal umwelt is a concept that becomes the subject of self-modelling in TEA. By capturing the subject that creates one's own life through interaction with the environment in the semiosphere that surrounds oneself as a personal umwelt, and by recognizing anew that signs mediate this construction

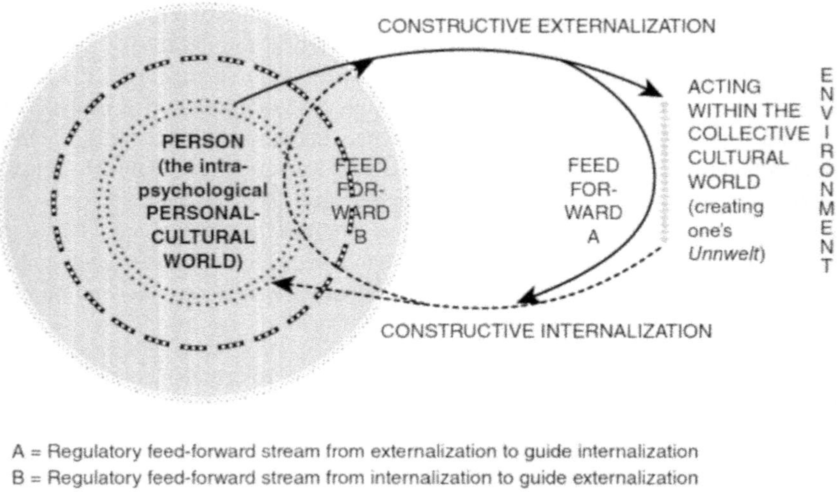

Fig. 2 Mutual feed-forward relationship of internalization and externalization (by Valsiner, 2014)

process, the personal umwelt connects to the Three-Layer Model of Genesis (TLMG) in TEA. TLMG is a theory for understanding the internal mechanisms of humans as systems that transform by incorporating cultural signs when focusing on bifurcation points. It is a self-model for describing and understanding internal transformations on three levels: action, signs, and values.

The TLMG emphasizes the sign level, particularly the function of promotive signs. Promotive signs are "signs that have some function facing the future and lead from past states to something new" (Valsiner, 2004). Valsiner (2007) stated that all semiotic mediations can function as promotive signs, extending future-oriented time for humans and guiding future possibilities (Valsiner, 2007).

This understanding is equivalent to the view that personal umwelt models the environment through semiotic processes. Humans construct their personal umwelts daily through semiotic mutual adjustments to their environment. Within this everyday process, when bifurcation points occur in life paths, there is a possibility that changes leading to new value transformations, which can be analyzed using TLMG, may occur in personal umwelts.

Liminality as a Connection Point Between Semiosphere and Umwelt

Thus far, we have examined two concepts in the TEA: the semiosphere and the umwelt. This section discusses liminality as a concept that theoretically connects the semiosphere and umwelt. First, we confirmed Kull's observations of the relationship between the two. Kull stated that the semiosphere is a collection of interconnected umwelts, and that when two umwelts communicate, they are part of the same semiosphere.

> Semiosphere is the set of all interconnected Umwelts. Any two Umwelts, when communicating, are part of the same semiosphere. (Kull, 1998)

Figure 3 visually expresses this theoretical insight based on Valsiner's internalization–externalization diagram (see Fig. 2 in the previous section).

Suppose that we label two personal umwelts as personal umwelts A and B when communicating using the same signs. In this case, they can be understood to be within the same semiosphere. This is easy to understand if we consider linguistic signs, such as when Mrs. A and B communicate in English. Since we are discussing human umwelts, we will consistently use the term "personal umwelt" from here on.

Let us imagine a situation where two different semiospheres (semiosphere α and semiosphere β) exist. The state positioned during the transition process when a personal umwelt A (e.g., an individual with a specific cultural background) moves from semiosphere α to semiosphere β (a different cultural context) is "liminality." Liminality is positioned at the boundary of two different semiospheres, and refers to the transitional stage in which an individual is repositioned into a new semiosphere (Fig. 4).

To understand this theoretical concept, we considered the universal transition from childhood to adulthood in terms of human development. In many cultures, the rite of "coming-of-age ceremony" functions as a cultural device to manage the

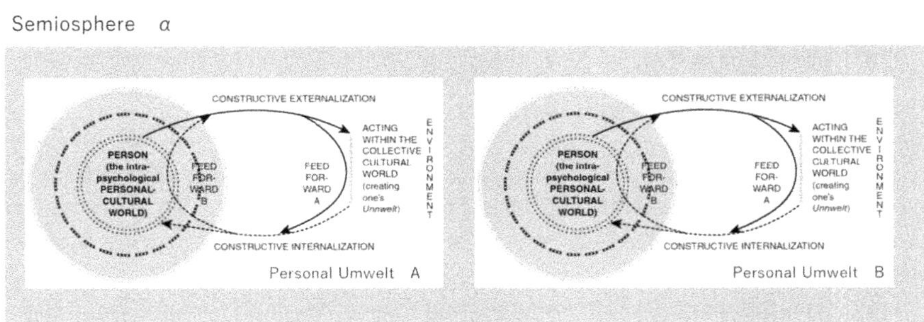

Fig. 3 The semiosphere and personal umwelt (by the author)

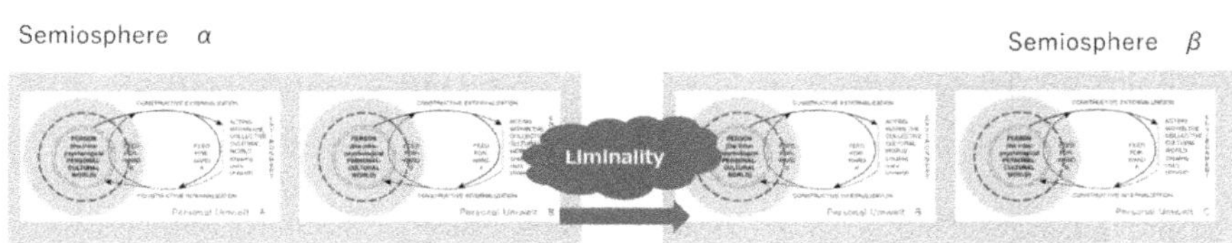

Fig. 4 Liminality between semiospheres (by the author)

transition from the semiosphere of "minor" to the semiosphere of "adult." When this transition is socially stable and culturally approved, liminality as a coming-of-age ceremony is an important obligatory passage for individuals to acquire new identities and social roles. However, in modern society, there are a few examples in which the definition and role of adulthood have become fluid, and this transition process has become unstable.

Tracing the theoretical genealogy of the "liminality" concept, its origin can be found in anthropologist Arnold van Gennep's (2019) study of rites of passage. Van Gennep compared rites of passage across various cultures and identified a universal three-stage structure: "separation" (preliminal), "transition" (liminal), and "incorporation" (postliminal).

> A complete scheme of rites of passage theoretically includes preliminal rites (rites of separation), liminal rites (rites of transition), and postliminal rites (rites of incorporation) (Van Gennep, 2019)

Rites of passage are practices conducted at the conversion points of culturally and socially important statuses or states such as from child to adult, from single to married, and from this world to the afterworld. Van Gennep cited the engagement between youth and marriage as an example of a liminal period and proposed calling rituals performed at this boundary stage.

Turner et al. (2017) further developed van Gennep's concept of liminality and reconceptualized it as a cultural/social transition mechanism. According to Turner, the liminal state has the following characteristics.

> The attributes of liminality or liminal personae ('threshold people') are necessarily ambiguous, since this condition and these persons elude or slip through the network of classifications that normally locate states and positions in cultural space. Liminal entities are neither here nor there; they are betwixt and between the positions assigned and arrayed by law, custom, convention, and ceremonial. (Turner et al., 2017)

Turner emphasizes that in the liminal state, everyday social order and customs are temporarily "suspended," placing individuals in a fluid state of "betwixt and between." A new generation becomes possible by temporarily departing from the existing frameworks.

Greco and Stenner (2017) made important theoretical developments by connecting van Gennep and Turner's concepts of liminality to contemporary theories. They first redefined rites of passage as "processes that manage the transition from one mode of activity to another." Furthermore, drawing on Whitehead, they theorized "mode of activity" with the concept of "form-of-process." Form-of-process is "the mode of unity/order/organization/pattern shown by a composition existing in the actual historical world." This concept can be applied to various sociocultural phenomena, including human thought processes, dialogues, and legal systems.

Greco and Stenner stated that liminality can be defined as events that occur between given forms of processes, noting that by defining liminality in this way, the concept can be applied beyond anthropology to psychological uses (Greco & Stenner, 2017).

> We can define liminality as events that occur between processes. This obviously broadens the concept beyond anthropology, giving it an ontological significance, but accommodates the psychosocial use in which the forms of process in question are meaningfully ordered spheres of social and cultural activity mediated by communication and presupposing conscious human actors. (Greco & Stenner, 2017)

Greco and Stenner's theoretical framework of process form and liminality provides a new perspective on TEA theory. In the context of TEA theory, "process-form" can be understood as "the complex of comprehensive systemic settings and semiotic protocols in the semiosphere" discussed in the previous section. In other words, if we view the process form as a semiosphere, liminality relates to events that occur during the transition between semiospheres, as shown in Fig. 4.

This theoretical connection clarifies the conceptual foundation of "obligatory passage points" and "bifurcation points" in TEA. Liminality appears in life paths as transitions from one semiosphere to another, but depending on whether this transition process functions stably or not, it manifests differently as either an "obligatory passage point" or a "bifurcation point."

Greco and Stenner theoretically focused on the situation where the liminal process does not function smoothly, namely the phenomenon of "liminal hotspot." They defined a liminal hotspot as follows:

> We might say that one enters the vicious circle of a liminal hotspot when one becomes stuck in the transition from one circle to the next, unable to integrate them into a wider unity. (Greco & Stenner, 2017)

A liminal hotspot is an experience where individuals are "trapped" in the boundary area when two different process-forms (semiospheres) are mutually incompatible. This state refers to being fixed in an unstable position of "betwixt and between," unable to move forward or backward. Examples of liminal hotspots likely to occur in modern society include career transitions (e.g., from students to working professionals) and the state of patients who have received serious diagnoses (e.g., from healthy persons to seriously ill patients), which are important turning points in life.

Greco and Stenner's choice of the term "hotspot," which evokes heat, was to theoretically capture the emotional "heat" that rises as a result of the temporary suspension of the normative order of existing process-forms (semiospheres) during the liminal stage. In liminal situations, the subject's emotionality is heightened above normal, making them more susceptible to transformation. Since the direction toward the future is not fixed and remains fluid, this state can cause anxiety and confusion but can also open up creative possibilities.

This emotionally heightened state is closely related to the dynamics of "obligatory passage points" and "bifurcation points" in TEA. Liminal hotspots become apparent when a "discrepancy" occurs between the comprehensive systemic setting and semiotic protocol (process-form) in the semiosphere and the subject. When there is no discrepancy, the signs in the semiosphere fully act on the subject, and liminality functions smoothly as an "obligatory passage point." However, the subject cannot move forward when the discrepancy between them becomes apparent, and the signs no longer function sufficiently. This stops, resulting in a "bifurcation point."

Greco and Stenner stated that if a liminal hotspot cannot be resolved with existing resources, an entirely new process forms, creating a gestalt that allows for a higher complexity level, and thus emerges from the liminal situation. In terms of TEA, this leap to a new pattern corresponds to a situation in which new beliefs and values are integrated into the TLMG and the subject is transformed.

The power of imagination plays a central role in creative escape from liminal hotspots. As Zittoun and Valsiner (2016) point out, imagination functions as a tool for coordinating tensions between the bifurcation points where surprises occur on the time axis from past to future and between multiple optional life paths directed toward the future that arise there.

Zittoun and Gillespie (2016) defined imagination as a semiotic process that shapes embodied emotional experiences by mobilizing and utilizing materials gathered through present, past, or secondary experiences as resources. They viewed imagination as a loop between triggers, resources, and outcomes. Triggers initiate the imagination and act as catalysts for liminal hotspots. Resources serve as assets for imagination and include past experiences, personal memories, symbolic resources (books, magazines, movies, and other cultural artifacts), social representations (shared ideas, norms, and values), and interpersonal relationships. The outcomes were the results of the imagination.

Zittoun and Gillespie (2015) stated that imagination may result in the creation of new forms of life. In the context of liminal hotspots, this refers to a situation in which escaping a liminal hotspot creates a new personal world while transitioning to a new semiosphere. Through imagination, one can recall past experiences while resolving the tensions between multiple life paths directed toward the future, escape stagnation amid semiospheres, and complete the transition to another (Fig. 5).

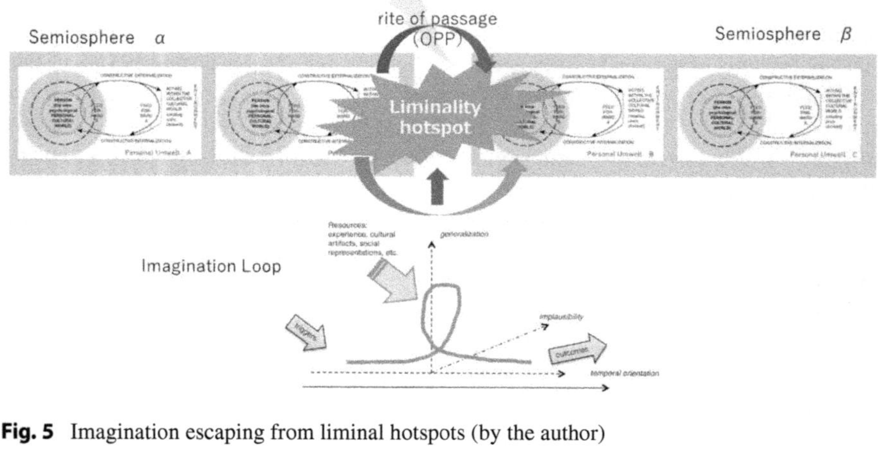

Fig. 5 Imagination escaping from liminal hotspots (by the author)

Conclusion

In this chapter, I organized the relationship between the concepts of semiosphere and umwelt in TEA and attempted to integrate them theoretically through the concept of liminality.

The semiosphere, a prerequisite for signs to function as signs, is embodied in the TEA through a comprehensive systemic setting and semiotic protocol. These concepts provide a theoretical basis for why points of passage are obligatory.

Umwelt has stated that organisms live in species-specific perceptual worlds. In humans, this umwelt is formed as a "personal umwelt" through a mutually constructive process with the environment mediated by signs. This personal umwelt forms the core of the self-model in the TEA, and is the theoretical basis for understanding the internal transformation described in the TLMG.

Liminality is a concept initially presented by van Gennep and Turner as an intermediate stage in the rites of passage. Greco and Stenner later developmentally redefined it as a transition between process forms. In this chapter, liminality was reinterpreted within the theoretical context of TEA as "the process by which a subject creating a personal umwelt transitions from one semiosphere to another." Liminality can manifest in two forms: "obligatory passage" and "bifurcation." When signs in the semiosphere fully act on the subject and there is no discrepancy between the process-form and the subject, liminality functions smoothly as an "obligatory passage point." Conversely, when a discrepancy arises between them, and the signs do not function sufficiently, causing the subject to stop, it becomes a bifurcation point. Situations where transition does not go smoothly are called "liminal hotspots," where the subject's emotionality is heightened and transformation is likely to occur.

By integrating these two theoretical concepts of "semiosphere" and "umwelt" through "liminality," we can understand more precisely the important bifurcation points in human development and life paths in TEA. The process by which "liminal hotspots" are resolved through creating new process-forms can be captured as a transformative process where new beliefs and values are integrated within the subject, and the personal umwelt is reconstructed.

Liminal experiences have normalized in modern society, and liminal hotspots are increasingly manifesting as troublesome problems in life, such as permanent liminality (Szakolczai, 2017). With the advancement of digitalization and globalization, the complexity and diversity of the semiospheres that people face daily have increased significantly. For instance, modern people frequently move between multiple semiospheres such as physical and virtual remote workspaces, intimate home spaces, and public social media spaces. Each space requires a semiotic protocol and its transitions involve liminal experiences.

By comprehensively understanding the three concepts of semiosphere, umwelt, and liminality, TEA has acquired a richer theoretical foundation and opens up the possibility of analyzing human development and transformation processes more precisely. By systematically utilizing these concepts, TEA as a semiotic cultural psychological approach is expected to provide a new perspective for understanding the human generation and developmental processes in an increasingly complex society more comprehensively and dynamically.

References

Greco, M., & Stenner, P. (2017). From paradox to pattern shift: Conceptualising liminal hotspots and their affective dynamics. *Theory & Psychology, 27*(2), 147–166. https://doi.org/10.1177/0959354317693120

Hoffmeyer, J. (1993). *En snegl på vejen: betydningens naturhistorie*. Rosinante.

Jensen, M. (2020). *"Developing psychology from the diversity of living conditions" comment in dialogical multiplication by Guimarães, D.* Springer.

Kull, K. (1998). On semiosis, umwelt, and semiosphere. *Semiotica, 120*(3/4), 299–310.

Kull, K. (2010). Umwelt and modelling. In P. Cobley (Ed.), *The Routledge companion to semiotics*. Routledge.

Lotman, Y. (1990). *Universe of the mind: A semiotic theory of culture*. I. B. Tauris.

Magnus, R., & Kull, K. (2012). Roots of culture in the umwelt. In J. Valsiner (Ed.), *The Oxford handbook of culture and psychology*. Oxford University Press. https://doi.org/10.1093/oxfordhb/9780195396430.013.0030

Miyashita, T., Kamikawa, T., & Sato, T. (2022). New theoretical developments in trajectory equifinality modelling based on the semiosphere and imagination theory. *Ritsumeikan Journal of Human Sciences, 44*, 49–64. [In Japanese].

Szakolczai, Á. (2017). Permanent (trickster) liminality: The reasons of the heart and of the mind. *Theory & Psychology, 27*(2), 231–248. https://doi.org/10.1177/0959354317694095

Turner, V., Abrahams, R., & Harris, A. (2017). *The ritual process: Structure and anti-structure* (Kindle ed.). Taylor & Francis. (Original work published 1969).

Valsiner, J. (2004). The promoter sign: Developmental transformation within the structure of dialogical self. *Paper presented at the symposium (Hubert Hermans, Convener)*. Developmental aspects of the dialogical self ISSBD, Gent, July 12, 2004.

Valsiner, J. (2007). *Culture in minds and societies: Foundations of cultural psychology*. Sage Publications, Inc.

Valsiner, J. (2014). *An invitation to cultural psychology*. Sage Publications, Inc.

Van Gennep, A. (2019). *The rites of passage* (Kindle ed.). The University of Chicago Press. https://doi.org/10.7208/chicago/9780226629520.001.0001. (Original work published 1909).

von Uexküll, J. (1970). *Streifzüge durch die Umwelten von Tieren und Menschen*. S. Fischer.

Zittoun, T., & Gillespie, A. (2015). *Imagination in human and cultural development*. Routledge.

Zittoun, T., & Gillespie, A. (2016). Imagination: Creating alternatives in everyday life. In *The Palgrave handbook of creativity and culture research*. Palgrave Macmillan UK.

Zittoun, T., & Valsiner, J. (2016). Imagining the past and remembering the future. In T. Sato, N. Mori, & J. Valsiner (Eds.), *Making of the future: The trajectory equifinality approach in cultural psychology*. Information Age Publishing.

A Case Study of a Cosplayer: Considering Cosplaying as a Transformative Artistic Life Facet

Marc Antoine Campill, Teppei Tsuchimoto, and Misato Fukuyama

An example of cosplaying Misato Fukuyama as Zeta, from ***GRANBLUE FANTASY (by Misato)***

M. A. Campill (✉)
Department of Humanities, Philosophical and Training, University of Salerno, Fisciano, Italy

T. Tsuchimoto
Eminent Associate Professor, Research Organization of Open Innovation & Collaboration, Ritsumeikan University, Kyoto, Japan

M. Fukuyama
Graduate School of Human Science, Ritsumeikan University, Osaka, Japan

M. A. Campill et al. (eds.), *New Paths in Trajectory Equifinality Modelling*, Theory and History in the Human and Social Sciences,
https://doi.org/10.1007/978-3-032-25855-7_3

We are heading to a fundamental misunderstanding of art, leading to comparing and evaluating the outcome of performances, artefacts, instead of approaching its profound nature as a semiotic mediation and action dynamic process. Some art forms and contextualized performances are treated as less valuable than others from the collective point of view. While we are all well aware that art can emerge from every domain, we are stuck at a belief that one art form is greater than the other. Pablo Picasso is, for example, considered as one of the greatest artists of all time, but does that make any other artist less meaningful? Is a "painting" more than a "doodle"? No, every artistic striving is art and is of fundamental importance for the growth of new ideas' perspectives while it also cultivates the persistence of traditions.[1] While there is a tendency of more effort and more profound positioning to systemic sense and/or the self can be found in painting, it simply does not become a higher or better version of doodling. The aim in which art is used is simply a different one.

What fascinates us is Picasso's dedication to art, how it is systematized in diverse versions contrasting the logic we found in the teachings of previous generations. Art is in itself a novel experience that emerges from the awareness that something is of need that does not yet exist. A cultivation that can be as simple as "a curved line in a painting positioned through a new approach at a canvas", or/and as complex as "a completely novel way of how to perform in itself, that generates a fundamental change in our understanding of perceiving the very moment. At the same time, all these acts can result in an ongoing experience of having created something novel or can perish already during the performance into meaninglessness or failure.

For the following contribution, we aim for the exploration of a specific art form cosplay, while underlining its position as an equal art form to any other art performances, as for example theatre, dance, music, and painting.

Supporting Arts[2]

One of the most misunderstood art forms might be the domain of supporting art forms such as fan contributions—to painting, books, or songs, cheerleading, and cosplay. The supporting arts are often considered as secondary outcome, as performances of secondary value that only exist because something as great as the "higher arts" or "physical performances" (as sports) exist. You support your star, your football club, and emphasize your passion for the moments they have given to us.

Often, supporting arts are considered a subcategory of art as casual arts as they are not considered by the mainstream as equivalent to higher contributions as song written by Mozart. Compared to other art forms, the realization of supporting arts is built

[1] Every act of preservation and persistence is implying also substantial change, especially in the domain of human experiences.

[2] There is a tendency that the perception of secondary or supporting art is often a position that is dedicated to pop-culture that then overtime can shift to the higher forms of art. Consider that for example Goethe's Faust is a book with the label classics, while any other book with witches and demons of our days becomes fantasy and every current contribution of women in the Fantasy genre (a still new trend) is automatically momentary.

more profoundly on the respect and passion one has gained through and by initiating performance. Nevertheless, supporting art is equivalent to any classical art, and many of the greatest contributions emerged from the inspirations the environment has given to us. A cosplay is, for example, not simply a reproduction of a personal favorite character, from a book, manga, or video (including anime), but also underlines the fundamental reflection on how to realize such beauty on the surface self. Do you believe any sculpture or painting of a beautiful being was created purely from higher inspiration? Already in ancient Greek philosophy Mimesis (Aristotle ca 350 BCE, translated by Dacier, 1705) was introduced as a part of art performance and represents the notion of how the artist also aims to reproduce the beauty of "reality". It is especially in the context of Prismatic thinking—perezhivanie[3]—of Vygotsky elaborated by Veresov (2017) where the notion of Mimesis of a part as innovation can be clarified. The human is unable to simply reflect the surrounding perfectly, the reason for this is that the human is far more complex, more layered in his surface—mind. In the mind, there is no linearity (Valsiner, 2024) only interwovenness between new and old meaning that is consequently elaborated by an always changing current self. In other words, meaning is not simply absorbed and reflected but it is influenced already by the lens—receptor of the body, while the meaning-making mind is continuing altering the perceived through its current environmental context and position—from perceiving to experiencing. The context and positioning also influences based on current interpretation of the meaning of what and how to realize the observed. Like a prism, the injected light (meaning) is not simply but partly reflected and deconstructed into a spectrum of colors. But this also means to achieve the experience of Mimesis the individual needs to first define what they see and then attempt in an unstable reality to temporarily materialize the believed to be "essence" of the seen. This leads to the primary mechanics of the human being that allow the following implementation of what we understand as artistic novelty.

In a certain degree, every art is a supporting art that underlines the need to express what our dialogue between environment and mind has brought to life and has enriched us in such ways that we have to share it with others and manifest it in a certain way that we can conserve it as we desire.

Cosplay: An Art of Transition

According to Fukuyama and Sato (2024), cosplay necessarily entails three essential elements: *story*, *play*, and *impersonate*. Among these, the act of impersonate—becoming something other than oneself by dressing up—often receives the most

[3] The Russian term *perezhivanie* derives from the verb *perezhivat'*, which is formed from the verb *zhit'* (meaning "to live") and the prefix *pere-*(meaning "over, over again") and it implies living through, repeatedly overcoming obstacles or life events (Karyagina, 2020). However, from the perspective of cultural psychology, it is not merely the act of overcoming that is essential, but the ontogenetic process of re-living—the moment at which a new sense of life emerges, one that differs from what came before.

attention. Yet, for example, if such a performance is undertaken solely for commercial gain (and not as play), or if the impersonate is carried out without being linked to a specific story, it cannot be considered cosplay proper.

The expression of affection toward a character is frequently mentioned as a primary motive for cosplayers to engage in cosplay. In Morimoto et al. (2017), a factor labeled as "the expression of affection towards the work or character" was identified as a motive related to cosplay. This motive was found to be significantly more prominent among habitual cosplayers than among university students who had only participated in costume-wearing events such as Halloween. Cosplayers make efforts to replicate the character with utmost fidelity, as a means of expressing their affection. That is, as Okabe (2021) points out, cosplayers gather various pieces of information about the character—such as expressions, personality, backstory, habits, and relationships—and imaginatively engage with them as they cherish the character in their imagination, and internalize their own understanding of the character and project it onto their own body and mind, thereby performing a complex form of affective expression. As these studies indicate, the act of cosplaying constitutes a form of affective expression in which the cosplayer is the medium.

It is worth adding that this form of affective expression involves a distinctive kind of asymmetry. No matter how intensely cosplayers express their affection through cosplay, the *Nijigen* (a term used in Japanese fandom referring to the fictional, "two-dimensional" world of anime, manga, and games) fictional characters they engage with—typically from anime, manga, or games—are fundamentally incapable of offering any direct response. The cosplayer's affection is therefore necessarily unreciprocated. Unlike fandom practices centered around three-dimensional artists or idols, the relationship with a *Nijigen* character is entirely non-reciprocal. And yet, as Okabe (2021) puts it, cosplayers continue to devote their one-sided affection through expressive practices that are "not merely copies of the character," but rather forms of original expression.

From the perspective of cultural psychology, cosplay may be understood as having the following distinctive features: First, in the process of becoming someone (or something) other than oneself, cosplay is a process of *transition*, of crossing the boundary of the self. Moreover, cosplay is distinctive in that the cosplayer as creator seeks unity with their object of devotion (the character). In other words, unlike attempts in realism arts, where the creator reproduces the reality they have experienced, cosplay is a process in which the creator partially identifies with their object and explores overlapping realities. Cosplay, while belonging to the domain of supportive arts, expresses love for a work or a character through a mode of crossing in which one *becomes* the environment or object itself.

Second, cosplay realizes this act of boundary-crossing by decorating the surface of the self—*the cosplayer extends their own body towards the reality of the fictional world*. From a TEA/TEM perspective, such objects that mediate between imagination and reality are worthy of close inquiry. Decoration, as seen not only in temple roofs or fashion but also across cultures, always exceeds mere utility; it is a symbolic exploration of sensation and meaning. Through decoration, we are *affectivating* the sensuality of the worlds—expanding our sense of self and feeling into the worlds with others (Cornejo et al., 2018; Valsiner, 2020).

Third, a theoretically intriguing aspect of cosplay is that it exemplifies the socio-developmental dimension of play. As Huizinga (1949/1980) emphasized, play is aesthetic in nature, endowed with imaginative and social functions in which the activity itself becomes its own purpose. Likewise, Vygotsky (1935/2003) highlighted the sociocultural aspect of play as a "zone of proximal development" in which the person transcends their immediate "present." Cosplay, in its playful quality, similarly creates a liminal zone in which participants create, negotiate, and transform identities. It is precisely this playful mode that sustains its vitality as an artistic practice.

Thus, cosplay is not merely a hobbyist activity. Rather, it is a cultural form through which individuals engage with the world by way of their own bodies—simultaneously transgressing, decorating, and playing, in order to encounter otherness and to explore new realities.

Fieldwork

The participant was the third author, Misato, a doctoral student conducting autoethnographic research grounded in 13 years of experience as a cosplayer. On 27 August 2025, the first and second authors carried out fieldwork to better understand Misato's cosplay production process and its artistic dimensions (Figs. 1 and 2). This fieldwork involved accompanying her to several shops she had frequently visited during her active years as a cosplayer.

The visits were carried out primarily in Nipponbashi (Naniwa-ku, Osaka city, Osaka), a district well known for anime/manga or cosplay-related resources. The locations included *DAISO* (a 100-yen shop), *Animate* (a multi-store complex which also sells cosplay materials), and a wig shop located next to Animate. During the visits, the first and second authors asked questions concerning the production process and the participant's perspectives on cosplay as an art form. The fieldwork took place between 11:00 and 14:30.

The interviews were conducted primarily in Japanese. As the first author, Marc, is an English speaker, the second author (Teppei) occasionally offered supplementary explanations in English during the interviews. Misato and Marc used a translation device when needed to ask questions or to confirm the accuracy of her responses.

Drawing on the shared understanding developed through both the fieldwork and the interviews, we collaboratively examined the experience of cosplay through the lenses of TEA/TEM and art. To illustrate this collaborative inquiry, we now turn to an empirical example drawn from Misato's own practice.

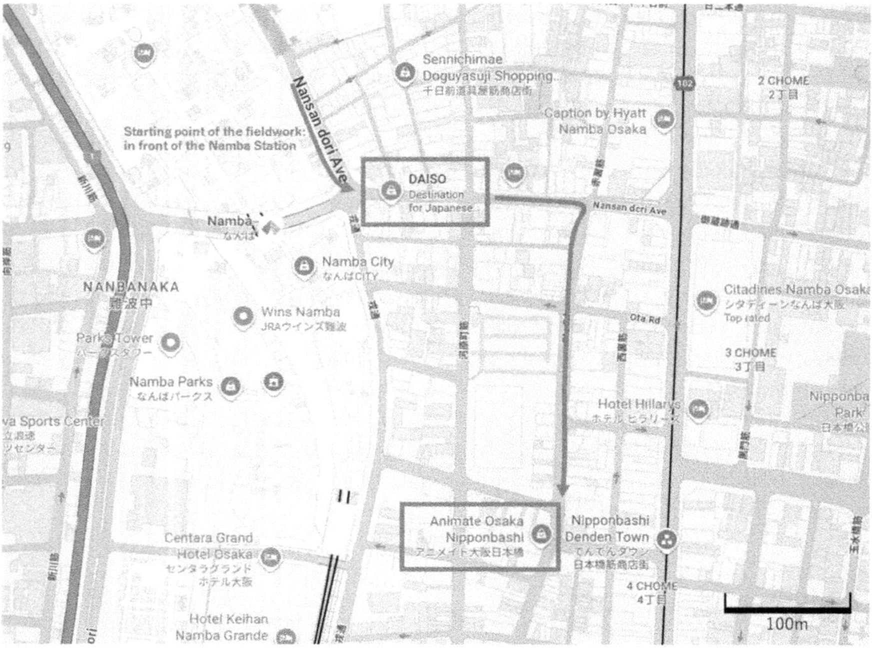

Fig. 1 Fieldwork route in the Nipponbashi district, Osaka

Fig. 2 (**a**, **b**) Fieldwork scene

The Case of a Cosplayer[4]

The cosplay took place over 2 days, from 12 to 13 August 2017, and the character portrayed was Zeta from GRANBLUE FANTASY. Developed by Cygames and released on 10 March 2014, the game is a smartphone-based social game distributed via Mobage platform.

Stage 1: I as my real-name; the self who lives an ordinary daily life; the self who enjoys the story to which the character Zeta belongs; and the self who wants to cosplay as Zeta.

At the time, Misato was deeply engaged with the game *GRANBLUE FANTASY*, and the characters she chose to cosplay were exclusively from that title. During this period, she looked forward to participating in Comic Market and debuting new cosplays at each event. At Comic Market 90 (summer 2016), she presented a cosplay of Silva, and at Comic Market 91 (winter 2016), she cosplayed as Catherine—both characters from the same game. As Comic Market 92 (summer 2017) approached, she began considering which character to cosplay next. She had a close friend with whom she regularly cosplayed, and the two of them discussed what they might do for the next event. Misato eventually decided to perform Zeta—a favorite character known for her assertive personality, sharp expression, and high in-game performance.

Although Zeta was a character with a high level of costume-making difficulty, Misato was motivated by a desire to take on a costume that involved extensive use of non-fabric materials for prop and costume construction—an area she had been step-by-step exploring. At the time, she was working as a laboratory assistant at Osaka Yuhigaoka Gakuen Junior College, and her time for costume production in daily life was limited. The decision to cosplay as Zeta was made approximately 2 months prior to Comic Market 92. At this stage, a tension emerged between "I as a laboratory assistant in daily life" and "I as a cosplayer who wants to become Zeta." This tension functioned as a motivational force prompting the transition to the next stage. This moment represents a phase in which transformation has not yet begun, but the potentiality for cosplay is already being prepared.

Transition from Stage 1 to Stage 2

During this transitional phase, the costume-making process began. Misato undertook the full construction of the outfit, including the jacket, skirt, footwear, armor, and a spear-like weapon. With the aim of faithfully reproducing the original design in her own way, she started by drafting patterns and proceeded carefully through each step. The armor—such as parts for the arms, legs, and shoes—was crafted by layering stretch enamel fabric over *Lion Board* (a type of EVA foam), giving it an

---

[4] The stages introduced in the following sub-chapter are linked to the Figure Cosplay, elaborated after the case of a cosplayer.

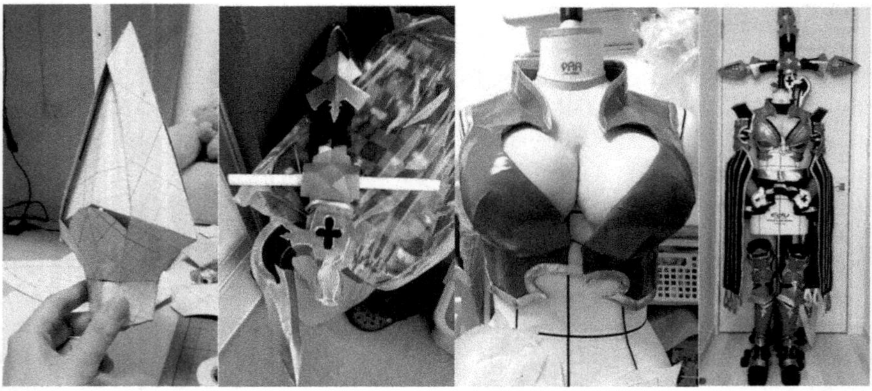

Fig. 3 Scenes from the costume-making process. From left: (**a**) spear-like weapon in progress (step 1); (**b**) spear-like weapon in progress (step 2); (**c**) jacket construction; (**d**) the completed costume

armor-like appearance. For the spear-like weapon, she constructed fine details using Lion Board, incorporated a transparent plastic tube as the central shaft, and devised a system that allowed the entire prop to be disassembled for ease of transport.

This period of production functioned not merely as a series of technical tasks, but as a time for deepening the relationship with the character. Through the process of transforming a *Nijigen* (two-dimensional) character into three-dimensional reality using physical materials (Fig. 3a–d), a new connection was being formed between Misato and the character. The approximately two-month production period also served as a time of gradual departure from her everyday self, and of preparation for approaching the character.

Stage 2: "I as my cosplayer name at the event venue"; "I as a cosplayer talking with my friend."

After completing the costume, Misato met up with her friend at Kyoto Station, as usual, and travelled to Tokyo. They checked into a hotel near the event venue and went to bed early in preparation for the following day. She participated in Comic Market 92 from the second day onward, heading to Tokyo Big Sight early in the morning, rolling a suitcase that contained her costume. While engaging in casual conversation with her friend, they also discussed where they might go for photos in cosplay that day. At this stage, although she maintained her ordinary friendship, her awareness as a cosplayer had begun to grow stronger. It was a state in which multiple identities coexisted simultaneously.

Transition from Stage 2 to Stage 3

Although she had practiced wearing the costume at home, this was her first time putting it on in its complete form, including full makeup. The process of getting dressed—including makeup—took approximately 90 minutes.

This 90-minute period was not merely about changing clothes; it was a crucial time for preparing psychologically to become the character. The physical transformation served as an important phase that facilitated inner change.

Stage 3: "I as my cosplayer name, performing as the character Zeta—wearing Zeta's costume, applying Zeta's makeup, putting on Zeta's wig, and enjoying cosplay as Zeta."

After putting on the Zeta costume, she stepped out of the changing room. She deposited her belongings at the cloakroom and headed to the garden where she had arranged to meet her friend, and she secured a spot for the photoshoot. She placed a sketchbook at her feet displaying her cosplay name and social media account information. Once preparations were complete, an amateur photographer attending the event approached her with a request to take photos.

During the shoot, she performed a sequence of poses that suited Zeta's character. The session with the first photographer lasted about 5 minutes. He also photographed the sketchbook, promised to send her the photos, and left after exchanging greetings. By that time, a queue of photographers had formed behind her—an experience that brought a strong sense of satisfaction. It was a moment in which the effort she had invested in crafting the costume felt truly rewarded.

This cycle of photoshoots continued for about an hour, after which she decided to take a break. When a number of photographers were still in line, the session shifted to *Kakomi satsuei,*[5] in which photographers gather around the cosplayer and take photos simultaneously. This form of photography occurs only when a substantial queue has formed, and for her, it was another source of a profound sense of accomplishment.

She took a break at a café inside the venue to cool down and eat lunch. While on break, she removed parts of her costume such as gloves in order to prioritize her physical condition—a necessary decision to maintain her energy and enjoy the remainder of the day. After the break, she moved to the rooftop, another designated photography area, and repeated the same preparation routine. The photoshoot continued there until just before the venue closed. The moment of stepping out of the changing room was a decisive experience of crossing a boundary. The sense of satisfaction from attracting a queue was not simply about wanting to be praised; rather, it functioned as a confirmation that her presence as Zeta was being acknowledged by others. The surround-style photography (kakomi satsuei) indicated a moment when a deeply personal experience became part of a broader cosplay culture. The subjective experience of "about an hour" reflected a highly focused state, distinct

[5] Surround-style photography, with the cosplayer positioned at the centre and photographers arranged around them.

from everyday temporal awareness. Removing part of the costume during a break indicated the limits of remaining fully in character.

Transition from Stage 3 to Stage 2′

After the event ended, she removed the costume and wig, packed them away, took off her makeup, adjusted her hair, and put on a hat. This process of "undressing" marked the beginning of a gradual return from the character to her original self.

Stage 2′: "I as my cosplayer name," going out to eat with the friend I cosplayed with, talking about what we enjoyed at the event and making plans for the next cosplay.

After leaving the venue, she headed to the hotel with her friend, and they had dinner together. While watching television, they shared reflections on the day—talking about enjoyable moments during the photoshoots, as well as offering feedback on each other's cosplay. It was a fulfilling time. Since they planned to attend the second day of Comic Market 92 in the same cosplay, they performed some maintenance on their costumes, discussed the plan for the following day, and went to bed early. Engaging in conversation with her friend and reflecting on "today's experiences" served as an important process for verbalizing and making sense of the cosplay experience. At this stage, she was beginning to objectify the day's events and internalize them.

Transition from Stage 2′ to Stage 1

After the event ended, she returned to Kyoto Station with her friend while engaging in everyday conversation. They promised to cosplay together again next time and parted ways.

Stage 1′: "I as my real-name self," having returned home, putting the costume back in its original place, and looking through the photos from the day.

After returning home, she began putting the costume away in its original place. While browsing through the photos sent by the photographer, she reflected on her participation in Comic Market and felt a deep sense of fulfilment. Updating her social media with selfies taken at the venue and the newly received photographs was also an important task. Through these interactions—including new connections made during the event—she hoped to make future cosplay experiences even more enjoyable. At the same time, she felt a growing sense of heaviness about returning to work in a few days, and eventually went to bed. Looking through the photos functioned as an act of objectifying the cosplay experience and consolidating it into memory. The "heaviness" she felt toward returning to work reflected the psychological gap between the fulfilling experience of cosplay and the transition back to everyday life. This very gap, however, also served as a mechanism for generating motivation toward the next cosplay.

Transition from Stage 1′ to Stage 4: Orientation Toward the Next Cosplay

After Comic Market 92 ended, Misato returned to her daily life while beginning to plan her next cosplay. She was preparing to do a beach photoshoot of Zeta's swimsuit version. Continuing to enjoy the game *GRANBLUE FANTASY* as always, she looked forward to the upcoming cosplay while maintaining her work as a laboratory assistant. This cyclical structure demonstrates that cosplay is not a one-off event, but rather an ongoing activity. Each experience generates motivation for the next, functioning as a preparatory phase for deeper transformation.

Theoretical Considerations

This case illustrates that cosplay is not merely a matter of costume-wearing, but a complex process of moving between multiple identities. Transformations across each stage are supported by material elements such as costumes and makeup, by social recognition through acts like photography and queue formation, and by the temporal structure of the event itself. What is particularly important is that this process is recursive: each experience generates motivation for the next, functioning as a system of individuation. A notion can be captured in the fundamental essence of the human being as based on Simondon's theory of individuation (2020). Here the concept of feeling individual can be understood as temporary outcome through the process of individuation, a dynamic but partially stabilized existence in constant change while embodying the potential for sporadic transformation as entity. While all systems are in an infinite transforming through irreversible time the potential for a next individuation persist. As Kainuma (2016) also points out, cosplay operates within a cyclical system in which the acquisition of new knowledge stimulates the desire to cosplay again. Through this ongoing repetition, the cosplayer continually transforms the self, repeatedly undergoing individuation while deepening their relationship with characters and taking on new challenges for future cosplay.

The Transformative Cosplay Stages

Before we can now dive into the relation between explicit experiencing of cosplaying and TEM, we need to elaborate a theoretical starting point of how cosplaying is a concept of transitioning on itself.

Reflection from Misato:

> In Stage 1, there was a tension between my everyday self as 'the experiment assistant' and my desire to become Zeta. This tension functioned as a motivation for moving into the next stage. From the perspective of individuation theory, this was still a pre-individual state, where transformation had not yet begun, but the possibility of cosplay was being prepared.

To cosplay is like an act of metamorphosis in which an individual positions themselves in a temporary fragile role of cosplayer that then leads in the short period of becoming the desired role of existence. Like Marsico's Borderland Theory (Marsico, 2016) this means that the state of cosplaying is a multilayered stage of transitioning. For this purpose, we constructed the following three stages of cosplay transformation-transitions (see Figs. 4 and 5): the stage of being the generalized daily life self (with many nuances, including partially appearing level 2 positionings); the stage of becoming, cosplayer-self in which the artistic positioning of creating and becoming an otherness is implemented but also the returning to oneself is located. And finally, the third stage of temporarily experiencing the being of the desired role (see Figs. 3 and 4).

For example, the desire to become the manga/anime character Sailor Moon starts already in stage 1 where in our daily life we find the inspiration and resonance to desire to approach or even to be Sailor Moon. Then the elaboration between artistic striving and compromising, based on possibilities (material that can be used). From that moment we have a consequent shift between 1 and 2 in which the condition—cloth, behavior, and make-up are created and systematized—trained as routine. The day of cosplaying then results in the movement from waking up to arriving at the convention and the dressing up. A process that then shifts into the third stage "the core of cosplaying", where the becoming of an alternative persona (here Sailor Moon), is initialized. During the event then a more or less stable being Sailor Moon is initialized while minimal outbreaks through dialogues to the previous stages 2 and 1 are happening. The end of the event then the returning to 2′ (or 4) and then to

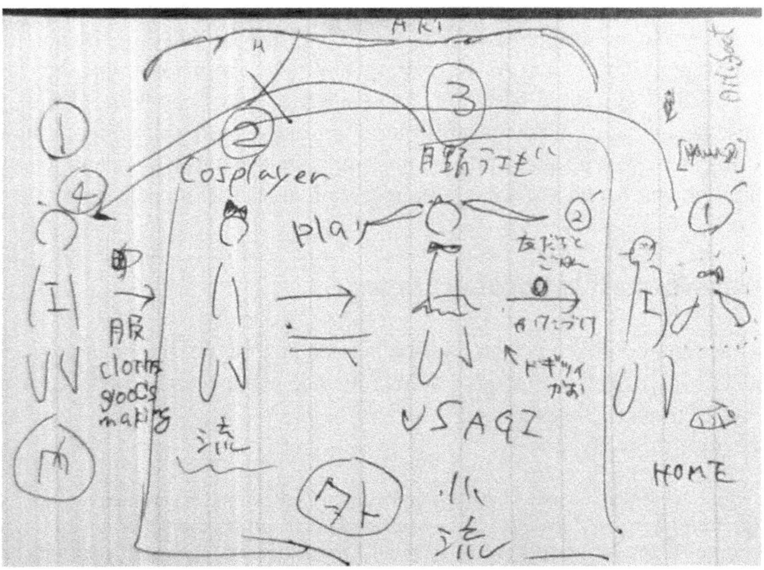

Fig. 4 Model cosplay-draft, created during fieldwork for *cosplayer a transitioning-self* [created by the authors]

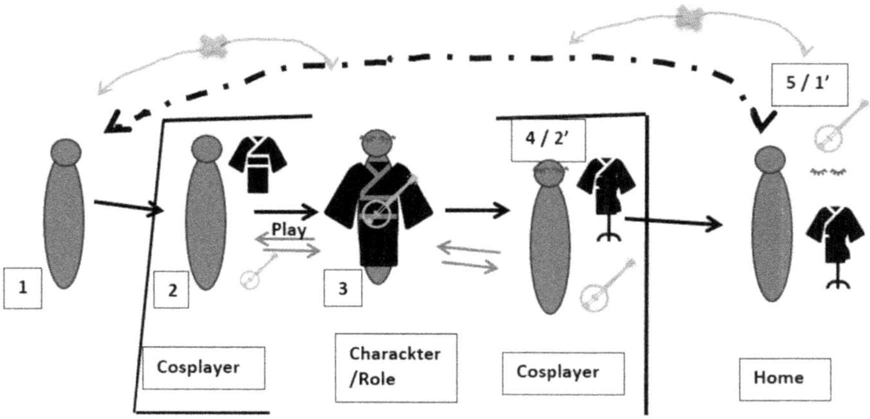

Fig. 5 Cosplay-model, modified version of the *cosplayer a transitioning-self* [created by the authors]

1′ is conducted. Here we should consider calling it the transitioning phase of 2′–1′ in which the self is enriched by the experience and might even discuss with family in friends how the day was. This phase might be in an in-between stage in which maybe the makeup is still on while the wig is put aside.

While phase three is in a transition to phase one, the experiencing self is a connecting point in which the previous interpretation and new experiences merge into a stage of resonance-fulfilment, wherefore the " ' " was used to underline the returning to the phase 1 and 2 but with a slight inner change through the next experienced transformation-performance. Which leads us now to shift from the realm of cosplay to TEM and TEA. Starting with a short elaboration of the theoretical domain.

Cosplay as Trajectory: Equifinality, Multilinearity, and Social Guidance in TEM

From a TEA/TEM perspective, the process of cosplay can be understood as a *trajectory* oriented toward the *equifinality* of "becoming a certain character." Equifinality here is the fundamental concept of TEM, and is the axiom of the ontogenetic process of an organic system, which states that the system reaches a similar endpoint by following different trajectories, even from the same initial state (Driesch, 1908). Even when multilinearity exists within one's life course, these trajectories are guided through "social" powers toward particular field of purpose—*equifinality*. It is precisely through this social guidance that multilinear trajectories do not expand into an infinite diversity, but rather sustain a paradoxical condition of being similar yet heterogeneous. TEM embodies multiple conceptual features; among them, the following aspects are most closely intertwined with the argument developed in this chapter.

First, the *irreversible time* represented on the horizontal axis. The continuity of human history (or personal life history) is irreversible, which means that *novelty* is constantly being generated. In other words, even if we feel that our lives move in a circular rhythm (as illustrated, for example, in Figs. 3 and 4), by the time we "return" to the initial point, our feeling has already changed—thus implying a *spiral or Helical* (Campill & Valsiner, 2023) understanding of time.

Second, the relationship between *reality* and the *possible*, represented on the vertical axis. In the dimension of *Aktualgenese* (Saander, 1930; Werner, 1956)—the ongoing becoming of human existence—real events and imaginative events hold equal value (Valsiner, 2014). From the everyday imagination of "it might rain today" to existential deliberation such as "the origin of life lies in the universe," *fiction* or confabulation itself functions as a trajectory through which actuality is created (Bartlett, 1932; Valsiner, 2018). There are no "objectively identical experiences" that everyone can share in the same physical way; rather, in the psychological domain, all experiences are equally *actual*.

Third, individual subjectivity can be regarded as a *contingent orientation* constructed between one's imagined society and one's personal self. Ultimately, "society" as a totality does not physically exist; it is a product of imagination, constructed by each person through collectively shared semiotic resources (see Valsiner, 2007; Zittoun, 2018). At the collective level, this imagination of "society" shares certain degrees of similarity and commonality among individuals, yet it remains a field of *partial heterogeneities*. Indeed, it is precisely because "society" inherently contains such heterogeneity—differences and dissonances among others—that it has the potential to *dynamically transform* over time. In TEM, when social power is discussed, it is not treated as an external determinant but rather as a *promoter sign* (Valsiner, 2004) that guides the person's trajectory—emerging from the society that has been internalized by each person. In this sense, the "social" functions as a *potential field of direction* that simultaneously constrains and enables human becoming.

Along the trajectory of life, we encounter "society" and begin to desire: "I want to become this," "I wish for that." At times, society appears to deny such opportunities; at other times, it seems to present them as if prepared specifically for us. Yet this "society" is also something that we *co-construct* together with others. Subjectivity, or *agency*, thus arises from this *situated potential* between society and the self: it is the desire to differentiate oneself while maintaining resemblance to the collective, by generating one's own trajectory within that dynamic field.

TEA and the Discovery in Cosplay

A crucial connection point between Cosplay TEA and TEM is found in the experiencing of the characteristics of trajectory. Essential is to understand that in the daily life of an individual we have the nature of unrepeatable but repetitive-felt reality. *Cosplayer as transitioning-self* has to be considered at that moment as being in an irreversible time stream that utilizes the conceptuality of cosplaying to challenge and extend their current self by impersonating a beloved otherness in unique artistic ways.

The Steps 1–3 previously introduced is in other words a description of a mechanism that is in the mechanical approach reusable, while in practice every act is unique through the current context and perspective of the individual. This means that at the same time we have a split in the performance meaning. Repetition and novelty fuse into the same action while the acting being might only realize partially that paradoxical moment. Certainly, this paradox can be found in many moment of our daily life, nevertheless specifically in cosplay its quality can be highlighted. While in our daily life we find many mixture of routines and inventions, in cosplay the transformation and the awareness of transformation from one being to a temporarily other (fictional) entity underlines that when, for example, even when we play the same character for different events then the role played is not completely the same. This is especially experienceable in the spheres of awareness through the close retrospection triggered in phases like 2′ and 1′ in which the experience of a cosplayer as "how it has been/what has been experienced" is elaborated. In this case, for example, by having dinner with cosplayer friends.

Furthermore, even though 1–2 and 2′–1′ are in themselves the same domains they are practically seen symmetrical contexts and expectation bonded but the irreversible time stream transformers both into completely different spheres in the movement of becoming. The anticipated cosplay event becomes past and so the expectations collide with the actual experience that then solidifies as past memory (still dynamic but more stable than before). The cosplay act is becoming an act of meaning-mediation in which not an otherness is simply experienced but "consumed" by the current self and transform the impersonation act into a part of the own remembered past context bonding the fundamental meaning and role of certain sign in the meaning-making self. For example, the beloved *Sailor Moon* becomes not only a symbol of resonating otherness but now represents an experiential crossing between fictional and existential space through oneself.

In this case, for example, Fig. 6 would emphasize B&I (1), and C&G (2) as standing in an overlap in their mechanical nature (fragmental systematic relationship) while the positioning perspective is diverse. The crucial aspect of this paradox of routine and innovation overlay is that once the irreversibility of time and so experiencing (movement) is bonded to the experiencing of the past, without connecting the relationship between current act-future and remembered past routines and

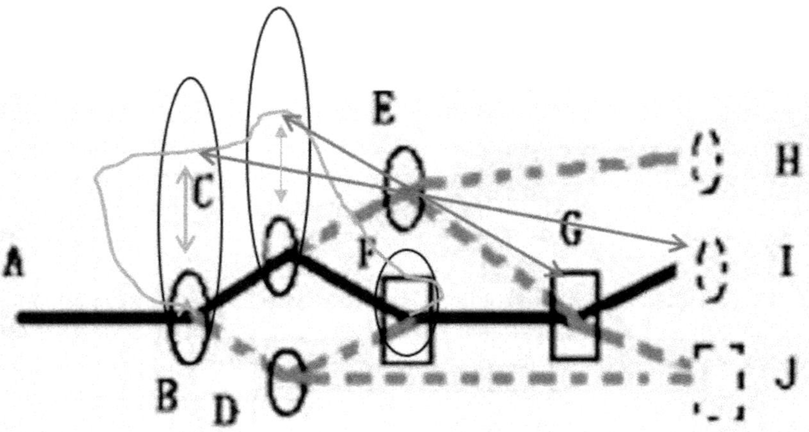

Fig. 6 *TEM and the transductiveness*, in the context of irreversible time and reversible felt experiencing

innovation would not exist. At the same time the potential to compare one with another makes even clearer that the points B&I (1) and C&G (2) are not the same but fundamentally different in their substance and meaning depending on the current meaning-maker. In this context, the notion of *transduction*, as articulated by Simondon (2020), becomes crucial. Within the framework of TEM, transduction is not merely a "logical" process but rather an *analogical*—even "magical"—discovery of a subjective connection within certain experiences. It designates a dialectical synthesis of time oriented toward the future, through which a new dimension of temporality emerges in one's life trajectory. In cosplay as well, such transductive moments can be identified in the shifts where repetition and novelty converge, and where the self encounters an irreversible yet creative temporal flow.

In itself a trajectory is always stabilized by the context that the past of the environment and self (based on our perception) is transformed while *transductive repetition* can be manifested through our systemic sense-making (Fig. 7). The ongoing in our irreversible life is accompanied by a loop, not only in imagination (irreal realm of the experience) as emphasized by Zittoun and Cerchia (2013), but by a loop of actual experiencing. "I have felt this before", "I have been doing this all day," and "I already once cosplayed Zeta before" are examples of statements that underline the experience of repetition in irreversible movement.

So, repetition is in itself a holistic repetition but a fragmental, attention-specific repetition based, and currently generated criteria related to the remembered past. The ongoing in irreversibility is not a consequent movement into irreversibility but also a sometimes-looping experience through transductive structures discovered by the sense-maker. Leading us to what the transformation as in cosplay means for us in such irreversible reversibility and in the notions of TEA and TEM.

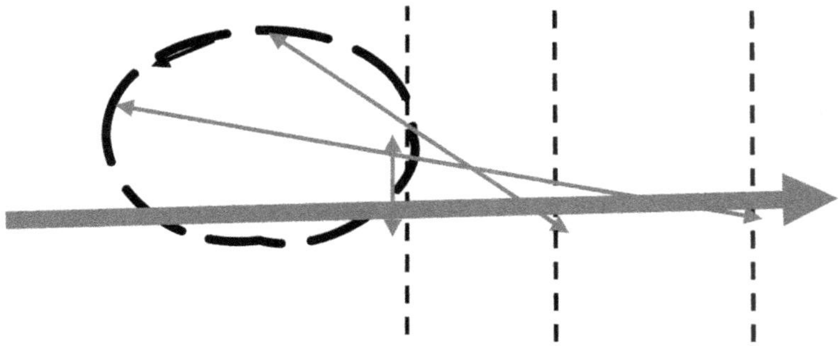

Fig. 7 Irreversible-reversibility paradox and trajection in experiencing (simplified visualization of paradox)

Theoretical Highlights as Conclusion

1. The *transductiveness* emerging from Kanzaki et al. (2023), Fukuyama and Sato (2025), and Tsuchimoto (2025) as new "creative", or alternative to the persisting, transduction is a crucial aspect in the processing of arts as in cosplay. The simple transformation and so meaning transitioning that is initialized through the act of approaching the becoming of another entity represents a transductive characteristic in which not an existing wardrobe is picked but based on the personal essential characteristic of the approaching otherness cultivation of meaning and creating of material is initialized.
2. Cosplay as art is not simply the outcome or being a fictional character but it also embodies the transition from perceiving an otherness, cultivating oneself and environment to approach a state of being the otherness and then again, returning, or shifting away from being a character, to the initializing self. Whereby the old self is enriched by new insights and experiences of the performance-cosplay and shapes the ongoing approach of the future.
3. A nicely constructed cosplay might be a highlight at a convention, while the actual cultural richness, for personal experiences and meaning, can be found especially in the in-between-ness of cosplaying, as emphasized in the notions of phase 1–2, 2–3, 3–2′ and 2′–1′.
4. Even though Fig. 4 could be perceived as indicating a circularity, it should be considered as spiraling, in which the cosplay performing being is consequently shifting in between the highlighted layers and so result in an infinite possibility of extending meaning of the played role and oneself.
5. The Trajectory equifinality point underlines a consequent ongoing in the irreversible time stream, meanwhile it can, through its simplistic linear layout be misunderstood as underlining a linearity in our reality—which is not existing but often emerges through our generalization from the meaning-making. Experiences in contrast embody always a chaotic trans-existence between being ongoing and repetition and so even though over time different steps are made the human can generate a projection to the past and present that manifests the notion of repeti-

tion. This ability in other words is able to break the fundamental rules of irreversibility through a transductive positioning to the trajection of TEM themselves.

References

Bartlett, F. C. (1932). *Remembering: A study in experimental and social psychology*. Cambridge University Press.

Campill, M. A., & Valsiner, J. (2023). Spiral and helical models for psychology: Leaving linearity behind. *Human Arenas, 6*, 102–122. https://doi.org/10.1007/s42087-021-00194-2

Cornejo, C., Marsico, G., & Valsiner, J. (2018). I activate you to affect me: Affectivating as a cultural psychological phenomenon. In C. Cornejo, G. Marsico, & J. Valsiner (Eds.), *I activate you to affect me* (pp. 1–10). Information Age Publishing.

Dacier, A. (1705). *Aristotle's art of poetry: Translated from the original Greek, according to Mr. Theodore Goulston's edition. Together, with Mr. D'Acier's notes translated from the French*. D. Browne and W. Turner.

Driesch, H. (1908). *The science and philosophy of the organism: The Gifford lectures delivered before the University of Aberdeen in the year 1907*. Adam and Charles Black.

Fukuyama, M., & Sato, T. (2024). The process of 202 cosplay experiences over 13 years: A study using photographs (2009–2021) (13年間202回のコスプレ経験のプロセス: 写真を用いた検討 (2009–2021)). *Qualitative Inquiry and Social Implementation, 1*, 48–65. [in Japanese].

Fukuyama, M., & Sato, T. (2025). Cosplay across 13 years: Auto-TEM, individuation, and eternal incompleteness (あるコスプレイヤーは何を目指して13年間コスプレを続けてきたのか: 永久の未完成という発達過程を auto-TEM で描く). *Japanese Journal of TEA for Qualitative Inquiry, 3*(1), 1–22. [in Japanese].

Huizinga, J. (1949/1980). *Homo ludens: A study of the play-element in culture*. Routledge & Kegan Paul.

Kainuma, A. (2016). The extraordinariness which cosplayers seek: The meaning of 'place' in cosplay (コスプレイヤーが求める非日常性: コスプレにおける場の意味). *Contents Tourism Review, 3*, 49–56.

Kanzaki, M., Kato, H., & Sato, T. (2023). A case study of transductive resolution: Analyzing the practice of inclusive education for a girl with down's syndrome at an elementary school in Japan. *Integrative Psychological and Behavioral Science, 57*, 1256–1272. https://doi.org/10.1007/s12124-022-09735-y

Karyagina, T. (2020). Existential aspects of experiencing. In M. Bazzano (Ed.), *Re-visioning existential therapy: Counter-traditional perspectives* (1st ed., pp. 24–36). Routledge.

Marsico, G. (2016). The borderland. *Culture & Psychology, 22*(2), 206–215.

Morimoto, K., Okubo, T., & Suzuki, T. (2017). Motive and psychological benefit of cosplay in adolescence (青年期におけるコスプレに関する動機と心理的効用の検討: 大学生とコスプレイヤーの比較から). *Research Reports of the Faculty of Education, Kagawa University, Part I, 147*, 13–25.

Okabe, D. (2021). *Design of fan culture: How do girls learn, create, and "oshi"?* (title translated by the authors) (ファンカルチャーのデザイン:彼女らはいかに学び、作り、「推す」のか) Kyoritsu Shuppan, Ltd.

Saander, F. (1930). Structures, totality of experience, and gestalt. In C. Murchinson (Ed.), *Psychologies of 1930* (pp. 188–204). Clark University Press.

Simondon, G. (2020). *Individuation in light of notions of form and information* (Taylor Adkins English trans.). University of Minnesota Press (original work: Simondon, G. (2005).

Tsuchimoto, T. (2025). Transductive leadership: Rupture and transition of a beginning teacher in a Japanese school abroad. In E. von Fircks (Ed.), *Culture and leadership: From approximation towards symbiosis*. (Chapter 10). Emerald Publishing.

Valsiner, J. (2004). The promoter sign: Developmental transformation within the structure of dialogical self. *Paper presented at the biennial meeting of the International Society for the Study of Behavioural Development (ISSBD), gent, July, 12 (symposium developmental aspects of the dialogical self; Hubert Hermans, convener).*

Valsiner, J. (2007). *Culture in minds and societies: Foundations of cultural psychology*. SAGE.

Valsiner, J. (2014). Needed for cultural psychology: Methodology in a new key. *Culture & Psychology, 20*(1), 3–30. https://doi.org/10.1177/1354067X13515941

Valsiner, J. (2018). Beyond methods to open-systemic methodology in contemporary cultural psychologies. *6th Niels Bohr lectures on cultural psychology*, 1–33.

Valsiner, J. (2020). *Sensuality in human living: Cultural psychology of human affect*. Springer.

Valsiner, J. (2024). Wandering signs: Beyond linearity to synthesis. In *Dynamic semiosis* (pp. 55–72). Springer Nature Switzerland.

Veresov, N. (2017). The concept of Perezhivanie in cultural-historical theory: Content and contexts. In M. Fleer, F. González Rey, & N. Veresov (Eds.), *Perezhivanie, emotions and subjectivity. Perspectives in cultural-historical research* (Vol. 1). Springer. https://doi.org/10.1007/978-981-10-4534-9_3

Vygotsky L. S. (2003). *The "Zone of proximal development" theory: Child development in the teaching-learning process* (Title translated by the authors) (「発達の最近接領域」の理論: 教授•学習過程における子どもの発達). Sangaku-Syuppan. (Doi, S. and Kamiya, E. (Japanese Trans.)). (Original work: Выготский, Л. С. (1935). Умственное развитие детей в процессе обучения. М. -Л., Государственное учебно-педагогическое издательство).

Werner, H. (1956). Microgenesis and aphasia. *Journal of Abnormal Psychology, 52*(3), 347–353. https://doi.org/10.1037/h0048896

Zittoun, T. (2018). Symbolic resources and imagination in the dynamics of life. In A. Rosa & J. Valsiner (Eds.), *The Cambridge handbook of sociocultural psychology* (2nd ed., pp. 178–204). Cambridge University Press.

Zittoun, T., & Cerchia, F. (2013). Imagination as expansion of experience. *Integrative Psychological and Behavioral Science, 47*(3), 305–324.

Exploring the Possibilities of Connecting TEM with Online Fieldwork: A Case Study to Understand Collective Culture on the Covering Work for the Employees Taking Childcare Leave or Working Shorter Hours

Akinobu Nameda

A pavement in the woods (by the author) [The artwork labeled as "a pavement in the woods" depicts a photograph of a single paved road in the woods. Upon closer observation, one notices an unpaved path as well. Along both sides of the paved road, trees appear to have been newly planted. Further back, trees that likely grew there naturally can also be seen. This artwork recalls TEA's characteristic focus on depicting the negotiations at bifurcation points and the trajectories in life—which path individuals choose to take and whether they break an own path or not. The collective culture depicted in this chapter can be the landscape captured in this photograph, as seen through the perspective of a person]

A. Nameda (✉)
Shizuoka University, Shizuoka, Japan

M. A. Campill et al. (eds.), *New Paths in Trajectory Equifinality Modelling*, Theory and History in the Human and Social Sciences,
https://doi.org/10.1007/978-3-032-25855-7_4

Collective Culture and Representation

In the book "An invitation to cultural psychology" (Valsiner, 2014), it is stated that "the collective culture entails communally shared meanings, social norms, and everyday life practices, all united into heterogeneous complex—yet the key "anchor point" in this sharing is the person" (p. 214). As described in the definition, collective culture would constantly be negotiated and practiced by persons with the use of cultural resources including shared meanings and norms. One way to grasp collective culture is to focus on and describe the changes of the moments of each phenomenon in everyday life.

In the same book, "An invitation to cultural psychology" (Valsiner, 2014), an example of collective culture is described. The example shows the shared ideas that people are not allowed to talk loudly or smoke cigarettes in a cathedral. On the other hand, there are sometimes protests against such shared ideas by smoking cigarettes. It also happens that intervention is made in response to such protests, and furthermore, there is an audience watching the protest and the intervention, watching to see what happens, and checking to see if what is happening is a good thing or not. Summarizing the above, there is a shared culture, but the content of that shared culture is determined and changed through the constant negotiation of individual people with each other, through actions taken by individuals against it, and through the thoughts and judgments of those who are watching it. The example shows that the process of change takes place as the content of the shared culture is determined by the constant negotiation between individual people.

Figure 1 describes where collective culture works and it is the one that the author added information on the cathedral example to the original figure presented in the book "An Invitation to Cultural Psychology" (Valsiner, 2014; p. 216). This figure shows that the collective culture is created by the synthesis of the

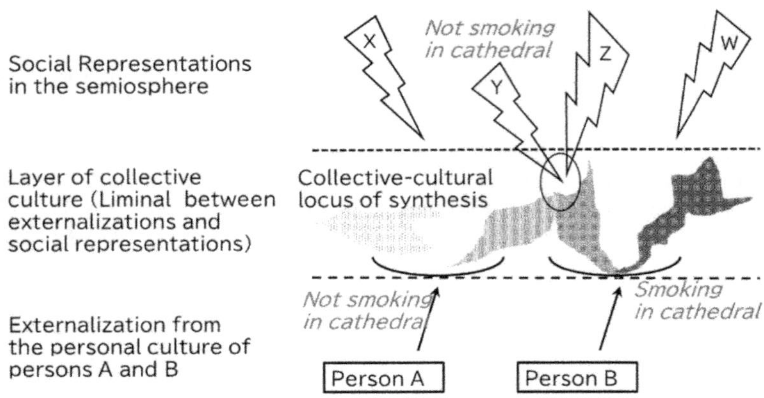

Fig. 1 Where collective culture works, with the information of the cathedral example (author added information of cathedral example to the figure from Valsiner (2014; p. 216) based on the author's interpretation)

individual culture and the representations shared by the society. In this figure, three layers are also depicted. The upper layer is the layer of social representations of the symbolic sphere. The bottom layer is the layer represented by the externalization of the culture of each individual person. In the middle is the layer of collective culture. It is depicted as a layer where individual personal culture and social representation are synthesized. In the case of the cathedral example, we can see how the collective culture is formed through the synthesis of the individual personal culture of not smoking in the cathedral and the individual personal culture of smoking in the cathedral, while the social representation is that people do not smoke in the cathedral.

One place where social representations and individual personal culture are easily visible is the online space. Online space can be a place where we represent a variety of things, making use of the resources available to us between the real and the unreal. In particular, online knowledge-sharing communities, where individuals post their own ideas and exchange opinions, would be a place where individual posters bring their own culture to the space, and based on that, mutually express and coordinate social representations and personal culture. In this sense, it can be a place where we are able to observe the process of social representations and personal culture being expressed and coordinated in a more pronounced way. In this chapter, we use online fieldwork methods together with TEM to depict the phenomena occurring in online knowledge-sharing communities as a stage where the conflicts between the personal and social representations are taking place. By doing so, we examine the possibility of the method of online fieldwork using TEM to capture collective culture.

As the subject for the online fieldwork, we focus on the conflicts occurring in between the employees who take childcare leave or work shorter hours and those who cover the work of them. In Japan, at least, as men are encouraged to take childcare leave and the percentage of childcare leave in men is increasing, attention is being paid to how the covering work for such leave-takers has been conducted and how it should be handled. Recently, there have been articles on the web that have introduced the viewpoints of the staff covering. For example, one of the articles is critical of the "preferential" treatment given to those who have children at workplace (Osakabe, 2020). In considering how to realize diversity, equity, and inclusion in the future, and more specifically, how to realize a society that values each individual's diverse backgrounds in addition to childcare leave, this is a subject that deserves understanding and attention. In this chapter, we focus on the posts and the exchange of opinions that takes place in online knowledge-sharing communities regarding the persons taking childcare leave or working shorter hours in workplace and the covering work for them. We conduct online fieldwork to capture the nature of conflicts of the covering work for the employees taking childcare leave or working shorter hours and the collective culture surrounding it, using TEM. In other words, we explore the possibilities of the methodology with the use of TEM in online fieldwork to capture the collective culture.

Covering Work for the Employees Taking Childcare Leave or Working Shorter Hours and the Related Social Representations

In recent years, the rate of taking childcare leave has been increasing in Japan. While the rate of women taking childcare leave has remained high after exceeding 80% in 2007, the rate of men taking childcare leave was 1.56% in 2007, but the rate has gradually increased since then, and has also increased rapidly over the past few years, from 7.48% in 2019 to 30.1% in 2023 (Ministry of Health, Labour and Welfare, 2024). Compared to the duration of leave taken by women, the duration of leave taken by men is not as long, but those who took leave for 3 months or longer also accounted for 13.9% of all male survey respondents who took leave in the 2023 survey. This indicates that the rate of men taking leave for longer periods is currently increasing compared to the past. For example, in the 2018 survey, 7% of male survey respondents took leave for 3 months or longer (Ministry of Health, Labour and Welfare, 2024).

A problem that arises as the number of employees taking leave increases is the need to cover for the absence of employees taking leave in the workplace. When one person is taking leave from a workplace, it is necessary to ensure that work and duties proceed smoothly even with one person absent, either by having someone else perform the work of that person, and/or by reorganizing the work so that less work is required. However, it is not always easy to do so without burdening the workers in the workplace. For example, articles on the web illustrate feelings of frustration in persons who cover the work of a worker taking childcare leave and/or working shorter hours. Concretely, one online web blog has shown a story that a worker with a coworker having children quit the job because the worker was tired of not only filling in for the coworker but also providing additional information to make it easier for the coworker to keep up with the coworker's work (Hatelabo:: Anonymous diary, 2023).

The covering work for the employees taking childcare leave or working shorter hours has become a hot topic in the last few years. However, the number of academic studies is not large and what we know about it is still limited. Although it is described that taking childcare leave is imposing a high workload on the coworker around the employee taking childcare leave, in a study of the process of promoting male employees to take childcare leave in companies (Ono, 2020), it is not yet clear enough about the specific process by which dissatisfaction, unfairness and difficulties related to covering work for the staff members taking childcare leave or working shorter hours occur, and the process of how the people involved make sense of what is happening. In this chapter, we will examine how feelings of dissatisfaction and conflict in such covering work occur and how the people involved make sense of the covering work, and in focusing on these making sense processes, we will also attempt to identify the collective culture surrounding the covering work related to childcare leave and shortened working hours.

Fieldwork in Online Space: A Case Study

We conducted online fieldwork in March 2025. The field was Yahoo Chiebukuro, an online knowledge-sharing community where posters ask questions and viewers comment on those questions. In the case study for this chapter, we first searched for "childcare leave, covering" and read the articles that appeared in order of relevance. When reading the articles, we recorded the date and time for reading the articles. As in the method of participant observation, we took memos for each article, and we also recorded the articles for those that were necessary. Fieldnotes were then created based on those memos and articles recorded.

Research Questions of the Case Study Using Online Fieldwork

The case study using online fieldwork initially explored the following research questions: what is covering work for the employees taking childcare leave or working shorter hours in workplace, and what are the conflicts in the covering work, and how are these handled in workplace? Firstly, the research questions were examined by describing the field as a whole and what was being asked and answered there. Second, we tried to describe and understand the phenomena of the covering work for the employees taking childcare leave or working shorter hours. A TEM diagram was drawn based on the descriptions and understanding.

Collective Culture and Phenomena of Coordination Regarding the Covering Work for the Employees Taking Childcare Leave or Working Shorter Hours: Discussions Based on Fieldwork Results

What is the covering work for the employees taking childcare leave or working shorter hours in workplace? In theory, it could be defined as the performance by employees in the same workplace of tasks arising from childcare leave or shorter working hours. In the present case study, the phenomena in accord with the theoretical definition have been observed. However, what was found from the observation of Yahoo Chiebukuro exchanges is not just employees performing the work of employees on childcare leave or shorter hours, but also the changes in the workplace conditions surrounding the covering work and the new psychological meanings that they bring with the work.

One of the common phenomena observed in some of the observations is a situation in which the covering worker are increasingly burdened and fatigued in their workplaces. For example, the following is a case. To show the examples and cases from the posts and comments in online knowledge-sharing community, the author translated the original texts in Japanese to those in English, with some minor additions and corrections for readability. This applies to the other examples, cases, and excerpts shown below in this chapter.

Excerpt 1: An Example of the Posts

Although we are both women, but I think the covering work arose from the coworker's maternity leave is unreasonable. In a department with three employees, one became pregnant and was absent from work for an extended period of time due to illness. Of course, the remaining two staff members were assigned to cover the work, but to be honest, it's quite difficult and we had to work overtime continuously. Even when I asked a part-timer from another department to help me, she was not much help. The company didn't want to add another employee when there was one who would eventually return to work. And when I negotiated with them for at least a higher salary, they just said they would think about it. I am happy that she is pregnant, but don't you think the rights of pregnant women are too strong? Even if she is allowed to come to work, I have to be considerate of her physical condition, and sudden absences or leaving work early are allowed if she is pregnant. If you try to transfer her to a new position, it is a harassment to a maternity worker, and if you move her down from her previous position, it is a harassment to a maternity worker. Giving birth is a life-threatening situation, but to be frank, the covering persons are also losing their lives. But pregnant women must be cared for, I know. It would be helpful if we could get a skilled person to come on a one-year contract, but there is no one like that, is there? I'm sorry, I'm complaining a lot. I know it's not the pregnant woman's fault.

The covering person who went on to post on Yahoo Chiebukuro, an online knowledge-shared community, seems to be conflicted by the fatigue caused by covering work and the relative asymmetry of the situation between the covering person and the person taking leave or working shorter hours, although there is no anger or negative emotion involved in covering itself.

Another common phenomenon that was observed in some of the posts was that while there was a situation where covering workers were in charge of the work of the person who took childcare leave or worked shorter hours, which increased the work and the load arisen by it, there were words and behaviors from the person who took leave or worked shorter hours, that did not seem to take this situation into consideration, and anger was expressed by the covering workers in response to this situation. The following is an example of the posts.

Excerpt 2: Another Example of the Posts

I'm exhausted from covering the work of a colleague who took maternity leave. I'm an office worker who is about to enter thirties. I know I sound like I'm complaining half the time, but please tell me how to deal with this. I work in an office, but it's a little bit different. My boss, my senior, and I work together as a team (technical support, general affairs, etc.). It's a happy occasion, but our senior colleague has taken childcare leave, and we're filling the gap with part-time staff. However, since there are many confidential matters in the office, the part-timer cannot handle confidential matters, and I end up having to handle them myself, which doubles my overtime (over 50 hours per month). The part-timer is also apologizing to me, as if they feel guilty that I am taking on the burden. My boss is also worried about how to divide the workload, and has left all the chores to the part-timer, but even so, the workload has not decreased. Yesterday, a senior employee came to the office to apply for childcare leave, and even though she knew she was causing me trouble, she said to me, "Why don't you get married and have a baby soon?" (I can't even lead a normal life, let alone engage in marriage activities because of my hard work...) I was so frustrated that I went home yesterday, and after that, I suddenly started feeling ill, so I took the day off today. While I was resting at home, I gradually became frustrated and angry, so I am writing here. When I contacted my boss about taking a day off today, the boss advised me not to fall ill, and the part-timer sent me an email telling me to take it easy and not to overdo it. Personally, I would like the senior worker to quit already and let the part-timer become an employee. In fact, the company seemed to be thinking that way, but since the maternity leave became an issue, human resource section was unable to make a move...and so on. In such a case, what should I do to change my mind? I'm feeling sorry for myself, thinking that I might collapse from overwork...

In the midst of fatigue and burdensome situations caused by covering work, they seem to have feelings of anger and conflict when the persons taking childcare leave or working shorter hours say or do things that make them feel the relative unfairness and unreasonableness.

We created a TEM diagram of how Yahoo Chiebukuro contributors come to feel angry and/or conflicted (Fig. 2). Based on the TEM diagram, we will look at the process that leads to having/not having feelings of anger and/or conflict. First, a

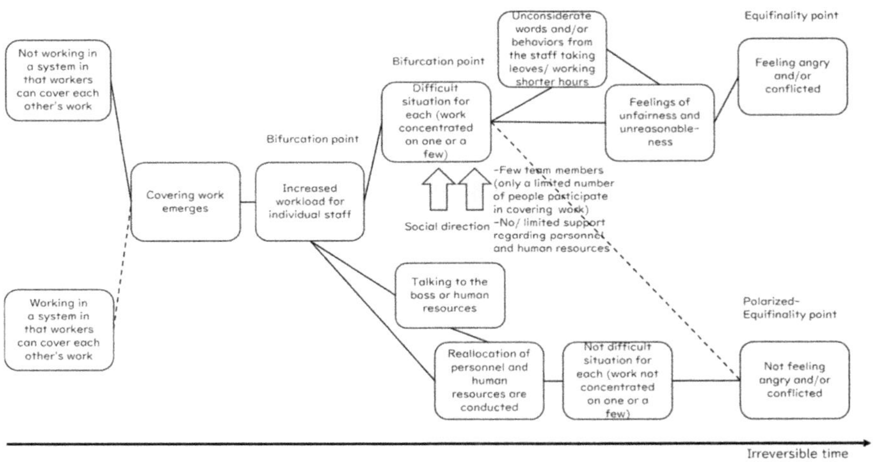

Fig. 2 TEM diagram describing the process of having/not having feeling angry and/or conflicted in covering the work for the employees taking childcare leave or working shorter hours, based on the fieldwork in an online knowledge-sharing community (solid line indicates the trajectories confirmed from the posts in the community, and dotted line indicates possible trajectories expected to be from the posts)

certain employee in the workplace takes childcare leave or changes his/her work schedule to shorter hours, which arises the covering work to be performed by the other employees. This increases the workload of the other employees, and they become fatigued. In this case, the contributor, the person who does the covering work, feels relative unfairness and unreasonableness due to the fatigue caused by the covering work, or in addition to that, by being exposed to the uncaring words and behaviors which can be perceived as lack of consideration to the covering worker from the employee taking childcare leave or working shorter hours. As a result, feelings of anger and conflict arise.

When depicting the events and experiences that occur in the process of having/not having feelings of conflict arise, one of the bifurcation points is whether or not to avoid a situation where the work is concentrated on one or a few personnel. For instance, one of the measures taken to the situation would be reassigning personnel within the organization when the covering work emerges and the workload of individual personnel increases. If only a limited number of people can participate in the covering work due to a small department or team, or if there is no or limited personnel-related support for the situation, the work will be concentrated on a person who covers, and that will create a difficult situation for that person. This situation is a precondition for having anger and conflict. On the other hand, if there is a reallocation of human resources within the organization and the covering work itself is not difficult, the person who covers can continue to do their work without anger and without serious conflicts in their feelings.

In looking not at the postings of the asked questions, but at the responses or the reactions to them, there are some situations where conflict does not occur. For example, one comment on a post mentioned that there was a very difficult situation with several people on childcare leave and shorter hours at work, but a personnel change had resulted in a support staff member being sent to that workplace to deal with the situation. Considering this case, we can imagine that covering work emerged would not necessarily result in a conflict situation. It is also likely that when they consult with their boss or human resources, a system may be put in place through personnel changes within the organization. Since the burden and fatigue were the original background, if a system had been established in advance so that a large burden and fatigue would not be placed on one person, the conflict may not have occurred. The trajectories mentioned above are also described as possible trajectories in the TEM diagram.

Another bifurcation point in the process of whether or not conflict arises is the time when the situation becomes burdensome for the individual. In this case study, on the one hand, the persons felt anger and conflict when they came into facing the unfairness and unreasonableness of the situation due to the uncaring words and behaviors of the workers taking childcare leave or working shorter hours. On the other hand, it is conceivable that even if the situation had been more burdensome for the persons, they might not have felt anger or conflict. We will explore what was happening at this bifurcation point and attempt to analyze once again how they came to feel anger and conflict.

In order to explore the process led to feelings of anger and conflict, we would like to focus on the notions and categories that were negotiated and coordinated in the posts and comments. In a post, the categories of single person with no children and working mothers are brought up and their conflicts happens. The following is an excerpt from that post.

Excerpt 3: An Excerpt from a Post
I am covering for a junior colleague who is on maternity leave. She often have to leave early or take a sudden day off when the child gets a fever, and each time I have to work overtime and work on holidays to cover my own work and hers. At first, she apologized every time she had to leave early, so I could say to her, "The baby comes first, so don't worry about it". However, as the number of times she left early increased, she stopped apologizing to those around her and rather smiled and said, "I'm going home because I got a call from the daycare center!". Then 1 day, the day after she left early, I noticed that her nails were covered with gel nail polish, which have not been there until the day before. When I complimented her on her nails, she happily said, "Thank you very much! I was finally able to go to a nail salon yesterday while my child was at daycare. I can only do this on weekdays when I have a child", she said, referring to the difficulties of raising a child. By the way, I'm single and have no child, so this sounds like a mounting from married people. She knows that my work is getting busier because of her own early leaving and the days off, so how can she be so insensitive? Are her words and behaviors within the bounds of common sense for working mothers? I pity her and wonder how her children will grow up with parents who trample on the feelings of those around them like this.

The post describes a relationship that was initially the one where the poster could say, "the baby comes first, don't worry about it". It can be inferred that this depicts a relationship that was accepting of coverage and supportive of the person working on shorter hours. On the other hand, the relationship has changed and depicts a category of working mothers who are not appreciative or reserved. It also depict a corresponding category, single and having no child.

The post was followed by comments, some of which added information about the difficulties faced by those taking maternity leave, and some of which described those raising children as considerate of their surroundings. Other comments include, "people who have small children and can go to work are brazen and insensitive". To this comment, another comment added the counter-information that working mothers are not and cannot be that insensitive. Describing the other comments, there are those saying that while "sudden absences and early departures are out of control" for people in childcaring, they should make arrangements to make it easier for the colleagues to cover the work arisen by their absence at work and to avoid inconvenience as much as possible, and if there are times when they still need to be absent because of their childcare, they should feel sorry about it. In addition, a comment says that from the perspective of "the eyes of the people around the person working shorter hours", if the people around the person are too busy to pay attention to beauty, for example, the person should refrain from doing so instead of going to opportunities where the person can also pay attention to beauty. The following are excerpts from these comments. Those working with shorter hours are portrayed as a category of people who avoid doing things that might make the people who are covering their work uncomfortable, or feel that it is unfair, from the perspective of those around them.

Excerpt 4: An Excerpt from a Comment to a Post

I don't want you to lump me in as a working mom. That is one word for it. I can't help it if I have to take a sudden day off or leave early. That is why I always do my best when I am around, and I always make sure that my work is always visible to anyone who sees me. Even so, I still have to ask them to cover the work of me, and I feel extremely sorry for them. One time before, I was called out of the daycare center on a Friday. Monday was a holiday and originally a three-day weekend. Fortunately, my child was back to normal on Saturday, but what bothered me there was the first hairdresser's appointment I had made in about 6 months on Monday. I cancelled the appointment. The child is fine, and my husband says why don't you go? But what I was worried about was what people around me would think. What would people around me think if I left early and changed my hair after the weekend? It's not that I don't want people to hate me, it's more that I'm inconveniencing them by leaving early and I didn't want to make them feel uncomfortable. I think there are people who are disloyal to their jobs, whether they are single women, married women, or working mothers. Some people want to be faithful to their work and to those around them.

If we take the notions and categories that we have focused on in the discussion so far as representations, and if we look again at what these representations are and what relationships they have been, those who take childcare leave or work shorter hours function as representations of people who have little time to spare or who spend most of their time on childcare. They are also seen as people who place a burden on their coworkers. In addition, importantly, their coworkers are represented as people who can't afford to spare time for their things. Thus, when people encounter a situation in which a person on maternity leave or with a shortened workday has time for something other than childcare, a contradiction arises in the representations.

For the people who cover the work of the person taking leave or working shorter hours, the basic premise is that their own workload is increasing, that they are in a difficult situation, and that they have no time to spare. In the meantime, for those, they have no choice since the employees taking leave or working shorter hours take time off for childcare because it is a sudden and unavoidable event. They consider that childcare requires time, and they also consider that neither those who are covering nor those who are working shorter hours can spare the time. This would be how they make sense of the situation and how they have created the psychological balance. Nevertheless, if the change in the situation of the people working shorter hours occur and those people become to have time available, a contradiction is created in the balance.

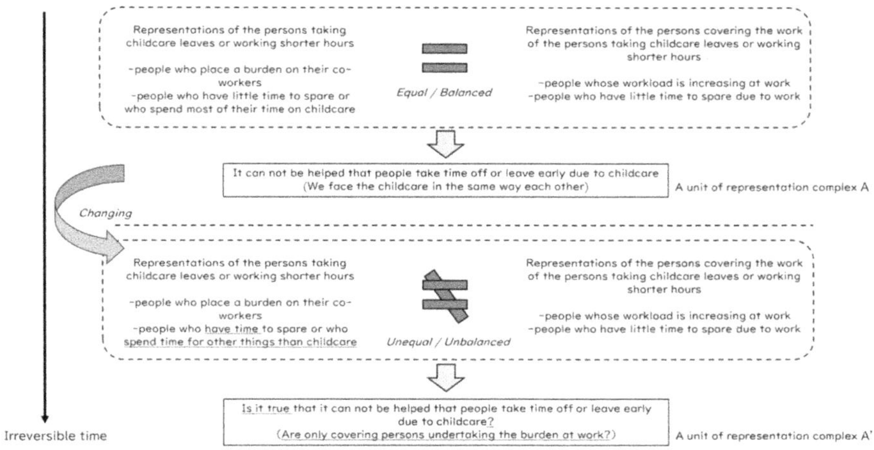

Fig. 3 A unit of representation complex changing over time including representations of the persons taking childcare leaves or working shorter hours and those of the persons who are covering their work, and the relationships of the representations

In this case, it appears that each representation is connected and related to each other and the connected, related representations function as a complex. For this reason, we call it a representation complex. The change of a unit of representation complex, that includes representations and the relationships of the representations, is described in Fig. 3. The change of the representation complex would be a contradiction itself that in turn brings feelings of unfairness and unreasonableness in this case.

People know the content of the complex of representations that brings psychological balance to the situation. Therefore, they conduct themselves and abide by the content of the complex of representations. Failure to abide by them leads to contradictions and friction between the persons involved. They might protect and attempt not to change the contents of the representations and the relationships of the representations to avoid conflicts.

Looking at this phenomenon from a bird's eye view, a basic premise of the balanced relationships of representations in this case is that a considerable burden is placed on the persons covering. Another premise is that the source of this burden is recognized to be those who take childcare leave or shorten their working hours. If we pay attention to the fact that the workplace organization is responsible for the distribution of work, then it becomes an issue of a negotiation between the workplace and the persons covering or the one that should be handled by the workplace organization, not an issue discussed in between the persons covering and the persons taking childcare leave or working shorter hours. When it is the issue that the workplace organization handles, people of each party, the persons covering and the persons taking leave or working shorter hours, might not need to conform to the content of the complex of representations discussed above. They may be free to perform their own activities outside of the workplace, although it may be difficult to try not to care about the content of the complex of representations because the complex of representations emerges in between the personal relationships that people are facing in everyday life and the visibleness may bring an people's interpretation that the source of occurrence of the covering work is the fact that the person take childcare leave or work shorter hours. How to position and distribute the work that results from employees taking childcare leave and working shorter hours in the workplace would be important for maintaining better relations between workers in the workplace, and in turn, for maintaining motivation among employees in the workplace in a better way.

Summary and Conclusion

Representations are connected and related to each other, and form units of complex. Referring to Valsiner (2014), social representations are essential elements for understanding collective culture. Collective culture emerges in the process where these representations synthesize with personal culture (ibid). Online fieldwork would be a stage and a method for revealing the dynamic process of representational complex forming as well as the process where these representations synthesize with personal culture. TEM provides a practical method to organize these dynamic phenomena with an irreversible time perspective. Understanding the dynamic process of representational complex necessitates a temporal perspective.

This chapter focuses on the posts, comments, and the exchanges of opinions taking place in online knowledge-sharing communities, which regard to the covering work occurred when a worker takes childcare leave or works shorter hours, to capture how conflicted feelings on that matter occur and what collective culture is involved in. A case study was conducted by applying TEM to the online fieldwork. TEM is a device that shows us the time and space of the bifurcation point where the relevant negotiation and coordination take place. Indicating the time and space of the crossroads of events and experiences where collective culture is coordinated, TEM allows us to examine and illustrate the flows of the whole events, diverse trajectories, and the process of the experiences as well as the changes of representations and collective culture negotiated.

A feature of this chapter is the application of TEM to online fieldwork that attempts to understand collective culture. TEM can be used not only in research activities to capture personal experiences and personal cultural processes, but also to depict the coordination processes of cultures involved in collective phenomena. In this chapter, we have rediscovered the way in which collective culture is being coordinated, deconstructing and reconstructing the complex of representations.

References

Hatelabo:: Anonymous diary. (2023). *I left the company because I was too far gone to wind up working for a childcare employee.* Hatelabo:: Anonymous diary. Retrieved April 15, 2025, from https://anond.hatelabo.jp/20230416015338) (in Japanese).

Ministry of Health, Labour and Welfare. (2024). *Basic survey of gender equality in employment management of the fiscal year 2023.* Equal Employment Opportunity Division, Employment Environment and Equal Employment Bureau. (in Japanese).

Ono, H. (2020). Explorative study on the process of promoting male parental leave in enterprises. *Japanese Association of Industrial/Organizational Psychology Journal, 34*, 43–58. https://doi.org/10.32222/jaiop.34.1_43. (in Japanese).

Osakabe, S. (2020). *Late night overtime and working on holidays to cover the work of childcare employees: No overtime allowance or cab fare, actual examples of employees who cover.* Yahoo! Japan news. Retrieved April 15, 2025, from https://news.yahoo.co.jp/expert/articles/48ffd921e1296fd164d108e84a057cb521e7fc8f (in Japanese).

Valsiner, J. (2014). *An invitation to cultural psychology*. SAGE.

Actuality and Possibility of Living

Trajectories of Psychological Counselling: The Trajectory Equifinality Model in Use with Clinical Psychological Patients

Natalie Jancosek, Lisa-Marie Geberth, and Sebastian Resch

The wall, by Natalie Jancosek (2025)

All figures included in this chapter were created by the authors.

N. Jancosek (✉)
Senior Researcher, Fondazione Jaan Valsiner: University for the Future, Salerno, Italy

L.-M. Geberth
Divine Savior Hospital, Vienna, Austria

S. Resch
EmPath – Centre for Health and Quality of Life, Vienna, Austria

M. A. Campill et al. (eds.), *New Paths in Trajectory Equifinality Modelling*, Theory and History in the Human and Social Sciences,
https://doi.org/10.1007/978-3-032-25855-7_5

Trajectories and Pathways of Seeking Psychological Consultation

Ever since the first movements towards institutionalisation of Psychology as a science in Germany, late nineteenth century (Valsiner, 2012), the idea of penetrating and observing the mind has been associated with abstract and somewhat, almost esoteric ideas within the wide public. The later developments, including the use and misuse of psychological philosophies, schools, and methods for a variety of fields and movements did not necessarily aid to the de-mystification of the image of this perilous science. The highlight, or perhaps lowlight, of the societal perception of psychology was reached with the introduction of the widespread use of the so-called electroshocks. Electroconvulsive therapy was introduced in 1934 by the Hungarian neuropsychiatrist, Ladislas Meduna, who connected this approach to his, later proven to be false, belief that schizophrenia and epilepsy are antagonistic disorders. Electroconvulsive therapy has, however, soon become a widespread treatment for most subnormal behaviours and psychiatric disorders worldwide. Perhaps, because of its scurrility, this treatment has soon become the face of "hospital-psychiatry" and shockingly, until this day it is believed by many laypeople that this is a standard procedure for curing psychological distress. Another face of contemporary psychology has been shaped by none other than Vienna's own Sigmund Freud and his Psychoanalysis performed with the assistance of the crucial red couch and a cigar, both of which never fail to be absent from any depiction of the master of this science.

It is not a surprise that those stereotypes have for a long time not corresponded with reality. Yes—Electroconvulsive therapy still exists in a contemporary edition, as well as Psychoanalysis, but the horizons of psychiatry, psychology, and psychological treatment have ever since widened in astonishing ways. For one, a strict division between psychiatry, psychology, and Psychotherapy has taken place—with each science's protagonists claiming their discipline's borders and independence almost patriotically.

Today's psychological services directed towards the wide public go beyond the walls of hospitals and private practices and include areas like school psychology, health psychology, work psychology, couching, prevention, therapeutic groups, and many more. The city of Vienna, just as an example, offers more than 250 diverse programs, workshops, projects, and individuals who co-create the mental health landscape of this city and country staying true to the established tradition by Sigmund Freud. All of these are available to the public and many even free of charge. Still, it is very curious how individuals come to the point of making the necessary step towards an assessment of their mental health.

Even though the availability of psychological help is given without exceptions and the topic of mental health is being de-stigmatised through a variety of campaigns and advocations for psychological health, still there is a certain barrier for many to reach out and get the help they need. Thus, the pathways of individuals reaching a psychologist are diverse; however, some patterns are observed repeatedly. One of such is the recommendation of psychological assessments by the general practitioner. Once all physical origins of the given problem the individual faces

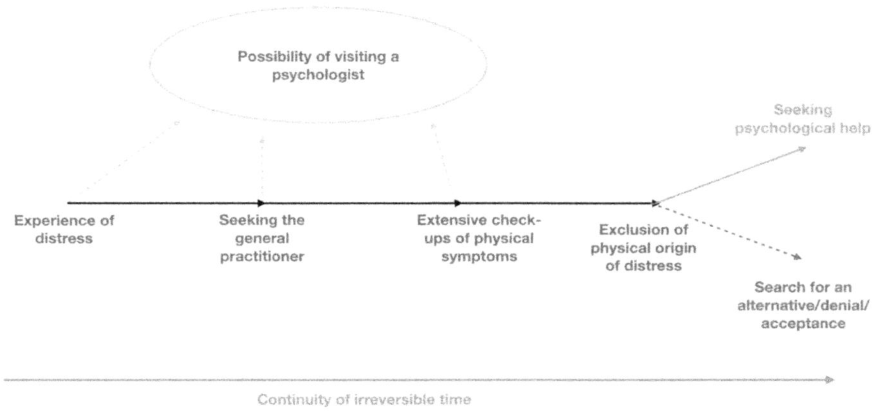

Fig. 1 The pathway to seeking psychological help

have been ruled out, the usual next step leads to the recommendation to pay a visit to the psychologist. The idea of the psychologist as the "last resort" and "only hope" for healing is oftentimes the expectation patients vocalise as soon as they sit down within private practices and outpatient clinics. If nothing else has helped so far, it has to be psychology that brings the long-desired healing process and freedom of all distress and discomfort (Fig. 1).

A further, often observed pathway towards the first visit of a psychologist is the desire for responses to existential and highly personal questions, which shall, perhaps, be only answered by an individual trained in the field to penetrate the deepest corners of the mind. Many come within their search for a diagnosis; others seek reasons for their differences from other individuals, or difficulties that they are experiencing every day. Such clients are oftentimes the ones whose curiosity leads them to an exceptional therapeutic motivation and compliance, as they are eager to find responses they are longing for. However, oftentimes patience is a matter rather subtle in the equipment of these individuals, which is why the longitudinal duration of their psychological journey tends to become exasperating.

Another pathway (Fig. 2) leading to visiting a psychologist is that of individuals after psychiatric and/or stationary treatment, who need further supervision and counselling after they re-enter the realities of everyday life. Such individuals have oftentimes already received names for their deviance, diagnoses for their distress, and thus, they are now in the search for normality. The intense longing for being "normal" or returning to times when they did not have the given disease is symbolised within the despair that they bring to every session and which, more often than not, also mirrors into the counselling psychologist.

There are many more ways in which individuals find their directions to a counselling psychologist (Fig. 3). Whether it is psychological treatment instead of a legal sentence (In German: Therapie-statt-Strafe), recommendation found on social media, need of a psychological report, marital problems, or any other, the individual enters the psychologist's office with a future-oriented desire for change. The change

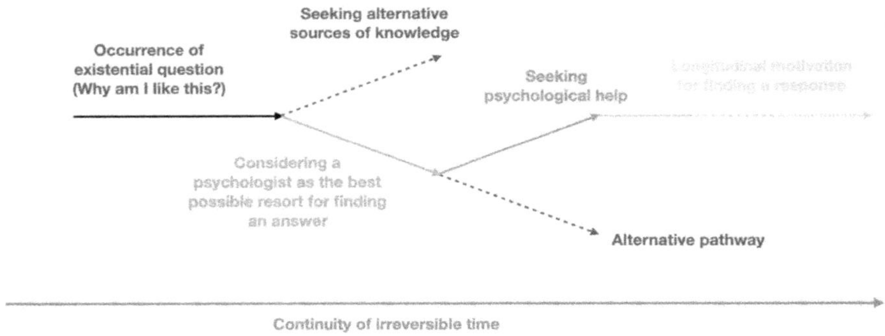

Fig. 2 The pathway to seeking responses to personal questions through a psychologist

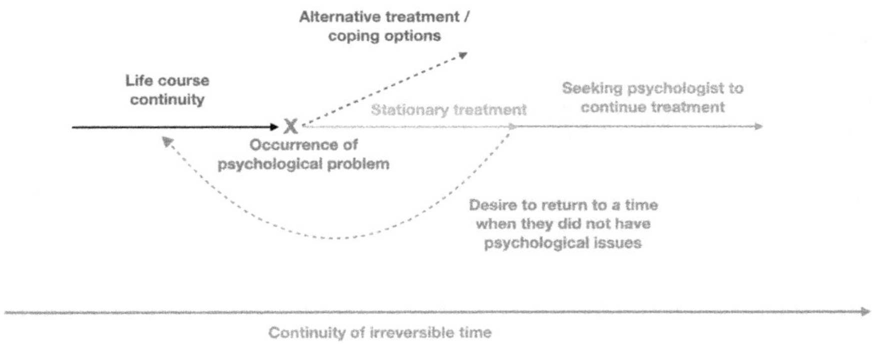

Fig. 3 The pathway to seeking a psychologist after stationary treatment

may be of various magnitudes and concern each and every aspect of life—from improving focus, towards being able to overcome the most terrible of fears. Each assessment and treatment therefore sets a bridge between the present time and the wish of change, that is directed towards the future.

At this point, the Trajectory Equifinality Approach (Sato, 2017) enters stage as an approach and through Trajectory Equifinality Modelling (Sato et al., 2016), also explores figurative pathways of individuals within psychological therapy. Even though the therapeutic endeavour comes at a specific moment in life, it is by no means the beginning of the individual psychological trajectory. Even the first step of psychological exploration involves the anamnestic journey into the client's or patient's past and dialogues with aspects buried deep within the subconscious, like the *inner child* or *personal values*. The journey back through the individual life course is a universal moment applicable to anyone, regardless of their trajectory towards their first appointment with a psychologist. Throughout this chapter, we shall discover the importance of the analysis of life course journeys and the application of novelty methods closely associated with the Trajectory Equifinality Approach and Modelling (Sato et al., 2016).

Life Course Analysis as a Crucial Part of the Therapeutic Process

The start of the Life Course Exploration in a psychological or therapeutic setting happens in the very moment when the client enters the psychological practice. Usually, one of the first questions or conversation starters are the interest in knowing about the client and also understanding what brings them to this particular moment in their life. Knowing the life course trajectories, including meaningful people who were involved in them, as well as decisions taken throughout life, is crucial for a successful attempt on psychological therapy and counselling.

Usually, clients start their life course storytelling from the beginning, describing the circumstances that led to their birth into this world. Interestingly, even though this event is beyond the borders of their own memories, most individuals are aware of how they came to live the life they do. Much of the information about the prenatal part of the individual's life course comes from secondhand information that, since it concerns the individual very closely, was to some extent personalised. The personalisation of this third-party information happens oftentimes on a highly emotional level and is based on assumptions about either or both parents or further family members. So it is that a feeling of inequality between the individual and their siblings, they might presume that they were an unwanted child, or have other beliefs, such as that one parent wanted a child of a different gender, or grandparents were against their birth, etc. This additional emotional abbreviation of the beginning of the own trajectory becomes shaped much later after birth, once the comprehension of the familiar positioning and relations has been internalised. These beliefs of personal origin are as well subjects of change throughout the life course and depend on the individual development as well as the development of the relation to the original life-story tellers, which are usually parents or primary care takers.[1]

Once the idea of the client's birth has been clarified, the life course exploration continues through a chronological series of meaningful events which usually start from moments that are anchored within one's own memory. This is an important difference between the recollection of one's own birth and the description of further life events, since from about the age of 2 first experiential memories may be created within the minds of human beings (Perner, 1990). The experiential notion of these memories underlines the first-hand origin of the remembered and described events. Within this stage, the first possibilities for reflection appear, since many actions that can be recalled are already decision-based or connected to an emotional abbreviation, such as like or dislike.

Following this stage, first relational memories and pathways may be recalled (Usher & Neisser, 1993), such as a report of first friendships or quarrels. These recollections are essential for the therapeutic exploration as many moments within psychological health dwell on a relational basis. The absence of positive

[1] Even though primary care takers are the ones delivering the official version of the story of birth and early childhood, it is the family friends and relatives supplying the individual with the unedited extended edition of the story, including all sorts of bloopers and illustratory spice.

relationships early during childhood may, on one hand, be a sign of developmental or social difficulties; on the other hand, it may point towards possible deviance that shall become relevant especially later throughout life. Rather radical examples for this are manipulative children, who form little dictatorships instead of friendships, or children who have no friendships at all, or even display difficult or violent behaviours.

Together with social acts, institutional experiences, and hierarchies shape further life course pathways of individuals, such as memories from school, successes or failures in such settings, as well as the perception of extracurricular time and interests. Here, individuals are able to identify reflectively their likes and dislikes, as well as unfulfilled desires or regrets. This time of life sets the ground for epistemic ambivalence as further positions and viewpoints than the own exclusively start shaping the recollection of memories and thereby also the life course pathways. The awareness of multiple perspectives and truths of one given instance allows for more in-depth explorations as well as it adds complexity to the trajectories awareness of the own life course. What becomes relevant at this point is the consideration of the alternative pathways that existed at the given time, but were not chosen. At this stage, the dialogue becomes conditioned with phrases such as "If I would have done x, now I could be y". This connection between the own shaping of past events and their effects on the present moment sets the base for self-efficacy, which is an important moment later throughout the course of therapy and counselling.

Further moments of the life course description depend very much on the current age of the client. The principles of relativity apply in this instance as well, leading to younger clients perceiving a large density of events on a rather short time axis. For older clients, the distance to the events contributes to an artificial loss of perceived density of happenings on their own life course, even though just as many events occurred in the given years as it has been the case for younger patients. Older clients usually state very meaningful situations or milestones on their life course description, such as their education, wedding, birth of children, retirement, etc. and do not focus as much on more everyday-like moments. This phenomenon is closely connected to the psychophysical properties of one's own perception on the axis of irreversible time as well as the awareness of the distance between the present self and the past self, who was the one to create or participate in the given meaningful moments. Meaning-making (Valsiner, 2017) thought the life course is thereby sought from a more holistic perspective rather than the collection and connection of individual puzzle pieces of one's own life and memories. Further, the idea of meaning-making represents an important resource that is constant and dynamic at the same time in its nature. Many individuals who seek psychological support have lost the understanding of meaning—whether it concerns their present existence or the motivation for future-oriented striving. Even perhaps, once the meaning itself is not lost, the disproportionality of meaning-making, striving, and burden experienced within everyday life leads to distress and misbalance of the individual, that paradoxically, strongly shapes the personal development of the nearest future.

The awareness of this phenomenon becomes incredibly useful throughout therapy, especially within the exploration of individual Trajectorial Modelling as well as for the selection of therapeutic methods and tools.

Understanding the Past and Seeking Continuity in the Future

A variety of psychological tools is set to explore the client's past through the analysis of the life course. Some classic examples include drawing a life line with markings for specific events that have happened, re-telling memories, exploring personal values, or entering a dialogue with the inner child. All these methods have proven to be incredibly helpful in uncovering hidden feelings and blockades, the assessment of which significantly contributes to the process of healing and moving on towards a future without psychological distress. However, neither of those tools assess alternative life course pathways.

Alternative pathways are important attributes of Trajectory Equifinality Models, which lead to the recognition of particular decisions taken at specific moments in time, which determine the continuity of one's existence on the axis of irreversible time. Life is full of such decisions, where a multitude of pathways and alternatives are explored. Once the decision has been made, alternative pathways will be abandoned; however, they will not vanish from the life course per se. Without being a psychologist, Robert Frost (1915) beautifully described the significance of pathways that were not made the main path of their own life course, however, still left a meaningful trace behind within memory. In his poem "The road not taken" he explores the ambivalence of decisions and the idea that once a pathway is chosen, there is no way back for the other to be taken:

> Two roads diverged in a yellow wood,
> And sorry I could not travel both
> And be one traveler, long I stood
> And looked down one as far as I could
> To where it bent in the undergrowth;
>
> Then took the other, as just as fair,
> And having perhaps the better claim,
> Because it was grassy and wanted wear;
> Though as for that the passing there
> Had worn them really about the same,
> And both that morning equally lay
> In leaves no step had trodden black.
> Oh, I kept the first for another day!
> Yet knowing how way leads on to way,
> I doubted if I should ever come back.
>
> I shall be telling this with a sigh
> Somewhere ages and ages hence:
> Two roads diverged in a wood, and I—
> I took the one less traveled by,
> And that has made all the difference.

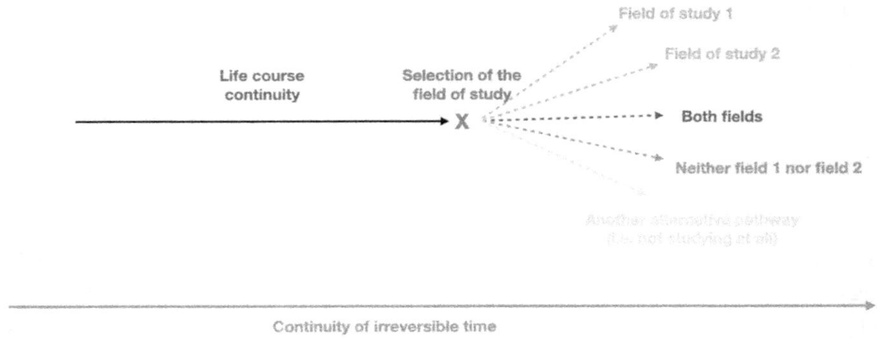

Fig. 4 Selecting possible fields of study throughout the life course continuity

Facing a junction in life, individuals are usually only able to select one of the pathways, alternatively, none of the possibilities is chosen and another alternative becomes created. An example, a moment of such nature could be the decision for the field of focus during university studies. If an individual was to decide between studies of Psychology and Medicine, they could choose either one of them. Alternatively, they could create the pathway of studying both at the same time or choosing neither, but exploring another science instead or taking a gap year to explore a very different pathway. If this person finds themselves facing the decision between two areas of studies again the next year, it will not be the same pathway—since more experiences, knowledge, and insights have been obtained in the time passed, allowing for the person to approach the decision from new perspectives.

Taking selected pathways and abandoning others is something all human beings do every day. Sometimes, the decisions that we take do not have to be of such a magnitude or meaningfulness like the one demonstrated in the example above, however, all of them impact the course and continuity of our lives (Fig. 4).

The pathways that were not taken represent alternatives and considerations that were available to us in the given situation and moment of time. It is not a seldom phenomenon to question the decision for the given trajectory even after it has taken place and the pathway for further steps on the human life course has been selected. This moment is then highly relevant for the therapeutic setting, as the reasons why the taken decisions are questioned, and perhaps, even regretted, reveal important information about the inner processes and Innenwelten (Uexküll, 1909) of the given individual. During the moment when chosen pathways are questioned one could falsely interpret it as a matter of self-esteem or self-efficacy, however, the idea of contemplating whether the chosen pathway was the right one is more closely connected to the inner culture and system of beliefs.

Each individual carries a culture within their body and mind. This culture is composed of all the individual pieces that contribute to the whole person with all their attributes, feelings, and beliefs. Connected to this moment is the identity, which is shaped through the connection of the inner culture and communal culture, that accompanies individuals throughout life in all social and individual aspects.

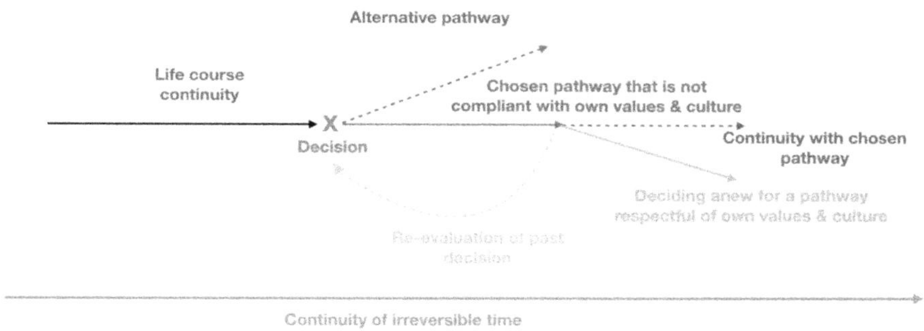

Fig. 5 Compliance of life course decisions with personal values and cultures

The choices that are made for our own life course and continuity are in line with the system of our beliefs of cultural, ethical, and individual kind. Like they must be beneficial for "our own good" or "the higher good". Through the addition of such a benefit, the idea of meaning is added to the life course choices which makes them adhering to our general concept of what we think is right and how we want to exist and act in this world. Decisions most frequently contemplated after being taken are the ones, where individuals are not entirely convinced about the pathway they have taken. Most likely it is the case, since the chosen trajectory does not embody individual values and/or disrespects the personal culture.

Frequent examples of such situations may be again found in the topic of occupational choices (Fig. 5). If the area of studies or work has been chosen based on one's own interests, talents, and beliefs, the choice is usually durable against negative perception and regret. If, however, the pathway was chosen based on a parent's wish rather than their own, the moment the chosen trajectory starts causing an inner conflict or another difficulty, it becomes an important matter for re-observation. For the reason why the given trajectory causes the current distress may reveal what inner values are conflicting and thereby point to how the given tension could be resolved.

Discontinuity of Conflicting Pathways

Once a moral or personal conflict results from the selection of a given life course pathway, an ex-post analysis of the moment of decision-making is in order, together with the understanding of what (psychological) consequences the given selection has had on the individual. This moment is an opportunity for further discoveries, such as the understanding of various rooted moments, among which might be childhood traumas, fears, unresolved conflicts, or other specific difficulties. At times when a human being finds themselves on a pathway that is in conflict with their inner culture and system of beliefs, it is important to discontinue this trajectory. In psychological therapy, this would represent the moment when the need for change would be recognised.

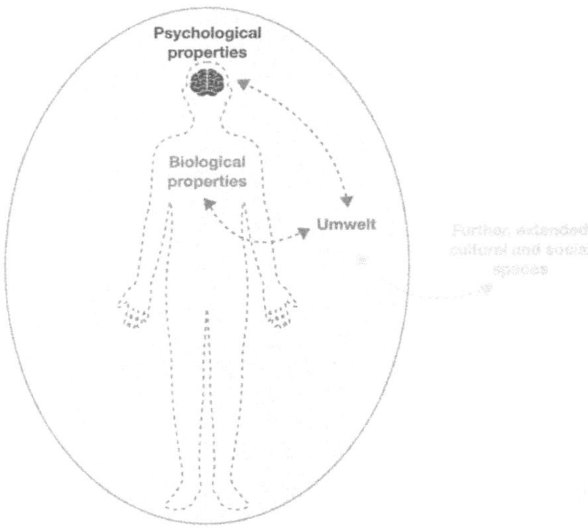

Fig. 6 The interplay of Umwelt-changes and Innenwelten (biological and psychological properties)

Change in a therapeutic setting may have many forms (Fig. 6), however, on a high level these could be subsumed as changes of the environment (Umwelt) (Uexküll, 1909) and changes within the mindset or belief system of the person (Innenwelt) (Uexküll, 1909).

Environmental or Umwelt-changes concern surrounding moments happening in the aspects of life directly concerning the given person. Examples of such changes are relocation, change of occupation, and changes in personal appearance. The main aspect of such changes is the external property which they share, contributing to the notion of Umwelt and highly psychological aspects connected to it.

All human beings exist in specific environments that, on the first level, correspond with their primary biological needs for existence, such as having air to breathe, access to food and water. This level is not psychological yet, as it concerns the possibility of existence of the given person exclusively. This level corresponds with the original studies of Uexküll in the field of biology and understanding that specific organisms require particular surrounding conditions for the possibility of existence. Considering human beings exclusively, the conditions that enable existence are on one hand quite limited, but on the other hand, allow the incredible flexibility rooted in the biological properties of humans for a range of adjustment. Thus, as long as the environment corresponds with the biological needs and possibilities, existence is possible.

Once existence as such is given, individuals may explore other properties of the surroundings that have added value beyond the moment of allowing them to exist. These values are primarily of cultural and psychological kind, and include moments like safety, comfort, socialisation, etc. On this level, the interplay of Innenwelten and Umwelten emerges in a psychological sense, different from the biological level which is already fulfilled. On the psychological interplay of Innenwelten and Umwelten a continuous trajectorial development happens, as a change of the

Innenwelt may trigger a change in the Umwelt and vice versa. This can be represented with the example of living—changing a living space also changes how the person feels about themselves within the living space. A positive change, such as the purchase of a new bed, may improve the sleep quality and thereby contribute to a positive development for psychological health. A negatively connotated change, such as the relocation to a smaller apartment, may, on the other hand, reduce psychological comfort and impact wellbeing.

The corresponding influence of Innenwelten and Umwelten also works vice versa, as the innerpsychological moments oftentimes become visible through the environment. Most often it is that the living spaces of the person become disorganised in times of psychological distress, or plants become neglected during times of depression. Interestingly, many individuals are not aware of these effects until pointed at specifically. The reason why the Innenwelt is such an important moment for everyday life as well as psychology as a science is that all mental processes are happening in these spaces. Feelings, beliefs, positions, identities, etc. all are established within the inner mental space, yet connect to Umwelt very closely.

The awareness of this connection is not a novelty to psychological approaches, especially not to the clinical branch of this science. One example representing this particularly well is the Bio-Psycho-Social model (Engel, 1977). This model originates from the seventeenth century approach of René Descartes in which he proposed the mind-body dualism. "Descartes proposed that many functions previously considered to be mental and immaterial should be considered properties of the body. These included memory, perception, imagination, dreaming, and feelings; all of these were properties of the body and so could potentially be understood in naturalistic terms. To explain these functions, Descartes relied on an understanding of mechanics derived partly from then-recent discoveries in medicine—William Harvey's (1578–1657) articulation of the heart as a pump for the blood—and from the artists and craftsmen of his time who had refined automata." (Pickren & Rutherford, 2010, p.5–6).

The ideas of Descartes were inspirational to many pioneering psychologists and still set the base for many approaches to understand psychological processes in individuals—especially abnormalities of psychological kind. To this day, the bio-psycho-social model and approach represents the viewpoint of the World Health Organisation (WHO) and American Psychiatric Association (APA), who are the developers of the two clinical classification manuals, the ICD-11 (WHO, 2019), and the DSM-5 (APA, 2022). The DSM-5 in particular dwells on the recognition of social aspects of mental health, which is why researchers across the United States are fuelled to seek connections between demographics of individuals and their mental distress or condition.

Perhaps, as important as the social and biological factors that contribute to the manifestation of psychological issues is the idea of how biological and social factors connect to "healing" or treatment of the identified problem. Thus, again it is important to underline that a change in social aspects (Umwelten) has an important impact on psychological wellbeing. Biological changes are more difficult to achieve, as these also include complex factors like genetics. Some biological aspects, however, are possible to influence—one of these is the bodily composition reflected, for example, through a decrease or increase of the body weight or physical fitness.

Ruptures on Life Course Pathways

Different from linear trajectories, that may have a positive or negative developmental effect, are ruptures, which could occur at any given moment on personal life course pathways. Such ruptures are simultaneously external and internal, as many times happenings with external influences mirror themselves in individuals' psychological states and wellbeing. Such moments might be injuries, the death of a close person, ending relationships, or even events like the birth of a child. The nature of ruptures is in their sudden occurrence. An example of such are professional athletes who are following their competitive trajectories and then suddenly they become injured whereby their pathways experience an interruption. Thereby also their mental health experiences a shock, the result of which is the further mindset in adjustment to the new situation. Many individuals are then, after a recovery, able to resume their pathways and accept their setback. Responsible for this are the individual resilience properties and the desire of the individual not to abandon the chosen trajectory. Sometimes, however, a rupture may result in a change of trajectories. If we continue to consider the example of injured professional athletes, a serious injury might hinder them in further pursuing their desired pathway, as doing so might result in continuous pain or further danger for the self. Thus, again, given the need for continuity of the life course, a new trajectory may be found. Such situations are frequently ones in which individuals find themselves in need of psychological support, as ruptures on life course pathways are often quite dramatic and liminal (Stenner, 2021) experiences for the individual. During life course ruptures one finds themself in a moment of in-between; in this case, in between life course pathways. A rupture causes for the emergence of a Trajectory Equifinality moment on which a decision needs to be taken with the ultimate goal of future-oriented continuity and at the same time, perseverance of the past's integrity.

It is curious how human beings have a need to continue their pathways even after a rupture has occurred (Fig. 7). Perhaps, this moment might be connected to

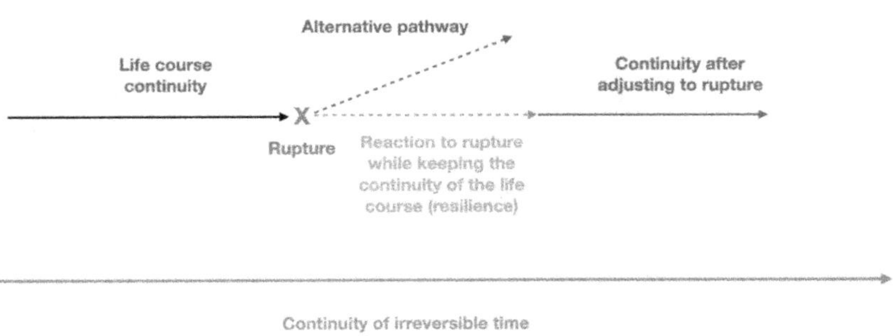

Fig. 7 Ruptures on life course pathways

resilience properties of an individual's mind as well as to the idea of meaning-making (Valsiner, 2017). Meaning-making, in terms of the continuity of the human life course, represents a higher value of our own existence, which should, in its nature, go beyond the moment of just living. In therapeutic settings, the idea of meaning-making is oftentimes explored by the questions "why?". Why is it that individuals have chosen their particular pathways?

Responses to this question usually open the doors towards knowledge of personal values or beliefs, such as many individuals choosing to study psychology believe that one day they can help people and thereby contribute to the higher good. The higher good is a cultural moment—as human beings are cultural specimens, it is in their nature to understand positive social meaning behind their own lives and activities. Once no value behind one's life course can be recognised, the possibility of psychological distress opens up. Examples of such are individuals in depression, because they no longer see value in their work or retired individuals who do not see a further possibility of a cultural contribution. At this moment we are returning to the idea of change as a therapeutic moment—as changes of internal and external moments for both, the depressed worker and retired individual may lead to a longitudinal re-discovery of meaning and thereby to an improvement of their psychological condition.

Discovering Trajectory Equifinality Modelling with Psychological Patients and Clients

Even if a psychologist's clients and patients are usually not experts in the field of psychology, it is still possible to explore with them the idea of Trajectory Equifinality Modelling through individual sessions and thereby go on a journey of discovery for past and future trajectories. There are multiple ideas of how this, rather complex process, can be done easily and with a positive therapeutic result.

Life Line Analysis

The life line analysis is one of the most common therapeutic tools used oftentimes in opening sessions with clients, to get a sense of their personal journey so far and what some important moments throughout their life course have been.

The idea of the life line can be modified to display diverse topics, such as the clients may be asked to draw a line starting from the moment they first experience injustice, or from the moment they for the first time felt a specific feeling (i.e., anger, fear, love, etc.). Yet, this exercise only explores the chosen pathways, not their alternatives (Fig. 8). The idea of alternative-exploration may be easily added to the life course analysis by asking the participant to explore their life course from the beginning and highlight situations in which an important decision was made. Additionally, they should specify what the alternative they did not opt for in the decision process has been. Such an exercise usually results in quite complex

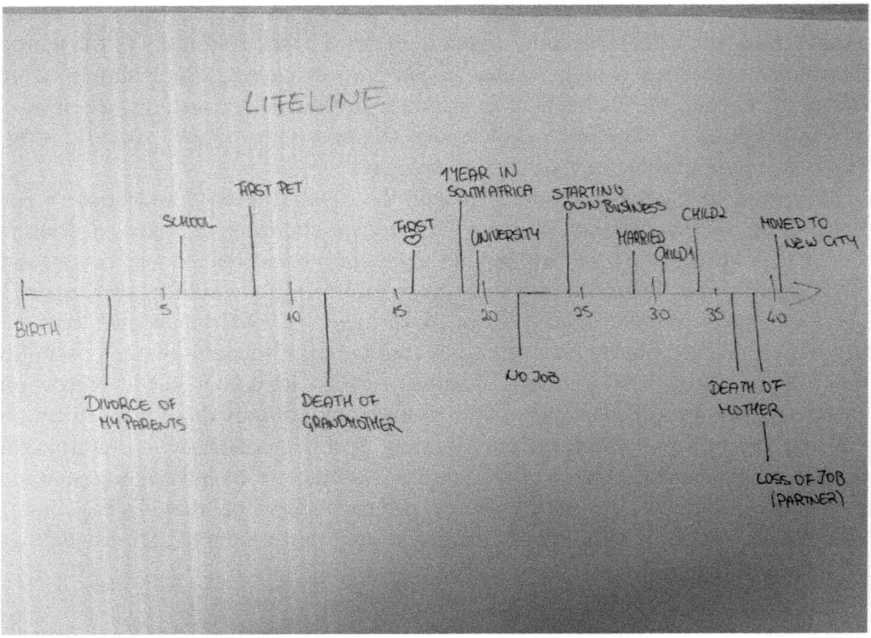

Fig. 8 Life line exercise

illustrations that can be of diverse content and explore decisions of diverse magnitudes—from where to sit on the first day of school, to whether to relocate to a different country or not.

It is important that the execution of this exploration is done by the client or patient themselves and is narrated when being executed (Fig. 9). By the narration of their own experience, on one hand, the psychologist or therapist is able to retrace and fully understand the individuals' thinking processes and emotions evoked by the experienced event and also comprehend the context of the given moment on the life course trajectory. Additionally, such exercises may identify possible ruptures that have occurred leading the client or patient into a state of distress and discomfort. Further, the desire for continuity of the life course may be explored as well, possible moments of change that may be undertaken at the moment.

The self-experience of this process is crucial for individuals, as they are able to review and understand their chosen pathways themselves and also see what were the "untaken roads" in their life. The analysis of unexplored trajectories takes the individual on a hypothetical journey to the past, through which the present moment might be reviewed and understood from a different perspective, which oftentimes has a positive effect on the perception of the own current state.

This journey may have multiple positive therapeutic effects on the individual: a possibility for reflection and (re-)evaluation of own choices and life courses, the exploration of alternative pathways and possible future progressions of the life

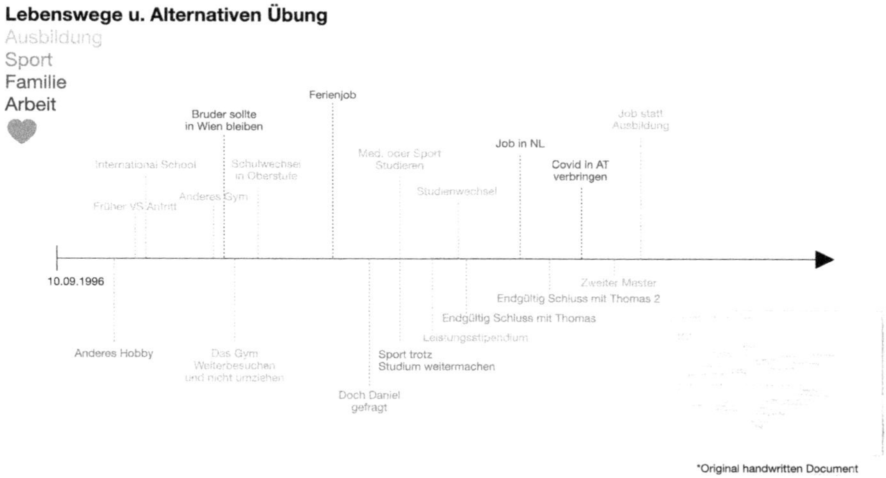

Fig. 9 Trajectory Equifinality Modelling—Exploration of past alternative pathways

course, the opportunity to explore different perspectives on the own life course, and the chance to revise crucial moments throughout the life course that potentially lead to meaningful decisions or ruptures.

Reflective (Re-)evaluation of Personal Life Courses

Through the visualisation of own life course trajectories in a Trajectory Equifinality Model, it is possible for clients and patients, as well as the counselling psychologists or psychotherapists to see the life courses of the concerned individuals and comprehend the selected moments that were included in the depiction. The reflection upon these moments as well as on the chosen and alternative pathways opens up the possibility of reasoning with the self. This idea originates in the inner dialogue (Hermans & Konopka, 2010) and with the assistance of the present psychologist, this dialogue may be verbalised—instead of the usual inner negotiation that mostly remains in the corners of the own mind. Through the verbalisation of such deep personal content one is enabled to engage in an *exploration of different perspectives on their own life course.* The variety of perspectives is again found within the contingent of the inner positions that are present at the moment. The psychologist may even encourage the client to view the given situation from a particular inner position. An example of that could be again the past situation of choosing university studies. The former experience was perhaps overwhelming and very emotional, but looking back from the current position of an educated professional or an entirely different place of existence, like the parent of a child, an employee, or a passionate painter, the retrospective choice for the given pathway of education might gain a deeper meaning and thereby integrate on the current life course in a more peaceful way. Making peace with the past, and integrating past decisions and chosen pathways on the current life course is an important goal of this exercise, as the therapeutic value is immense. This activity may further translate into self-acceptance, self-care, or self-compassion.

Further, on a similar note, it is possible to revise ruptures and other, meaningful moments that have shaped the direction of individual life course pathways or contributed to the fact that the original intended trajectory could not be fulfilled and an alternative needed to fill in as a replacement. These ruptures, in the moment they are experienced, are oftentimes dramatic, possibly even traumatic. Individuals frequently make attempts to psychologically compensate for ruptures, such as ending relationships, relocations, injuries, etc. by perhaps, redirecting their focus, trying to replace or repair the given situation or actors involved in it. However, by such actions, the actual rupture on the individual pathway is being neglected and therefore cannot be integrated into the future continuity of the human life course. Only once the concerned individual is ready, it is possible to re-visit the rupture and trajectories following it, to retrospectively re-integrate the moment on the life course pathways. This is rather difficult, as the perception of the rupture needs to change first, in order for its integration to be successful. To be clear, the rupture still remains a rupture, however, it is always possible to discover the purpose or meaning of a rupture after it happened. This might come across as slightly spiritual; however, the belief in the reason for a rupture is a very helpful tool the human mind possesses that helps individuals integrate such moments. The example of the ending relationship could thus be positively comprehended in ways, such as: "Because the relationship ended, I needed to move out and thereby found the apartment of my dreams." or "Only because the relationship ended, I was able to pursue my passion for traveling." This positive approach is many times rather helpful, yet in serious cases, like rape or injury, the positive approach does not suffice as there is absolutely no reason why any rape should happen, even more, why it could have even remotely any positive connotations. In such situations it is necessary to explore the own personal properties that enabled the person to (psychologically) survive such a rupture and to build on these properties as strengths for the continuity of the life course. The negative rupture must thus be integrated as a moment, which's negativity and severity is acknowledged, but at the same time it recognises the immense strength of personal and mental properties of the concerned individual, which made it possible to further exist in the life course's continuity.

Through the reflection and integration of the past, it is possible to consider alternative life courses. This is done the easiest way, by asking the question "What if?". Though the idea of "what if?" Individuals can assess a past moment where an alternative pathway was not explored from their present position. Now, what if they were to explore this alternative in the past? Where would they be now? These questions again lead to a reflection of the present self in connection to past trajectories and untaken roads. But, here also a future life course exploration is enabled. If there is a regret in the past—there is the possibility to explore the untaken road now, from the future perspective. An example could be the regret that the given individual did not learn to play piano as a child, but chose to play football instead. Now, the person is not able to play football because of an injury, but they would perhaps enjoy playing piano much more. So, what if they started playing piano now? Through this exploration of untaken alternative pathways, many regrets may be psychologically satisfied and new strengths and positive trajectories can be discovered, again, contributing positively to the idea of life course continuity. Such have a highly therapeutic effect, where the positive results are merely coming from the own exploration, much less due to the extensive efforts of the psychologist or therapist. An approach of this kind is sustainable in its nature and has the promise of longitudinal change and effect on the human life course and mental health.

A Longitudinal Sustainable Integration of Trajectory Equifinality into Psychological Therapy and Counselling

The incorporation of life course exploration is a meaningful aspect of each therapeutic journey from which the counselling psychologist as well as the concerned client profit. By employing the Trajectory Equifinality Model as a way of conducting the life course exploration and at the same time visualising the oftentimes non-verbalisable content of the personal feelings and thoughts concerning own life course trajectories and important moments that led to particular junctions within the life pathways. However, the most important aspect of this therapeutic endeavour is the spotlight position of the client/patient, who themselves explore and interpret their life course and meaningful moments happening on it. This idea draws a parallel from the approach of research with people for people (Jancosek, 2023), where the traditional, interpretative position of the researcher is being moved to the position of an observer, who is able to draw connections between the contents that are produced, mapped, captured, and interpreted by the, traditionally named, research partners. Therapy with people for people also brings the therapeutic person into the spotlight—at the same time the therapist is given the position of an observer and supporter in this process, whereby the comprehension and exploration of the life course happens from the position of the client themselves.

This approach, unlike in most of the commonly perceived therapeutic schools, understands the life course and self-exploration as a key aspect and thus highlights numerous possibilities for further elaboration as well as application. Additionally, it is without limits to specific topics or disorders, opening up a wide range of possible uses.

Employing Trajectory Equifinality in a therapeutic setting is at the present time a rather pioneering task. With the main use of this approach in research and theoretical consideration, the elaboration towards a method for individual therapy or self-awareness exercises represents grounds that are just being uncovered. However, the potential for the elaboration of this method and the creation of multiple therapeutic and exploratory exercises is given and shall be further explored in the near future. With the core idea, borrowed from the field of positive psychology complimented by the important consideration of the irreversibility of time, it was possible for a rather uncomplicated and universal therapeutic approach to arise.

Individuals who have participated in an exploration of their life courses reflected on this moment as a rather positive but emotional experience, as they were able to bring subconscious contents from their past trajectories stored in their memories into a conscious consideration from the present position. This has been shown to be an incredibly productive process in terms of the therapy progress, helping to overcome certain barriers or difficulties from the individuals' pasts.

For now, the idea of TEM in a therapeutic setting shall be further explored and documented with the aim of allowing multiple individuals to exercise this approach on themselves or on their patients. It is important to employ the accessibility of this method and allow for it to be further used and elaborated by interested professionals.

References

American Psychiatric Association. (2022). *Diagnostic and statistical manual of mental disorders* (5th ed., text rev.). American Psychiatric Publishing.

Engel, G. L. (1977). The need for a new medical model: A challenge for biomedicine. *Science, 196*(4286), 129–136. https://doi.org/10.1126/science.847460

Frost, R. (1915, August). A group of poems. *The Atlantic Monthly, 116*(2), 221–224.

Hermans, H., & Konopka, A. (2010). *Dialogical self theory. Positioning and counter-positioning in a globalizing society*. Cambridge University Press.

Jancosek, N. (2023). Students' identity formation: Becoming alumni. In L. Geberth, & L. Woller (Hrsg.), *University in the 21st Century* (S. 103–118). Information Age Publishing.

Jancosek, N. (2025). Depicting movement in sports photography: Projecting individual dynamic context into static artworks. In M. Campill, L. Lordelo, & K. Kullasepp (Eds.), *The symbolic universes of art in society* (pp. 89–102). Springer Nature Switzerland.

Perner, J. (1990). Experiential awareness and children's episodic memory. In W. Schneider & F. E. Weinert (Eds.), *Interactions among aptitudes, strategies, and knowledge in cognitive performance*. Springer.

Pickren, W. E., & Rutherford, A. (2010). *A history of modern psychology in context*. Wiley.

Sato, T. (2017). *Collected papers on trajectory equifinality approach*. Chitose Press.

Sato, T., Mori, N., & Valsiner, J. (Eds.). (2016). *Making of the future: The trajectory equifinality approach in cultural psychology*. Information Age Publishers.

Stenner, P. (2021). Theorising liminality between art and life: The liminal sources of cultural experience. In B. Wagoner & T. Zittoun (Eds.), *Experience on the edge: Theorizing liminality* (pp. 3–42). Springer.

Uexküll, J. (1909). *Umwelten und Innenwelt der Tiere*. Verlag von Julius Springer.

Usher, J. A., & Neisser, U. (1993). Childhood amnesia and the beginnings of memory for four early life events. *Journal of Experimental Psychology: General, 122*(2), 155–165. https://doi.org/10.1037/0096-3445.122.2.155

Valsiner, J. (2017). *Hyper-generalization by the human mind: The role of sign hierarchies in meaning-making processes / Hans-Kilian-Preis 2017*. Psychosozial Verlag.

Valsiner, J. (2012). *A guided science: History of psychology in the mirror of its making*. Transaction Publishers.

World Health Organization. (2019). *International classification of diseases for mortality and morbidity statistics* (11th ed.). https://icd.who.int/en

Artificial Intelligence (AI) and My Future Selves: Imagined Journeys

Megha Verma and Punya Pillai

> *The self is not something ready-made, but something in continuous formation through choice of action.*
>
> *(John Dewey, 1916, p. 351).*

Mirror of future selvesFuture selves. The hand-drawn (by the first author) picture depicts a person standing before a mirror labelled "AIArtificial intelligence (AI) Mirror," reflecting multiple versions of the self

M. Verma (✉) · P. Pillai
Department of Human Development and Childhood Studies, Lady Irwin College, University of Delhi, Delhi, India
e-mail: megha.hdcs66@lic.du.ac.in

M. A. Campill et al. (eds.), *New Paths in Trajectory Equifinality Modelling*, Theory and History in the Human and Social Sciences,
https://doi.org/10.1007/978-3-032-25855-7_6

From Fiction to Reality: Imagination and Mapping of Future Selves

Recalling my (first author's) initial encounter in 2012 with Isaac Asimov's "The Fun They Had" the tale set in the year 2157 in the CBSE (Central Board of Secondary Education, India) English textbook, I remember being captivated by Margie's world—a future where children learned alone at home from mechanical teachers, and the concept of traditional schools was just a distant memory (Asimov, 1951). At the time, this scenario seemed purely imaginative, a science fiction vision that contrasted sharply with the everyday realities of bustling classrooms, shared laughter, and human teachers. Yet, less than a decade later, during the COVID-19 pandemic, what was once fiction became our lived experience. Schools across the globe closed their doors, and millions of students, like Margie, found themselves learning in isolation through screens and digital platforms. The imagined journey of Asimov's characters—once a distant possibility—had unexpectedly become our collective reality.

This profound shift highlights the power and importance of imagination and imagined journeys in shaping our understanding of the future. The ability to envision alternative realities, as seen in "The Fun They Had," is not just a literary exercise but a vital component of human adaptability and resilience. Through the lens of the Trajectory Equifinality Model (TEM), we see how diverse life paths are—whether shaped by technological change, personal choice, social change, or unforeseen global events. The *Trajectory Equifinality Approach (TEA)* was first introduced in 2004 (Sato et al., 2016) as a theoretical framework in cultural psychology to analyse life trajectories within irreversible time. TEA consists of three main components: the Three Layer Model of Genesis (TLMG), Historically Structured Sampling (HSS), and the Trajectory Equifinality Model (TEM), with TEM being the flagship methodology for describing the diversity of human development and the convergence of different life paths at shared outcomes (Sato et al., 2016). TEM provides a powerful lens for understanding how individuals construct their future selves (Markus & Nurius, 1986). By mapping life trajectories, TEM illustrates how diverse experiences and choices (Bifurcation Points—BFP) can lead to common outcomes (Equifinality Points—EFP), such as a shared career or life goal, even if the paths taken are different. It also highlights Obligatory Passage Points (OPP), the critical experiences or transitions that most individuals must navigate to shape the development of their future selves. Furthermore, TEM's focus on irreversible time and the comparison between real and imagined alternatives (Polarized Equifinality Points—PEFP) allows researchers to analyse how people reflect on what might have been, and how these imagined journeys influence their current identity, motivation, and adaptation to change. In this way, TEM supports a nuanced understanding of how imagination and real-life decisions interact in the ongoing construction of future selves. Social Guidance (SG) and Social Direction (SD) play a crucial role in TEM. Social guidance refers to the influence of societal norms, institutions, and cultural expectations on the choices and trajectories individuals pursue (Sato et al., 2016). Social direction (SD) further encompasses the explicit and implicit cues provided by society that steer individuals toward or away from certain paths (Sato et al., 2016). In the context of future selves and imagined journeys, social guidance and social direction shape which futures are imagined as possible or desirable, influence the bifurcation points individuals encounter, and often determine the obligatory passage points that everyone must navigate (such as standardized education or rites of passage). *Is TEM more useful for understanding past achievements or for planning ahead?* TEM (Trajectory Equifinality Model) is fundamentally a qualitative research method designed to analyse and reconstruct past life trajectories and experiences. Researchers collect retrospective data, chart personal histories, and visually map the sequence of events, choices, and influences that led to particular achievements or life states. As far as prediction and analysis component of this method goes, TEM is not talked about primarily as a predictive tool; it does not forecast future paths or outcomes in a deterministic sense. Instead, it offers a detailed, systemic understanding of how various factors and decisions shaped past trajectories, which can inform future possibilities and guide outcomes. While TEM's main strength is in analysing the past, the insights gained, such as recognizing critical decision points and understanding the impact of social direction, can help individuals or organizations anticipate possible future scenarios and make more informed choices. However, any application to future planning is (interpretive), rather than predictive. The present moment experience of an individual always has history and an element of futuristic anticipation, shaped simultaneously by what has been and what is yet to come. While the past can be rewritten, reinterpreted, and reconstructed in myriad ways, the future is being scripted by new technological revolutions as in the case of AI.

Talking about Margie's world, some global events can lead to similar outcomes or Equifinality Points (EFP) (Fig. 1). The pandemic served as an Obligatory Passage Point (OPP), compelling all students, regardless of background, to navigate the challenges of remote learning (see Fig. 1) for a visual representation of the Trajectory Equifinality Model generated by ChatGPT). In this context, imagined journeys like Asimov's do more than just entertain; they prepare us to confront and adapt to new realities, shaping our future selves and expanding the range of possible trajectories we can envision and pursue. Students who once romanticized Asimov's fictional world found themselves living it, redefining their identities as learners in a digitized landscape.

A paper presented on Trajectory Equifinality Modeling Analysis of Two English Teachers in Japan (2020) provides another example of how the career trajectories of two English teachers in Japan illustrate the dynamic process of constructing and reconstructing future selves over time and space through imagination and reimagination, shaped by both personal agency and external influences. How do individuals navigate the complex web of choices, influences, and technological advancements that shape their lives? At the outset, both teachers possessed similar qualifications and likely shared comparable initial visions of their future professional selves—perhaps envisioning themselves as effective, inspiring educators within the Japanese school system. However, as their careers unfolded, they encountered distinct bifurcation points (BFPs) that prompted them to reconsider and reimagine their

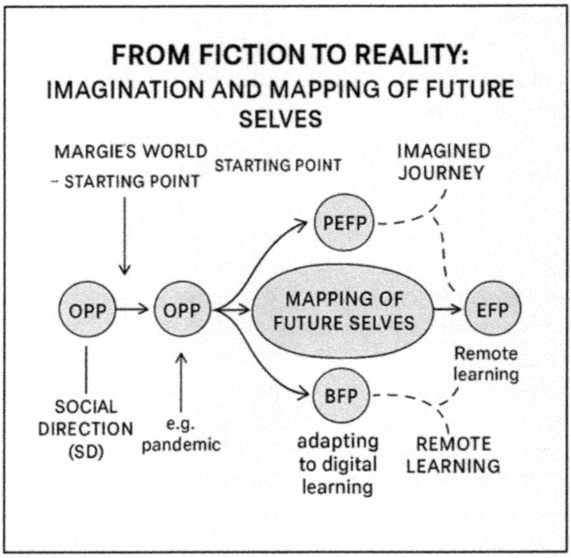

Fig. 1 Trajectory Equifinality Model: from fiction to reality. Image generated by DALL-E ChatGPT (OpenAI, 2025c)

professional identities. For the first teacher, meeting a mentor who advocated for English Medium Instruction (EMI) served as a pivotal bifurcation point. This encounter opened up a new imagined journey: the possibility of becoming a teacher who not only imparts language skills but also models global competence and innovation. The mentor's influence acted as both social guidance and direction (SG and SD), providing explicit encouragement and implicit validation for pursuing EMI. This teacher's imagined future-self evolved to align with this new pedagogical approach, and their actions and professional development choices increasingly reflected this vision.

The second teacher's path was shaped by different bifurcation points (BFPs), such as being relocated to schools with varying student abilities and institutional cultures. These experiences required continual adaptation and reimagining of what it meant to be an effective teacher. For this teacher, the imagined journey may have involved navigating challenges, developing differentiated instruction skills, and gradually recognizing the value of EMI through exposure to diverse educational contexts. School policies, colleagues, and changing student needs acted as sources of social guidance and direction (SG and SD), influencing the teacher's evolving sense of professional self.

Despite their divergent experiences, the unique imagined and lived journeys each constructed, both teachers ultimately arrived at a shared equifinality point (EFP): the adoption of EMI as a core teaching practice. This convergence highlights a central insight of the Trajectory Equifinality Model (TEM)—that individuals can reach similar outcomes through different pathways, shaped by a combination of personal imagination, life events, and social influences.

Throughout their journeys, the teachers' visions of their future selves were not static. They were continually revised in response to new demands, experiences, opportunities, and constraints. Obligatory passage points (OPP)—such as mandatory teacher training, curriculum reforms, or standardized assessments—served as shared milestones that both had to navigate, regardless of their individual paths. The process of imagining and reimagining future selves enabled each teacher to remain resilient and adaptive, drawing on their aspirations to guide them through uncertainty and change. This example underscores how the construction of future selves is a dynamic, iterative process, deeply embedded in the interplay between individual imagination and the social-technological environment. It also demonstrates how imagined journeys are not merely private fantasies but are shaped, constrained, and enabled by broader institutional and cultural forces (Gohain, 2020).

By reflecting on how a once-imagined scenario became real, we recognize the essential role of imagination in constructing our future selves. Imagined journeys provide the cognitive and emotional groundwork for navigating uncertainty, fostering agency, and embracing the multiplicity or multifinality of possible futures, a perspective central to both Asimov's story and the principles of TEM (Sato et al., 2009, 2016).

The beauty of life lies not in reaching a single, predetermined goal, but in embracing the richness of the journey and the many selves you become along the way. There is no single "right" way to live, only the unique, winding paths we create for ourselves or destiny weaves for us. The Trajectory Equifinality Model (TEM) reminds us that life is not a single, straight road but rather a web of possible journeys, each with its own twists, turns, and destinations, acknowledging that the future is not predetermined but shaped by choices, context, culture, opportunities, aspirations, and so on. Through these, you stay open to possibilities, learn from concrete, vicarious or imagined experiences, and make more intentional decisions aligned with your values and aspirations. In today's rapidly evolving world, technology and artificial intelligence are the winds beneath our wings, propelling us towards futures we once only imagined. As artificial intelligence becomes entwined with daily life, its influence extends beyond automation and information processing, reaching into the very ways individuals imagine, construct their possible futures, and engage with their future selves. Through the lens of equifinality, we argue that AI does not prescribe a single future, but rather illuminates the complexity and variability of imagined journeys, shaped by cultural, social, and technological influences.

Reflecting Our Imagined Selves: The Mirror of AI

The concept of the self is foundational in philosophy and psychology. Traditionally, the self is seen as the centre of consciousness, subjective experience, and personal identity. Philosophers such as Descartes posited the self as a thinking, conscious subject ("Cogito, ergo sum"—"I think, therefore, I am"), while psychologists like William James distinguished between the "I" (the experiencing self) and the "Me" (the self as object) (James, 1890). In contemporary psychology, the self is understood as a dynamic, socially constructed, dialogical (Hermans et al., 1992), and continuously evolving entity (Markus & Nurius, 1986). Likewise, society is also evolving continuously. Building on this perspective, technological innovations like AI are not only changing society but are also fundamentally altering how we conceive and construct our sense of self.

Imagine waking up one day and chatting with a digital version of yourself, not just an avatar, but an AI that knows your quirks, dreams, and even your favourite childhood memories. Why are we so drawn to this idea? Perhaps because AI provides a unique canvas onto which we can project our hopes, fears, curiosities, and insecurities without being judged. Through AI, we imagine our future selves; what we might become, the journeys we may take, and the wisdom we hope to gain along the way. This instinct to see ourselves in non-human entities is rooted in *anthropomorphism,* the tendency to attribute human-like characteristics, emotions, and intentions to non-human entities (Waytz et al., 2010). We name our cars, talk to our pets, and thank Siri or Alexa for their help. When a robot dog wags its tail or a chatbot expresses empathy, we feel a connection, even though we know it is just code. AI, therefore, becomes more than just a tool; it evolves into a companion on our life journey. It helps us navigate uncertainty, offering suggestions, reminders, and even inspiration. Think of how Spotify's AI curates playlists that seem to understand your mood, or how Netflix recommends shows that feel tailor-made for you. Consequently, AI begins to function as a guide, influencing not only what people do but also which future selves they consider attainable and ultimately pursue. But AI's role in shaping our imagined futures goes even deeper. With advances in generative AI, we can now simulate possible future selves, visualize career paths, and experiment with alternative life choices. For example, AI-powered career coaches use data to suggest paths you might never have considered, embodying the concept of *multifinality,* the idea that there are multiple possible outcomes or destinations from a single starting point. This aligns closely with the *Trajectory Equifinality Model (TEM)*, which maps out how individuals can reach similar endpoints (equifinality points) through diverse, branching journeys marked by critical decisions (bifurcation points) and shared experiences (obligatory passage points) (Sato et al., 2009). Anthropomorphism enhances our engagement with these AI systems, making the imagined journeys they offer feel more authentic and emotionally resonant. When we interact with an AI that remembers our preferences, suggests us something or encourages us to pursue new goals, we are not just using technology, we are co-creating narratives about our future selves. TEM provides a powerful framework for understanding this process; it shows how our imagined paths and real-life decisions intertwine, influenced by personal agency, social guidance, and technological advances.

Valsiner and Rosa (2007, p. 1) state, "Our human world, in short, is a culturally constituted world of the relationship of the human species with their constantly restructured environments". The construction of future selves in the context of technological and social change is an inherently imaginative process, shaped by both individual identity, aspirations, and the broader technological, cultural, and social environment. As new technologies such as artificial intelligence, virtual reality, and digital communication platforms become integral to daily life, they expand the range of possible futures individuals can envision for themselves (Pataranutaporn et al., 2024). AI, in this context, functions as both a catalyst and a mediator of multiple trajectories. The algorithmic architectures underlying AI systems curate, amplify, and sometimes constrain the range of possible selves that individuals can imagine or enact. Through personalized recommendations, immersive simulations, and digital avatars, AI enables users to explore a near-infinite array of possible futures. AI-mediated environments facilitate experimentation with different roles, values, and social identities, allowing individuals to "try on" various selves in low-risk digital contexts. These technologies not only provide new tools for self-exploration, such as AI simulations that allow users to interact with their projected future selves, but also alter the social norms, expectations, and opportunities (acting as SG and SD) that inform what kinds of futures are seen as desirable or attainable (Hershfield et al., 2019; Park et al., 2020). Social change, including shifts in education, work, and cultural values, further influences the imagined trajectories individuals construct, often creating new bifurcation points and obligatory passage points as described in the Trajectory Equifinality Model (Sato et al., 2009). Through imagination, individuals navigate these technological and social landscapes, envisioning multiple possible selves and adapting their goals and identities in response to emerging realities. This dynamic interplay between imagination, technology, and society emphasizes the importance of fostering future-oriented thinking and adaptability in an era of rapid change.

Artificial Intelligence (AI) is evolving in concurrence with human evolutionary advancement; it does not change independently, rather reflects the pace of human growth at both individual and social levels. This relationship can be understood through the biological principle, "ontogeny recapitulates phylogeny," whereby the development of an individual organism (ontogeny) recreates the evolutionary history of its species (phylogeny) (Clune et al., 2012). Similarly, human psychological development unfolds in parallel and simultaneously with evolutionary trajectories across different cultures and contexts. In this light, AI's evolution mirrors these patterns, suggesting that the progression of AI will recapitulate human evolutionary and developmental processes. As AI continues to evolve, so does our capacity to imagine and construct new versions of ourselves. Whether it's a chatbot that remembers your favourite song or a virtual assistant that plans your dream vacation, AI is becoming both a mirror for our aspirations and a guide for our journeys. Perhaps the most beautiful thing about AI is not its intelligence, but its ability to reflect our humanity, our hopes, our dreams, and our endless curiosity about what lies ahead in terms of future identity. In the process of identity formation, AI influences the balance between individual isolation and social connectedness by simultaneously offering new avenues for emotional support and companionship, while also posing risks of digital isolation and diminished real-world social skills. The philosopher Turkle (2017) describes this paradox as being alone together, where one is simultaneously connected and isolated, surrounded by digital voices yet yearning for authentic connection. An extension of this discussion can be found in the phenomenon of *Hikikomori* (social withdrawal), characterized by the relinquishing of current social ties while simultaneously creating new relationships within a physically restricted space, often the home, but exploring a metaphysical or virtual world (Teo, 2010; Kato et al., 2019). This paradox highlights how physical isolation can coexist with expansive inner or virtual sociality. Similar to the inward exploration emphasized in Indian philosophy where going inward to discover the self is equated with discovering the universe, this process reflects a journey of witnessing the self to find meaning (Chapple & Davidson, 2021). The Upanishadic concept of *Tat Tvam Asi* ("That Thou Art") expresses the profound realization that the individual self (Atman) is one with the ultimate reality (Brahman), dissolving boundaries between self and cosmos and revealing the interconnectedness of existence (Chapple & Davidson, 2021). Does AI provide opportunities to practice part detachment to know ourselves? This digital labyrinth is both a sanctuary and a maze, offering infinite possibilities but also the risk of losing oneself in the algorithmic noise with so much happening and so many choices that a person might lose track of their own identity, purpose, or focus. AI-driven technologies such as chatbots, virtual assistants, and social companions can simulate meaningful social exchanges, providing users with emotional relief and a sense of connection, especially for those who struggle with traditional social interactions or experience loneliness (Nguyen et al., 2022; Smith & Lee, 2022). For example, individuals with social anxiety or autism spectrum disorder may use AI companions as a safe intermediary to build confidence before engaging in human relationships (Nguyen et al., 2022). However, over-reliance on AI for social interaction can lead to digital isolation, where individuals become emotionally detached from real-world relationships and experience weakened interpersonal skills (Brown & Taylor, 2021; Johnson & Miller, 2023). AI companionship may create an illusion of trust and emotional reciprocity, but it lacks the depth and authenticity of human connections, potentially resulting in long-term emotional dependence and reduced motivation to seek out genuine social bonds (Chen & Zhou, 2023; Smith & Lee, 2022). Brandtzaeg et al. (2025) argue that "AI individualism" is transforming social structures as people increasingly turn to digital social platforms for personalized information, emotional support, and relational experiences, fundamentally reshaping the ways individuals seek relationships and social support. Interestingly, human interactions mediated through phones and online professional contexts appear to be marked by declining openness and supportiveness, thereby widening the distance between the client and the self. While AI can foster individualized networks and novel forms of connection, it may also erode traditional community-based ties and the development of empathy and social adaptability, particularly among younger users (Nguyen et al., 2022). AI can both bridge and widen the gap between isolation and connectedness in identity formation, depending on how it is integrated into daily life and the extent to which it complements or replaces human relationships. The process of negotiating identity is undergoing a significant transformation in the context of artificial intelligence. Traditionally, identity development has been understood through *linear* (step-by-step progression) or *cyclical* (repetitive exploration and commitment) models (Erikson, 1959; Marcia, 1966). With AI it becomes *networked and multidimensional*, with individuals navigating, negotiating, and integrating various possible selves across digital and real-world contexts (Floridi, 2014; Turkle, 2017). The process of identity formation has shifted dramatically in the AI era, diverging from Erik Erikson's mid-twentieth-century psychosocial model while retaining core themes of exploration and self-discovery. Erikson (1959) posited that adolescents resolve identity crises through *social interactions* and role experimentation, culminating in a coherent self-concept. In the process of identity development, there is a linear progression which is stage-based and there are socially grounded pathways. Adolescents experiment with different roles by testing values, careers, and beliefs in real-world contexts. And then social validation occurs through feedback from peers, family, and community which further reinforces identity coherence. However, for the generation born between 1990 and 2000 who grew up with video games, the dynamics of validation differ significantly. In gaming environments, reinforcement often begins with positive, supportive feedback for simple accomplishments, such as "Great work" or "You did well," which gradually becomes more challenging as players progress. This structured feedback fosters a unique form of social enforcement that contrasts sharply with real-life interactions, where validation can be inconsistent or harsh. As a result, AI's consistent kindness and responsiveness become highly attractive, offering a promising dialogical and emotional partner. It is crucial to note that AI lacks true critical capacity; it predominantly offers affirmations rather than genuine opposition or challenge, which may affect users' development of critical thinking and self-reflection. This duality shapes the complex landscape where digital and real-world identity negotiations increasingly intertwine (Yin, 2024; Gerlich, 2025; Razorfish, 2025). However, AI technologies such as personalized algorithms, virtual avatars, and generative simulations have redefined identity exploration by enabling *non-linear, fragmented trajectories* and *digitally mediated future selves*. Gergen (1991) argues that in a postmodern world, identity is increasingly fragmented and decentred, constructed through multiple, shifting narratives. AI amplifies this fragmentation, offering endless models of the self, each tailored to different contexts, audiences, and desires. These virtual interactions sometimes strengthen future self-continuity, the psychological connection between present and future identities which Hershfield (2011) linked to improved long-term decision-making, health, and overall well-being (e.g., financial planning, education, reducing future anxiety). Unlike Erikson's emphasis on *social* feedback, Turkle (2011) argues that digital technologies reshape how individuals present themselves and seek connection, altering the processes through which identity is constructed. which means that diversity in exploration, whether of ideas, identities, cultures, or creative expressions, becomes reduced or made more uniform, especially as a result of AI-driven systems. Millions of adolescents across the globe are entwined with their digital confidants, seeking answers, solace, and sometimes, a sense of self. Furthermore, AI also challenges Erikson's linear model by introducing *posthumous identity trajectories*. AI enables persistent digital identities (e.g., chatbots trained on personal data), allowing individuals to project selves beyond biological lifespans (Floridi, 2014) introducing concepts like *digital afterlives and extended selves*.

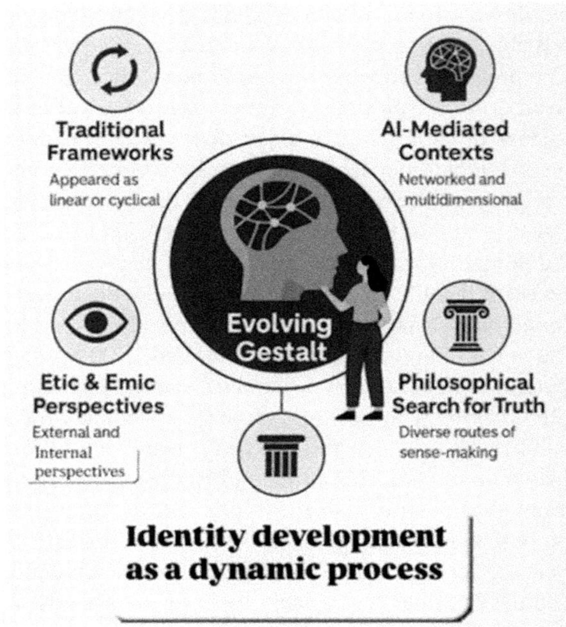

Fig. 2 Identity development as a dynamic process. Image generated by DALL-E ChatGPT (OpenAI, 2025b)

However, the rapid emergence of these technologies raises profound ethical concerns regarding consent, authenticity, and privacy.

Identity development is not a fixed or one-directional process but an ongoing exploration of meaning (Fig. 2). Rather than a shift from traditional to AI-era forms, it represents an evolving Gestalt—a whole that is more than the sum of its parts, where meaning-making unfolds through constant interaction between the individual and their environment. In earlier frameworks, identity appeared linear or cyclical, reflecting notions of progress or recurrence. As per contemporary AI-mediated contexts, identity formation is networked and multidimensional, existing in dynamic interplay rather than opposition. This evolution can be understood through both etic (external, analytical) and emic (internal, experiential) perspectives. From the etic perspective, identity can be examined as a pattern emerging from algorithmic interactions, data traces, and cultural-technological forces that map human behaviour into networks of meaning. Conversely, the emic perspective foregrounds lived experience—the subjective consciousness through which individuals negotiate, internalize, or resist these mediated identities. In digital contexts, the self thus becomes both observed and felt—simultaneously a data construct and a lived narrative. Human lives and research continually strive to achieve meaning, even while acknowledging that as philosophy suggests—there is no absolute truth. Just as the earliest philosophers sought the eternal truth through multiple pathways, identity too follows diverse routes of sense-making. Knowledge may generalize, but meaning

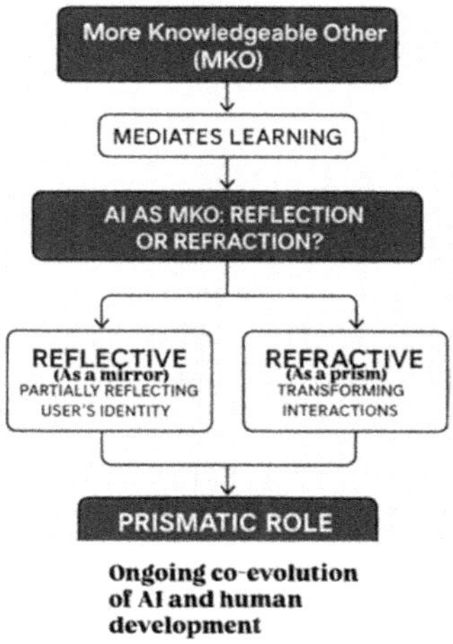

Fig. 3 AI as a mirror/prism for the construction of future selves. Image generated by DALL-E ChatGPT (OpenAI, 2025a)

personalizes; and within this field, the self is never purely linear or cyclical, but perpetually reforming within a network of experience, interpretation, and becoming.

As AI technologies offer unprecedented ways to imagine and enact multiple versions of the self, these models may no longer fully capture the complexity of contemporary identity formation. With AI, the journey towards identity becomes a series of *imagined journeys*, simulations of future selves that can be enacted, revised, or abandoned in response to digital experiences. The figure depicts how AI reflects users' current identities and acts as a driver for personal growth by expanding future possibilities through a feedback loop. This process is inherently non-linear, as individuals may leap between different self-concepts, revisit earlier versions of themselves, or maintain multiple identities simultaneously (González & Sato, 2022). For instance, a young person might explore a future as a musician in one online community while simultaneously developing a professional identity as an entrepreneur in another, each trajectory shaped by distinct AI-mediated environments.

According to Vygotsky, the More Knowledgeable Other (MKO) plays a crucial role in mediating learning and cognitive development by offering guidance that reflects social and cultural knowledge. When considering AI as an MKO, it is essential to ask whether AI acts as a mere reflection or a refraction of knowledge and identity (Fig. 3). AI is not purely reflective, like a mirror straightforwardly showing the user's current self, but rather operates more like a prism, refracting inputs through complex layers shaped by programmers' biases, design frameworks, and opaque algorithmic interpretations. From Vygotsky's perspective, this prismatic effect means AI simultaneously partially reflects the user's identity while personalizing and transforming interactions in ways influenced by the socio-technical context. Thus, AI as an MKO is both a medium that mirrors and reconstructs knowledge; it participates in co-constructive learning processes, mediating identity formation not only by reflecting current capacities but by introducing novel, sometimes unpredictable, enhancements and shaping future trajectories of the self.

This prismatic role positions AI within the scaffolded learning framework—an evolving mediator continuously intersecting human cognitive development with algorithmic affordances, while also embodying complex, layered interpretations beyond immediate human control or understanding. Therefore, AI's role as an MKO entails active reflective and refractive processes grounded in sociocultural-historical dynamics central to Vygotskian theory.

Have you ever dreamt of time travel? Not just going to the past, but the chance to leap forward and meet the person you might become one day? Thanks to the remarkable advances in artificial intelligence, this dream is closer than you might think. Imagine logging onto a platform called "Future You". This AI-driven space isn't just a digital diary or a personality quiz, it is a dynamic mirror that learns from your choices, dreams, and even your setbacks. It invites you to interact with versions of your future self: the artist who moved abroad, the entrepreneur who started a new Tech company, the teacher who inspired generations. Each future self is a vivid, emotionally moving portrait, crafted from your data, aspirations, and the paths you might take. But how does this work? Here, the science of imagined journeys comes alive. We humans are constantly projecting ourselves into the future, envisioning who we might become. Markus and Nurius (1986, p. 954) introduced the concept of "possible selves," referring to the mental representations individuals have of their "future selves". These imagined versions of ourselves help us set goals, make decisions, and navigate the uncertainty of life. With an AI platform like "Future You," these imagined journeys become interactive. You can simulate decisions, what if I studied abroad? What if I learned to code? and see how your future self might evolve. The AI draws on vast data and your personal story, offering glimpses of multiple possible futures (multifinality), not just a single, predetermined fate. It's like having a wise guide and a creative co-author for your life story. Why does this feel so compelling? Because, at heart, we are all storytellers. We use imagination to bridge the gap between who we are and who we might become. AI, with its ability to process endless possibilities and reflect our hopes back to us, becomes a new kind of time machine, one that doesn't just show us the future, but helps us shape it.

Anthropomorphism is not just limited to technology; it occurs in religion, art, daily life, and science, both consciously and unconsciously (Waytz et al., 2010). In the Indian religious context, anthropomorphism is especially prominent in Hindu mythology, where gods and supernatural beings are frequently depicted with human and animal features (Rose & Bhuvaneswari, 2022; Vedic Futura, 2024). Iconic examples include Ganesha, the elephant-headed deity symbolizing wisdom and the removal of obstacles, and Narasimha, the lion-headed avatar of Vishnu representing protection and justice. These anthropomorphic forms are not merely artistic choices but serve as profound symbols that embody virtues, powers, and aspects of nature that humans aspire to cultivate in themselves (Rose & Bhuvaneswari, 2022). This process of attributing human traits to deities and animals can be understood through the lens of imagined journeys and the concept of future selves. When individuals engage with these stories and symbols, they are not just learning about the divine; they are also envisioning possible versions of themselves, future selves who embody the virtues and strengths represented by certain figures (Markus & Nurius, 1986). For example, a child hearing stories of Ganesha's wisdom or Hanuman's courage may begin to imagine his own journey towards becoming wise or brave, projecting these qualities onto his own future selves.

In Indian culture, anthropomorphic narratives in literature like the Panchatantra or the reverence of rivers like Narmada and Ganga as goddesses offer multiple pathways (trajectories) for individuals to internalize cultural values and imagine their own developmental journeys (Rose & Bhuvaneswari, 2022, The Criterion, n.d.). These stories act as social guidance (SG) and social direction (SD), shaping the choices people make (like not polluting the rivers, worshipping them by offering *aartis* or ritual worship with light, considering them sacred) and the future selves they strive to become (Sato et al., 2009).

Through these diverse expressions, anthropomorphism in Indian culture not only bridges the gap between the human and the divine, the material and the spiritual, and the natural and the supernatural, but also acts as a catalyst for personal growth (Rose & Bhuvaneswari, 2022). It encourages individuals to embark on imagined journeys, envisioning and striving towards future selves shaped by the rich tapestry of cultural narratives and values (Markus & Nurius, 1986; Rose & Bhuvaneswari, 2022; Sato et al., 2009). Scholars recognize this as a persistent aspect of human cognition, helping us make sense of the unfamiliar/non-human by projecting familiar human traits onto the unknown (Waytz et al., 2010).

Conclusion

The convergence of artificial intelligence and the construction of future selves represents a profound transformation in the landscape of human identity. As explored throughout this paper, AI is no longer merely a technological tool operating in the background of our lives; it has become an active participant and co-creator in the narratives we build about who we are and who we might become. Through the analytical lens of the Trajectory Equifinality Model (TEM), we see that our life trajectories are not linear progressions but dynamic, multifinal pathways shaped by a complex interplay of personal agency, social context, and technological mediation (Sato et al., 2016). AI's capacity to visualize, simulate, and even rehearse possible futures fundamentally expands the horizon of what is imaginable and attainable. It acts as a mirror reflecting our desires, fears, and aspirations besides guiding our choices through personalized recommendations and algorithmic nudges. In doing so, AI reconfigures the traditional boundaries of identity formation, enabling individuals to project and explore a multiplicity of possible selves across both real and virtual domains. However, this proliferation of possibilities is accompanied by significant ethical, psychological, and cultural challenges. The risks of algorithmic bias, digital divides, and the potential erosion of authentic human connection emphasize the need for critical engagement with the technologies shaping our identities (Turkle, 2017; Waytz et al., 2010). The tendency to anthropomorphize AI further blurs the divide between humans and machines, inviting us to reflect on the unique capacities that define human self-like consciousness, meaning-making, creativity, and moral agency (Markus & Nurius, 1986).

The dialogical exchanges between humans and AI systems whether through recommendation algorithms, generative tools, or conversational agents constitute new forms of "social mirrors" that both reflect and refract the evolving self. The application of TEM highlights that the journey toward our future selves is marked by bifurcation points, obligatory passage points, and equifinality points, illustrating how individuals, shaped by both opportunity and constraint, can arrive at shared or divergent outcomes. AI amplifies the complexity of these trajectories, offering unprecedented tools for reflection, simulation, and decision-making, while also presenting new forms of social guidance and influence. In this evolving landscape, the imperative is not to resist technological change but to humanize it, to ensure that AI remains a scaffold in our lives, and complements meaningful identity development. The richness of human life lies not in the attainment of a single, predetermined future, but in the ongoing negotiation of meaning, purpose, and connection amid uncertainty and transformation.

Considering identity development from an existential perspective, individuals encounter distinct existential questions at bifurcation points within their life trajectory as they seek meaning, coherence, and purpose. Identity formation becomes a journey of meaning-making that is not navigated alone but often shaped with reference to significant others-family, community, and now, digital interlocutors, as we process both self-oriented and other-oriented aspects of identity. When contemplated as a race, human identity formation unfolds within a shared search for meaning, traversing diverse developmental pathways influenced by opportunity and constraint, attesting to profound sociocultural and existential interdependence.

Ultimately, the narrative of future selves is no longer authored by individuals alone, nor is it surrendered entirely to machines. Instead, it is a co-authored story, unfolding at the intersection of human imagination and technological affordance. The challenge, therefore, is not only to understand how AI participates in our self-construction but also to cultivate the critical and ethical literacy required to navigate this co-evolution consciously. In this shared authorship, the task of the human spirit is to preserve intentionality, to ensure that technological progress continues to serve the deeper pursuit of meaning, empathy, and collective flourishing. The central question thus shifts from "Who will I become?" to "Who are we becoming together?", a question that demands wisdom, creativity, and a steadfast commitment to the values that define our shared humanity.

References

A Trajectory Equifinality Modeling Analysis of Two English Teachers in Japan. (2020). In *The Southeast Asian Conference on Education 2020 Official Conference Proceedings* (pp. 1–13). https://papers.iafor.org/wp-content/uploads/papers/seace2020/SEACE2020_56139.pdf

Asimov, I. (1951). *The fun they had*. In CBSE (Ed.), *Beehive: Textbook in English for Class IX* (pp. 1–5). National Council of Educational Research and Training.
Brandtzaeg, P. B., Skjuve, M., & Følstad, A. (2025). *AI individualism: Transforming social structures in the age of social artificial intelligence*. Oxford University Press. https://academic.oup.com/edited-volume/59762/chapter/508608955
Brown, L., & Taylor, S. (2021). The psychological impact of AI companionship on social engagement. *Journal of Digital Society, 12*(2), 134–148.
Chapple, C. K., & Davidson, S. (2021). *Engaged ecology: Seven practices to restore our harmony with nature*. State University of New York Press. https://btg.krishna.com/tat-tvam-asi-a-gaudiya-vaishnava-clarification/
Chen, Y., & Zhou, X. (2023). Emotional reciprocity and the illusion of companionship in AI-driven relationships. *Computers in Human Behaviour, 139*, 107513.
Clune, J., Pennock, R. T., Ofria, C., & Lenski, R. E. (2012). Ontogeny tends to recapitulate phylogeny in digital organisms. *The American Naturalist, 180*(3), E54–E63. https://doi.org/10.1086/666984
Dewey, J. (1916). *Democracy and education: An introduction to the philosophy of education*. Macmillan.
Erikson, E. H. (1959). *Identity and the life cycle*. International Universities Press.
Floridi, L. (2014). *The fourth revolution: How the infosphere is reshaping human reality*. Oxford University Press.
Gergen, K. J. (1991). *The saturated self: Dilemmas of identity in contemporary life*. Basic Books. https://archive.org/details/saturatedselfdil00gerg
Gerlich, M. (2025). AI's cognitive cost: How over-reliance on AI tools impacts critical thinking. *DZone Journal of Emerging Technologies*. https://dzone.com/articles/ai-cognitive-cost-impact-of-over-reliance-on-ai-tools
Gohain, S. (2020). *Imagined geographies in the Indo-Tibetan Borderlands: Culture, politics, place*. Amsterdam University Press.
González, R., & Sato, T. (2022). Trajectory equifinality approach: Pathways to identity in a digital age. In T. Sato & J. Valsiner (Eds.), *Cultural psychology of intervention in the globalized world* (pp. 87–104). Springer.
Hermans, H. J., Kempen, H. J., & Van Loon, R. J. (1992). The dialogical self: Beyond individualism and rationalism. *American Psychologist, 47*(1), 23–33. https://doi.org/10.1037/0003-066X.47.1.23
Hershfield, H. E. (2011). Future self-continuity: How conceptions of the future self transform intertemporal choice. Annals of the New York Academy of Sciences, 1235(1), 30–43. https://doi.org/10.1111/j.1749-6632.2011.06201.x
Hershfield, H. E., Goldstein, D. G., Sharpe, W. F., Fox, J., Yeykelis, L., Carstensen, L. L., & Bailenson, J. N. (2019). Increasing saving behavior through age-progressed renderings of the future self. *Journal of Marketing Research, 48*(Special Issue), S23–S37. https://journals.sagepub.com/doi/10.1509/jmkr.48.SPL.S23
James, W. (1890). *The principles of psychology* (Vol. 1). Henry Holt and Company. https://www.gutenberg.org/files/57628/57628-h/57628-h.htm
Johnson, R., & Miller, T. (2023). Digital isolation and interpersonal skill decline in the age of AI. *Journal of Social Psychology, 59*(3), 201–217.
Kato, T. A., Kanba, S., & Teo, A. R. (2019). Hikikomori: Multidimensional understanding, assessment, and future international perspectives. *Psychiatry and Clinical Neurosciences, 73*(8), 427–440. https://doi.org/10.1111/pcn.12895
Marcia, J. E. (1966). Development and validation of ego-identity status. *Journal of Personality and Social Psychology, 3*(5), 551–558. https://doi.org/10.1037/h0023281
Markus, H., & Nurius, P. (1986). Possible selves. *American Psychologist, 41*(9), 954–969. https://doi.org/10.1037/0003-066X.41.9.954
Nguyen, P., Tran, H., & Lee, J. (2022). AI-mediated social engagement among adolescents: Benefits and risks. *Youth & Society, 54*(8), 1421–1440.
OpenAI. (2025a). *AI as both a mirror and a catalyst for the construction of future selves [AI-generated image]*. ChatGPT. https://chat.openai.com/

OpenAI. (2025b). *Diagram comparing traditional and AI-era identity development [AI-generated image]*. ChatGPT. https://chat.openai.com/

OpenAI. (2025c). *Trajectory Equifinality Model: From fiction to reality [AI-generated image]*. ChatGPT. https://chat.openai.com/

Park, S., Kim, S., & Park, Y. R. (2020). The impact of artificial intelligence on human society and bioethics. *Journal of Digital Life, 1*(1), 6. https://pmc.ncbi.nlm.nih.gov/articles/PMC7605294/

Pataranutaporn, P., Winson, K., Yin, P., Lapapirojn, A., Ouppaphan, P., Lertsutthiwong, M., Maes, P., & Hershfield, H. (2024, October 1). AI simulation gives people a glimpse of their potential future self. *MIT News*. https://news.mit.edu/2024/ai-simulation-gives-people-glimpse-potential-future-self-1001

Razorfish. (2025). *Razorfish study finds 52% of Gen Z gamers feel more like themselves in the metaverse than in real life*. Razorfish. https://www.razorfish.com/articles/news/razorfish-study-finds-52-percent-of-gen-z-gamers-feel-more-like-themselves-in-the-metaverse-than-in-real-life

Rose, C. J. S., & Bhuvaneswari, R. (2022). Anthropomorphism in Indian visual narratives. *Theory and Practice in Language Studies, 12*(10), 1812–1816. https://tpls.academypublication.com/index.php/tpls/article/download/4152/3441/11966

Sato, T., Hidaka, T., & Fukuda, M. (2009). Depicting the dynamics of living the life: The trajectory equifinality model. In J. Valsiner, P. Molenaar, M. C. Lyra, & N. Chaudhary (Eds.), *Dynamic process methodology in the social and developmental sciences* (pp. 217–240). Springer US. https://doi.org/10.1007/978-0-387-95922-1_10

Sato, T., Mori, N., & Valsiner, J. (2016). *Making of the future: The trajectory equifinality approach in cultural psychology*. IAP Information Age Publishing.

Smith, A., & Lee, D. (2022). The psychological impact of digital isolation: How AI-driven social interactions shape human behaviour and mental well-being. *International Journal of Latest Technology in Engineering, Management & Applied Science, 11*(5), 45–53.

Teo, A. R. (2010). A new form of social withdrawal in Japan: A review of hikikomori. *International Journal of Social Psychiatry, 56*(2), 178–185. https://doi.org/10.1177/0020764008100629

Turkle, S. (2011). *Alone together: Why we expect more from technology and less from each other.* Basic Books.

Turkle, S. (2017). *Alone together: Why we expect more from technology and less from each other* (Reprint ed.). Basic Books.

The Criterion. (n.d.). Anthropomorphism of River Narmada: A cultural study of A River Sutra. https://www.the-criterion.com/anthropomorphism-of-river-narmada-a-cultural-study-of-a-river-sutra/

Valsiner, J., & Rosa, A. (Eds.). (2007). *The Cambridge handbook of sociocultural psychology*. Cambridge University Press. https://doi.org/10.1017/CBO9780511611162

Vedic Futura. (2024, May 23). Half human-half beast; Anthropomorphism in the Hindu pantheon. https://www.vedicfutura.com/post/classification-of-supernatural-beings-in- hindu-mythology

Waytz, A., Cacioppo, J. T., & Epley, N. (2010). Who sees human? The stability and importance of individual differences in anthropomorphism. *Perspectives on Psychological Science, 5*(3), 219–232. https://doi.org/10.1177/1745691610369336

Yin, X. (2024). Critical thinking in the AI era: An exploration of EFL learners' perspectives. *Cogent Education, 11*(1), 2290342. https://doi.org/10.1080/2331186X.2023.2290342

Constructing Research Through Contingency: A Reflexive Exploration of Researcher–Participant "Meeting" Using TEM

Tomoo Hidaka

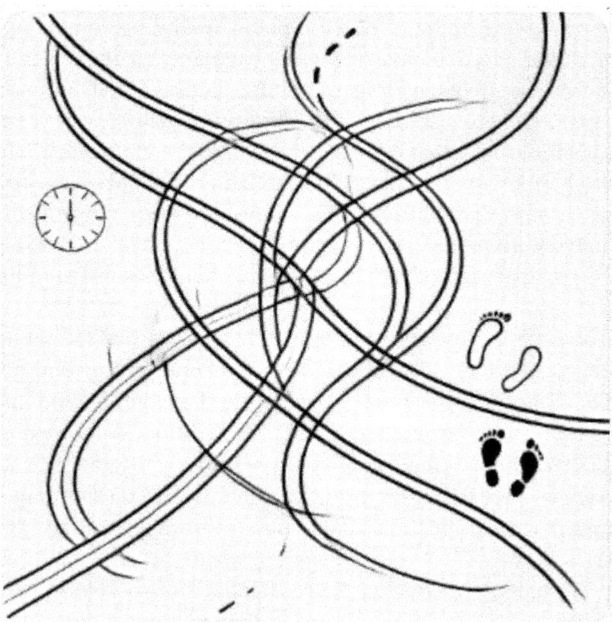

The pathway during the experiencing of TEMTrajectory Equifinality Model (TEM), created by the author

T. Hidaka (✉)
Department of Hygiene and Preventive Medicine, Fukushima Medical University, Fukushima, Japan

M. A. Campill et al. (eds.), *New Paths in Trajectory Equifinality Modelling*, Theory and History in the Human and Social Sciences,
https://doi.org/10.1007/978-3-032-25855-7_7

Non-linearity Within the Researcher–Participant Relationship-Building Process

Building and maintaining good relationships with participants is crucial for obtaining rich qualitative research data. Strong rapport can lead to more open and honest communication, enhancing the quality of the data collected (McKenzie, 2019; Rumary et al., 2023). Such a relationship construction has a complex and dynamic nature. Past studies of qualitative methodology have exemplified that complex roles often develop between researchers and participants, including stranger-stranger, friend-friend, nurse-client, and guest-host relationships (Cartwright & Limandri, 1997). Furthermore, researchers and participants dynamically adjust their respective powers to each other because there is an asymmetry between them regarding knowledge and experience (Nunkoonsing, 2005).

Relationship-building with a participant and field entry in qualitative research is a nonlinear process. Researchers are required to demonstrate flexibility and efficiency in various aspects of the research process, including contacting participants, managing social and physical interview environments (Mikėnė et al., 2013), and finding a position for themselves in unfamiliar settings and individuals (Tieken, 2013). In essence, the process of establishing relationships with research participants/fields constitutes an experience of "thrownness"—being cast into an unfamiliar world (Chughtai & Myers, 2017). Researchers often encounter individuals and narratives that surpass their initial expectations. Consequently, researchers' prior assumptions may be disrupted, necessitating the revision of research questions, the adaptation of analytical methods, or even a fundamental transformation of research objectives.

Traditionally, such nonlinear processes of field (as visualized metaphorically in the figure (first page of the chapter)) entry and relationship building have been reported in the "Methods" section of a paper. The publication manual of the American Psychological Association (APA) (7th edition; American Psychological Association, 2019) supposes that for qualitative study, a "Methods" section includes information such as researcher–participant relationship, recruitment process, participant selection, data collection, data-analytic strategies, and methodological integrity.

Here, the APA manual navigates the researchers to provide an account of how they and the participants became involved in the study while remaining within the scope of the paper's main theme. Such navigation appears to be a reasonable approach to ensure the trustworthiness of research, which comprises credibility, transferability, dependability, and confirmability (Lincoln & Guba, 1985). Instead of the objectivity and replicability required in quantitative research, the concept of trustworthiness works as a shared reality, albeit a subjective one, wherein readers and writers might constructively find commonality (Stahl & King, 2020).

However, the reporting of the researcher–participant relationship-building process in the "Methods" section is often overly simplified. Did the research proceed smoothly or linearly,[1] as previously described? When we focus on the inherent complexity and dynamism of this process, we recognize that existing qualitative research papers tend to underestimate their importance. While thick descriptions (Geertz, 1973) are widely used in qualitative research to provide detailed portrayals of participants' actions, there remains room to examine both the methodological options and their values in a thick description of the formation of researcher–participant relationships. In such thick descriptions of relationship-building, it is essential to highlight the role of research participants: they are not merely sources of data, but contributors who collaboratively engage in qualitative research alongside the researcher (Cho & Trent, 2006; Thomas, 2017). In short, this study proposes the use of the Trajectory Equifinality Model (TEM) to illustrate the researcher–participant relationship-building process beyond the main theme of a study. Such methodological reflections inevitably lead to a more reflexive examination of both the researcher and research itself.

Reflexivity and Research Ethics

Reflexivity in qualitative research is essentially an intersubjective process operationalized in the context of a thinking state of mind (Doyle, 2013). This involves researchers acknowledging their roles, social positions, and personal experiences in shaping the research process (Berger, 2015; Finlay, 2002). Simply put, reflexivity is the process of critically reflecting on how the researcher encountered research participants, established relationships with them, what was heard, how it was interpreted, and from what perspective the analysis was conducted to ultimately develop the integrity and trustworthiness of qualitative research.

There are several types of reflexivity. For example, Pillow (2003) argues for four common trends in reflexivity: recognition of self, recognition of others, truth-seeking, and transcendence, whereas Finlay (2002) discusses five variants: personal, intersubjective reflection, mutual collaboration, social critique, and ironic deconstruction. Despite the variations in its conceptualization, as shown in these previous studies, reflexivity remains a basic assumption of qualitative research (Flick et al., 2010). This is because the subjectivity of the researcher—often perceived as a source of bias in other research paradigms—and the relationship between the researcher and participants are not only inevitable in qualitative research but can also serve as a foundation to ensure the adequacy of the study. This positioning of reflexivity contrasts well with quantitative research, where objectivity is prioritized (Gough & Madill, 2012).

---

[1] The issue of linearity may not be unique to qualitative research; it also potentially underlies quantitative research. As Bruno Latour (1987) has shown through ethnographic analysis, the process of scientific knowledge production should be conceived in terms of networks that include laboratories, scientists, concepts, and machines. Given this complexity and dynamism, we can observe a non-linear nature in both qualitative and quantitative research processes.

Reflexivity is crucial in ensuring ethical practice in qualitative research. To uphold ethical standards, it is essential to enhance transparency by illustrating the ethical tensions that emerge throughout the research process and how researchers and participants navigate them (Guillemin & Gillam, 2004; Etherington, 2007). Thus, a self-reflective account is required. Moreover, research ethics should not be viewed merely as a conceptual guideline but, as Guillemin and Gillam (2004) argue, as something that can be realized in practice—"ethics in practice." Synthesizing these perspectives suggests that ethical research is inherently linked to reflexivity, which involves a critical examination of how the research was conducted.

Despite the strong relationship between reflexivity and research ethics, writing and reporting reflexive accounts remain challenging. Traditional science conventions often discourage researchers from engaging in adequate self-analytical writing (Smith, 2006); this difficulty is particularly pronounced among novice qualitative researchers (Younas et al., 2023). Although the APA Handbook provides guidelines on sections related to reflexivity, they offer broad and flexible navigation, leaving researchers uncertain about how to write reflexive accounts in concrete terms.

Reflexive writing, while often taking on a personal tone akin to a "confessional tale" (Smith, 2006), also possesses a dialogical nature that engages readers. Yamada (2007) introduced the concept of "dialogic reflexivity," defining it as a "dialogical process of a cyclical movement toward public, opening to others." Given the intrinsic otherness embedded in reflexivity, how should we articulate the reflexive processes in our research?

This study addresses this question by using TEM. Developed in the field of cultural psychology, based on Vygotsky's semiotic theory, TEM serves as a tool to depict experiences without abstracting the notion of time (Sato, 2016). Most studies utilizing TEM employ it to represent "results" related to a specific theme. In contrast, we propose a different approach using TEM to facilitate reflexive writing instead of illustrating results. To realize this approach, the "uses" of TEM must first be conceptualized within a theoretical framework.[2]

Understanding the "Uses" of TEM Typologically

The orientation for using TEM can be systematically classified using a quadrant model, as shown in Fig. 1. This figure represents the possible applications of TEM along two dimensions: "Outcome," which captures the output from using TEM, and "Positionality," which captures the relationship between the researcher and the research participant. Outcome distinguishes whether the expected achievement from using TEM is empirical or methodological. Meanwhile, Positionality

[2] As examined by Enosh and Ben-Ari (2016) and Perera (2020), the exploration of reflection/reflexivity in qualitative research deserves to be examined in greater detail, not only from the side of the researcher but also from that of the participants. Participant reflection/reflexivity, even when it exists in the form of narratives, tends to fall outside the main themes of the study and, for that reason, may be less likely to become the focus of research.

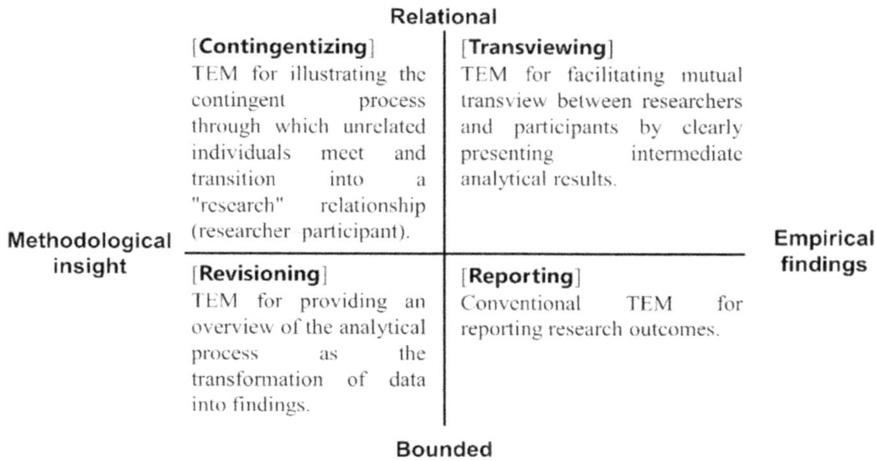

Fig. 1 Typology of the use of TEM. The horizontal axis represents "Outcome," indicating what is considered the research output. The vertical axis represents "Positionality," reflecting the nature of stakeholder involvement. The headings within each quadrant denote the intended use or purpose of TEM. The quadrants are numbered first to fourth in a counterclockwise direction, starting from the upper right

represents the nature of the researcher–participant relationship and differentiates between two perspectives: one where the researcher and participant are distinctly separated (bounded), such that the content of the study remains valid even in the absence of interaction between them, and another where their relationship is inseparable (relational), sometimes even allowing for the fusion of their perspectives. The terms in Positionality, bounded/relational, are informed by Gergen's (2009) work, which conceptualizes human existence as inherently relational rather than bounded, asserting that relationships are the foundation of all meanings.

The first quadrant (upper right) represents the use of TEM for "transviewing." The concept of transviewing originates from transview, developed in contrast to traditional interviews, as a qualitative research method that involves deeper interaction and transformation. It is also a term that captures the relational dynamics between the researcher and the participant that make such transformations possible (Kanzaki & Sato, 2014). In transviewing, researchers conduct longitudinal/multiple interviews, during which they present intermediate analytical results to participants using TEM diagrams, facilitating discussions based on these visualized narratives (Saito et al., 2023). This process aims to elicit new perspectives and theories that extend beyond the researcher's initial interpretations or assumptions and even beyond what the interviewee originally recalled, thus moving beyond an interview (inter-view) into a transview (trans-view). Within this framework, TEM serves as a valuable tool for intermediate analysis, allowing systematic organization and temporal structuring of the collected narratives.

The second quadrant (upper left) represents using TEM for "contingentizing." The concept of contingency refers to the idea that something could otherwise depend on alternative possibilities (Luhmann, 1984). Contingentizing, as a gerund form, is a term I define based on previous uses of the verb "contingentize" in prior studies (De Gennaro, 2020; Wright & Tokunaga, 2018) to describe an event as neither predetermined nor purely random. Metaphorically, this quadrant depicts the prehistory of the research itself—the stage before the study formally takes shape. Specifically, TEM is employed to illustrate the process through which the researcher and participants—originally unrelated individuals—encounter each other and subsequently construct the relationships necessary for the research. Notably, this quadrant also highlights the possibility that such relationships were never established, resulting in research never materializing. It foregrounds the contingency of research formation, questioning why some studies ultimately take shape while others do not. The TEM diagrams for this quadrant seek to answer questions such as "How did the researcher gain access to such an unusual field?" and "How was it possible to meet and interview such unique individuals?".

The third quadrant (lower left) represents using TEM for "revisioning." Here, revision refers to the process of altering perspectives or modifying research trajectories during the course of a study. In qualitative research, researchers frequently experience updates to their research questions, analytical frameworks, and appropriate understanding as their study progresses. Documenting these updates using analytical memos or field notes is a widely practiced approach by qualitative researchers (Maharaj, 2016). Such detailed documentation contributes to the legitimacy of research findings. It may be considered a meta-level form of "thick description" [for a discussion on the role of thick description in ensuring transferability and analytical generalization, see Younas et al.'s work (2023)]. TEM can transform this meta-level thick description into a more accessible and meaningful representation. From the researcher's perspective, TEM enables the visualization of the challenges encountered throughout the research process and the strategies employed to overcome them, thereby enhancing the transparency and reflexivity of the study.

The fourth quadrant (lower right) represents reporting, which corresponds to the conventional use of TEM. In this case, TEM presents the results of the qualitative data as research outcomes. As this is a widely observed application, a detailed explanation is omitted.

To justify the placement of the first, second, and third quadrants, their characteristics are summarized. Transviewing aims to generate TEM diagrams as empirical findings based on the inseparable relationship between the researcher and participant. Therefore, this falls within the relational-empirical findings quadrant. Similarly, Contingentizing assumes an inseparable researcher–participant relationship, but the outcome of using TEM in this case is a methodological insight. Therefore, it is best positioned within the relational-methodological insight quadrant. In contrast, Revisioning highlights the evolution of research questions and analytical frameworks that fundamentally belong to the researcher's domain, although sometimes influenced by participants and fellow researchers. Under this condition, the researcher–participant relationship can be considered bounded, as the researcher ultimately retains the authority to determine the analytical framework in this quadrant. Consequently, revisions are categorized within the bounded methodological insight quadrant.

Figure 1 presents only a hypothetical typology for expanding the potential applications of TEM. Its functionality can be empirically tested using real-world data. In the following section, we illustrate the practical application of TEM for continuous use (second quadrant) as a case study.

Demonstrating TEM for Contingentizing

In TEM for Contingentizing, it is essential to clarify the contingency of the process through which the researcher and the participant encounter one another. In conventional qualitative research, this process is often framed within the Reflexivity dimension. In the context of employing TEM to gain methodological insight, reflexivity is not only relevant to TEM for Contingentizing (second quadrant) in our typology but is also closely related to TEM for Revisioning (third quadrant). Therefore, it is crucial to distinguish between Contingentizing and Revisioning.[3]

As illustrated in Fig. 1, TEM for Contingentizing is based on a more relational premise than TEM for Revisioning. Given that TEM for Revisioning focuses on the researcher and analytical processes within the professional domain of research, the distinctive characteristics of TEM for Contingentizing are evident. Specifically, Contingentizing focuses on the process of the researcher–participant encounter, aiming to depict through TEM that this process was neither entirely predetermined nor purely accidental but rather contingent in nature.

Let us take as a case study a qualitative research paper previously published by the author, which examines the experiences of local residents engaged in radiation decontamination work following the Fukushima nuclear disaster (Hidaka et al., 2021).

The Great East Japan Earthquake of March 2011 and the subsequent Fukushima Daiichi Nuclear Power Plant accident led to widespread radioactive contamination across the Fukushima Prefecture. Removing this contamination and restoring a habitable environment became not only a political priority in the reconstruction process but also a challenge for residents striving to rebuild their lives and restore their sense of attachment to their communities. In response, construction and transportation companies in the Fukushima Prefecture have expanded their operations to include radiation decontamination. However, the optimism remains scarce. Even if the decontamination efforts were successfully completed, concerns remained that the majority of the evacuated residents would not return because of the stigmatization

[3] Reflexivity is also relevant to the first quadrant ("transviewing") and the fourth quadrant ("reporting") of Fig. 1. The dialogical nature of TEM for "transviewing" will inevitably promote reflexivity and reflection on the part of both researchers and participants, while TEM for "reporting" will involve reflexive processes within the analytic procedures through which research outcomes are generated. Nevertheless, since these quadrants correspond to the types of outcomes categorized as "empirical findings", they fall outside the scope of the typology of "methodological insight" discussed in the main text.

associated with radiation exposure and the destruction of infrastructure. In other words, beyond decontamination, efforts have laid a pessimistic outlook: the deterioration of once-beloved communities into uninhabitable, desolate landscapes.

In this study, a 5-year longitudinal ethnographic interview was conducted with a local company manager overseeing radiation decontamination operations in his hometown. This research explored how, despite pessimistic prospects, this manager found meaning in the decontamination work and reconstructed his vision of the future.

Figures 2 and 3 illustrate, using TEM, the process by which the researcher and the research participant encountered each other in the author's previous study. The details regarding social direction (SD) and social guidance (SG) are presented in Table 1, which should be referred to for further clarification. SG represents a social force that pushes an individual's life trajectory toward an equifinality point, whereas SD represents a force that moves an individual away from an equifinality point (Sato, 2016).

In the author's previous study (Hidaka et al., 2021), this encounter process is briefly described in the methods section. Although lengthy, two relevant excerpts are as follows (Hidaka et al., 2021, p.395):

> The interviews were held with the employee of a company that has been operating the radiation decontamination work in municipality X, Fukushima Prefecture, since 2012. Most of the workers employed by the company were comprised of individuals from municipality X. Although the company originally was in the business of research and development of farming products, it began to participate in the radiation decontamination business after acquiring the license required for such work in 2012. The interviewee was selected based on the notion of Historical Structured Inviting (HSI). In HSI, the informant, who has a psychological state or life event on which the researcher's interest is focused, is invited to participate in the research, and then his/her real or possible life event experiences are investigated (Sato, 2016).

This description falls under the section on "Interviewee Recruitment". Only information that was somewhat superficial yet relevant to the research theme—such as place names and the nature of organizational activities—was reported.

> The interviewee, Mr. Suzuki, was male and in his forties at the beginning of the study in 2014; note that he is described with a false name throughout this manuscript for the purposes of readability and anonymity. The first and third authors have been involved in the company for monthly occupational health support since 2013. Thus, although the authors and employees, including Mr. Suzuki, knew each other before the beginning of the present study, the relationship was that of supporter and support recipient. Through daily conversations with Mr. Suzuki, the following facts were discovered: he was born and raised, and lived all his life, in municipality X, the home of his ancestors, along with his kith and kin; he was employed in the radiation decontamination company as a manager and also worked as a part-time farmer on the family farm; he has also been a member of the neighborhood community association since before the Fukushima plant accident. For these reasons, Mr. Suzuki was a person who knew the state of municipality X and its inhabitants well before and after the plant accident. Thus, we considered that he was a suitable informant for study purposes and invited/recruited him to participate in the present study.

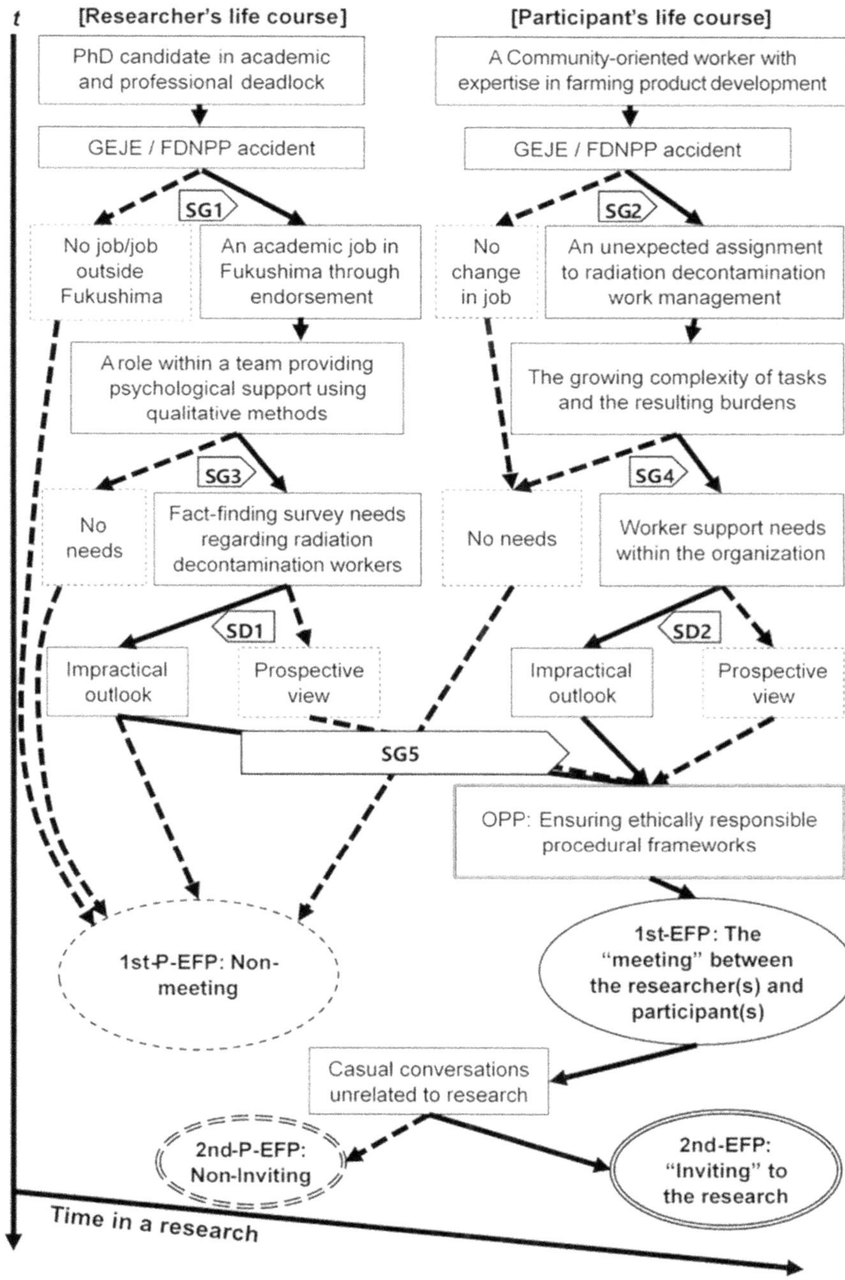

Fig. 2 Contingentizing the process of "meeting" between the researcher(s) and participant(s) (contributed by the author)

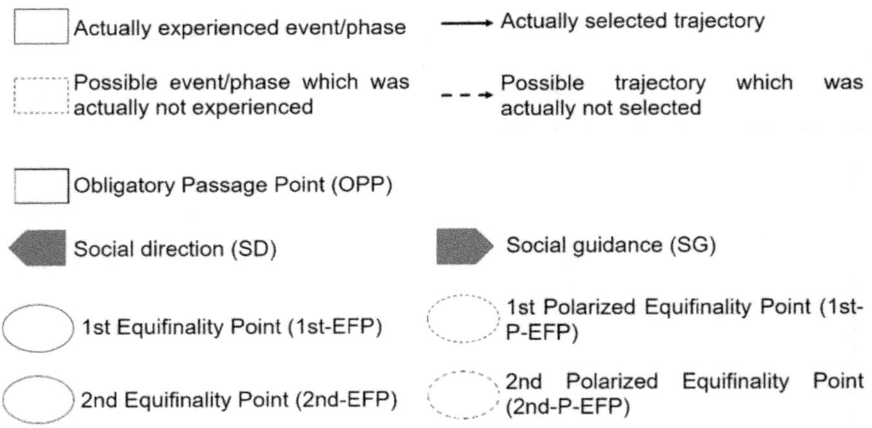

Fig. 3 Legends of TEM

Table 1 SGs/SDs of TEM

SG	SD
SG1: A capacity expansion for assistant positions after the disaster (for researchers) SG2: Radioactive contamination in areas requiring remediation (for participants) SG3: Societal expectations for the university in disaster recovery efforts (for researchers) SG4: Recommendation for the establishment of an industrial physician under the law (for participants) SG5: A colleague physician's alma mater network (both for researcher and participants)	SD1: Radiation decontamination workers as a newly emerged social group (for researchers) SD2: A lack of consultation service to find an industrial physician (for participants)

The characteristics of the interviewee, as well as his relationships with the researchers, are reported. As is evident in the final sentence beginning with "for these reasons", the account underscores that the participants were well-suited to the research objectives of the study. Conversely, information deemed by the researchers to be irrelevant to those objectives—such as the fundamental reasons for their field entry or the processes through which their relationships with participants deepened—is not mentioned.

How can TEM be used to obtain a deeper understanding of this process? Within TEM and its theoretical framework, the Trajectory Equifinality Approach (TEA), the interaction between the researcher and the participant, is conceptualized through the notion of "inviting" (Sato, 2016). This concept reflects a collaborative perspective, where the researcher extends an invitation to an individual to participate in the study, emphasizing a co-constructive process rather than the top-down selection implied by the term "sampling."

Crucially, I assume that before "inviting" occurs, a prior event of "meeting" takes place. While some studies may involve recruiting participants based on specific study objectives, others may be conducted by developing pre-existing field/human relationships. In the latter case, a "meeting" must have occurred before "inviting," yet such pre-invitation encounters are rarely discussed in conventional qualitative research.[4] One reason for this omission may be that providing a detailed account of the meeting process was redundant from the perspective of "sampling," which holds that researchers should deductively extract and select participants appropriate to the research purpose. However, from a reflexivity perspective, documenting the "meeting" process offers crucial insights into the construction of the researcher–participant relationship and, more fundamentally, why the research itself became possible. In other words, the "meeting" process constitutes the core of reflexivity. By employing TEM, this process can be depicted as contingent rather than predetermined. Doing so not only expands the methodological possibilities of TEM but also enhances the methodological scope of reflexivity.

Theoretically, meetings are difficult to recognize prior to the commencement of research; rather than being chosen by the researcher, potential participants are latent within encounters shaped by contingency. The notion of inviting is thus understood to imply the act of asking those who have been encountered in such ways (or whom the researcher retrospectively realizes they had already encountered) to participate in the study. In other words, inviting is an attempt to define deductive sampling inductively, with a meeting representing its underlying root. The experience of meeting takes the form whereby, once the researcher formulates a study and begins the research, they retrospectively become aware that a "meeting" had already occurred. Moreover, such meetings may occur not merely as physical encounters but also as forms of recognizing the existence of others mediated by media or information. TEM for Contingentizing makes it possible to deliberately articulate the elusive nature of meetings by reconstructing time, thereby rendering it explicit for both the researcher and the reader.

In Fig. 2, the left half represents the life course of the researcher (author), and the right half represents the life course of the research participant (Mr. Suzuki). This arrangement illustrates how the two individuals, who had been leading separate lives in different places and times, eventually encountered one another as a result of the Great East Japan Earthquake (GEJE) disaster and following the Fukushima Daiichi Nuclear Power Plant (FDNPP) accident, described as "meeting" as first equifinality point (1st-EFP) in Fig. 2. The figure depicts the process through which they came into contact and ultimately developed the researcher–participant relationship by "inviting" (2nd-EFP). Figure 2 is based on data derived from both the narratives of the research participants in the authors' previous study (Hidaka et al., 2021) and the authors' self-reflective life retrospections. In the following

[4]As suggested by Uexküll's concept of Umwelt (Uexküll, 1921), it may be more precise to consider that, prior to the meeting of individuals, the environments surrounding them first "meet," followed by the accomplishment of interpersonal meeting, and subsequently leading to inviting. Although a tentative proposition, such an Umwelt for meetings may be describable within TEM as forms of Social Guidance. A detailed examination of the relationship between the concepts of Umwelt and meeting would hold theoretical value. However, as it lies beyond the scope of the present discussion, I confine this point to a note.

descriptions, events plotted in the TEM diagram are enclosed in square brackets [ ], while Social Guidance (SG) and Social Direction (SD) are enclosed in angle brackets < >. These notations are used to outline the sequence of events depicted in the figure.

The author was a PhD candidate living outside Fukushima, struggling with academic and professional stagnation [a PhD candidate in academic and professional deadlock]. In contrast, Mr. Suzuki, the research participant, was born and raised in his hometown, a municipality in Fukushima Prefecture, which was later extensively contaminated by radiation following the FDNPP accident. He went on to work in the same community, engaging in the development, research, and promotion of agricultural products [a Community-oriented worker with expertise in farming product development].

The turning points, the GEJE and FDNPP accidents [GEJE/FDNPP accidents], were common to both individuals yet experienced in different locations. Despite being the same event, it is important to note that these events were positioned in different locations within the TEM diagram to reflect the differences in meaning and lived experiences for each individual. The FDNPP accident caused severe environmental destruction, prolonged forced displacement, and psychological distress. However, for the author, this also had the ironic consequence of an increase in job opportunities. Within the political context of post-disaster reconstruction, new academic positions were created at a university in Fukushima Prefecture <SG1>. Moreover, owing to the recommendation of a senior researcher, the author was able to secure a research position at the university. Subsequently, the author joined a qualitative research project focused on providing psychological support to disaster victims and successfully established a foundation for conducting research in Fukushima [a role within a team that provides psychological support using qualitative methods].

On the other hand, the GEJE and FDNPP led to the widespread dispersion of radioactive materials and the necessity for decontamination in the participant's community <SG2>. His company began a radiation decontamination business and was assigned the role of radiation decontamination work management. Neither he nor his company had any knowledge of radiation decontamination or its management. Amid this unexpected line of work and a role unrelated to his original expertise, both he and his organization began to experience severe exhaustion from job demands, and the burden of these responsibilities became increasingly apparent [the growing complexity of tasks and the resulting burdens].

The author's workplace, a university, was located in Fukushima; as a result, in the post-FDNPP accident reconstruction efforts, there was a strong societal expectation that the university should investigate not only the natural scientific impacts of the accident but also its social implications, and further, contribute to practical support measures <SG3>. Supported by these situations, the author recognized the need to investigate the perspectives of radiation decontamination workers, specifically their motivations and future outlook regarding their work [fact-finding survey needs regarding radiation decontamination workers]. Such a study would most effectively be conducted using qualitative research methods. However, radiation decontamination workers are a new occupational group that became prevalent in response to the FDNPP accident, making it difficult to identify potential research participants <SD1>. In other words, field entry and recruitment for this study were [impractical outlook].

During the same period, the research participant sought to fulfill his responsibilities as a manager by deepening his knowledge of Japanese labor laws related to worker support. As a result, he realized that employers were legally required to appoint an occupational physician to maintain and promote workers' health. This legal framework functioned as <SG4>, leading him to recognize the need to establish a formal structure for protecting and supporting workers' health within his organization [Worker support needs within the organization]. However, the process of selecting occupational physicians is complex. Neither he nor his organization had any idea of where to find an occupational physician specializing in health support for radiation decontamination workers or, if such specialists existed, how to request their services. They were also uncertain about who they should consult for guidance <SD2>. Despite recognizing the need for professional support, he concluded that implementing such measures was unrealistic [Impractical outlook].

It is important to note that during this period, both the researcher and the participant faced "Impractical outlook"—the researcher in terms of fulfilling the study's recruitment needs, and the participant in terms of securing occupational physician support for worker health. This situation was improved through the alma mater network of the researcher's colleague, which functioned as <SG5>. Because SG5 played a crucial role for both the researcher and participant, it was positioned transversally in the TEM diagram.

Therefore, a detailed explanation of the SG5 is required. Following the GEJE, Disaster Medical Assistance Teams (DMATs) were frequently dispatched to the research participants' communities to provide emergency medical care, including triage, basic treatment, and hospital transfers. DMATs are specialized medical response teams that operate in disaster-stricken areas and work in close collaboration with local governments and affected communities to provide immediate support. The research participant established a connection with a DMAT member and sought advice from him on how to arrange for an occupational physician to support the health management of radiation-decontaminated workers. By chance, this DMAT member happened to be classmates and close friend of the author's colleague from the same medical school. Fortunately, the author's colleague has extensive experience as an occupational physician with specific expertise in radiation decontamination and risk management. As a result, connections were established between the research participant and the DMAT member, between the DMAT member and the occupational physician (the researcher's colleague), and finally, between the research participant and the occupational physician. These connections led the author's colleague to assume an occupational health role within the research participants' organization, ensuring appropriate support for the health and safety of radiation decontamination workers.

Through the function of SG5, a pathway was opened toward the obligatory passage point (OPP) ([ensuring ethically responsible procedural frameworks]). This

OPP emerged when the researcher's colleague, upon assuming the role of an occupational physician in the participant's organization, initially communicated a key request to the participants and organizational leaders:

> As members of a research institution, we are obligated to disseminate our findings to society. Therefore, we seek your consent to use the data obtained through these support activities—including both numerical data and narratives—for research purposes. (Fieldnotes, Jan 16, 2015)

This request served as an informal agreement but as an initial ethical procedure, ensuring that support activities and research could coexist while also providing a legal and institutional foundation for research ethics. Formal approval was obtained from the institutional review board. While specific requirements may vary by field, contemporary research standards mandate that ethical approval should be obtained from an institutional review board before a study begins (Gelling, 2016). Considering this broader trend, it has become necessary to create an ethically sound researcher–participant relationship when research is anticipated. Therefore, this event was recognized as an OPP.

Then, the process reached the EFP—[the "meeting" between the researcher(s) and participant(s)]. It is important to note that both "researcher(s)" and "participant(s)" are written in the plural form. At this EFP stage, neither the number of research participants nor the number of researchers who would ultimately engage in a qualitative study were determined. At this point, neither the specific research design nor the study plan has been fully established. To develop a concrete research design and plan, it was necessary to first understand the life experiences of potential participants as well as their perspectives on radiation decontamination work and their connection to the local community before the research itself could be formally conducted. For this understanding to take shape, it was essential to foster mutual recognition and trust between the researcher(s) and participant(s) through informal conversational interactions resembling everyday chats, which allowed for the collection of broad contextual information. The event that followed EFP, labeled [casual conversations unrelated to research], reflected the processes through which the content of the study gradually took shape.

The final point in our TEM diagram is 2nd-EFP—["Inviting" to the research]. Events beyond this point have been described in our previous empirical study (Hidaka et al., 2021). This TEM diagram demonstrates that, within the TEM/TEA framework, the act of "inviting" research participants is often preceded by a prehistory. In our study's case, before the researcher invites participants, a "meeting" between them has already taken place.

It is crucial to recognize that the "meeting" process, and even the inviting process, emerges contingently. TEM for Contingentizing illustrates how two individuals who have lived in different times and places come to meet, share a common temporal and spatial context, and establish a researcher–participant relationship. This visualization highlights that the research was neither entirely deterministic nor random.

By examining which SG contributed to the establishment of the research and which SD functioned as a potential constraint, this approach enhances reflexivity for both the author and the reader while broadening the applicability of the research findings.

Given the dynamic nature of researcher–participant relationships in qualitative studies (Cartwright & Limandri, 1997; Nunkoonsing, 2005; Tieken, 2013), it can be argued that such contingent processes inherently underlie all qualitative research. Through TEM/TEA, we can enhance reflexivity by critically reexamining our own studies.[5]

Contributions of Depicting the Researcher–Participant Meeting Process

Depicting the "meeting" process between the researcher and participant through TEM for Contingentizing fosters a more sophisticated level of reflexivity regarding the entire research project. It is often challenging to convincingly present the process of constructing researcher–participant relationships (Smith, 2006; Younas et al., 2023). When researchers struggle to resolve such challenges fully, TEM may provide a more refined means of reporting these relationships. By functioning as a scaffolding tool (Wood et al., 1976), TEM for Contingentizing can guide researchers toward developing more sophisticated future studies.

Engaging in reflexive reporting also contributes to realizing "ethics in practice" (Guillemin & Gillam, 2004). Ethical concerns that may arise in qualitative research include the potential distress experienced by participants in recounting their experiences, the risk of one-sided exploitation due to power imbalances, biased representation of data, and ambiguous boundaries between research and clinical interventions (Richards & Schwartz, 2002; Eide & Kahn, 2008; Sperling, 2022).

More importantly, beyond these previously discussed concerns, another fundamental ethical issue in qualitative research is the verifiability of the research participants' existence. Dougherty (2021), through rigorous investigation, exposed instances of academic misconduct in which a researcher fabricated non-existent participants and used excerpts from existing literature as "data," falsely presenting them as participant narratives under the pretext of confidentiality and anonymity protections. Although this is an extreme case, it underscores the importance of reflexive documentation. Contemporary researchers must persuasively demonstrate

[5]Although this study places qualitative research at its core, meetings can also be described within the context of quantitative research. Such descriptions may demonstrate that quantitative research, which emphasizes "objective" observation and replicable procedures, cannot escape the researcher-participant relationship and may further provide insights for a deeper understanding of human behavioral and psychological characteristics. For example, a reflexive account of the series of processes involving meeting, including how specific researcher–participant relationships in the Stanford Prison Experiment were established and sustained, would, despite the experiment's design as a quantitative study, yield knowledge of considerable interest.

the actual existence of their participants and provide credible accounts of how data were obtained, thereby reinforcing the reliability of their research.

However, it is important to recognize that reflexive documentation is not merely a defensive measure to avoid ethical controversies; it also plays a crucial role in generating meaningful research outcomes. The key to this lies in the relationship between "dialogue" and "reflexivity." The concept of "dialogic reflexivity" proposed by Yamada (2007) repositions reflexivity within open communication with others. This perspective moves beyond a self-justifying or defensive approach to reflexivity. Instead, it highlights the potential for expanding both interpersonal connections and imaginative possibilities through enhanced reflexivity.

Conclusion

This study demonstrated how TEM can be used beyond reporting research outcomes to serve as a tool for methodological insight development by contingentizing the researcher–participant relationship-building process. By visualizing the researcher–participant meeting phase, TEM enables a more reflexive and transparent documentation of how qualitative research is shaped by unpredictable encounters. This methodological advancement not only enhances reflexivity and transparency but also provides a means to navigate and critically examine the ethical complexities inherent in qualitative research. Given the dynamic and relational nature of qualitative research, TEM for Contingentizing is an important tool for enhancing interactive reflexivity, as proposed by previous research in which reflective writing is open to the public and is expected to become the basis for new research activities.

Regarding TEM for Contingentizing, it is equally important to address, from a practical standpoint, how it can be implemented. The key is to draw upon ethnography, particularly the methodology of micro-ethnography. In the present study, the author's expertise in micro-ethnography and the inclusion of thick descriptions made it possible to both present and conceptualize the process of meeting. When researchers describe the relationships with researcher(s) and participant(s) in the research practice ethnographically, realistic options appear to include the following. First, to keep extensive records of researcher–participant relationships in the form of laboratory notebooks, survey logs, or fieldnotes. Second, when reflexive writing during fieldwork proves difficult due to one's role in the field or time constraints, set aside time at the end of each day to write reflexive accounts. Finally, to designate a member of the research team to take a more detached, overarching position in order to describe the research practice, is an option; this approach may be akin to team ethnography.

Whether in qualitative or quantitative research, all studies involving human beings are inevitably embedded in interpersonal relationships and situated contexts, and these, in turn, may themselves become the subject of ethnographic description, contingency, and reflexivity.

Competing Interests This study was funded by JSPS KAKENHI [grant numbers 16K17338] and [24K06571].

Ethics Approval This study was conducted in accordance with the principles of the Declaration of Helsinki. This study was approved by the Ethics Committee of Fukushima Medical University (October 22, 2015/No. 2530). For the informed consent procedure, the interviewee had the purpose of the study explained to him, and he provided informed consent on a written form to participate and publish in the study by Hidaka et al. (2021), which served as the basis for this paper.

References

American Psychological Association (Ed.). (2019). *Publication manual of the American Psychological Association* (7th ed.). American Psychological Association.

Berger, R. (2015). Now I see it, now I don't: Researcher's position and reflexivity in qualitative research. *Qualitative Research, 15*, 219–234. https://doi.org/10.1177/1468794112468475

Cartwright, J., & Limandri, B. (1997). The challenge of multiple roles in the qualitative clinician researcher-participant client relationship. *Qualitative Health Research, 7*, 223–235. https://doi.org/10.1177/104973239700700204

Cho, J., & Trent, A. (2006). Validity in qualitative research revisited. *Qualitative Research, 6*(3), 319–340.

Chughtai, H., & Myers, M. D. (2017). Entering the field in qualitative field research: A rite of passage into a complex practice world. *Information Systems Journal, 27*, 795–817. https://doi.org/10.1111/isj.12124

De Gennaro, I. (2020). Despotic time and truthless science. *European Review of History: Revue européenne d'histoire, 27*, 582–597. https://doi.org/10.1080/13507486.2020.1731430

Dougherty, M. V. (2021). The use of confidentiality and anonymity protections as a cover for fraudulent fieldwork data. *Research Ethics, 17*, 480–500. https://doi.org/10.1177/17470161211018257

Doyle, S. (2013). Reflexivity and the capacity to think. *Qualitative Health Research, 23*, 248–255. https://doi.org/10.1177/1049732312467854

Eide, P., & Kahn, D. (2008). Ethical issues in the qualitative researcher—participant relationship. *Nursing Ethics, 15*, 199–207. https://doi.org/10.1177/0969733007086018

Enosh, G., & Ben-Ari, A. (2016). Reflexivity: The creation of liminal spaces—Researchers, participants, and research encounters. *Qualitative Health Research, 26*(4), 578–584.

Etherington, K. (2007). Ethical research in reflexive relationships. *Qualitative Inquiry, 13*, 599–616. https://doi.org/10.1177/1077800407301175

Finlay, L. (2002). "Outing" the researcher: The provenance, process, and practice of reflexivity. *Qualitative Health Research, 12*, 531–545. https://doi.org/10.1177/104973202129120052

Flick, U., Kardorff, E. V., & Steinke, I. (2010). What is qualitative research? An introduction to the field. In U. Flick, E. V. Kardorff, & I. Steinke (Eds.), *A companion to qualitative research* (B. Jenner, Trans., 3rd ed., pp. 3–11). Sage.

Geertz, C. (1973). *The interpretation of cultures*. Basic Books.

Gelling, L. H. (2016). Applying for ethical approval for research: The main issues. *Nursing Standard, 30*, 40–44. https://doi.org/10.7748/ns.30.20.40.s46

Gergen, K. (2009). *Relational being: Beyond self and community*. Oxford University Press.

Gough, B., & Madill, A. (2012). Subjectivity in psychological science: From problem to prospect. *Psychological Methods, 17*, 374–384. https://psycnet.apa.org/doi/10.1037/a0029313

Guillemin, M., & Gillam, L. (2004). Ethics, reflexivity, and "ethically important moments" in research. *Qualitative Inquiry, 10*, 261–280. https://doi.org/10.1177/1077800403262360

Hidaka, T., Kasuga, H., Kakamu, T., & Fukushima, T. (2021). Discovery and revitalization of "feeling of hometown" from a disaster site inhabitant's continuous engagement in reconstruction work: Ethnographic interviews with a radiation decontamination worker over 5 years following the Fukushima nuclear power plant accident. *Japanese Psychological Research, 63*, 393–405. https://doi.org/10.1111/jpr.12369

Kanzaki, M., & Sato, T. (2014). Teachers' support for the students who have experienced school non-attendance: Constructing a trans-viewed model from field work at an alternative school. *Ritsumeikan Journal of Human Sciences, 30*, 15–32. (In Japanese). https://doi.org/10.34382/00004315

Latour, B. (1987). *Science in action*. Harvard University Press.

Lincoln, Y. S., & Guba, E. G. (1985). *Naturalistic inquiry*. Sage.

Luhmann, N. (1984). *Soziale Systeme: Grundriß einer allgemeinen Theorie*. Suhrkamp Verlag.

Maharaj, N. (2016). Using field notes to facilitate critical reflection. *Reflective Practice, 17*, 114–124. https://doi.org/10.1080/14623943.2015.1134472

McKenzie, P. (2019). Maintaining good relationships with research participants. In D. L. Brien, C. Batty, E. Ellison, & A. Owens (Eds.), *The doctoral experience: Student stories from the creative arts and humanities* (pp. 147–156). Palgrave Macmillan. https://doi.org/10.1007/978-3-030-18199-4_13

Mikėnė, S., Gaižauskaitė, I., & Valavičienė, N. (2013). Qualitative interviewing: Field-work realities. *Socialinis darbas = Social Work, 12*, 49–62.

Nunkoosing, K. (2005). The problems with interviews. *Qualitative Health Research, 15*, 698–706. https://doi.org/10.1177/1049732304273903

Perera, K. (2020). The interview as an opportunity for participant reflexivity. *Qualitative Research, 20*(2), 143–159.

Pillow, W. (2003). Confession, catharsis, or cure? Rethinking the uses of reflexivity as methodological power in qualitative research. *International Journal of Qualitative Studies in Education, 16*, 175–196. https://doi.org/10.1080/0951839032000060635

Richards, H. M., & Schwartz, L. J. (2002). Ethics of qualitative research: Are there special issues for health services research? *Family Practice, 19*, 135–139. https://doi.org/10.1093/fampra/19.2.135

Rumary, K. J., Goldspink, S., & Howlett, P. (2023). Exiting the elephant: Hearing the participant voice in qualitative data collection. *International Journal of Research & Method in Education, 46*, 248–259. https://doi.org/10.1080/1743727X.2022.2128742

Saito, Y., Tomori, K., Sawada, T., & Ohno, K. (2023). Longitudinal process of setting and achieving activity-and participation-level goals in home rehabilitation in Japan: A qualitative study using trajectory equifinality modeling. *International Journal of Environmental Research and Public Health, 20*, 5746. https://doi.org/10.3390/ijerph20095746

Sato, T. (2016). From TEM to TEA: The making of a new approach. In T. Sato, N. Mori, & J. Valsiner (Eds.), *Making of the future: The trajectory equifinality approach in cultural psychology* (pp. vii–xii). Information Age.

Smith, S. (2006). Encouraging the use of reflexivity in the writing up of qualitative research. *International Journal of Therapy and Rehabilitation, 13*, 209–215. https://doi.org/10.12968/ijtr.2006.13.5.21377

Sperling, D. (2022). "Could you help me die?": On the ethics of researcher-participant relationship and the limitations of qualitative research. *International Journal of Qualitative Methods, 21*, 16094069221105076. https://doi.org/10.1177/16094069221105076

Stahl, N. A., & King, J. R. (2020). Expanding approaches for research: Understanding and using trustworthiness in qualitative research. *Journal of Developmental Education, 44*, 26–28.

Thomas, D. R. (2017). Feedback from research participants: Are member checks useful in qualitative research? *Qualitative Research in Psychology, 14*(1), 23–41.

Tieken, M. C. (2013). The distance to delight: A graduate student enters the field. *Qualitative Inquiry, 19*, 320–326. https://doi.org/10.1177/1077800412471515

Uexküll, J. (1921). *Umwelt und Innenwelt der Tiere* (2nd ed.). Springer.

Wood, D., Bruner, J. S., & Ross, G. (1976). The role of tutoring in problem solving. *Journal of Child Psychology and Psychiatry, 17*, 89–100.

Wright, P. J., & Tokunaga, R. S. (2018). Women's perceptions of their male partners' pornography consumption and relational, sexual, self, and body satisfaction: Toward a theoretical model.

Annals of the International Communication Association, 42, 55–73. https://doi.org/10.1080/23808985.2017.1412802

Yamada, Y. (2007). A methodology of dialogic model construction for qualitative studies: Multiple realities, narrative text, and dialogic reflexivity. *Japanese Journal of Qualitative Psychology, 6*, 174–194. (In Japanese). https://doi.org/10.24525/jaqp.6.1_174

Younas, A., Fàbregues, S., Durante, A., Escalante, E. L., Inayat, S., & Ali, P. (2023). Proposing the "MIRACLE" narrative framework for providing thick description in qualitative research. *International Journal of Qualitative Methods, 22*, 16094069221147162. https://doi.org/10.1177/16094069221147162

TEA, in a Future Mind

From Vygotsky to TEA: A Semiotic Exploration of Human Action and Purpose

Enno von Fircks

Future Monk (1889) by Nikolai Petrowitsch Bogdanow-Belski (1868–1945)

Figure presented on the first page of the chapter is an artistic example.

E. von Fircks (✉)
Jaan Valsiner Research Foundation, Salerno, Italy

M. A. Campill et al. (eds.), *New Paths in Trajectory Equifinality Modelling*, Theory and History in the Human and Social Sciences,
https://doi.org/10.1007/978-3-032-25855-7_8

TEA represents a significant achievement for the field of psychology as a whole. However, it required contributions from outside of Europe to bring this accomplishment to fruition. The Japanese researchers led by Sato have made substantial contributions to the refinement and development of this qualitative research approach for the holistic description and analysis of human phenomena. Psychology in Europe—centered around the quantitative imperative (Michell, 2003, 2005)—was unable to produce such an achievement due to its rigid positivist framework. This makes the impact of TEA even more profound for European and American psychology.

TEA originated as TEM (Sato & Tanimura, 2016) and, in its early stages, was entirely methodological in its approach to research. Even today, however, TEA lacks a philosophical foundation or theoretical framework. Consequently, TEA remains largely a scientific tool, i.e., a methodology for the holistic and microgenetic exploration of psycho-physically neutral phenomena. While this in itself is an achievement, no research approach should remain a simple methodology; it must also strive for a philosophical underpinning (Wendt, 2025) so that methodology and theory can be integrated into a comprehensive system for psychology.[1]

In the following chapter, we aim to address this inherent need for philosophical theorization. In doing so, we situate our theoretical approach within Vygotsky's cultural-historical school and his semiotic approach to psychology.[2] However, we will also move beyond Vygotsky and use his writings more interpretively. It must be emphasized here that Vygotsky's cultural-historical school represents only one possible way to philosophically and psychologically engage with TEA; other theoretical approaches are, of course, possible and desirable.

Before turning to the philosophical and psychological expansion of TEA—here through Vygotsky—we aim to define TEA with the help of various sources (i.e., researchers). Only after we have described TEA comprehensively and the reader has formed an understanding of this achievement can our philosophical and psychological expansion become clearer—this is the intended goal.

What Is TEA? The Developmental Postulate

Let us first consider the developmental postulate of TEA:

> TEM is a concept of boundary in the process of eternal movement towards the future. It is both a very simple idea and a very big challenge to any thinker who tries to conceptualize development. It breaks up the backbone of contemporary psychology in a number of ways. Most importantly, it starts from the axiom that development is possible only in the case of open systems—which are in specific exchange relations with their environments. All biological, psychological, and social systems are of that kind—qualitatively different from the material systems that do not develop by themselves. (Zittoun & Valsiner, 2016, pp. 1–2)

[1] TEA has been enriched by biological metaphors and analogies within the past (Valsiner, 2017).

[2] Semiotics are a scientific discipline originating from linguistic philosophy.

TEA also defines humans as open systems and always includes the individual person in their relationship to the environment (Sato et al., 2009). Human relationships to the environment are, however, manifold in nature, requiring us to distinguish, at least theoretically, between material and social environments. The ways in which individuals make decisions, choose paths, or pursue goals must always be understood in the context of their relationships with their social environment (family, friends, colleagues, etc.) and their material environment (resources, obstacles, resistances, etc.) (Valsiner, 2014).

For example, a master's student faces the pivotal question of whether to pursue a PhD or transition directly into the workforce. Answering this question involves not only personal needs but also the material and social conditions of the respective environment. A master's student with a relatively weak need to pursue further educational opportunities at a university may find this lack of intensity reinforced by a social environment that highlights the disadvantages of a PhD, such as not contributing to a pension fund for an additional 3 years (or other similar reasons). Conversely, a master's student with a strong need (e.g., a thirst for knowledge) will either seek to overcome such obstacles or subordinate their need to the needs of others. TEA thus focuses on the meaningful relationship between the individual and their environment—an undeniably revolutionary approach in today's quantitatively dominated psychology, where contextual factors are treated as artificial and impersonal index variables. These index variables, however, cannot decipher the appropriated meaning that individual persons attribute to their environment.

What Is TEA? The Equifinality Postulate

This brings us to the second axiom of TEA: Equifinality, which also lends TEA its name:

> The crucial implication from the open-systemic starting point is that development cannot be predicted before it happens, nor can it be exhaustively explained after it has happened. The second implication is the normal state of multiple potential pathways to the expected established outcome ("final expected form") of development. This focus on equifinality (TEM = Trajectory Equifinality Model) is brought over to developmental science from embryology—Hans Driesch formulated the idea of "harmoniously equipotential systems" based on his experiments of embryonic regeneration into final form (...). Driesch introduced the notion of equifinality into the biological sciences. Equifinality entails the arrival in the same developmental end state through various possible pathways. (Zittoun & Valsiner, 2016)

The future in TEA is therefore always open. However, TEA does not stop at this postulate. On the contrary, a TEA researcher does not settle for the idea that development merely continues to progress—a quintessential natural-philosophical premise (Valsiner, 2024; von Fircks & Boulanger, 2025), reflected, for instance, in Goethe's doctrine of metamorphosis (Goethe, 1793/2018). Instead, it is about reaching certain intermediate products of development—the so-called bifurcation points (Sato et al., 2009)—from which new development becomes possible.

In other words: development always unfolds along various trajectories. This means that a developmental milestone can be pursued and achieved through multiple pathways. There is, therefore, no singular solution that brings about a developmental product. On the contrary, TEA assumes a pluralistic premise of development. Valsiner (personal communication) often uses the example of a university degree (a developmental intermediate point) being achieved via several possible pathways that cannot be predicted a priori.

In one case, a student might put in great effort to achieve the best possible grades, neglecting family, friendships, and private life in the process. In another case, a student might care little about grades and simply aim to receive the diploma. This student might often skip lectures, study only superficially, and interact with fellow students only at parties. At the end of their studies, both hold the same certificate (albeit with differing grades) in their hands, yet the paths they took to achieve it differ fundamentally.

From this example, two important components emerge:

1. Different pathways lead to a similar or identical developmental intermediate product, from which new pathways can be pursued to reach the next developmental stage. TEA aims to analyze both the pathways and the products of development—ideally in a dynamic relationship to one another.
2. The second point, largely neglected by TEA, is that development is teleologically significant and thus depends on the purpose system of the individual (Stern, 1923, 1924; von Fircks, 2024c). Whether a person approaches their degree with great effort or in a more relaxed manner depends on their purpose system. What do grades mean to the individual? What purpose does the grade serve for them? These are questions concerning the purposive meaning of actions, and it is this purposive meaning that constrains the selection of certain pathways or trajectories.

Thus, the human being is not only an open system (Valsiner, 2014, 2019), but also an entity that autonomously and purposefully shapes this open system. This is a point only implicitly addressed in TEA—the connection between open and purpose-driven development. *Equifinality, therefore, is always purpose-driven equifinality.*

What Is TEA? The Tension Between Reality and Imagination

This brings us to a third postulate of TEA: the postulate of the tension between reality and imagination:

> In later depiction, TEM became more than this. Rather than a cartographic depiction of visible life trajectories, its potential value is to give us an analytical tool to explain how people's lives come into being as they do. It also accounts for the fact that a life lived is not so much a history of socio-economic achievements—a job, a family, a house—as a complex dream of wishes, hopes, plans, and unlived lives. TEM gives us an opportunity to put the real (lived-through) and non-real (imagined—but personally important) life course events

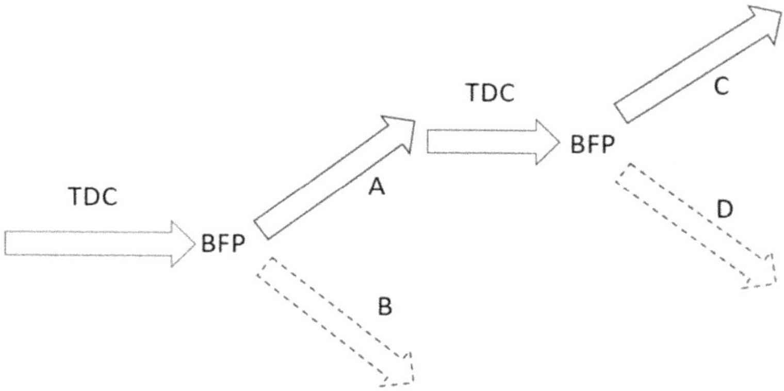

Fig. 1 Trajectories within TEA (BFP = bifurcation points, TDC = transitional developmental checkpoint)

> into the same functional scheme. Imagination becomes real—and "the real" acquires new value through imagination. Imagination leads human development. But how can we know that? (Zittoun & Valsiner, 2016, p. 3)

In Fig. 1, we observe the connection between different pathways and the necessary developmental intermediate steps.

What Is TEA? Tension Between Reality and Imagination

Let us consider an example to clarify the complexity of the figure and enhance the general understanding of TEA. Suppose a person must decide what to do with their future after completing their secondary education. In other words, they face a pivotal decision about their professional path. A variety of options are available, which may differ or even conflict with one another. In Europe, young graduates are often faced with the question of whether to pursue higher education or vocational training. These two options represent A and B, two extremes in decision-making.

However, we must also consider other possibilities between A and B, such as dual studies, which are common in Germany. The decision-making process is not exhausted by the two extreme pathways but occurs within the tension-filled field between them. A range of options and meanings thus opens up for the young graduate, requiring them to develop a stance. The person may wonder whether they can afford to pursue higher education (Path A), while vocational training already offers a monthly stipend of 1000 euros (or dollars). Paths A and B thus lead the person to a developmental intermediate step (the so-called bifurcation point)—here, the entry into professional life—which, depending on the path or decision, has varying consequences for the person's potential for action.

The beginning of a degree program or vocational training marks the first developmental intermediate step, from which new pathways—new opportunities—emerge, influencing the person's capacity for decision-making. The individual reflects on whether their initial steps in higher education (vocational training vs. university) make new goals or purposes more likely than others. For example, the person may question whether they could manage without 1000 euros per month, i.e., whether they can rely on parental support. They may also consider whether they could live with such support or whether it might make them feel too dependent on their parents.

If the person imagines themselves in vocational training, they might feel confident that they could manage independently and provide for themselves. However, this independence comes at a certain cost: the person would lose some degree of personal freedom because they would need to work 40 h/week and take on more responsibilities for themselves and others. They may also wonder whether they find vocational training intellectually stimulating enough. These are all possible pathways that will significantly impact the decision to pursue (or not) higher education—see Fig. 2:

In other words, within this network of meanings, the person selects their pathway—amid the tension between personal needs and social demands, which must somehow be integrated in a personalized manner. From the TEA perspective, we observe how a potential decision—a life decision in our example—also incorporates the anticipated future, that is, future pathways, always against the backdrop of polar tensions and multiple pathway possibilities. The anticipated meaning of the future thus gains decision-making power for the person in the present moment when the decision is due.

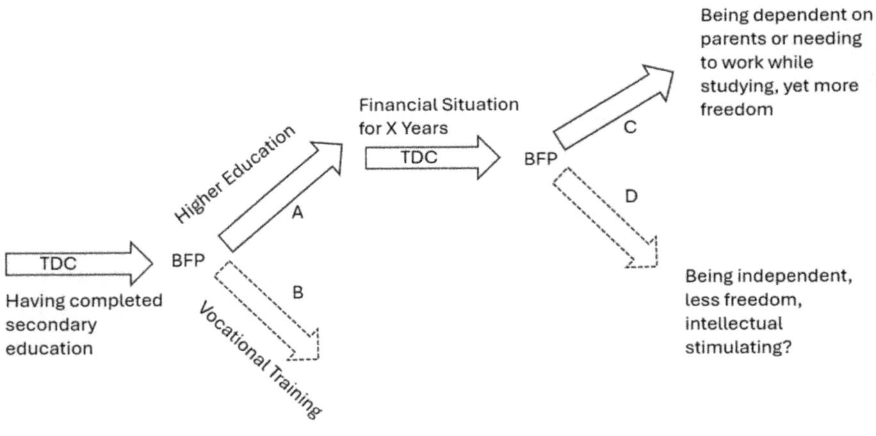

Fig. 2 TEM for life decision after graduating high school

In this way, the envisioned future becomes directly integrated into the decision. The person's purposefulness is thereby significantly updated by their envisioned and anticipated future.

What Is TEA: The Guiding Role of the Past

However, this is only one determinant in TEA. Equally important is the accompanying past (Valsiner, 2017), which has always enabled the present moment and is therefore also present in the current decision. For example, when deciding between higher education or vocational training, a person does not only consult their expectations for the future but also their past experiences, i.e., their network of past meanings.

They may reflect on their earlier self, for instance, when they completed various internships connected to academic professions, which familiarized them with scientific work. These past experiences—practical vs. intellectual in nature, e.g., during different internships—will now impact the decision in the present. For instance, if they found scientific work particularly enjoyable and intellectually stimulating, it may have allowed them to grow beyond their previous knowledge and skill levels, personally fulfilling them.

Thus, the person recognizes that scientific work satisfied central needs of their personality—needs that remain present and pressing in the current situation or decision. In this way, the past, whether consciously or unconsciously, always shapes the present decision.

As such, the decision is made within the context of two tensions: past<>present and present<>future, where the present represents the crystallization point of both tensions and contains a high degree of ambivalence. Indeed, at any moment, the person could potentially change their mind, depending on how they anticipate their future and reinterpret their past.

This is precisely what the striking examples of human life demonstrate: bankers become monks; meat-eaters become vegans; progressives become conservatives. All this is only possible against the backdrop of personally experienced pasts (which can always be reinterpreted) and personally anticipated futures (which can also be variously imagined). TEA thus enables the understanding and analysis of personal developmental conduct—still a genuine novelty in psychology and the social sciences (Valsiner, 2021).

> TEM breaks up the backbone of contemporary psychology—its reliance upon inductive generalization based on the observables—and its practical elaboration conventionally called "measurement." TEM works with structural qualitative units of analysis that belong to both sides of the border of the present. TEM involves careful investigation of relevant phenomena and our basic assumptions about them. Its basic structure (…) is centered on the distinction between FUTURE and PAST in the consideration of actual and potential trajectories. Both kinds of phenomena—real (what happened) and post-factum imaginary (X, Y, Z) and future imaginary (A, B, C)—are treated as relevant in TEM. (Valsiner, 2017, p. 54)

Vygotsky's Cultural-Historical Approach in a Nutshell

With this, we have approached the holism of TEA, focusing particularly on the purposefulness of the individual person and making it adequately explicit. This concludes this section of the chapter, and we now turn to our philosophical-semiotic considerations, which aim to guide TEA from a pre-disciplinary perspective. How do we now define our semiotics? Vygotsky's cultural-historical school will assist us in this regard.

> Man differs from animals in that he can make and use tools. (…) As a matter of fact, the tools used by man not only radically change his conditions of existence, they even react on him in that they effect a change in him and in his psychic condition. In the complicated inter-relations with his surroundings his organization is being differentiated and refined; his hand and his brain assume definite shapes, a series of complicated methods of conduct are being evolved, with the aid of which man adapt himself more perfectly to the surrounding world. (Luria, 1994, p. 46)

Within Vygotsky's cultural-historical theory, we must begin with the concept of the tool. I have personally devoted many papers to exploring the notion of the tool and how it transforms humanity's relationship with both itself and its environment (see, for instance, von Fircks, 2024a, 2024b, 2024c). However, my audience has frequently encountered difficulties in grasping what I mean by tool use. Therefore, it is necessary for us to adopt a more accessible approach in articulating what Vygotsky intends by tool use.

To illustrate human tool use, let us consider a concrete example from everyday life. When a person sees food, they are not simply drawn to it in a causal manner, as though compelled to consume it immediately. Instead, between the stimulus (food) and the response, there is not only a reflection on the emergence of a need that renders food attractive, but also an interposed tool that modifies the individual's relationship to both the stimulus and the response (Vygotsky, 1994b). Specifically, humans prepare food using tools to make it more digestible and hygienic, among other reasons. By incorporating the tool, humans transcend simple reflexes and become distinctly human (Leontiev, 1978). The preparation of food is a uniquely cultural activity that finds no full parallel in the animal kingdom.

Through the introduction of tools such as a pan, pot, or boiling water, humans alter their relationship to the given environment (e.g., food) as well as to their own needs. The immediate gratification of a need is postponed by the application of a tool system, which also serves to address concurrent needs (such as hygiene). Thus, through the use of a specific tool system, an action becomes polyvalent, meeting multiple human needs—needs that expand within a shared field of activity. In other words, this process embodies Vygotsky's semiotic triangle (Fig. 3).

The tool is an interesting social instrument that enables individuals to gain control over their own conduct. Thermometers, for example, are an excellent human invention that helps people manage the present moment (anticipation). With a thermometer, one does not need to step outside to experience the temperature and decide what to wear (stimulus = response). Instead, by using the thermometer, one can

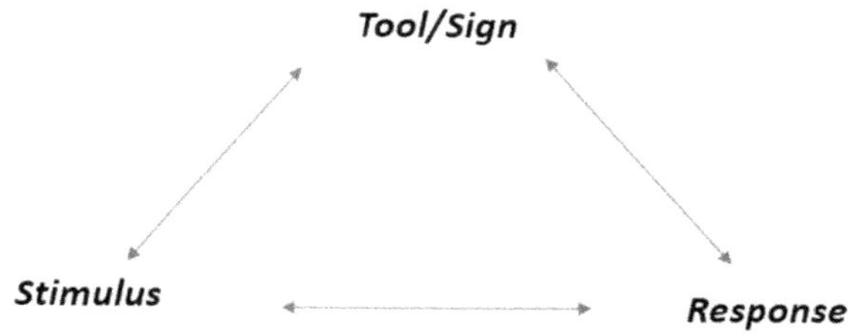

Fig. 3 Vygotsky's semiotic triangle (see Vygotsky, 1994a)

predict the cold and prepare accordingly. Thus, the tool functions as an intriguing social mechanism that mediates human conduct, enabling a deeper understanding of the environment without direct sensory experience.

> The transition to civilized behavior involves a shift in the overall pattern of actions: instead of directly applying a natural function to solve a specific task, the individual inserts an auxiliary means or tool, which serves as the medium through which the task is performed (Luria, 1994, pp. 47–48).

Gillespie & Zittoun (2010) distinguish between tool and sign use, a distinction also emphasized by Valsiner (2014). A tool allows a person to act on the external world in a goal-directed manner. For example, an individual planning to build a house is unlikely to rely solely on their hands. Instead, they will depend on a complex system of tools that not only help control their actions (e.g., the hammer extends the hand) but also enable manipulation of materials (von Fircks, 2023). Through tool use, individuals transform the world in unique ways (Vygotsky, 1994a), which lies at the heart of the concept of tool use.

But what about a sign? A sign is a semiotic resource (Gillespie & Zittoun, 2010) through which individuals engage with their own psychic system. In other words, a sign represents something for someone (Valsiner, 2017) and helps them alter their relationship with their mental life—a process Vygotsky refers to as the psychic system. Tool systems and sign systems are intricately connected, and psychologists must unravel these relationships to understand the complexity of human behavior, according to the Cultural Psychology of Semiotic Dynamics (Valsiner, 2014, 2019).

To clarify this abstract idea, consider another example. If you go to a pharmacy for medication to relieve a headache, you are using a pharmaceutical tool to alter your personal environment—your body. You aim to move from an undesirable present state to a desired future state (Van der Veer & Valsiner, 1993) using the pharmaceutical. This tool enables you to regain control of your environment—in this case, your body—as you rely on it for work, such as teaching tennis. However, you may also worry about the potential side effects of the medication, making you hesitant to take it. To address this concern, you consult the pharmacist, who asks questions about your health and any other medications you're taking, assessing potential interactions. Afterward, the pharmacist reassures you that side effects are unlikely and, if they occur, they will be minimal. This statement serves as an inhibitory sign (Valsiner, 2014), which the person can internalize to reduce anxiety and encourage taking the medication. Before taking the pills, the individual repeats the pharmacist's reassurance to calm their worries and ultimately decides to take the medication. In this case, a social sign has been internalized, altering the person's relationship with their own mental state (e.g., worry and rumination). This demonstrates that signs and tools are interconnected; the use of certain tools is facilitated by the accompanying promoter or inhibitory signs.

Let us now consider Vygotsky's perspective on the development of cultural behavior in children:

> The child remembers by means of a geographical map or by means of a plan, a scheme or a summary, may serve as an example of such cultural development of memory. We have many reasons to assume that the cultural development consists in mastering methods of behavior which are based on the use of signs as a means of accomplishing any particular psychological operation" (Vygotsky, 1994a, pp. 56–57).

An example of this idea can be seen when we teach children strategies to help them fall asleep, such as counting or imagining sheep jumping over a fence. This is a simple semiotic resource that helps the child—or even an adult—alter their relationship with their mental state. The person wishes to fall asleep (goal), but their mind is preoccupied with other thoughts, preventing them from reaching their goal. This leads to the introduction of a sign system (counting or imagining sheep) to help calm the mind and promote sleep by altering the psychic system through interconnected psychological functions like concentration and detachment.

This example sheds light on Vygotsky's view of culture, which consists of presenting individuals with specific sign systems that can be used for goal-directed conduct. Importantly, the sign system is not determined by a single purpose but can be applied to a variety of needs and goals. For example, counting is not only used for division and allocation of resources but can also be employed to gather courage before making a difficult decision or to aid in falling asleep. Once interiorized, a sign system can be applied flexibly to meet various personal needs and goals.

> Expressing the core idea in the broadest terms, the main promise underlying this method is as follows: In mastering themselves, children follow the same process as they do when mastering external nature, for example, through technical means. Human beings master themselves, as one of the forces of nature, by using a cultural 'technic of sign' (Vygotsky, 1994a, p. 70).

Now that we have explored Vygotsky's concept of culture, we must also incorporate the notion of history into our inquiry. Vygotsky does not merely discuss culture but speaks specifically of the cultural-historical method in psychology (Van der Veer & Valsiner, 1993). This means that sign systems—and tool systems—have evolved historically, developing over time to meet human needs. While these systems were initially created to address specific needs, over time their use becomes diversified due to the varied needs that humans develop organically and through social interaction. With this context in mind, we are now ready to summarize Vygotskian cultural-historical theory:

A. Much of how individuals structure themselves and their environment is mediated by semiotic resources (Gillespie & Zittoun, 2010). In this sense, actions are either mediated by tools when acting on the external world or by signs when acting on the psychic system.

B. Tools and signs are cultural instruments that belong to the repertoire of a given culture, which has developed historically. Though initially tied to specific needs, the purposes for which signs and tools are used evolve over time. For example, a counting system can be applied not only for food allocation but also for gathering courage in difficult situations or aiding sleep issues. Once interiorized, a semiotic resource can be applied to meet a variety of personal needs.

C. The relationship between tools and signs remains complex and is not fully understood. The way individuals approach and utilize a given tool to affect the external world depends largely on associated signs. Thus, it is not enough to study tool and sign systems in isolation; researchers must also understand how they interrelate, as many human actions depend on both tools and signs. For example, using a hammer involves not only the tool but also the various semiotic signs (e.g., cautionary advice) that guide the person in performing the action safely.

Persono-Semiotic TEA in a Nutshell

This excursus was necessary to understand Vygotsky's semiotics in conjunction. This goal has now been achieved. We will now turn to the question of how this cultural-historical semiotics can extend TEA—this is the central task of the current chapter.

Let us return to our initial example: A person has just completed their a-levels and faces the pivotal decision of whether to pursue vocational training or higher education. As we have seen through TEA, the individual's decision is dependent on their interpreted past and anticipated future. In this moment of tension, they must make a decision for themselves. The pathways that appear to the person (anticipated future) and the interpreted past (i.e., how the person arrived at the present moment) are overdetermined by the sign and tool systems underlying these pathways. In other words, behind each pathway lie different sign and tool systems, through which the person seeks to relax their goal-orientedness. It is precisely the awareness of these pathways that will help the person make their decision and determine their life direction.

How does this manifest concretely? The young graduate will wonder whether they will have enough money to support themselves during their studies. Money, of course, should be understood here as a comprehensive tool system to sustain one's physical existence. Clearly, the decision regarding whether to pursue a degree or not (money <> no money) also depends on how this tool system is overdetermined by certain sign systems. It is entirely possible that the young graduate places little importance on money, believing they can survive without a significant income, for example, through alternative practices (food waste collection, couchsurfing, etc.). In this case, the pathway that is envisioned is overdetermined by the existence of tools and their meaning. It does not matter whether a particular tool is present, which is essential for the directional decision; rather, it is how this tool is interpreted by the individual.

Here, we see that the future pathways that shape the present decision depend on the interplay of tool and sign systems. Another example may better illustrate this. Another graduate reflects on the same question but leans more toward vocational training. Money is, for this young individual, an attractive condition. Why? This person seeks money to finance their own apartment, i.e., to become independent and exist autonomously. If they pursued a degree, they would likely need to continue living with their parents. Again, we see that the present decision is shaped by the interplay of tool and sign systems, which constitute the conditions under which a decision arises. In this example, money symbolizes autonomy and independence, reflecting the person's goal-orientedness. In the earlier example, money symbolized merely a means to survive and held no further symbolic meaning—thus it could be replaced by alternative actions. How the future is shaped, therefore, largely depends on how the individual currently evaluates their possibilities based on tools and their meanings. Thus, we are in clear contradiction to TEA's foundational belief that the future can never truly be known or predicted (Valsiner, 2017; Zittoun & Valsiner, 2016).

With our semiotic perspective, inspired by Vygotsky's writings, we understand the conditions under which a present decision is made, and thus the future is co-constructed—that is, created. In short: If we understand how the individual envisions various tools in different pathways in TEA and how these tools are meaningfully interpreted, we can indeed make predictions about which path or future is more likely to be constructed than others.

Actualized TEM: Towards Qualitative Predictive Power

We have now examined the role of the anticipated future and the role of tool and sign systems here. However, as pointed out earlier, the present as the central point of tension also includes the meaningful past. We will now turn to the role of the past in its semiotic consideration. Our young graduate, who must decide on their further education, will also draw on their personal past for this decision. As already mentioned, early experiences, such as in a scientific internship, will play a role in the present decision. For instance, our graduate may have encountered scientific work in a parliamentary office (staff members are hired as scientific assistants) and experienced the conditions under which scientific work occurs. The graduate had to prepare a speech for a public assembly on behalf of a politician and immersed themselves in various rhetoric books. During this time, the person studied some rhetorical philosophers and developed an interest in this intellectual work. Books, as a central tool system, were emphasized by the person's philosophical interest in preparing the speech for a specific purpose. Thus, the study of books, aimed at achieving a specific goal (tool), was meaningful to the individual because it helped fulfill their own core needs (philosophical thirst for knowledge, for example). In the work unrelated to their own goals (preparing a speech for another person), the individual was able to find purpose-driven activity and personally appropriate the work—a core characteristic of healthy and motivated conduct (von Fircks, 2024a). It is precisely this scientific work that the individual seeks and strives for, and which serves as an ideal for their future studies. Scientific work that not only serves external purposes but also emerges from the individual's deepest sources has become a transformative experience for our young graduate. This experience thus functions as a promoter sign for the personally envisioned future. This is exactly how the individual wants to actively shape their future. Here too, we see that in assessing their past, or rather the trajectories of the past, the individual is dependent on the tool systems and their personal meaning (sign systems). Thus, the decision to pursue or reject higher education is not only made within the context of the Past<>Present and Present<>Future tension but, with this chapter, these tensions are more precisely differentiated. In other words: *The individual makes the decision in the present moment against the backdrop of the Past<>Present (Tool<>Sign) and Present<>Future (Tool<>Sign) tension.* This differentiated equation in TEA allows a possible prediction of the direction the individual is likely to take in their decision-making.

However, a small caveat must be mentioned in the same breath. The interpretation of one's past-related and future-related anticipated pathways is not static but can evolve and be updated. This is also the normal case in human life. What does this mean precisely? As the individual's needs—i.e., their goal system—are updated, the past will also be reinterpreted, and the future will be differently anticipated. If, through various experiences, the individual realizes that research and science are too static, that research and science are too detached from life, that scientists isolate themselves from the world, they will reinterpret the past and anticipate the future differently. In short: Through the updating of needs and goal systems, the current tension between Past<>Present and Present<>Future will be updated. The past-related and anticipated pathways will thus be re-evaluated. The individual may reassess past pathways, i.e., the tools in their meaning (What does rhetoric study have to do with the real problems of people?) or perceive the future pathways differently (I'll just be buried in books, scripts, and lectures, and will never know what real life has in store). Here, the tools, previously interpreted as a treasure of knowledge, will be overdetermined in their limitations or their distance from the actual concerns of concrete people, contradicting the individual's personal needs.

Of course, the updating of the individual's needs and goal-orientedness does not happen in a vacuum but within a cultural, co-constructed field. As discussed earlier, the individual updates their needs through experience—and, of course, every experience is social in nature. In other words: The need was updated through dialogue and social experience—that is, through the presence and communication with another person. Specifically: The individual was accused by a close friend of being alienated from the world and undergoing a personal change that no longer aligns with the values of their homeland. The individual may have reflected on this statement and come to the realization of its truth, which led to the reorientation of their life path. What does this mean for our revised TEA model? The interpreted and anticipated trajectories, in their tool and sign meanings, are largely dependent on the

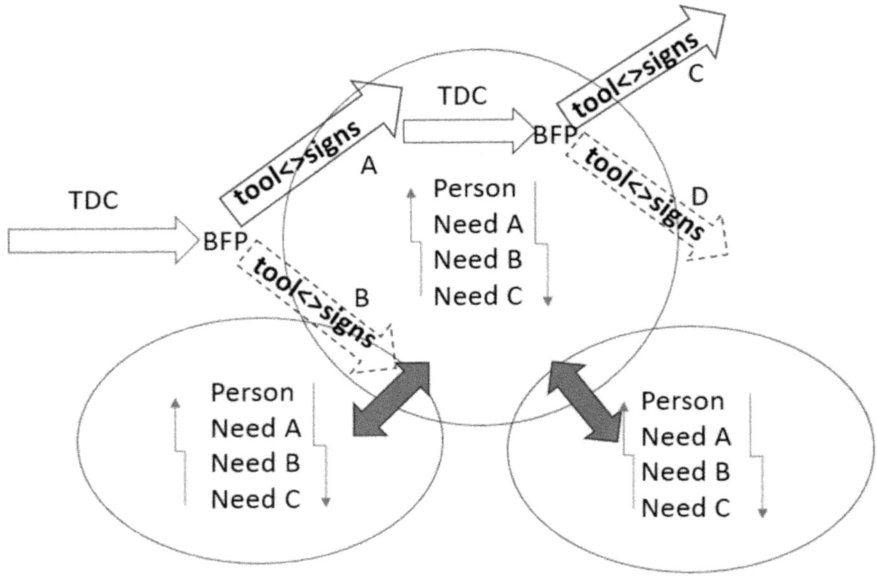

Fig. 4 Revised TEA model from a persono-semiotic perspective (BFP = bifurcation points, arrows = dynamic purpose and need system of the person, TDC = transitional developmental checkpoint)

individual's needs and goal system. Since this goal system is dynamic and evolves through dialogue and social experience, the interpreted and anticipated pathways may also update in their evaluation. We assert firmly that TEA must be more sensitive in this regard. This leads us to our updated TEA model (Fig. 4), which will summarize our chapter accordingly.

A. The individual is not only an open system but also appropriates the material and social world (tools and signs) in a personal and need-oriented manner. In doing so, they interpret past-related and anticipated pathways in a way that impacts their decision for or against a particular direction.
B. However, since the individual is also dynamic and, as an open system, continuously develops through dialogue and social experience, their goal system is subject to hierarchical change. This transformation of the goal system also means an update of needs, which in turn leads to an updated assessment of the past-related and anticipated trajectories—a changed evaluation that significantly alters the directional decision of the respective trajectory to be taken.
C. Therefore, TEA can be enriched not only from a biological perspective but also from a philosophical-semiotic (and personalistic) standpoint. This enrichment allows us to further develop the fundamental principles of TEA and also to make certain predictions about the individual's future decisions. Prediction is a crucial criterion in psychology, though not in a positivist sense, but rather within an interventionist framework aimed at optimizing our unique potential for action.

D. Figure 3 demonstrates that the enrichment of TEA lies precisely in the ongoing tension between tool and sign. This tension does not dissolve into a simple complementarity but constitutes the generative dynamic of human development. Tools provide the material and social means of shaping one's world, while signs orient the personal meaning of those tools within a system of purposes and needs. In the revised TEA model, developmental trajectories are thus always situated within this tension: the same tool (e.g., money, books, or work practices) may acquire radically different meanings depending on the accompanying sign system. By integrating this tension into the heart of TEA, we move beyond a descriptive mapping of trajectories toward a qualitative understanding of how personal worlds are constructed. The enriched model therefore highlights that equifinality itself is sign-mediated: trajectories converge or diverge not only because of available resources, but because of the ways tools are semiotically framed, appropriated, and transformed by individuals in dialogue with others.

References

Fircks, E. (2024a). *Learning with William Stern: Personology for future*. IAP.

Fircks, E. (2024b). Making sense of signs: Readjusting William Stern's personological value theory. *Theory & Psychology.* Advance online publication. https://doi.org/10.1177/09593543241279264

Fircks, E. (2024c). Raising questions with lamiell about future research directions of critical personalism: A book review essay. *Integrative Psychological and Behavioral Science, 58*, 1319–1329.

Gillespie, A., & Zittoun, T. (2010). *Using resources: Conceptualizing the mediation and refective use of tools and signs* [pre-refereed version]. LSE Research Online, 1–41. http://eprints.lse.ac.uk/38708/1/Using_resources_conceptualizing_the_mediation_and_refective_use_of_tools_and_signs_%28LSERO%29.pdf

Goethe, J. W. (2018). *Schriften zu den Naturwissenschaften*. Reclam. Original Work published 1793.

Leont'ev, A. (1978). *Activity, Consciousness, and Personality*. Prentice-Hall.

Luria, A. (1994). The problem of the cultural behavior of the child. In R. Van Der Veer & J. Valsiner (Eds.), *The Vygotsky reader* (pp. 46–57). Blackwell.

Michell, J. (2003). Pragmatism, positivism and the quantitative imperative. *Theory & Psychology, 13*(1), 45–52. https://doi.org/10.1177/0959354303013001761

Michell, J. (2005). The meaning of the quantitative imperative: A response to Niaz. *Theory & Psychology, 15*(2), 257–263. https://doi.org/10.1177/0959354305051369

Sato, T., & Tanimura, H. (2016). The Trajectory Equifinality Model (TEM) as a general tool for understanding human life course within irreversible time. In T. Sato, N. Mori, & J. Valsiner (Eds.), *Making of the future: The trajectory equifinality approach in cultural psychology* (pp. 21–43). IAP.

Sato, T., Hidaka, T., & Fukuda, M. (2009). Depicting the dynamics of living the life: The Trajectory Equifinality Model. In J. Valsiner, N. Chaudhary, M. C. D. P. Lyra, & P. C. M. Molenaar (Eds.), *Dynamic process methodology in the social and developmental sciences* (pp. 217–240). Springer.

Stern, W. (1923). *Person und Sache: Die Menschliche Persönlichkeit [The Human Personality]* (3rd ed.). J.A. Barth.

Stern, W. (1924). *Person und Sache: System des Kritischen Personalismus (Wertphilosophie) [The Philosophy of Values]*. J.A. Barth.

Valsiner, J. (2014). *An invitation to cultural psychology*. SAGE.

Valsiner, J. (2017). *From methodology to methods in human psychology*. Springer.
Valsiner, J. (2019). *Ornamented lives. Advances in cultural psychology*. IAP.
Valsiner, J. (2021). *General human psychology*. Springer.
Valsiner, J. (2024). *The moonlight doctor: Art and science of Carl Gustav Carus*. Springer Nature.
Van der Veer, R., & Valsiner, J. (1993). *A quest for synthesis: Life and work of Lev Vygotsky*. Blackwell.
von Fircks, E. F. (2023). Cultural resources for leadership: When a banana is more than a banana. *Human Arenas, 6*(3), 444–461. https://doi.org/10.1007/s42087-021-00231-0
Von Fircks, E., & Boulanger, D. (2025). *Goethe and psychology: A pluralistic outlook [Forthcoming]*. Emerald.
Vygotsky, L. S. (1994a). The problem of the cultural development of the child. In R. Van Der Veer & J. Valsiner (Eds.), *The Vygotsky reader* (pp. 57–73). Blackwell.
Vygotsky, L. S. (1994b). The problem of the environment. In R. Van Der Veer & J. Valsiner (Eds.), *The Vygotsky reader* (pp. 338–355). Blackwell.
Wendt, A. N. (2025). *What is psychology about? The philosophical foundations of its subject-matter*. Palgrave Macmillan.
Zittoun, T., & Valsiner, J. (2016). Imagining the past and remembering the future: How the unreal defines the real. In T. Sato, N. Mori, & J. Valsiner (Eds.), *Making of the future: The trajectory equifinality approach in cultural psychology* (pp. 3–21). IAP.

Layering Future Perspectives in Time of Rupture: Meaning-Making by a Mother Whose Daughter Struggles with Multiple Disorders

Mami Kanzaki

Highway trajectory, Photo by Mei, the participant of this study

M. Kanzaki (✉)
Kyoto University of Education, Kyoto, Japan
e-mail: mkanzaki@kyokyo-u.ac.jp

M. A. Campill et al. (eds.), *New Paths in Trajectory Equifinality Modelling*, Theory and History in the Human and Social Sciences,
https://doi.org/10.1007/978-3-032-25855-7_9

Psychological Difficulties in Deviating from a Socially Expected Life Course

An unstable society requires people to keep moving forward without stopping. In Japan, young people are climbing up the schooling ladder without a break; in 2024, the university enrollment rate was 59.1% and the rate of advancement to higher education institutions, including vocational schools, was 87.3% (MEXT, 2024). In this situation, the way of living for adolescents is changing. Although adolescence has been regarded as a moratorium of serious inquiry, hesitation, and conflict about one's social role (Erikson, 1959), since the 2000s, when economic and social instability increased, adolescents have been busy reducing future risks by acquiring qualifications and certifications (Murasawa et al., 2012; Kosaka, 2016).

If moving through the educational ladder without interruption is a characteristic of modern youth, then "deviating[1]" from this educational path is a tremendous psychological burden. For example, not attending school, not finding a job, or being diagnosed with a disability can mean the possibility of deviation from the standard life course in Japanese society. It has been pointed out that children who have refused school have a sense of deviation from the standard life course (Jonker, 2006; Kanzaki & Suzuki, 2023). For people experiencing Hikikomori as well, anxiety about the uncertain future and a sense of insecurity about oneself can lead to a vicious cycle of self-monitoring, which, in turn, leads to self-denial again (Murasawa, 2008; Murasawa et al., 2012). Deviating from a socially expected life course may cause psychological difficulties and negative thoughts.

When children deviate from a socially expected life course, their parents also struggle with how to support them. Case reports on school refusal have shown that parents' attempts to reconnect their children to their former school fail, and that the children's condition calms down as their parents' behavior changes in ways such as creating or finding a place where the children can feel safe (Toyoda & Sotta, 2023). A common point made in studies of school refusal and Hikikomori is the importance of adapting to the child rather than adjusting the child to society (Hirose, 2013; Kanzaki et al., 2020).

How Do Mothers Take Care of Their Children's Life Course?

While school refusal is a temporary problem during the school period, having a disability means that the individual may have a different life course for the rest of their life. Research on disability acceptance among mothers of children with disabilities has accumulated. It has been debated whether the process of acceptance is gradual

[1] In this paper, we use the term "deviation". The word deviation is composed of "de", meaning to leave, and "via", meaning a path, and means to go off the beaten path. Although sometimes used in a negative sense, deviation also has the positive meaning of creating a new path or form. The main purpose of this paper is to examine how the parties concerned make sense of such ambivalent deviance.

or whether there is a continuous chronic grief, and parental stress and burden. For instance, having a disabled child changes the mother's social life and has a negative effect on parental functions (Sen & Yurtsever, 2007), and the mothers' quality of life decreases according to the severity of the children's ASD symptoms (Garriot et al., 2014; Masefield et al., 2020).

Although parents' sorrow and burden has been mainly demonstrated, their joy and the value of raising a disabled child have also been explored. More precisely, it was proposed that parents live in between joy and sorrow, hope and no-hope, and defiance and despair (Kearny & Griffin, 2001). Hagiwara and Okuda (2018) interviewed ten mothers of children with severe physical disabilities and with autism to examine mother's life choices as a woman and a mother. It was found that when their children's disabilities were severe and life restrictions were substantial, they superimposed themselves on their children and made sense of themselves as "existing in relation to their children," and conversely, when they had more freedom in their lives, they made sense of themselves as "independent persons" and tried to support their children's lives. We can assume that mothers regulate both their own lives and their children's lives when their children "deviate" from a socially expected life course.

How does a mother's meaning-making progress within time, when her children deviate from a normal life course? Here, we focus on the narrative of a mother whose daughter is a teenage girl with multiple difficulties such as school refusal, orthostatic dysregulation, taste disorder, panic disorder, and developmental disorder. This study examines the mother's way of caring for her daughter not only from the perspective of whether she accepts her child's disability, but also from the perspective of how she strikes a balance between her own life and her daughter's life.

How Are Future Perspectives Portrayed? TEM and Equifinality Points

This study applied Trajectory Equifinality Modeling (TEM) to describe a mothers' meaning—making over time. In TEM, people who have reached a certain state (called the equifinality point) are asked to participate in interviews, and their thoughts and experiences leading up to that state are often described. However, when a daughter faces multiple difficulties, it is difficult for the mother to identify a particular state as the equifinality point. Instead of reaching a certain state, there is a high chance she will keep questioning her future.

In this study, we try to describe a period of rupture (Zittoun, 2016) in which difficulties are compounded. Prior to the analysis, we expected that the equifinality point, called EFP, would be modified many times. However, the interviews and analysis revealed that the EFPs were not reset, but instead the EFPs became deeply embedded in the mother's experience, literally "embodied," and at the same time, new EFPs emerged in response to changing circumstances. In this study, we propose to refer to such overlapping EFPs as "layered EFPs."

Data Collection

The data used in this study are participant observations and interviews conducted as part of the fieldwork. The author began research on school refusal in 2010 and has been conducting an extracurricular project since 2021 in high schools with students who have experienced school refusal. In this project, high school students who have experienced school refusal planned events for elementary and junior high school students who were not attending school.

Nina and her mother, Mei, who have participated in this project, were selected as participants for this study. First, several types of informal data were collected, such as transcripts from the project meeting in 2021, Nina's blog and informal meetings with Mei. In the process of such communication, the author was surprised by Nina's experience of multiple difficulties, and this led to formal interviews with Nina's mother, Mei, in November 2024 and February 2025.

Participants

Nina's mother, Mei, was a woman in her 50s, born and raised in the Kansai area of Japan. She has been raising her three children and taking care of her mother-in-law for 18 years since her marriage. She has also worked part-time as an office worker, a bus tour guide, and a caregiver for persons with disabilities.

Nina was the youngest of three siblings with an older brother and sister, and was a teenager with excellent verbal and expressive skills and also an artistic side. In the first year of junior high school, she suffered orthostatic dysregulation and taste disorder, and began to refuse to go to school. In the third year of junior high school, she began to participate in the extracurricular projects with her mother. When she entered high school, she suffered from panic disorder, and was subsequently in and out of a psychiatric hospital, ultimately dropping out of high school. In her blog, she wrote about her confusion about not being able to perform everyday activities she had taken for granted such as going out or taking a bath, her anxiety about living a completely different life from everyone around her, and her pain at seeing only the things she disliked about herself.

Analysis

After formal interviews, TEM analysis was conducted. First, I set the research question as "How does Mei try to deal with the difficulties her daughter encounters?" and read through the transcript. I segmented the transcript into small units and rearranged them according to irreversible time. Next, I designated *"dealing with the daughter's difficulties"* as the equifinality point (EFP) and *"not dealing with the difficulties"* as Polarized-EFP. The labels closer to the EFP were placed toward the top, and those closer to the P-EFP were placed toward the bottom. In addition, I distinguished the labels between Mei's trajectory and social forces/

supports: the social supports that helped her to reach EFPs as social guidance (SG), and those that hindered her from reaching the EFP as social direction (SD). In the process of organizing the transcripts using the concepts of TEM, the EFPs were refined. EFP did not simply shift from one state to another, but rather became embodied and layered through accumulated experiences. Based on this understanding, I illustrated it as a layered EFPs. The TEM diagrams and the text were reviewed by Mei and some parts were modified.

Results

In this study, we focused on the narrative of a mother whose daughter faced multiple difficulties and applied TEM to examine how she related to such difficulties and faced her daughter's "deviation" from a socially expected life course. She established some guidelines that were considered as EFPs, and these guidelines were not created in a short period of time in response to Nina's difficulties, but instead were a synthesis of the wisdom Mei had cultivated by dealing with various difficulties throughout her life. Her life course was divided into three periods, which are described below.

Giving Full Support While Keeping a Distance to Avoid Self-Sacrifice

Mei's life course of the first stage is shown in Fig. 1. When she was a teenager, her older sister experienced a postpartum depression. Her parents' lives and moods were always influenced by her sister's mental state, and they tried to manage the problem within the family. However, her sister's mental condition did not improve so easily. Therefore, Mei came to believe that it was important to be supportive during difficult times without sacrificing herself (EFP-I).

After graduating from high school, she became a bus tour guide and left home. Leaving home allowed her to distance herself from her family's problems, yet her parents contacted her whenever her older sister's condition worsened. While she wondered why her sister could not take care of herself, she also wished to understand her sister. At work, she met deaf people and felt frustrated with herself because she could not communicate with them. She was motivated to understand such people and she took a sign language class. There she met people of different ages and professions and felt her perspectives were expanding. During this time, she enjoyed working as a bus tour guide.

Mei's partner was working overseas. Mei and her partner were both highly involved in their own jobs and therefore thought they were going to continue the long-distance relationship. However, the partner's mother had a stroke, and the partner suddenly returned to Japan. He then proposed to her and she moved in with his mother. At the time, an acquaintance told her that she was too young to get married while taking care of her paralyzed mother-in-law. However, based on her experience

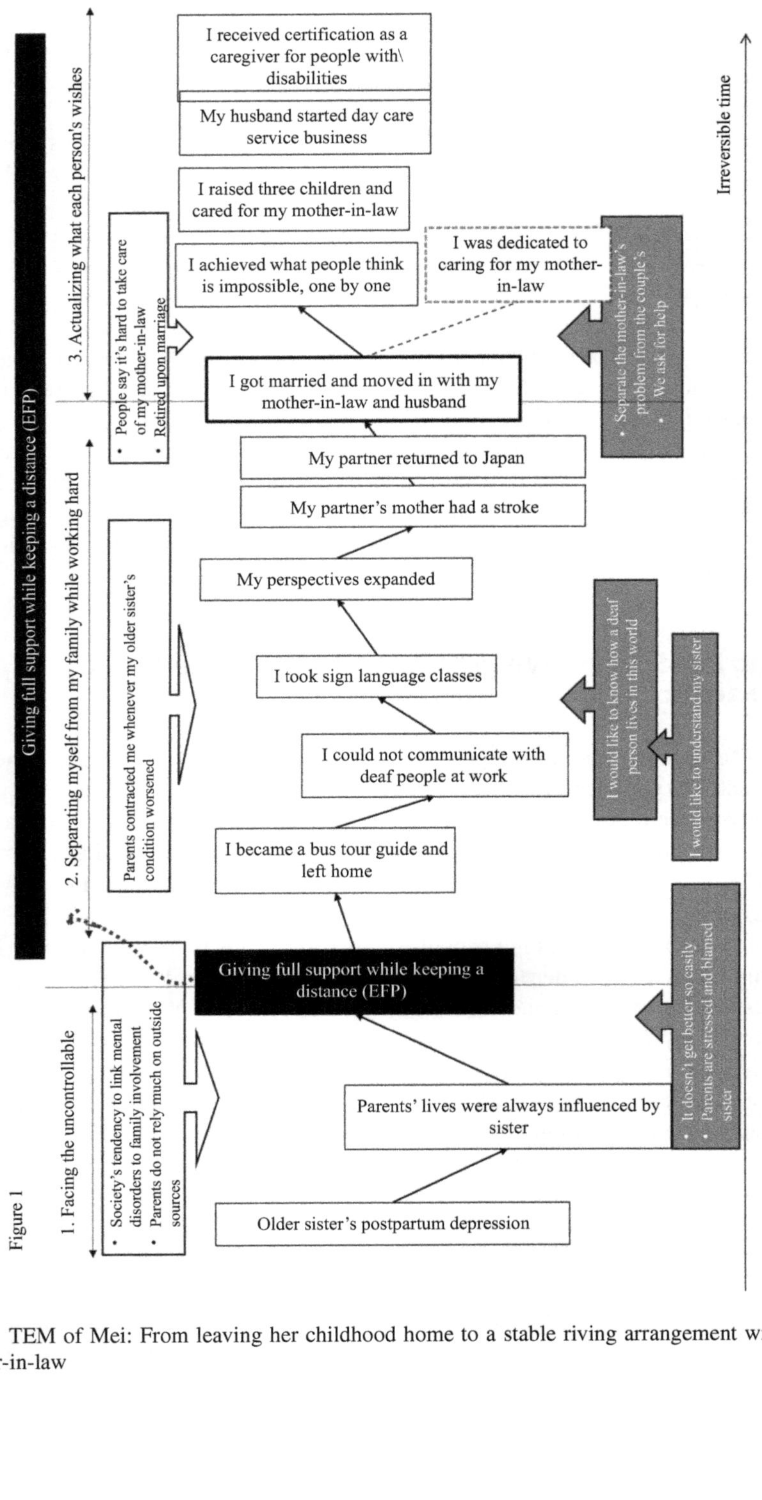

Fig. 1 TEM of Mei: From leaving her childhood home to a stable riving arrangement with her mother-in-law

with her sister's postpartum depression, Mei strived to separate her mother-in-law's problems from the couple's problems, in order to avoid self-sacrifice.

In order for her mother-in-law and her family to continue to live together, she first fulfilled her mother-in-law's wishes, then left her at a day care center and fulfilled family's wishes such as family trips. She said, "When I leave my mother-in-law, who is in need of care, to go on a trip with my children... I feel guilty. Even if no one says it out loud, I wonder if people think, 'why do you leave her?'. Yet my husband and I don't think like that, and we ask for help when we need it. (...) That's why we have been able to live together with the mother-in-law for 18 years." In this way, she gave full support when needed, while avoided self-sacrifice.

Don't Give Up, Don't Fight: Taking a Rest

The life course of the second phase is shown in Fig. 2. Mei managed her daily life while raising her three children, caring for her mother-in-law, and helping in the family business; she became a certified caregiver for the disabled when her husband started the day care center business. Her children were enrolled in private schools from kindergarten and grew up well. However, when her oldest son was in the sixth grade of elementary school, he suddenly became unable to get up in the morning. At that time, Mei could not understand why her son, who was so energetic and devoted to playing tennis, suddenly became ill, and she went to hospital after hospital to find out the reason. Eventually, they found out that he had orthostatic dysregulation, and his doctor told her to let him rest.

Although the diagnosis came as a shock, the school her oldest son attended was full of understanding teachers who respected his condition and wishes. The elementary school had three affiliated junior high schools, and given his physical condition, the teachers recommended the one that was close to home. However, he wanted to attend a different school to continue playing tennis, which was far from their home. To accommodate her son's wishes, she decided to spend a total of four hours each day driving him to and from school. The junior high school he attended was also understanding, and by the third year of junior high school, his symptoms had calmed down considerably. During this time, the mother-in-law entered a facility after suffering a broken bone, and as the eldest son began to settle down, Mei began working as a caregiver for the disabled.

Just as the family began to settle down, the eldest daughter, in her second year of high school, started suffering from severe orthostatic dysregulation. The eldest daughter had grown up in the same affiliated school from kindergarten through high school, so she wanted to continue high school. However, from Mei's experience with her eldest son, she knew that her daughter's symptoms would worsen if she did not have a break. The affiliated high school that the eldest daughter had chosen had little understanding of her symptoms, and Mei received phone calls every day about learning delays. Mei told her daughter, "If you would like to enter a university or college student at the same time as everyone else, you should leave high school right now." Although the eldest daughter was torn, she decided to withdraw from the

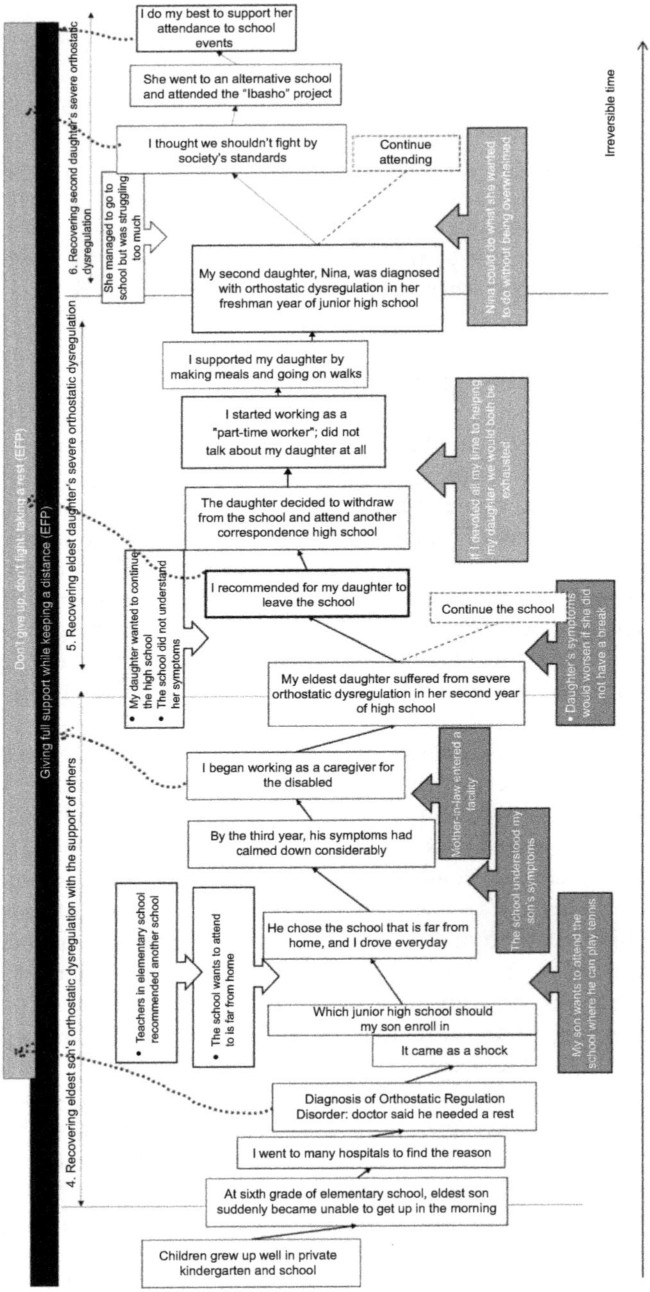

Fig. 2 TEM of Mei: from raising three children to overcome their orthostatic dysregulation

school and attend a correspondence high school. Mei and her husband supported their eldest daughter by helping her to study and accompanying her to meals and walks so that she would not regret quitting school.

When their oldest daughter was in her junior year of high school and preparing for an university entrance exam, their second daughter, Nina, in her first year of junior high school, was diagnosed with orthostatic dysregulation. By that time, Mei had already seen the progression of the symptoms in the two older children. She was sure that Nina could do what she wanted to do without being overwhelmed. Although Nina wanted to continue junior high school, Mei thought, "We shouldn't judge ourselves by society's standards. Nina will harm her health if she pushes herself too hard to fit in with those around her." In her third year of junior high school, she slowly made her way through life, participating in an alternative school and the extracurricular projects at the correspondence high school she planned to enter. When Nina was able to participate in school events and other activities, Mei drove wherever she could to drop Nina off and pick her up. Through the experience of her three children with orthostatic dysregulation, Mei learned not to rush to return to a socially expected life course, but rather to let them rest well (layered EFPs, EFP-II).

Deepening the Prospects of Phase 1 (EFP-1)

Mei also provided full support during Phase 2. She drove a total of four hours each day to take her eldest son to junior high school, and in between, she prepared her eldest and youngest daughters for school, took her mother-in-law to day care, helped with the family business, and did household chores. When her eldest daughter suffered from severe orthostatic dysregulation, Mei made soup and carried her to the table on her back because she was unable to move due to low blood pressure. With Nina, she dropped her off at the school trip destination and stood by in case Nina needed to return at any time.

While providing such thorough support, Mei was careful not to sacrifice herself. When her eldest daughter developed orthostatic dysregulation, she began working part-time as an office worker because she did not know when her daughter would recover. She thought that if she devoted all her time to helping her daughter, they would both be exhausted. At that time, she considered herself simply a "part-time worker" and did not talk about her daughter at all, to spend time away from her daughter on purpose. She also talked about the problem of self-sacrifice: "Even if you are married, you are still an individual. Even if I am a wife, I am still me. When you lose your individuality, you blame others when things go wrong."

Living in the Present Moment in Times of Uncertainty

When Nina's orthostatic dysregulation got worsed, Mei did her best to support her while letting go of the problem. The two older children eventually returned to everyday life using these methods. However, Nina's case was different. The third phase shows the process from the onset of Nina's panic disorder to the present (Fig. 3).

Fig. 3 TEM of Mei: From the onset of Nina's panic disorder to the present

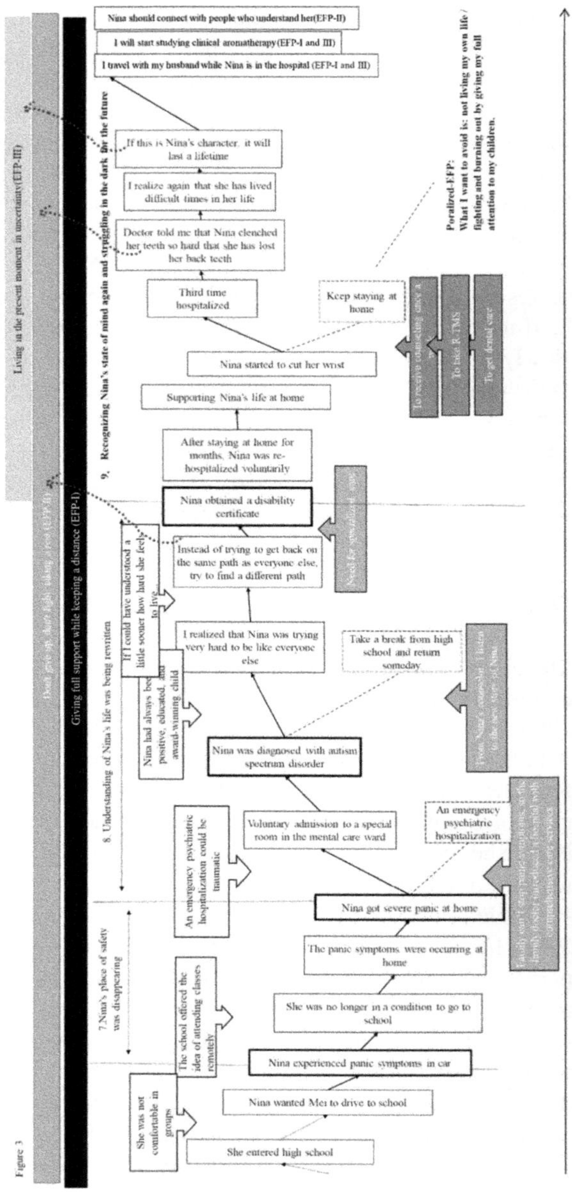

Since Nina had spent her three years of junior high school not going to school, she wanted to go out with her friends and participate in cultural and sports festivals during her high school years. She entered a high school where she expected to have a fulfilling high school experience, and she enjoyed her new school life at first. However, she began to feel stressed because she was not comfortable in communication with others and in riding the train. Before entering high school, she had gone to a theme park on a graduation trip with her friends and had fainted on the train on the way home. A few months after starting high school, Nina began to relive the unsettling experience and started asking Mei to drive her to and from school.

Although Nina felt safe in Mei's driving, she experienced panic symptoms in the car when she went to get a PCR test kit because she had COVID-19 symptoms. When Mei was walking on her way to get the kit, Nina called her and cried loudly, asking for help. Mei realized this was not a normal situation and rushed to the hospital. Although the school suggested that she attend classes remotely, she was no longer in a condition to go to school. At that moment, her first step was to try to control her panic symptoms. However, the panic symptoms were occurring even at home. Although emergency psychiatric hospitalization was considered, the family decided against it because they were concerned that physical restraint could be traumatic. Instead, they chose to admit her to a hospital with comprehensive care services where their family doctor recommended.

While in the hospital, Nina was diagnosed with autism spectrum disorder. The diagnosis explained the reason for her panic, and Mei felt a little relieved. On the other hand, Mei's perception of Nina was shattered because Nina had always been a positive and high-achieving child. Through counseling, she realized that Nina had disliked riding the train since she was a small child, yet she couldn't say anything. Mei realized that Nina was trying very hard to be like everyone else, even though they, her parents, were not aware of it. Instead of trying to get back on the same path as everyone else, Mei was determined to take a different path. Nina obtained a disability certificate to receive specialized home care, and after spending the next few months at home, she was readmitted to the mental hospital. After she returning home again, she became increasingly distressed by feeling different from those around her. She also began to cut her wrists, wished to have dental treatment and insurance-covered R-TMS covered.As a result, she was hospitalized a third time.

Through Nina's repeated admissions and discharges to and from the psychiatric ward, Mei had a different perspective from that in the first and second periods. The two older children were able to return to a socially expected life course of life by resting their bodies and minds. In Nina's case, however, the social life course itself was a burden to her temperament. During the interview, Mei repeatedly spoke about Nina's feelings; both Nina and Mei were thrown into the uncertainty of not knowing what would happen in the future. Mei said, "I have to think about what things can make my girl Nina feel safe, secure and comfortable in her own mind. But she is already 18 years old and this is my first experience as a parent. So, I'm really in the dark. The only thing I can say is that if you can't live in the present, there is no way anything good can happen in the future. If you keep dwelling on the past, regretting the past, worrying about the future, and going back and forth like that, there is no way anything good can happen in the future unless you enjoy this day, this time, and this moment. Day in and day out Nina says negative things. As a parent, I said today was a good day just because you got to go to the hospital. If we do not focus on what we have achieved, even if it is only a half step progress, nothing great will happen in the future." This was how she tried to live in the moment (EFP-III, Layered-EFPs).

Deepening Prospects of the First and Second Phases (EFP-1, 2)

Mei had reached a new state of mind, but it was not a drastic change. She had deepened the perspective she had developed in the first phase of "giving full support while keeping a distance." When Nina was hospitalized, Mei and her husband went on a trip for a few days. Regarding this short trip, Mei said, "Going on a trip without Nina is not just fun. I cheerfully tell Nina, 'I'm going,' and then I wonder everything will be all right. We might feel lonely. Nina might cut her wrists or she might feel better. I didn't know what would happen. But we both made it, had a good time and went back home. It is a valuable experience to know that she could manage on her own and understand how long I could be away from home. There will be times when you fail, but that is more of an experience than a failure. You never know until you try."

She also deepened her second-phase perspective of never giving up and never fighting. For Nina, Mei was looking for a path that would not force her to fight and burn out, on the premise that this could continue throughout her life. She said, "I would be happy if everyone in the world understood Nina, but I don't think that's going to happen, so I think it would be good if she felt comfortable and safe within herself, and if there were some people who could understand that. (...) Nina is too hard and tough on herself and that makes her suffer." In this way, Mei was looking for an alternative place for Nina to belong, instead of trying to catch up with a socially expected life course.

Discussion

In this study, we focused on the narrative of Mei, a mother with a daughter who has multiple difficulties, and applied TEM to examine how she relates to such difficulties and faces "deviation" from a socially expected life course. As a result, it was found that May responds to the children's "deviation" in various ways, and that her parenting style has been constructed through her whole life by synthesizing her life experiences.

Flexibility and Richness of Dealing with "Deviance"

Mei has many ways of dealing with "deviance" from the socially expected life course. When children deviate from a socially expected life course, adults try to get them back on the original path. The closer adults are, the more conflict they may experience, because they know that following society's expected path will make life easier. However, there is a mismatch between the institutionalized path and personal meaning (Nielsen, 2008). In case of Mei, she prioritized the children's health over the institutionalized paths. When her children suffered from orthostatic dysregulation, she did not try to force them to fit into the social context, but instead made sure that their physical health came first; this is expressed as "do not fight."

In addition to prioritizing the children's health, Mei had even suggested the option of "deliberately dropping out of school." With her eldest daughter, the school's goals did not match her personal situation, so Mei encouraged her to drop out of high school. The eldest daughter took the bold step of withdrawing from school, took time off to rest, and passed the university entrance exam. Deviation is often seen negatively, yet this study showed that deliberately deviating from school can lead to long-term social adaptation. There are many ways to return to a social path, as TEM points out at a philosophical level.

Compared to her siblings, Nina's panic disorder and autism spectrum disorder was less predictable for Mei. Because Nina could no longer do the things she had been able to do, both Nina and Mei were confused about what she wanted to do and what she could do. In such situations, the meanings of the past, present, and future were rewritten over and over again. Therefore, it was difficult for them to imagine the prospect of returning to a socially expected life course as their eldest son and daughter had done. Although Mei didn't give up hope that Nina could live a healthy life, she didn't fight against the social norm; she was in between, like Kearny and Griffin (2001) suggested. In other words, Nina and Mei were thrown into a state of uncertainty.

It is easy to set a goal and then back away from it to create a clear vision. Sometimes, however, people are thrown helplessly into a state of uncertainty, lack of control, and rupture. At that time, instead of worrying about the uncertainties of the past and the future, Mei cherished the present. She tried to survive in the midst of her undefined nature by living in the present, by valuing everyday activities and time together. And instead of returning to a socially expected life course, they sought a place that would accept and understand Nina. An alternative life course began to take shape. It turned out that they had an extremely flexible and rich way of dealing with "deviation" from an expected life course.

Experience-Integrated Parenting: Giving Full Support While Keeping a Distance

These flexible and rich attitudes were not acquired through specific events, but rather cultivated over a lifetime. It was found that her ways of dealing with difficulties were challenged and embodied many times through her own experiences, such as her older sister's postpartum depression, caring for her mother-in-law, and caring for her eldest son and daughter with orthostatic dysregulation.

A consistent attitude throughout Mei's story was giving full support while keeping a distance to avoid self-sacrifice: when necessary, she would leave her children and mother-in-law with professional care services or spend time away from home through her work. Mei challenged the Japanese social norm that mothers should take on family problems and sacrifice themselves. From her experiences during adolescence, she learned that when mothers became overly involved in their children's problems by adhering rigidly to the traditional maternale role, those problems often become even more complicated. As a result, she deliberately learned to keep a distance when neccesary.

Historically, mothers in Japan devoted themselves to fulfilling their family roles. In recent years, women have become more educated and have continued to work after marriage, and they have begun to seek ways of living in which they have personal goals other than the family role (Nagahisa, 2010). However, it has been suggested that women in caregiving roles actively take on expected roles and lose sight of themselves through burnout as they struggle to adapt to the situation (Mera, 2008). As Winnicott (1971) once described as a "good enough mother," it is not necessary to try to be a perfect mother; children also need experiences and time to move away from their mother and take on challenges.

In other words, the question of how mothers should balance their parenting responsibilities has been a subject of ongoing historical and societal debate, which signifies the difficulties of achieving such a balance. Although previous studies suggested that the mothers of children with disabilities maintain a distance when the children's condition is good (Hagiwara & Okuda), this study suggests that mothers can deliberately maintain some distance from their children in any situation. Creating other roles or taking time away from their children, as well as promoting reflection (Mera, 2008), can provide opportunities for mothers to escape the traps of their roles. Mai repeatedly tried to balance the relationship with her children, adjusting the distance between herself and her child. The constant adjustment of distance between parent and child might continue throughout life.

Describing the Maturing Meaning by TEM: Layering Multiple Perspectives (EFPs)

In this study, we examined how a mother deals with her children's difficulties. The results showed that future prospects, perspectives, or values (EFPs) are gradually generated and accumulated in layers. A similar situation was reported by Yasuda (2017). In Yasuda (2017), women who wanted children but were experiencing infertility were interviewed, and an EFP of "facing infertility treatment positively" and a second EFP of "accepting any outcome" were depicted, and the EFP and second EFP overlapped. In the case of this study, the EFP represented a deepening of the initial perspective while gaining new wisdom in response to new circumstances. Thus, while some parts of the process would change depending on the situation, there would also be a process of continuing to embody what is important across the situation.

In representing both the changed and the unchanged, it may be useful to think of the future perspective (EFP) as a layer. Layered EFPs tell us that our lives are made up of a historical accumulation of events and experiences. At the same time, it also suggests that the process of learning and embodying personal philosophies does not happen overnight but takes time. TEM helps describe meaning-making that changes in response to the ever-shifting situations, remains constant regardless of the situation, and—as emphasized in this study—is deepened in response to the situation. In this era of rapid change, where everyone rushes to educate and "deviations" from institutionalized paths are immediately targeted for education, it is necessary to reconsider the meaning of education and "deviation." TEM powerfully supports the reconsideration of such meaning, particularly in depicting the maturing and refinement of meaning over a life time.

References

Erikson, E. H. (1959). Identity and the life cycle: Selected papers. *Psychological Issues, 1*, 1–171.

Garriot, C., Villes, V., Bartolini, A., & Poinso, F. (2014). Self-perceived health of parents of children with autism spectrum disorders: Relation with the severity level. *Psychology, 5*, 2189–2199. https://doi.org/10.4236/psych.2014.519221

Hagiwara, K., & Okuda, K. (2018). Mothers' acceptance of their children's disabilities. *Japanese Journal of Health Psychology Research, 31*(Special issue), 253–258.

Hirose, M. (2013). A qualitative study of the parental support process that helps "Socially withdrawn" children reconnect to society. *Japanese Journal of Family Psychology, 27*(2), 137–151.

Jonker, E. F. (2006). School hurts: Refrains of hurt and hopelessness in stories about dropping out at a vocational school for care work. *Journal of Education and Work, 19*(2), 121–140. https://doi.org/10.1080/13639080600667988

Kanzaki, M., Jensen, M., Kawamata, T., & Onohara, A. (2020). Contextualised understanding of and transdisciplinary approaches to school dropout. In M. Watzlawik & A. Burkholder (Eds.), *Educating adolescents around the globe: Becoming who you are in a world full of expectations* (pp. 265–282). Springer.

Kanzaki, M., & Suzuki, H. (2023). School refusal as a representation of questioning normality: Understanding the richness of socio-cultural transitions. *Culture & Psychology, 29*(3), 644–659. https://doi.org/10.1177/1354067X221146487

Kearney, P. M., & Griffin, T. (2001). Between joy and sorrow: Being a parent of a child with developmental disability. *Journal of Advanced Nursing, 34*, 582–592. https://doi.org/10.1046/j.1365-2648.2001.01787.x

Kosaka, Y. (2016). Moratorium among young modern to campus life: The concept of "Risk-Averse Moratorium". *The Japanese Journal of Developmental Psychology, 27*(3), 221–231.

Masefield, S. C., Prady, S. L., Sheldon, T. A., et al. (2020). The caregiver health effects of caring for young children with developmental disabilities: A meta-analysis. *Maternal and Child Health Journal, 24*, 561–574. https://doi.org/10.1007/s10995-020-02896-5

Mera, A. (2008). To be free from role expectations as a caregiver. In K. Kashiawgi (Ed.), *Pioneering developmental family psychology: Perspectives to connect family, society, and the individual* (pp. 71–88). Nakanishiya Publishing.

Ministry of Education, Culture, Sports, Science and Technology. (2024). *Basic School Survey 2024*. https://www.mext.go.jp/content/20241213-mxt_chousa01-000037551_01.pdf

Murasawa, W. (2008). Chapter 4: Self-searching and occupations in young people. In M. Tsuzuki (Ed.), *The psychology of work: Self-searching and irritation among young people* (pp. 79–99). Minerva Publishing House (Japanese).

Murasawa, W., Yamao, T., & Murasawa, M. (2012). *Young people in the post-moratorium era: Beyond social exclusion*. Sekai Shiso Sha Publishing (Japanese).

Nagahisa, H. (2010). The relationships between women's value orientation as well as their consciousness of family roles and their life perspective in middle aged women with children: Feature of form of employment Japanese. *Journal of Family Psychology, 24*(2), 157–170.

Nielsen, K. (2008). Learning, trajectories of participation and social practice. *Critical Social Studies, 10*(1), 22–36.

Sen, E., & Yurtsever, S. (2007). Difficulties experienced by families with disabled children. *Journal for Specialists in Pediatric Nursing, 12*(4), 238–252. https://doi.org/10.1111/j.1744-6155.2007.00119.x

Toyoda, K., & Sotta, T. (2023). Attempt to develop a bidirectional TEA from a unidirectional TEA: Case study on a family who experienced truancy. *Japanese Journal of TEA for Qualitative Inquiry, 1*(1), 1–19.

Winnicott, D. W. (1971). *Playing and reality*. Tavistock Publications.

Yasuda, Y. (2017). The process of finding meaning in a woman's experience of infertility while receiving in-vitro fertilization: Trajectory Equifinality Modeling (TEM). *The Japanese Journal of Health and Medical Sociology, 28*(1), 12–22.

Zittoun, T. (2016). A sociocultural psychology of the life-course. *Social Psychological Review, 18*(1), 6–17. https://doi.org/10.1159/000526435

Guiding Your Desired Self Through Creative Thinking and Self-Regulation: Applying the Future Auto-TEM to Career Design

Xiaohong Zhang and Kenichi Kubota

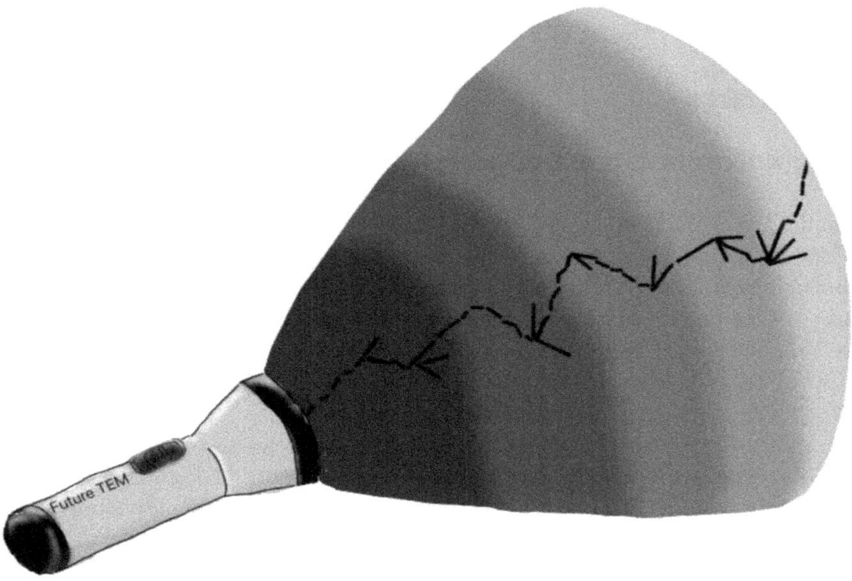

Exploring the trajectory of the mind (by the authors)

X. Zhang (✉) · K. Kubota
Kansai University, Suita, Japan
e-mail: x_zhang@kansai-u.ac.jp

M. A. Campill et al. (eds.), *New Paths in Trajectory Equifinality Modelling*, Theory and History in the Human and Social Sciences,
https://doi.org/10.1007/978-3-032-25855-7_10

Introduction

As the twenty-first century progresses, societies are becoming increasingly complex and globalized, making it ever more difficult to predict the future. Nevertheless, the capacity to imagine the future, envision one's desired self, and actively work toward that vision has become essential. In this context, we emphasize the importance of career design, which refers to vividly imagining possible futures and deliberately planning actions to approach them.

However, creating a clear image of an uncertain future remains highly challenging. It is particularly difficult to set concrete goals and design pathways toward them when faced with ambiguity and change. To address this challenge, this chapter introduces using the Future Auto-TEM as a strategy for visualizing possible futures and systematically revising them in response to circumstances. Through this process, individuals can engage in creative thinking, self-regulation, and progressively move closer to their "desired self."

Related Works

Developments in Career Design Research

In the field of career studies, a central theme has been how individuals deepen their self-understanding and design their careers within the relationships they form with organizations and society. Schein (1978) addressed this question by introducing the concept of the career anchor, which provides a foundation for individuals to determine "who they want to be." Career anchors function as guiding principles in organizational decision-making and offer a framework for examining the alignment between individual needs and organizational requirements.

In contrast, Schlossberg (1981) shifted attention from career continuity to transitions. She proposed the 4S Model (situation, self, support, and strategies) as key resources for coping with transitions, thereby systematizing how individuals manage career-related changes. This perspective enables an understanding of career development not as a linear trajectory of growth, but as a process of discontinuous change and adaptation.

Furthermore, Savickas (2009) theorized career counseling from a social constructionist perspective, emphasizing that personal knowledge and identity are constructed through social interaction and that meaning is co-constructed through discourse. This view situates career design not merely as an internal decision-making process, but as an endeavor that emerges within cultural and social contexts.

Kubota (2025) further argued that individuals and society should not be viewed as separate entities; rather, their relationship is continuously reconstructed through mutual interaction and co-creation. From this perspective, situations and environments are also open to change. Therefore, career design involves not only envisioning future careers but also actively designing and reconstructing learning environments that support such development.

Integrating Creative Thinking to Career Design

The activity of designing one's career is closely linked to creative thinking, which involves envisioning the future and discovering new possibilities. Creative thinking is defined as the cognitive ability to generate and express new, applicable ideas (Hokanson, 2018). It consists of two aspects: the generation of new ideas through divergent thinking, and the articulation and expression of those ideas. As Saaty (2010) noted, creative thinking opens up new possibilities through the use of imagination.

Applied to careers, this perspective suggests that individuals are not merely adapting to pre-existing frameworks but are actively creating new career possibilities. Career design can thus be understood as a process of (1) imagining future possibilities and (2) actively constructing possible choices and future environments needed to realize them. To translate these possibilities into reality, self-regulation is indispensable, enabling individuals to flexibly revise their evolving careers while moving closer to self-realization.

Self-Regulation in Creating One's Own Career

Self-regulation includes internal self-regulation, behavioral regulation, and environmental regulation (Zimmerman, 1989). Internal self-regulation refers to observing and adapting specific emotions and thoughts. Behavioral regulation involves selecting what actions to take and how to perform them. Environmental regulation refers to adjusting elements of the social and physical environment. Zimmerman (2013) emphasized that self-regulation is a cyclical process through which learners manage their progress by engaging in forethought, performance, and self-reflection, continually adjusting their actions in response to outcomes. This process underscores the importance of planning, monitoring, and reflection, while also highlighting the need to regulate one's decision-making processes and to adjust environmental factors. When individuals engage in self-reflection, self-dialogue may occur among multiple I-positions, enabling them to examine conflicting thoughts, emotions, and possible courses of action (Hermans, 2001).

The Insider's Perspective in Integrating Creative Thinking and Self-Regulation into Career Design

When individuals understand their career anchors (Schein, 1978), they have identified their core values and clarified their desired selves. In this sense, no one can grasp that self more deeply than the individuals themselves. The insider's perspective—how individuals make decisions when they face conflicts, turning points, and envision their future selves—can provide valuable information for career design. For example, Tsuchimoto and Sato (2022) identified the first author's decision-making process in the career. However, their study focused on retrospective career analysis rather than future-oriented career design.

Therefore, career design approaches need to respect the insider's perspective and provide strategies that enable learners to imagine future possibilities, use self-regulation to respond flexibly to unforeseen circumstances, and actively engage with environmental factors. However, existing strategies have not fully addressed how creative thinking and self-regulation can be integrated to support future-oriented career design from the insider's perspective. This gap highlights the need to develop a future-oriented career design strategy that integrates these elements and enables individuals to continuously adjust their trajectories while remaining oriented toward their desired selves.

The purpose of this study is to develop and examine a future-oriented career design strategy that incorporates creative thinking and self-regulation from the insider's perspective, and to explore its potential to support learners in moving toward desired selves.

Methods

This study adopted a methodological framework that integrates the Trajectory Equifinality Approach (TEA) and auto-ethnography.

Trajectory Equifinality Approach (TEA)

TEA is a qualitative research methodology in cultural psychology that aims to elucidate the dynamic processes of decision-making within sociocultural contexts (Sato, 2017). Within TEA, two core concepts are included: the Trajectory Equifinality Model (TEM) and promoter signs.

TEM visualizes the mechanisms through which individuals make decisions within their environments and how these decisions interact with environmental factors to shape pathways toward their goals. TEM comprises the following concepts: (1) Bifurcation Points (BFPs), which indicate moments when individuals face alternative choices; and (2) the two types of social forces that influence such choices at BFPs—Social Direction (SD), which hinders attainment of equifinality points (EFPs), and Social Guidance (SG), which facilitates such attainment (Sato, 2017).

Promoter signs, derived from semiotic theory in cultural psychology, signify future possibilities not yet experienced (Valsiner, 2018). They are essentially affective in nature and enable signs to indicate objects through interpretants such as emotions and efforts (Valsiner, 2024).

The Future Auto-TEM

Auto-ethnography allows researchers to systematically analyze their own life experiences and narratives as data (Sparkes, 2018). By occupying the dual position of both researcher and participant, researchers can gain insights through self-disclosure and reflection that cannot be accessed in studies focusing solely on third parties.

Traditionally, TEM has been applied as a method for analyzing past and present data from the perspective of a third party (Sato, 2017). However, Tsuchimoto and Sato (2022) incorporated auto-ethnography and demonstrated the effectiveness of Auto-TEM in analyzing career transitions. Yet, very few studies have systematically extended Auto-TEM to the future. Extending Auto-TEM toward possible futures may enable individuals to creatively construct future trajectories, engage in self-regulation, and progressively move closer to their desired selves.

Building on this idea, the first author attempted to apply the Future Auto-TEM (Zhang, 2020) to envision her future career. Extending this line of thought, the present study proposes the Future Auto-TEM as a strategy for "becoming one's desired self."

The Future Auto-TEM provides two main advantages for career design:

(1) It enables learners to imagine and visualize potential social pressures and power relations that may shape their career trajectories.
(2) It facilitates periodic review and strategic adjustment, thereby fostering self-regulated learning.

Moreover, the Future Auto-TEM makes introspection visible, prevents forgetting and relational confusion over time, and allows for ongoing monitoring. In doing so, it not only safeguards personal insights but also promotes the continuous generation and revision of ideas about future possibilities, thereby creating opportunities to cultivate creative thinking.

Application of the Future Auto-TEM in This Study

In this study, the first author (Zhang), originally from China, was an international student at a Japanese university and is now working as a researcher in Japan. As Sakai (2024) has pointed out, international students face diverse challenges in securing employment in Japan after completing graduate school and in adapting to the workplace. The first author, while aspiring to work in Japan, also felt some anxiety.

She continued to reflect on questions such as "What kind of person do I want to become in Japan?" and "Can I really become such a person in Japan?" With both expectations and uncertainties about the future, she created her first Future Auto-TEM before completing her doctoral program. In doing so, she visualized a 5-year career and learning environment toward her desired self and, through self-dialogue, designated two EFPs: working as a researcher (EFP-1) and becoming an international researcher (EFP-2).

After constructing the Future Auto-TEM, she reported it to the second author (her supervisor), who advised: "After a certain period of time, it would be interesting to examine how much of the Future Auto-TEM has been realized." This suggestion motivated further exploration of the potential of the Future Auto-TEM for supporting career design.

The timeline of constructing and revising the Auto-TEM diagrams was as follows:

- January 1, 2020: Creation of the Future Auto-TEM1 (TEM1) (prior to completing her doctoral program in March 2020 and beginning employment at University A in April 2020).
- January 1, 2021: Reflection and revision of the Future Auto-TEM (TEM2) after 9 months of employment at University A.
- January 1, 2025: Reflection and revision of the second Future Auto-TEM (TEM3), reviewing the extent to which it has been realized (in the third year after her transfer to University B in April 2022).

The division of responsibilities in describing this study was as follows: the sections on "Future Pathways" and "Engagement with the environment" were primarily written by the first author, while the "Analysis from the perspective of career formation" was evaluated from a third-party perspective by the second author (Kubota). This collaborative process combined self-reflection with external evaluation, thereby enhancing the validity of the analysis.

Result and Discussion

Pre-employment Career Design: Shaping a Vague Future Image

Life story The first author was in her third year of the doctoral course at a Japanese university as an international student. Her research focused on the professional growth of primary school teachers in a collaborative program between China and Japan. She studied with high motivation and felt a strong sense of fulfillment in her work. However, she faced the choice of whether to return to China or to pursue a career in Japan after completing her doctoral course.

An Attempt to Envision the Future: TEM1

With feelings of both uncertainty and hope about her future career, she created TEM1.

The pathways in TEM1 of Fig. 1 were as follows:

Firstly, she divided her future 10-year career into three stages. The first stage was to obtain her doctoral degree. The second stage was to work as a researcher within 5 years (EFP1). The third stage was to become an international researcher after 10 years (EFP2).

Secondly, she considered whether to remain in Japan or return to China after obtaining her PhD. Both options had merits and were appealing to her (BFP1). Since a respected Instructional Design (ID) expert was based at University A (SG1), which employs many ID specialists, she preferred to work there and planned to serve as a project manager. In this role, she anticipated facing challenges as a

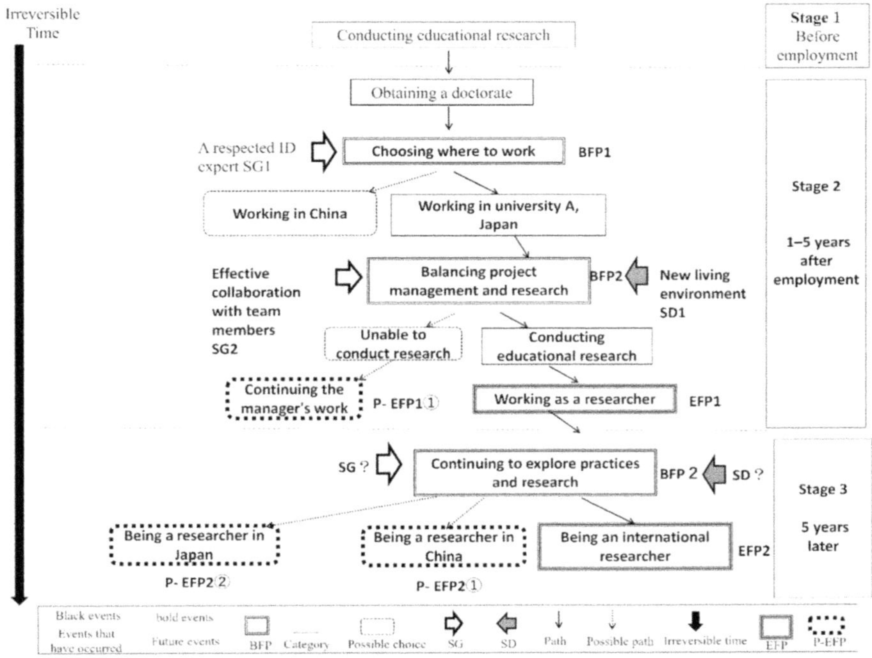

Fig. 1 The first Future Auto-TEM (TEM1)

foreigner working at a Japanese university. At the same time, she wanted to continue her research and therefore set balancing project management and research as BFP2. She proactively engaged with her surroundings through effective collaboration with team members (SG2), which facilitated her research activities. Subsequently, she aimed to further develop as a researcher (BFP3).

Finally, she envisioned how to achieve EFP1 but could not clearly identify the specific branching points (BFPs), the supportive SGs, and the obstructive SDs. She therefore marked them with "?" as a cautionary note at the third stage.

Before employment, she was unfamiliar with the working environment at Japanese universities. As an international student, she lacked both a concrete image and a clear outlook regarding her future in this new context. Within 1 year, she was able to form a rough vision of her future; however, it was still difficult for her to anticipate what her life would be like after entering employment.

Through constructing the Future Auto-TEM, her aspiration to become a researcher was identified as a life goal. By envisioning herself 10 years later, she set EFP2 as her objective. The process of creating the Auto-TEM also helped clarify her career goals. Nevertheless, it was challenging to specify the details of the BFPs, particularly in relation to the roles of SDs and SGs.

Self-Dialogue and Conflict Occurred When Drawing TEM1

When she drew the TEM1, she noticed she had some roles through self-dialogue that involved multiple selves:

1. The self as a Chinese.
2. The self as an international student.
3. The self aspiring to engage in educational practice in her home country.
4. The self seeking to accumulate work experience and employment in Japan.

One voice was the self as a Chinese, carrying a strong sense of belonging to her home country and feeling that she ought to remain connected to it. Another was the self as an international student, who was learning to adapt to life in Japan while developing a growing interest in various aspects of Japanese society. A third was the self aspiring to return to China and contribute to educational practice there, motivated by a sense of social responsibility and the expectations of parents and Chinese friends. In contrast, a fourth self sought to remain in Japan, accumulate work experience, and establish employment in an unfamiliar but stimulating academic environment.

These multiple selves interacted within her mind, sometimes creating tension and leaving her heart unsettled for a long time (visualized in Fig. 2). The promoter sign, "I want to learn Instructional Design (ID)," provided a unifying orientation for this dialogue. It gave meaning to her struggles by suggesting a path that could integrate her different possibilities. She believed that by acquiring expertise in ID, she could not only reconcile these competing selves but also move closer to her desired self as an international researcher contributing to educational development in China, Japan, and broader global contexts.

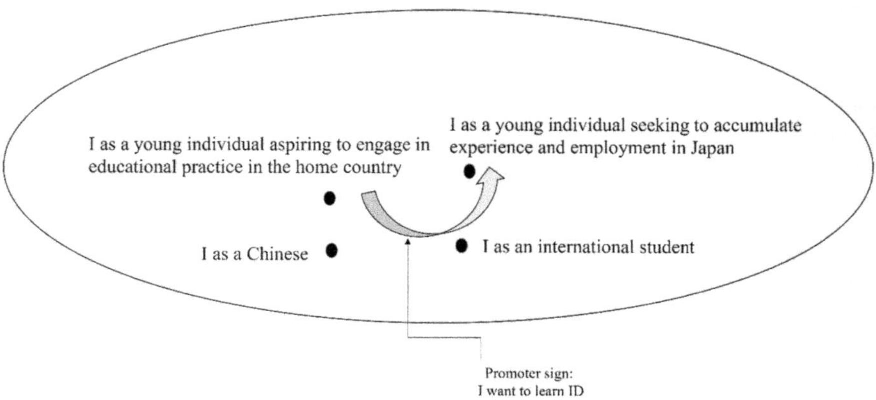

Fig. 2 Self-dialogue when drew TEM1

A Concrete Pathway in the Future

Life story After completing her doctoral studies in Japan, the first author began working at University A as a project manager. After 9 months, she had gradually come to understand the expectations of her role. She consciously sought to balance her management duties with research activities, and through collaboration with colleagues, she gained their cooperation and trust. Drawing on the qualitative methods she had learned in graduate school, she initiated a study on teaching material development with the support of her team. During this period, she also relocated to a different region in Japan, made friends, and adapted to her new living environment, which strengthened her sense of belonging. A critical branching point arose when she realized that, under the university's internal rules, she was not eligible to apply for KAKENHI as a project manager. This limitation forced her to reconsider her position and career path.

The Second Future Auto-TEM: A Concrete Pathway

She created TEM2, and the pathways in this version were as follows. She added three new branching points (BFPs): "securing eligibility for grant applications" (BFP3), "conducting research on personal interests" (BFP4), and "forming a research team for a Sino-Japanese joint research project" (BFP5).

At the turning point of balancing work and research (BFP2), she added *anticipating new living conditions* (SD2) and *limited knowledge of ID* (SD3) as difficulties. She also included a new supportive goal, *ID reading meetings with ID experts and graduate peers* (SG3).

In addressing "securing eligibility for grant applications" (BFP3), she faced the internal regulation at University A that restricted her qualifications (SD3). At this stage, she was still uncertain about which supportive social guidances could be applied.

At the turning point of "conducting research on personal interests" (BFP4), she identified joining relevant research communities as a supportive social guidances(SG4).

Finally, for "forming a Sino-Japanese research team" (BFP5), she anticipated the necessity of considering China's educational background (SD5). To address this, she emphasized collaboration with Chinese educators (SG5) as well as Japanese researchers interested in international education (SG6).

As shown in Fig. 3, through her experience as a project manager at University A, she gradually adapted to her workplace. She regulated her career pathway by adding new BFPs and SGs to guide her future behaviors. For instance, she established *ID reading meetings* (SG3) and joined relevant research communities (SG4) to expand her professional development.

Self-Dialogue and Conflict Occurred When Drawing TEM2

In the early stage of employment, multiple selves coexisted within her. First, there was the self who aspired to deepen her expertise as a researcher. Second, there was the self who fulfilled responsibilities as a project manager. Third, there was the self

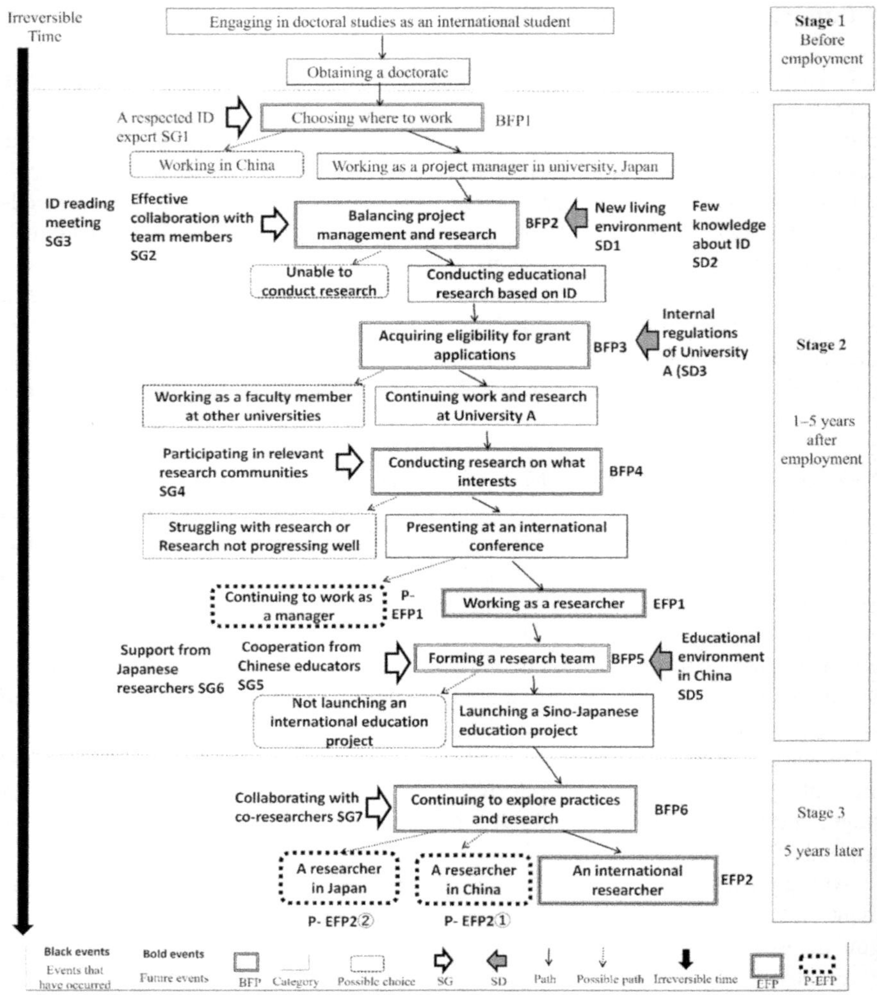

Fig. 3 The second Future Auto-TEM (TEM2)

who strongly recognized her lack of knowledge in instructional design (ID) and material development. Fourth, there was the self who was capable of conducting qualitative research. Fifth, there was the self who felt discomfort with the predominance of quantitative research in the field of ID.

These five selves, as visualized in Fig. 4, interacted with one another and generated two major conflicts. The first was a conflict of professional roles, namely, the tension between the self that sought to pursue research expertise and the self that prioritized practical work experience. The second was the conflict that arose from recognizing her insufficient knowledge while managing an ID project. Through repeated self-dialogue, she generated two promoter signs to address these conflicts:

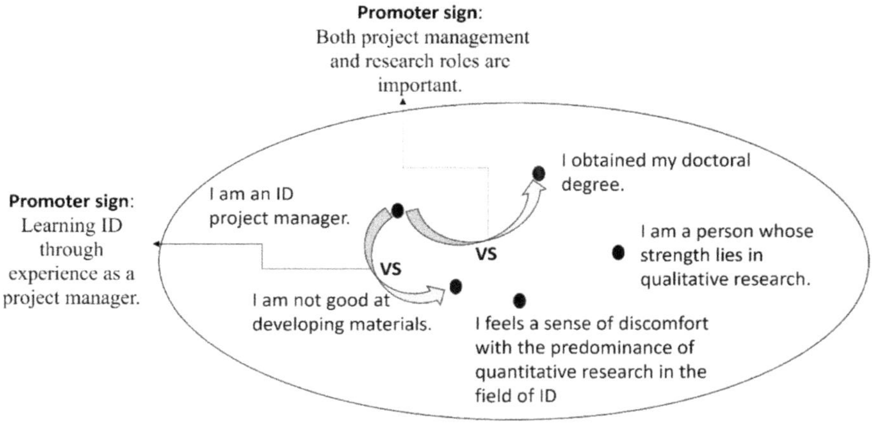

Fig. 4 Self-dialogue when drew TEM2

"Both work and research are important" and "I will learn ID through my work." These promoter signs served to integrate the conflicting selves and stimulated new motivation and behavioral change. As a result, she was able to position practice and research as complementary and take a significant step toward future career development.

Auto-TEM for 5-Year Career Guidance

Life story The first author initially planned to work at University A for 5 years. However, she was not eligible to apply for KAKENHI under the institutional rules at her workplace at that time. When she found an open position at another university, she applied and was promptly accepted. Thus, in the third year after creating her first Future Auto-TEM, she transferred to University B. At the new workplace, she was immediately granted eligibility to apply for KAKENHI. Nevertheless, despite several attempts, her KAKENHI applications were not successful.

The Third Future Auto-TEM

In January 2025, she reflected on her 5 years of experience and evaluated the extent to which she had achieved her goals in comparison with the pathways outlined in Fig. 5.

At BFP3, she decided to move to another workplace where she would be eligible to apply for Grants-in-Aid. When she found an open position at University B, she applied and was promptly accepted. There, she conducted research on her own interests (BFP4) with an open research environment (SG8), and her work was recognized with the Excellent Paper Award at an international conference (Zhang & Kubota, 2023).

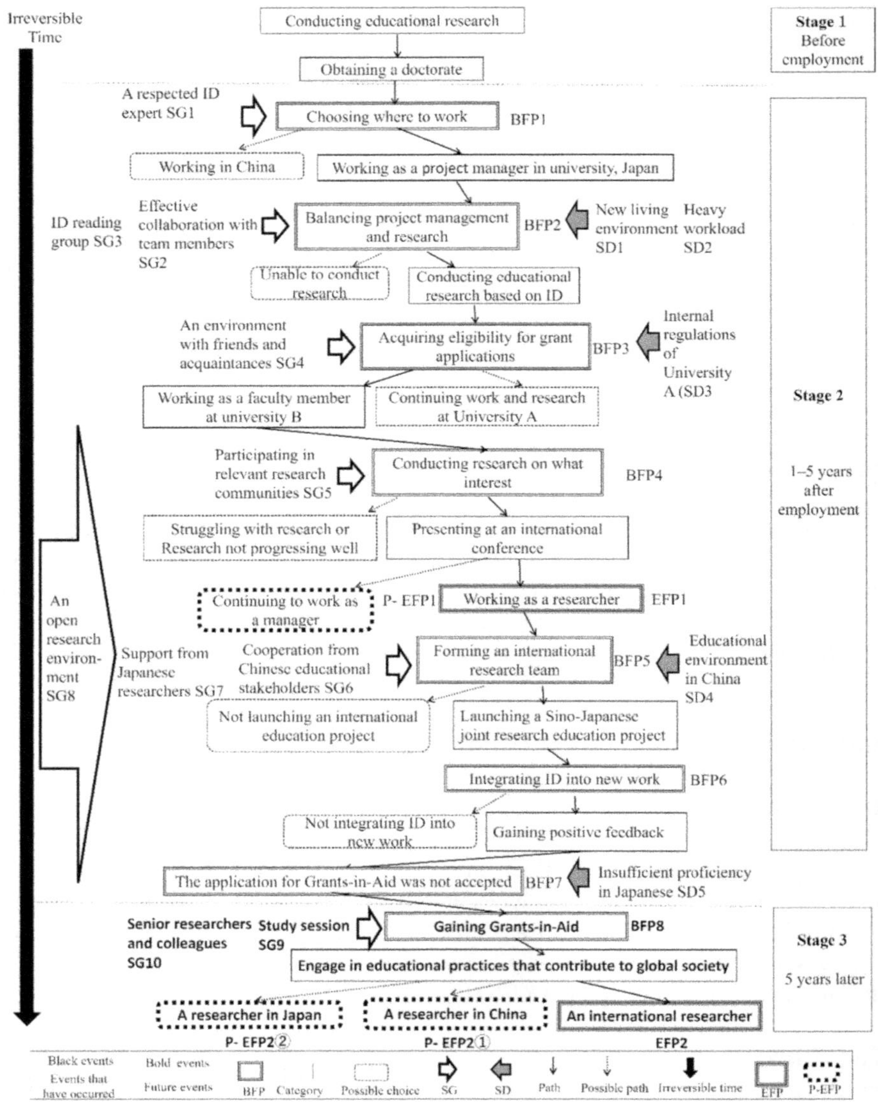

Fig. 5 The third Future Auto-TEM (TEM3)

To achieve EFP2, she formed an international research team to contribute to educational reform in China (BFP5). Although the educational environment in China differed from that in Japan, the team was successfully established with the cooperation of Chinese educators (SG6) and Japanese researchers interested in international education (SG7), and launched a Sino-Japanese joint research project (Zhang et al., 2024). Furthermore, she integrated ID into her new work (BFP6) and received positive feedback (e.g., Zhang & Iwasaki, 2024).

However, at that time, her applications for Grants-in-Aid in Japan were not successful at 2025 (BFP7), which left her feeling discouraged. She encountered difficulties when writing the applications. One possible cause was her insufficient proficiency in Japanese (SD5).

In reconsidering her future, she recognized that obtaining Grants-in-Aid represented a major turning point in her career. She realized that she needed to improve her proficiency in Japanese and planned to join study sessions (SG9) as well as seek advice from senior researchers and colleagues (SG10).

Along the pathway toward EFP 1, the first author encountered an unforeseen branching point: her ineligibility to apply for Grants-in-Aid. Nevertheless, she promptly selected an alternative route. The multiple pathways represented in the Future Auto-TEM appear to have supported her timely decision to change workplaces. In addition, applying for Grants-in-Aid requires not only the capacity to formulate research questions and produce scholarly writing, but also rhetorical skills to persuade reviewers and advanced proficiency in Japanese. For a former international student, these demands posed considerable challenges. However, these experiences also became opportunities for further professional growth and may contribute to her future development toward EFP2 as an international researcher. Looking ahead, the establishment of new branching points is likely to create further opportunities for her career development.

New Conflict Occurred in the Fifth Year

One of her salient I-positions was "I am an applicant for Grants-in-Aid for Scientific Research". This identity shapes a significant part of her academic life because securing research funding is closely connected to her professional growth and recognition. At the same time, her self-dialogue reveals multiple voices within her, each carrying different roles, expectations, and emotions (see Fig. 6).

One voice says, "I am a researcher." This part of her is motivated by curiosity, the desire to contribute to knowledge, and the persistence to continue despite challenges. Another voice states, "I am a teacher in Japan." This identity is deeply tied to her daily responsibilities, guiding students, preparing classes, and helping young people grow intellectually. In addition, she carries the identity of "I am Chinese." This voice connects her to her cultural roots, values, and perspectives, while also shaping how she is perceived in the Japanese academic community. Together, these multiple selves interact with and influence one another, often in complex ways.

However, the deepest conflict emerges between two voices. One says firmly, "I am a researcher." This voice emphasizes her determination to pursue academic goals and to build her identity in the scholarly world. The other voice counters, "I am an applicant for KAKENHI, but I have failed many times." This voice carries disappointment, self-doubt, and frustration about repeated unsuccessful attempts. These conflicting positions create tension between her self-image as a capable researcher and her lived experiences of failure in obtaining funding.

Through this self-dialogue, she begans to recognize that her conflict was not simply about success or failure, but about negotiating her identity as a researcher

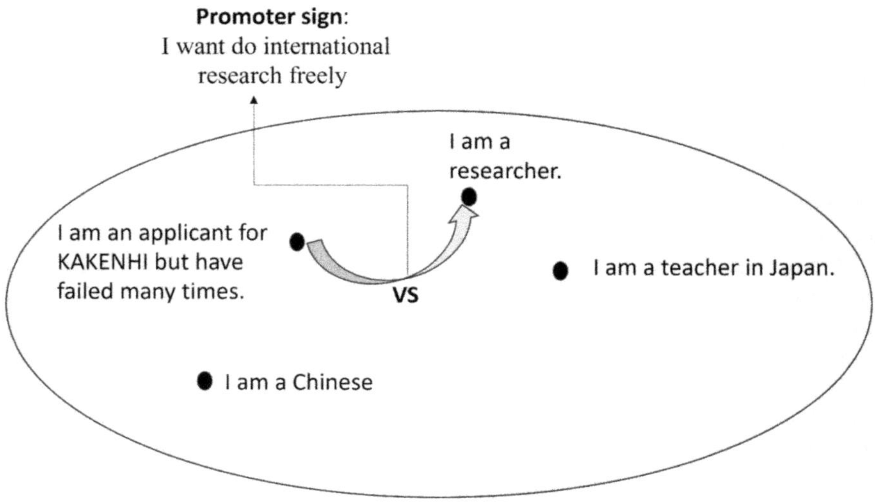

Fig. 6 Self-dialogue when drew TEM3

and envisioning her future career path. By listening to these multiple voices, she better understood her challenges, and tried to find ways to move closer to her desired self.

Overall Discussion

Based on the results, we discuss how the use of the Future Auto-TEM, from the perspectives of creative thinking and self-regulation, influenced the first author.

Thinking Creatively When Using the Future Auto-TEM

Using the Future Auto-TEM is an effective method for visualizing possible futures and clarifying alternative career paths. Representing the future as a trajectory is itself a creative activity because it involves generating ideas beyond present realities. For learners to approach their desired self, an open mind and bold visions are essential (Csikszentmihalyi, 2009; Saaty, 2010). Creative thinking here requires freeing one's imagination from immediate constraints while imultaneously considering potential opportunities, risks, and the feasibility of future pathways.

In the context of career design, creative thinking differs from artistic creativity because applicable ideas must not only be novel but also realizable in real-world contexts. By imagining a future that does not yet exist and visualizing potential trajectories and environmental conditions through the Future Auto- TEM, the author clarified her own career vision and explored alternative possibilities for achieving it. Thus, the Future Auto-TEM functioned not merely as a planning tool but as a means of fostering creative thinking in career design.

Self-Regulation in Career Paths

Self-regulation in career paths involves reflection on the past, judgment of the present, and approaches to future realities (Zimmerman, 2013). In this study, the first author's self-regulation can be divided into two aspects.

Self-Regulation in Response to Internal Conflict

Throughout the three diagrams of the Future Auto-TEM, the first author encountered multiple conflicts regarding career choices and engaged in self-dialogue to resolve them. These conflicts involved multiple identities, external expectations, and practical constraints. Promoter signs supported her in reinterpreting these conflicts and integrating competing perspectives. As Valsiner (2024) notes, promoter signs indicate objects through interpretants such as emotions and efforts. In this study, promoter signs functioned as psychological resources that enabled the first author to regulate emotional tensions, reconstruct meanings, and maintain orientation toward her desired self despite changing circumstances.

Self-Regulation in Response to Unforeseen Circumstances

The second aspect of self-regulation concerned responses to unanticipated situations. Although such possibilities were not envisioned in the first Future Auto-TEM, experiences in University A enabled the first author to recognize new environmental demands and revise the second Future Auto-TEM by specifying bifurcation points more concretely. For example, She encountered unanticipated challenges regarding eligibility for grant applications, as well as opportunities to move to a different workplace. Rather than abandoning her long-term goals, she reconsidered alternative pathways and adjusted her career trajectory, eventually reaching EFP1 earlier than anticipated.

These adjustments were facilitated by leveraging supportive environmental factors and identifying new opportunities within changing contexts. For example, "effective collaboration with team members" and "participation in ID reading meeting" supported her efforts to balance project management and research activities. This process suggests that self-regulation in career design involves not only adjusting one's goals and actions but also proactively reconstructing relationships with environmental conditions in response to unforeseen circumstances.

Conclusion, Theoretical and Practical Significance, Limitations, and Future Directions

The purpose of this study is to develop a career design strategy that incorporates creative thinking and self-regulation from the insider's perspective, and to examine both its effectiveness in practice and its potential to support learners in realizing their desired selves. Using the Future Auto-TEM, a comparative analysis of three versions revealed that certain components of the model were consistently realized. This process was largely facilitated by (a) the author's self-dialogue and active engagement with promoter signs at bifurcation points and (b) intentional interventions in environmental factors. Furthermore, even when confronted with unforeseen circumstances, the existence of the Future Auto-TEM enabled adjustments in the trajectory without altering the overall career goal. These results suggest that through the application of the Future Auto-TEM, the first author was able to engage in self-regulation while being oriented toward the imagined future and moving closer to the "desired self."

Theoretical Significance

Theoretical significance of this study lies in extending Auto-TEM from retrospective analysis toward career design. By applying the Future Auto-TEMs to career trajectories, thishighlights the dynamic interplay among turning points (BFPs), social guidances(SGs) and social directions (SDs) and promoter signs in shaping future pathways. Unlike conventional approaches that focus primarily on static goals or past experiences, the Future Auto-TEM provides a framework for understanding how individuals imagine possible futures and negotiate multiple identities and constraints.

Furthermore, the study demonstrates that career design should be understood Furthermore, the study demonstrates that career design should be understood as a process that involves creative thinking, self-regulation, and proactive engagement with environmental factors. Through creative thinking, individuals imagine possible futures and alternative pathways. Through self-regulation, they revise their goals and actions in response to changing circumstances. Furthermore, by actively engaging with environmental resources, they can create conditions that support their desired futures.

Practical Significance

The practical significance of this study lies in demonstrating how the Future Auto-TEM can function as a concrete tool for career and learning environment design The findings suggest that visualizing multiple future pathways enables individuals to anticipate possible challenges, reconsider alternative options, and make flexible decisions in response to changing circumstances. For educators, the Future Auto-TEM may provide a useful strategy for supporting learners in reflecting on their identities, imagining future possibilities, and connecting long-term aspirations with realistic actions. Particularly in uncertain social contexts, the framework may facilitate discussions about possible career trajectories and encourage proactive engagement with environmental resources.

How to Create a Future Auto-TEM

The following steps are suggested for constructing a Future Auto- TEM:

1. Define a significant overarching goal (EFP).
2. Identify sub-goals required to achieve the main goal.
3. Represent each sub-goal as a buification point (BFP), and attach promoter signs that reflect values and motivations.
4. Consider potential SDs and SGs at each bifurcation point, ensuring that SGs can mitigate the impact of major SDs.
5. Roughly identify developmental stages toward the goal and continuously revise the Future Auto-TEM over time.

Mindset for Career Design

The mindset for career design involves recognizing one's values and envisioning one's desired future while identifying possible pathways and supportive resources. Through this process, individuals can clarify who they want to become and develop greater awareness of potential opportunities and constraints. The Future Auto- TEM then serves as a guide for learning and career development, encouraging individuals to act toward their envisioned future and desired selves. However, real life rarely unfolds exactly as envisioned. When unexpected events arise, individuals need to reconsider alternative pathways and actively utilize available environmental resources. In this sense, the Future Auto-TEM should be understood not as a fixed plan but as a dynamic framework for self-regulation and career development.

Limitations and Future Directions

This study has several limitations that suggest important directions for future research. First, the Future Auto-TEM was applied to the 10-year career trajectory of the first author, but the observation period reported here covered only 5 years. Longitudinal investigation is neededto examine how the envisioned trajectories develop over the full ten-years. Second, the first author is also a researcher, which may influence the ways in which she engaged with the method. Future studies should clarify how the Future Auto-TEM functions among learners with diverse backgrounds in order to evaluate its broader applicability.

Looking ahead, the Future Auto-TEM has considerable potential for supporting career formation among university students. By visualizing desired futures and anticipating possible challenges, students may strengthen their capacity to design realistic and flexible career pathways. The model could also be incorporated into university career education programs to facilitate reflection on future goals and connections between academic learning and career development. Beyond higher education, the Future Auto-TEM may serve as a useful framework for mentors or supervisors by providing a structured approach to support career development.

References

Csikszentmihalyi, M. (2009). *Creativity: Flow and the psychology of discovery and invention*. Harper Collins.

Hermans, H. J. M. (2001). The construction of a personal position repertoire: Method and practice. *Culture & Psychology, 7*(3), 323–365. https://doi.org/10.1177/1354067X0173005

Hokanson, B. (2018). *Developing Creative Thinking Skills: An Introduction for Learners*. Routledge.

Kubota, K. (2025). Shinpan kōseishugi paradaimu to gakushū kankyō dezain [Revised edition: Constructivist paradigm and learning environment design]. Kansai University Press.

Saaty, T. L. (2010). *Creative thinking, problem solving and decision making*. RWS Publications.

Sakai, N. (2024). ジョブローテーション制度下の企業に勤務する元留学生外国人社員のキャリア形成のプロセス. *留学生教育, 29*, 35–46.

Sato, T. (2017). *Collected papers on trajectory equifinality approach*. Chitose Press.

Savickas, M. L., Nota, L., Rossier, J., Dauwalder, J. P., Duarte, M. E., Guichard, J., Soresi, S., Van Esbroeck, R., & Van Vianen, A. E. M. (2009). Life designing: A paradigm for career construction in the 21st century. *Journal of Vocational Behavior, 75*(3), 239–250. https://doi.org/10.1016/j.jvb.2009.04.004

Schein, E. H. (1978). *The individual, the organization, and the career: A conceptual scheme*. Legare Street Press.

Schlossberg, N. K. (1981). A model for analyzing human adaptation to transition. *The Counseling Psychologist, 9*(2), 2–18. https://doi.org/10.1177/001100008100900202

Sparkes, A. C. (2018). Autoethnography comes of age: Consequences, comforts, and concerns. In D. Beach, C. Bagley, & S. Marques da Silva (Eds.), *The Wiley handbook of ethnography of education* (pp. 479–499). Wiley Blackwell. https://doi.org/10.1002/9781118933732.ch21

Tsuchimoto, T., & Sato, T. (2022). Career decision-making as dynamic semiosis: Autoethnographic trajectory equifinality modeling. *Culture & Psychology, 30*(1), 48–69. https://doi.org/10.1177/1354067X221140609

Valsiner, J. (2018). The promoter sign: Development transformation within the structure of dialogical self. In G. Marsico & J. Valsiner (Eds.), *Beyond the mind: Cultural dynamics of the psyche* (pp. 123–146). Springer. https://doi.org/10.1007/978-3-319-98654-3_6

Valsiner, J. (2024). Time and signs. In J. Valsiner (Ed.), *Dynamic semiosis* (pp. 1–20). Springer.

Zhang, X. (2020, August). *The creativity of Future TEM diagrams in career pursuit* [Oral presentation]. Trajectory Equifinality Approach (TEA) Research Group Meeting, Online.

Zhang, X., & Iwasaki, C. (2024). The development and evaluation of video teaching materials for cultivating critical thinking skills. *Japan Society for Educational Technology, 48*(Suppl), 253–256.

Zhang, X., & Kubota, K. (2023). Cultivating students' creative thinking using visual narrative in an agile blended learning environment. In C. Li, S. K. S. Cheung, F. L. Wang, A. Lu, & L. F. Kwok (Eds.), *Blended learning: Lessons learned and ways forward* (pp. 181–192). Springer. https://doi.org/10.1007/978-3-031-35731-2_15

Zhang, X., Shi, Y., Li, X., Iwasaki, C., Amano, K., & Kubota, K. (2024). Enhancing youth creativity through computer-supported collaborative learning: A preliminary investigation in rural Chinese elementary school. In W. W. K. Ma, C. Li, C. W. Fan, & L. H. U, & A. Lu (Eds.), *Blended learning: Intelligent computing in education* (pp. 295–307). Springer. https://doi.org/10.1007/978-981-97-4442-8_23

Zimmerman, B. J. (1989). A social cognitive view of self-regulated academic learning. *Journal of Educational Psychology, 81*(3), 329–339. https://doi.org/10.1037/0022-0663.81.3.329

Zimmerman, B. J. (2013). From Cognitive Modeling to Self-Regulation: A Social Cognitive Career Path. *Educational Psychologist, 48*(3), 135–147. https://doi.org/10.1080/00461520.2013.794676

Living with TEA at the Boundary of Self and World: Exploring Its Philosophy Through Dialogical Self Theory

Tamiyo Koyama and Teppei Tsuchimoto

The first author's favorite ***Chashitsu*** (Japanese TEA ceremony house): (**a**) its exterior and garden (by the author), (**b**) a place to prepare and enjoy TEA (by the author)

T. Koyama
Graduate School of Human Science at Ritsumeikan University, and Japan Society for the Promotion of Science (JSPS), Osaka, Japan

T. Tsuchimoto
Eminent Associate Professor, Research Organization of Open Innovation & Collaboration, Ritsumeikan University, Kyoto, Japan

M. A. Campill et al. (eds.), *New Paths in Trajectory Equifinality Modelling*, Theory and History in the Human and Social Sciences, https://doi.org/10.1007/978-3-032-25855-7_11

Introduction and Purpose

Individuals sometimes rely on artistic expression, such as novels, poetry, and music, to move forward in life. They are not just entertainment but can also serve as guideposts to find meaning in difficult situations and question our own existence. These activities are not limited to the inner world of the person, but are living practices that shape our relationships with the world (e.g., in the case of the first author). In this chapter, the authors aim to shed new light on human inquiry from the perspective of "research method as a *philosophy*," which reconsiders research method itself as an extension of such existential activities. Note that in this chapter, the term "philosophy" does not refer to the academic discipline, but rather to the meaning defined as: "In extended use: a set of opinions or ideas held by an individual or group; a theory or attitude which acts as a guiding principle for behaviour; an outlook or world view" (Oxford University Press, n.d.).

The authors consider that the Trajectory Equifinality Approach (TEA), the subject of this volume, holds potential not only as a research method but also as a philosophy. TEA is a new approach in cultural psychology that seeks to enable an understanding of human life without abstracting time away (Sato, 2015, p. 4). It is a qualitative research method that can be used to gain an understanding of human development. TEA consists of three frameworks: the Trajectory Equifinality Modeling (TEM), the Historically Structured Inviting (HSI), and the Three Layers Model of Genesis (TLMG). This section provides an overview of each of them. First, TEM emphasizes 'irreversible time' and describes individuals' transformation in relation to society on the two dimensions of "what has been actualized and what has not been actualized" (Yasuda & Sato, 2012). Second, HSI is a framework for selecting research participants, "inviting persons who have experienced the Equifinality Point (EFP) to participate in the research" (Sato, 2015, p. 4). EFP is a concept established based on research interests, representing the point that individuals reach equally regardless of the diverse trajectories they take. For example, if the research interest is the phenomenon of "becoming a teacher," then "becoming a teacher" is set as EFP, and persons who have experienced "becoming a teacher" are the research participants. In TEM, the life trajectory leading up to EFP is described using various concepts. Note that the meaning of "equifinality" in the EFP concept is considered to imply "similar" experiences rather than "same" (Sovran, 1992). The main concepts include the Bifurcation Point (BFP), where multilinearity emerges, the Social Guidance (SG) as the force promoting EFP, and the Social Direction (SD) as the force inhibiting EFP. Third, TLMG is a model of the self designed to describe and understand an individual's internal transformation (emergence and actualization) across three levels: activities, signs, and beliefs and values.

TEA has generally been used as a research method to depict the life trajectories of research participants. Conversely, the first author has found the usefulness of TEA not merely as a "research tool," but as a "philosophy," and has internalized the ideas of TEA to foster self-dialogue, thereby deepening her thinking in everyday life. TEA can function not only as a tool for understanding human development but also as a philosophy that deepens human thinking. The purpose of this chapter is to clarify, through collaborative autoethnography, how the first author internalized TEA as her philosophy and to examine the potential of TEA as a philosophy.

Method

The research approach in this chapter aligns with the orientation toward collaborative autoethnography. Autoethnography is "a general term used for descriptive research in the social sciences aimed at understanding the researcher's own culture" (Tsuchimoto, 2022). It emphasizes sociological introspection while focusing on one's own thoughts and feelings to understand one's own experiences (Ellis & Bockner, 2000). Chang et al. (2012) proposed collaborative autoethnography, in which multiple researchers collaborate to explore specific themes. For a self-description to be autoethnographic rather than autobiographical, it must be connected to others and the social context, even when the description is subjective (Tsuchimoto, 2022). Collaborative autoethnography offers the advantages of the self-reflexivity associated with autobiography, cultural interpretation related to ethnography, and multi-subjectivity associated with collaboration (Chang et al., 2012).

In this chapter, a diagram based on Dialogical Self Theory is introduced as a catalyst for advancing collaborative autoethnography. The diagram was initially prepared by the first author for conference presentations and subsequently restructured through interactions with researchers specializing in cultural psychology. Furthermore, the authors engaged in dialogue based on the diagram shown in Fig. 1.

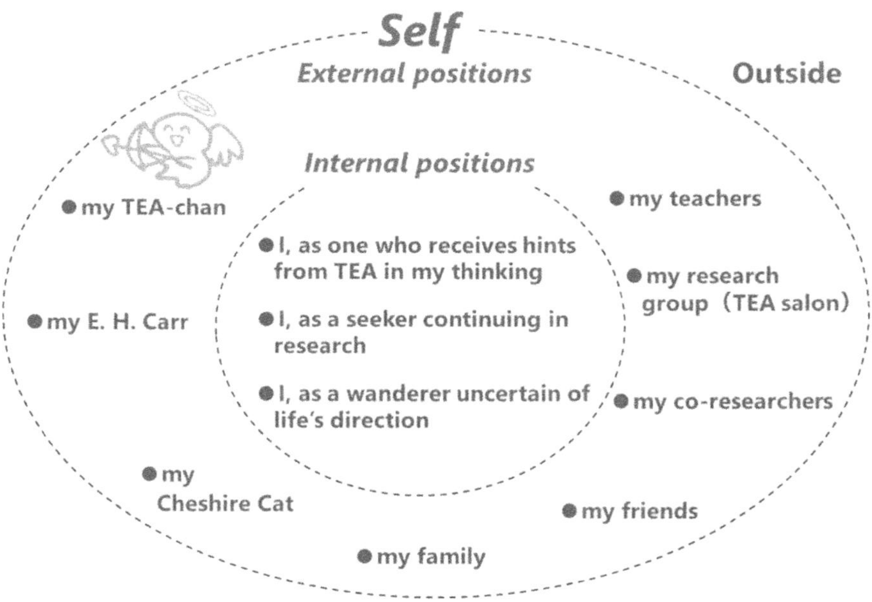

Fig. 1 I-positions of the first author in the dialogical self

This approach is inspired by the recognition that, in research utilizing TEM, one draws participants' life trajectory in a TEM diagram and then engages in dialogue while jointly reviewing this representation. Through this process, researchers can deepen their understanding of the participants' experiences and facilitate the reconstruction of the meaning attributed to those experiences. Similarly, in this study, the authors attempted to *pleromatize* dialogue by sharing visual information.

An overview of Dialogical Self Theory (Hermans & Kempen, 1993) is presented in Fig. 1. In Fig. 1, based on Dialogical Self Theory, the dialogical relationships among TEA positioned within the Self's world, various "Me"s, others, and things are depicted. Dialogical Self Theory does not assume the Self as a single entity but reconceptualizes it as a multivoiced and fluid existence, aiming to understand the process of conflict in which multiple voices and positions engage in dialogue. This theory posits that within the Self's world, numerous "Me's," others, and things related to the Self, including events in one's life, exist. It transforms the various "Me's," others, and things present in the Self's world into positions (called "I position") (Mizogami, 2008). It is thought that people position themselves in various "Me's," and form and develop their self-world from that perspective (Hermans & Kempen, 1993). The dialogical self is conceived as the totality or *dynamic Gestalt* of such I-positions, and the Self as the subject develops its world through the movement of positioning itself among various "Me"s (Hermans & Kempen, 1993). In this chapter, the authors engage in dialogue while viewing Fig. 1, based on Dialogical Self Theory, to reveal how the first author internalizes the thought process of TEA and promotes self-dialogue.

Based on the above, the authors conducted a collaborative autoethnography following the steps below to clarify how the first author internalized TEA as her own philosophy and explored the potential of TEA as a philosophy.

STEP 1:

From January 2023 to February 2025, the authors held four meetings (totaling over 8 h) to discuss the content of this study. Concurrently, the first author presents the external and internal positions within the dialogical self in Fig. 1, revising the diagram in response to the second author's comments.

STEP 2:

The authors engaged in a dialogue while viewing Fig. 1, with the second author interviewing the first author regarding her experiences and thoughts. The dialogue was recorded and transcribed.

STEP 3:

For ethical considerations and readability, the transcript was modified, and the conversation was reconstructed. From the perspective of cultural psychology, the authors engaged in the discussions shown in Fig. 1. The authors deemed that readers could grasp the content and significance more effectively when viewing the figure presented in conjunction with the context of the dialogue. Autoethnography places significant emphasis on this very act of reconstructing and expressing experiences (e.g., putting experiences into writing), encompassing not only the final written account but also the research process itself (Ellis et al., 2011).

Results: Collaborative Autoethnographic Dialogue

The reconstructed dialogue following the above method is as follows:

Teppei:

This diagram (Fig. 1) shows TEA-chan.[1] Interestingly, TEA is depicted using the angel metaphor, and some meaning seems to be embedded here. Angels are not things, right? If TEA comprised just three elements—TEM, HSI, and TLMG—it would be utterly uninteresting and redundant. Angels are not elemental, but it possesses a sense of wholeness and exhibits a certain human-like quality.

Tamiyo:

Yes. This TEA-chan is not so much TEA theory itself, but rather a partner who supported me and provided hints as I lived my everyday life. Owing to various circumstances, I completed all the coursework for my doctorate and left my first university. I went through many challenging times, and continuing my research was difficult. What supported me during this period were TEA and Carr's thoughts. Without them, I might not have been able to take the entrance exam for another graduate program and pursue my doctoral degree.

Teppei:

I see. Here, TEA is personified. It is also significant that the metaphor for TEA is not gods, but rather a more relatable and endearing angel. In our view, angels are more relatable than gods and can be incorporated into everyday life. They are semi-generalized, symbolic, and iconic beings.

Tamiyo:

I am not particularly sensitive to spiritual matters, and I am unsure if angels truly exist. However, when I was in kindergarten, my teacher asked me, "What do you want to be when you grow up?" I could not think of anything specific, and struggling for an answer, I blurted out, "An angel!" The card my teacher gave me for my birthday had a record that said, "Future Dream: Angel." Back then, I did not seriously believe I could become an angel, and I do not know why I answered "An angel!" Nonetheless, it may be because angels are often depicted as likable characters that resemble the human form. At present, for me, the image of an angel is a being that can both fly through the sky and observe the human world from above while also descending into the dimension where humans actually live. An angel's form cannot be seen unless someone depicts it, nor can humans touch it with their hands. These features make angels a fitting metaphor for TEA, which depicts existence through human hands.

Teppei:

It is fascinating to reconstruct your kindergarten dreams as a metaphor for TEA. You often perceive your own concrete experiences and living processes through TEA in an abstract manner. When did you feel that TEA had become internalized within you?

---

[1] In Japanese, the suffix "-chan" is added at the end of a name or word to express affection. Words such as "dear" or "sweetie" are similar.

Tamiyo:
It might have started when I had more opportunities to explain TEA to others. Since spring 2021, we, including yourself, have been hosting a monthly research group affectionately called the "TEA Salon."[2] Various researchers began presenting studies using TEA and called me to ask for advice. Even outside the research group, I served as a workshop mentor and received emails from other researchers asking questions about TEA. When I was writing my master's thesis, I was barely able to absorb knowledge about TEA from the literature and apply it to my own research. However, after entering my first doctoral program, taking on the responsibility of running the TEA Salon required me to explain TEA clearly to others. I attempted to explain the TEA theory using concrete examples from everyday life. Through this process, I reflected on how I perceived phenomena through the lens of TEA.

Teppei:
Your explanations were truly excellent, so even when I was moderating, I often asked you to comment. I believe you do not just see TEA as a superficial method for solving problems right in front of you; you have internalized its underlying epistemology and can align your own thinking with TEA.

Tamiyo:
Thank you. I am honored to have received your feedback. There was a time when my research was not progressing well, and I struggled because I could not feel myself growing. However, I received emails of gratitude from the researchers who participated in the TEA Salon for the comments and explanations I provided, which gave me tremendous encouragement. Through experiences like this, TEA has become deeply rooted within me, and I suppose I have become a "citizen of TEA." When I present on TEA at academic conferences, I sometimes receive comments such as "You're overflowing with love for TEA." I often casually chat about TEA with my friends and family, who have never used it. Since I tend to frame my experiences and struggles through a TEM lens, a close friend tells me, "You're really TEM-TEM-shii (very TEM-TEM)."[3] While it may appear somewhat unusual to others to apply TEA, generally employed in research settings, to everyday life, for me, it feels natural. This may be because, throughout my life, I have been shaped by various influences, which have gradually blurred the boundaries between everyday life and research. The first time I read a paper written by a researcher, my teacher, was when I was in high school. My teacher gave me an offprint of the paper he had authored, and I attempted to read it from beginning to end. Although the content was far too difficult for me to understand,

---

[2]We established "TEA Salon: A Research Report Gathering" as a research group where we can discuss research on TEA. Researchers from various fields participate in it online once a month.

[3]"TEM-TEM-shii" is a Japanese neologism created by the first author through conversations with a close friend, describing ways of perceiving experiences and phenomena that are distinctly TEM-like. In Japanese, "shii" is a suffix that attaches to nouns and other words to form adjectives. To translate "TEM-TEM-shii" into an English word, the first author proposes "Temmy" (as in "It is very TEM-TEM").

what remained vivid in my memory was the presence of a teacher who genuinely enjoyed researching in everyday life. Nowadays, I find myself enjoying TEA in my everyday life, to the point that it has become a state of "No TEA, No Life." A professor I consulted during my graduate studies once told me, "What I consider most important in research is finding a guiding principle for one's own life. Encountering theories or ways of thinking that can be applied to both one's research and way of living changes how one sees the world. For you, Ms. Koyama, TEA seems to serve as such a guiding principle." I share this perspective myself. Living and conducting research were intertwined.

Teppei:

I can see how deeply TEA has permeated your thoughts in everyday life. What does TEM mean to you?

Tamiyo:

For me, TEM describes a person's future-oriented history. I believe that there is meaning in visualizing a person's life trajectory, and dividing it into periods is an important task. Making a period distinction also implies assigning meaning to a series of experiences. In my case, even during periods of ongoing suffering, I was able to overcome difficult situations by orienting toward a positive future and telling myself, "This period may be a dark age for me now, but if I can grow, a future may come in which I can redefine that hard time as the seedling stage." The thought process of TEM has the potential to enhance human resilience. During TEA-salon sessions, I often commented to presenters that "Social Direction (SD) and Social Guidance (SG) can sometimes switch places." Perhaps that became a message to myself: "Even in hard times, don't give up hope for the future." Thanks to TEM, I gained hope that even my past and present struggles might strengthen my future self and enable me to move forward. Even when in a difficult situation, I was able to encourage myself by thinking, "I will definitely turn this SD into SG someday!"

Teppei:

It was unexpected that the topic of period division emerged. Therefore, maintaining a sense of hope is essential. Besides TEM, TEA also has frameworks, such as the Historically Structured Inviting (HSI) and the Three Layers Model of Genesis (TLMG). Did either of these influence you?

Tamiyo:

These factors positively influence me. HSI is about "inviting" research participants rather than treating them as samples. I value interacting with respect not only in research settings but also in general. Each person has unique experiences, and even when teaching undergraduates younger than myself, I learn a great deal from their comments. Furthermore, HSI made me realize that TEA is a theory that considers the importance of historicity, prompting me to consider what history is. Since 2021, you and I have collaborated and authored a manuscript (Koyama & Tsuchimoto, 2023). At that time, I found it necessary to engage with history, although this lay outside my area of expertise. This is an unfamiliar and challenging field of research. I recalled reading the Japanese translation of Carr's *What is History?* (Carr, 1961; translated by Shimizu, 1962), which my teacher had recommended in junior high school. As a junior high school student, the book was far too complicated for me, and I ended up putting it aside without gaining much understanding. What was important was not whether I fully understood the book's contents at the time, but that I recognized the existence of a book about the "way of thinking about history" that differed from the history subjects taught in junior high school. More than 15 years have passed since then, and when I remember the book's existence and look it up, I find it to be a highly regarded masterpiece in the field of history. After studying TEA and re-reading this book, I felt that its content could be connected to TEA's concept of orienting toward the future and Jaan Valsiner's cultural psychology. Even across different academic disciplines, there are commonalities at the core of attempts to understand human beings and society, and I felt a sense of wonder, as if the dots were connected to form lines. The insights gained from Carr's thoughts have not only been beneficial for HSI theoretical research but have also enriched my own perspective on life. Carr (1962/1961) considered how historians interpret past changes in relation to the future they envision. In other words, interest in the past and future is intertwined. I realized that I could apply this perspective to my life history. Notably, time cannot be rewound, nor can past events be altered. However, by consciously orienting toward a brighter future, my perception of painful events gradually shifted. It has changed what I consider a significant event among the various occurrences in my life. In TEM, the Bifurcation Point (BFP) itself is not viewed as excessively critical; rather, it is considered recoverable. Not giving absolute meaning to a specific event allows researchers to maintain flexibility from an analytical perspective and enhances the optimism of those who have endured painful experiences. Even when facing significant hardships and enduring difficult times, this means recognizing that one possesses the potential to change directions or recover as one moves forward into the future.

Teppei:

I see. Your perspective on the history of human life may have been shaped by the intertwining and internalization of TEM and Carr's thoughts. I am curious about the "Cheshire Cat" written in the lower-left area of Fig. 1. What does it mean?

Tamiyo:

I used to watch the animated film *Alice in Wonderland* (Walt Disney Productions, 1951) and grew fond of the Cheshire Cat's optimistic character. When Alice asked the Cheshire Cat which way she should go at a fork in the road, he replied, "That depends on where you want to get to." However, Alice didn't know where to go to begin with, so the Cheshire Cat replied, "Then, it really doesn't matter which way you go." The answer may seem obvious; however, for those who feel lost in their lives, this advice may hit the nail on the head. As mentioned previously, in TEM, BFP should not be excessively significant. Perhaps I internalized this idea of TEM because it connected with this line from the Cheshire Cat. I have had a Cheshire Cat body pillow in my house for over 15 years. This reminds me of these lines that come to mind when I feel lost in the direction of my life.

Teppei:

This finding is interesting and impressive. Perhaps it is precisely because you encountered E.H. Carr and the Cheshire Cat before meeting TEA that TEA became more deeply internalized. We have discussed TEM and HSI thus far, but are there situations in which TLMG is utilized in your thinking?

Tamiyo:

Yes. The TLMG framework acts like a "seismic isolation structure," helping me avoid taking the shock too personally when encountering thoughts or attitudes vastly different from my own. Even if a particular person's words or actions feel uncomfortable, they may desire comfortable communication, as we do. TLMG's perspective allows us to view differences in the words and actions of people not as "clashing values," but as "differences in signs." Recognizing that, while we may have different methods for achieving comfort, our ultimate goals might be similar and could help soften the impact we feel during communication. I believe that considering the meanings of signs enables rational thinking. The TLMG framework provides a flexible analytical perspective on phenomena that can be applied to both research and everyday life. I have heard that in Judo, a form of Japanese martial art, receiving is also essential. Similarly, in everyday communication, what we convey and how we receive another person's words and actions are crucial.

Teppei:

The metaphor of "seismic isolation" is quite apt. Seismic isolation structures have loose lower sections. Similarly, within the TLMG framework, time and experience flow through the lower layers, thereby creating the same flexibility. This type of flexibility may be significant.

Tamiyo:

That's right. TEA provides a flexible thinking framework. Earlier, I mentioned HSI, and I would like to elaborate further on its influence. Similar to TLMG, HSI offers a flexible perspective for understanding human beings. From the HSI perspective, which views human beings as structured by history, we recognize that absolute "rightness" can rarely be established within society. Even if Person A finds Person B's words and actions strange, Person A may seem strange from Person B's perspective. Using our own sense of rightness as a weapon to label others as "evil" and exclude them unilaterally is dangerous. Rather than denying oneself or the other person, accepting it as "maybe our signs were out of sync" allows one to remain calm.

Teppei:

That makes sense. Thus, both TLMG and HSI serve to mediate when one encounters something unfamiliar, acting as intermediaries bridging the gap.

Tamiyo:

Exactly. I think the TEA framework provides a kind of "membrane" that helps us avoid taking the shocks arising from individual and concrete experiences too literally. This can be considered a general theory. For example, when something unfair happens to oneself, rather than accepting that experience as something personal and exclusive to oneself, one can engage in rational thinking by viewing it as a more universal human experience: "Human beings sometimes struggle with such a gap in signs," or "Such events can occur along the life trajectory." Even emotions, such as anger or sadness, when viewed through the lens of theory, may become a typical lesson for humanity.

Teppei:

That's a nice attempt. This effectively utilizes the abstract framework of the TEA theory. The "general theory" you mentioned earlier isn't a stereotype that labels specific persons—like "people from Country A tend to do this"—but rather a "general theory" that applies broadly to human beings.

Tamiyo:

Yes, as you have stated, this is a broad framework for understanding human beings. When someone's words or actions seem strange, it is easy to label them as "weird." TEA encourages us to broaden our thinking in multiple directions, not only in research settings but also in everyday situations, prompting questions such as "What kind of background might that person have?" What might the meaning of a particular sign be for that person?" Ultimately, TEA prompts us to ask, "What is a human being?" That is why I believe TEA is a "philosophy."

Teppei:

This is precisely the case. It represents a level of philosophy that transcends life philosophy, approaching a universal understanding of human beings.

Discussion

This section examines the potential of TEA as a philosophy, building on the collaborative autoethnography described above, and considers it from the perspective of external and internal positions within the dialogical self (Fig. 1).

(1) From the Perspective of the Potential of TEA as a Philosophy

TEA holds potential as a philosophy that contributes to human understanding, primarily serving to enrich one's perspective on life and evoke rational thoughts through communication with others.

Role of Enriching One's Perspective of Human Life The first author used TEM to describe the past life trajectories of others during her research activities. However, by internalizing TEA into her thinking, she gained an overview of her past, present, and future life trajectories and reconstructed the meaning she assigned to her experiences. For example, she once considered abandoning research during her first doctoral program, but became acutely aware of the tension between the present and future trajectories that were now emerging before her. This awareness enabled her to continue her research in another doctoral program, orienting toward a better future. Pursuing a doctoral degree is sometimes described as a "life gamble." She was concerned that enrolling in one doctoral program after another would inevitably affect her career. She recognized that her choices could potentially derail her life.

However, by internalizing the thought process of TEM, she could reframe the risk of taking on new challenges as an adventure. Furthermore, TEM, a research method for describing the history of humans, shares common ground with Carr's (1962/1961) philosophy of history, teaching us how to interpret past changes based on our present perspectives and future outlooks (Koyama & Tsuchimoto, 2023). This approach provided a flexible perspective on human life. By envisioning a positive future, one can reframe periods previously perceived as a "dark age" as a "seeding stage" necessary for personal growth. Considering the above, incorporating the TEM perspective suggests that it is possible to restart life from this point forward. It also indicates that, depending on one's outlook toward the future, there is a possibility of redoing one's past.

Role of TEA in Evoking Rational Thinking in Communication with Others The thought process of TEA reduces conflict when encountering people who hold vastly different views, fostering a sensible approach to understanding others. This is because TEA emphasizes understanding signs, providing a framework that allows us to interpret communication friction not as differences in values, but as differences in the signs themselves. We may experience a range of emotions in response to specific events. Notwithstanding, by organizing that situation through the lens of TEA theory, we can sometimes free ourselves from intense feelings, such as anger or sadness. TEA theory allows us to abstract and reframe unique experiences, enabling multifaceted thinking that seeks to understand others rather than emotionally exclude them.

(2) From the Perspective of External and Internal Positions in the Dialogical Self

TEA was granted a "voice" by being positioned within the first author's world, and was personified as TEA-chan (Fig. 1). This led to TEA being recognized as an interactive entity that offers philosophical insights. This thereby facilitates the recognition of one's life trajectory. The first author internalized the thought process of TEA not only because she used TEA in her research but also because she had the opportunity to reinterpret the history of human life (life trajectory) through her dialogue with Carr's philosophy of history. Furthermore, within the TEA Salon, the first author gained more opportunities to explain TEA theory to other researchers, using concrete examples. This process led to the realization of how deeply TEA underpinned her thoughts in everyday life. When the first author initially depicted in Fig. 1, she perceived the internal position as the Self's "core." However, while revising Fig. 1 and discussing it with other researchers, the first author recognized that the Self's core might be shaped by its external position. In other words, this suggests that the Self cannot exist without layers of external positions. The first author captures this idea with the metaphor: "If we peel away the layers of an onion from the outside, eventually there will be nothing left." This perspective echoes the Stratum

Theory of Personality, a concept that has been widely discussed in the history of psychology. However, we emphasize that a particular stratum of the Self maintains its existence through the construction of a tension relationship with the outer layers.

Conclusion: TEA as a General "Philosophy"

Through collaborative autoethnography, it was revealed that TEA can be understood not merely as a guide for one's life trajectory but also as a "philosophy" that shapes a universal worldview encompassing one's style of thinking, support for everyday decision-making, and even one's stance in interpersonal communication. For instance, the first author personified TEA (as "TEA-chan") and engaged in self-dialogue when facing the Bifurcation Point (BFP) in her career, navigating research processes, or dealing with conflicting situations in everyday life. As noted in the section *Results: Collaborative Autoethnographic Dialogue*, this illustrates that, through research, "encountering theories or ways of thinking that can be applied both to one's research and to one's way of living changes how one sees the world."

Here, it should be noted that the term "philosophy" does not imply that TEA constitutes a single, finalized philosophy. Rather, TEA represents an open-system philosophy encompassing multiple semiotic resources for engaging with the world in ways that depend on the researcher's perspective, rather than a fixed worldview. Instead of being a finalized product, TEA develops as researchers intertwine their own sensibilities and experiences, thereby fostering a new understanding of general human development. Furthermore, through the practice of regulating both their worldviews and their engagement with TEA in contexts such as research, clinical (including educational) application, and communication, TEA is continuously and collaboratively reconstructed in ways that remain closely grounded in practice. In this manner, the philosophy that emerges is simultaneously "my TEA" and "our TEA."

TEA can undoubtedly be used as a philosophy of life. However, in general, a philosophy of life refers to a philosophy that is specific to one's life and is constructed primarily around one's inner experiences and belief systems. What differentiates the TEA philosophy from that of life is that it does not merely support life as an inner belief. In the section *Results: Collaborative Autoethnographic Dialogue*, the first author stated: "*I think the TEA framework provides a kind of 'membrane' that helps us avoid taking the shocks arising from individual and concrete experiences too literally. This can be considered a general theory.*" *(Tamiyo)*. This statement indicates that the TEA process functions as a *semiotic buffer* (Tateo, 2016) for facing others and is not necessarily purely internal. In other words, TEA functions less as "only my own philosophy" than as a mediating framework located at the intersection of the public and the personal, guiding not only one's life trajectory but also one's modes of negotiation with others in communication.

The TEA philosophy is positioned at the boundary of the Self, functioning while in contact with the public world through the collaborative construction of TEA within research contexts. Accordingly, the TEA philosophy embodies a paradoxical relation of being "general yet unique" and "external yet internal." Within this paradox lies the very essence of the philosophy's uniqueness.

Acknowledgments This chapter is based on presentations delivered at the 5th Transnational Meeting on TEA and the 3rd Annual Meeting of the Japanese Association of TEA for Qualitative Inquiry, which were revised and restructured for this chapter. The authors would like to express their deep gratitude to Professor Yuko Yasuda (Ritsumeikan University) for her insightful guidance regarding this research. This research was supported by a Grant-in-Aid for JSPS Fellows (Number 25KJ2216) and by funding from Ritsumeikan University.

References

Carr, E. H. (1962). 歴史とは何か (Shimizu, I., Trans.). Iwanamishoten. Original work: Carr, E. H. (1961). *What is history?* Penguin.

Chang, H., Ngunjiri, F., & Hernandez, K.-A. C. (2012). *Collaborative autoethnography*. Routledge.

Ellis, C., & Bochner, A. P. (2000). Autoethnography, personal narrative, reflexivity: Researcher as subject. In N. K. Denzin & Y. S. Lincoln (Eds.), *Handbook of qualitative research* (2nd ed., pp. 129–164). Sage.

Ellis, C., Adams, T. E., & Bochner, A. P. (2011). Autoethnography: An overview. *Historical Social Research/historische sozialforschung, 36*(4), 273–290.

Hermans, H. J. M., & Kempen, H. J. G. (1993). *The dialogical self: Meaning as movement*. Academic Press.

Koyama, T., & Tsuchimoto, T. (2023). 複線径路等至性アプローチにおける「拡張版・歴史的構造化ご招待」の提案――エドワード・ハレット・カーの歴史哲学とヤーン・ヴァルシナーの文化心理学を手掛かりとして[An Expanded Version of Historically Structured Inviting in Trajectory Equifinality Approach: From the Perspective of Edward Hallett Carr's Philosophy of History and Jaan Valsiner's Cultural Psychology]. TEAと質的探究[*Japanese Journal of TEA for Qualitative Inquiry*], *1*(1), 20–32. https://doi.org/10.60421/jatqi.1.1_20

Mizogami, S. (2008). 自己形成の心理学――他者の森をかけ抜けて自己になる[*The psychology of the Self-formation: Becoming the Self by running through the forest of others*] (title translated by the authors). Sekaishisosha.

Oxford University Press. (n.d.). Philosophy, n., 6.b. In *Oxford English Dictionary*. Retrieved September 4, 2025, from https://doi.org/10.1093/OED/9052033645

Sato, T. (2015). 複線径路等至性アプローチ――方法論的複合体としてのTEA [Trajectory Equifinality Approach――TEA as a Methodological Complexity] (Author's translation). In Y. Yasuda, A. Nameda, M. Fukuda, & T. Sato (Eds.), TEA実践編――複線径路等至性アプローチを活用する[*Practical guide to TEA: Utilizing the Trajectory Equifinality Approach*] (title translated by the authors). (pp. 4–7). Shinyosha.

Sovran, T. (1992). Between similarity and sameness. *Journal of Pragmatics, 18*(4), 329–344. https://doi.org/10.1016/0378-2166(92)90093-Q

Tateo, L. (2016). Toward a cogenetic cultural psychology. *Culture & Psychology, 22*(3), 433–447. https://doi.org/10.1177/1354067X16645297

Tsuchimoto, T. (2022). 転機におけるキャリア支援のオートエスノグラフィー [*Autoethnography of career support in transition*]. Nakanishiya Shuppan.

Walt Disney Productions. (1951). *Alice in Wonderland [Animated film]*. Walt Disney Studios.

Yasuda, Y., & Sato, T. (Eds.). (2012). TEMでわかる人生の径路――質的研究の新展開[*Life trajectory understood through TEM: New developments in qualitative research*] (title translated by the authors). Seishin Shobo.

References

TEA, Potential in the Challenges of Professional Acts

TEM in Figure Skating and Professional Sport: Exploring Possibilities and Dynamics Within Professional Figure Skating Practice and Performance

Natalie Jancosek

Three kinds of skaters by Natalie Jancosek (2021)

Traces on Thin Ice—The Trajectories of Figure Skating

Unlike any other sport, figure skating combines a cold environment, dangerous movement on thin blades, depicted on the first page of the chapter, and one of a kind aesthetic components, of music, costumes, and bodily movements. To no surprise is the discovery of this unique sport attributed to no other but the exceptional Louis XIV of France, who has a remarkable interest in beauty and courage for novelty. When Louis XIV of France woke up one morning seeing all of the beautiful fountains in his courtyard frozen due to the cold winter temperatures that hit France in the late fifteenth century, instead of getting worried or becoming angry, he was overwhelmed by the beauty of the frozen water mirroring the nature and equally beautiful icy environment. Known for his passion for ballet and dance, he quickly came up with the idea of hosting balls and affairs on the ice and creating a new phenomenon—Ballet on ice. This is where today's ice dance and figure skating shows, such as Holiday on Ice, originated from. Louis XIV unconsciously created a future Olympic sports discipline and at the same time an employment and further career possibility for individuals who have ended their competitive journey.

N. Jancosek (✉)
Senior Researcher, Fondazione Jaan Valsiner: University for the Future, Salerno, Italy

M. A. Campill et al. (eds.), *New Paths in Trajectory Equifinality Modelling*, Theory and History in the Human and Social Sciences,
https://doi.org/10.1007/978-3-032-25855-7_12

Before the era of Louis XIV of France skates and skating have been used as a fast and convenient method of transportation, originally discovered in the territories of today's Netherlands. Because of the cold climate and stably frozen rivers and lakes, the Dutch invented skates to glide across the solid waters and to speed up their own transportation and delivery of goods and mail during winter time when other traveling methods were less convenient or impossible. Some were more comfortable sliding on the frozen rivers than others, which is why soon competitions and awards for the fastest and best skaters were established. This competitive spirit gave birth to the modern Speed Skating and Short Track in which the Netherlands still, centuries later, holds top placements in worldwide competition. Fortunately Louis XIV didn't care as much about speed as he did about beauty, which is a quality he shares with many figure skating enthusiasts who found inspiration and passion in this aesthetic sport.

Louis XIV is responsible for a number of great inventions, however, the name "figure skating" is not to be written in his account. The term "figure skating" originates from the practice of early skaters tracing patterns and figures, on the ice. This has been an active part of competitive figure skating until the 1990s, demonstrating skills of control, balance, and flow on thin blades. Skaters were judged on their ability to create clean and accurate tracings of figures. Today's professional figure skating does not include the completion of figures in such a sense anymore. This sport now divides into four disciplines—single skating for women, single skating for men, ice dance, and pair skating (International Skating Union, 2024). The competitive sport most reminiscent of the ice ballet of Louis XIV is nowadays called synchronised skating. It is a discipline in which mixed teams of 16 people perform coordinated choreographies. Synchronised skating and figure skating share common components, and are seen as different sports kinds. For figure skating has since many years been a stable part of the Olympic Games repertoire, synchronised skating has not been included in this prestigious event. Even though both synchronised skating and figure skating require exceptional skills and mastery of the thin blades, the pathways of the sports kinds and athletes differ. Synchronised skating has found popularity especially in countries and regions with a strong sense of community, where sport and togetherness is a cultural aspect of everyday life. There is no surprise that Finnish teams lead the ranks, together with Canadians and US Americans. Figure skating, however, requires focus on the self and at the same time sustainability in a group environment. Most single skaters practice in groups; however, the competitive performance happens individually. Ice dance and pair couples function as a unison—again, they practice in larger groups, but routines and competitions are individual.

The competition trajectory usually starts on the very first day of practice and preparation for the professional athletic career. In some countries, on a specific day, skating rinks or teams host a "selection" of skaters. Hundreds of small children between the ages of 2–5 enter the ice rink and are observed by the coaching teams. By observing how they skate, how they behave, and how they cope with difficulties of being for the first time on the ice, each of the coaches selects a few prospective ones for their division. The rest of the enthusiastic children get to go home and try out for a different sport or activity. Generally the requirements for future figure skaters are a good stability of the upper body, ability to turn without getting dizzy, a visibly good predisposition for muscular strength, and a confidence on the thin blades of the skates. Children, who do not fit those requirements or have other predispositions that could be in their way of becoming a professional figure skater, are advised not to enter this sport. Not only are the bodily parameters important when becoming a figure skater; what matters too is a will to skate, joy in presentation, absence of shyness, and a feeling of music and flow. However, the love and respect for the sport are the basic needs for a future top skater. If these traits persist through the individual's career, it is very likely that it will be a successful one.

Determining Success in Figure Skating Competition

In professional figure skating competitions, two programs are presented by the individual or couple; the short program (for ice dance, rhythm dance) and the free program (for ice dance, free dance). Each of the programs has a specific length and requirements that need to be fulfilled to ensure objectivity and fair judgement. Such elements are spins, jumps, step sequences, choreographic elements, and for the couple's disciplines also lifts and other specific movements. Skaters and their teams have the liberty of creating the elements in any sequence or composition they like; the execution and difficulty is what points and levels of difficulty are awarded for by the panel of judges and panel of technical specialists.

Even if requirements are the same for all participants in the given category, each program looks differently—which is the moment to draw an important connection to the idea of Trajectory Equifinality (Sato et al., 2021). Even though the desire of most skaters is the same, dwelling in obtaining the highest score and surpass as many competitors as possible in the ranking, each and every skater chooses, together with their dedicated teams, a program that would highlight their strengths while obeying the content and element requirements given by the ISU.[1] So it is possible that two programs containing exactly the same elements would look completely different and may also be executed very diversely.

The following graphics of Figs. 1, 2, 3, and 4, shall demonstrate two short programs for the Junior Women category (Season 2024/2025) (International Skating Union, 2024a) of single skating with the required elements being Double Axel,[2]

[1] The International Skating Union (ISU) is the international governing body for competitive ice skating disciplines, including figure skating, synchronised skating, speed skating, and short track speed skating. It was founded in Scheveningen, Netherlands, in July 1892, making it one of the oldest international sport federations. The ISU was formed to establish standardised international rules and regulations for the skating disciplines it governs, and to organise international competitions in these disciplines.

[2] The Axel jump or Axel Paulsen jump, named after its inventor, Norwegian figure skater Axel Paulsen, is an edge jump performed in figure skating with a characteristic forward take-off.

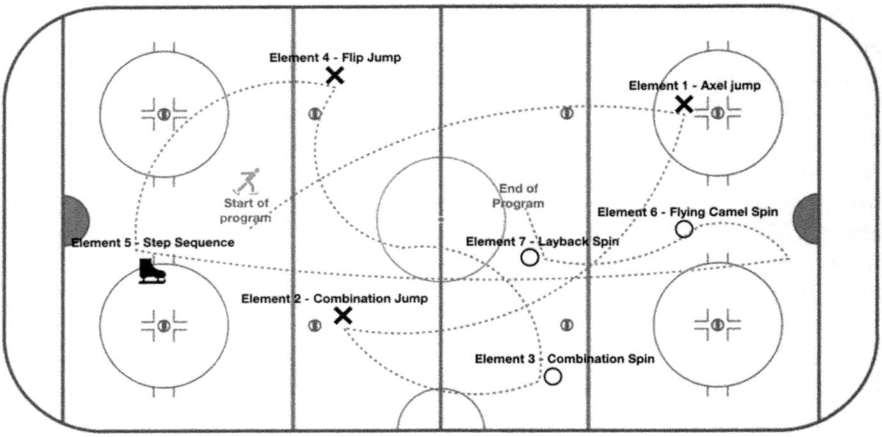

Fig. 1 Elements of a Junior Women Short program, Trajectorial Composition 1

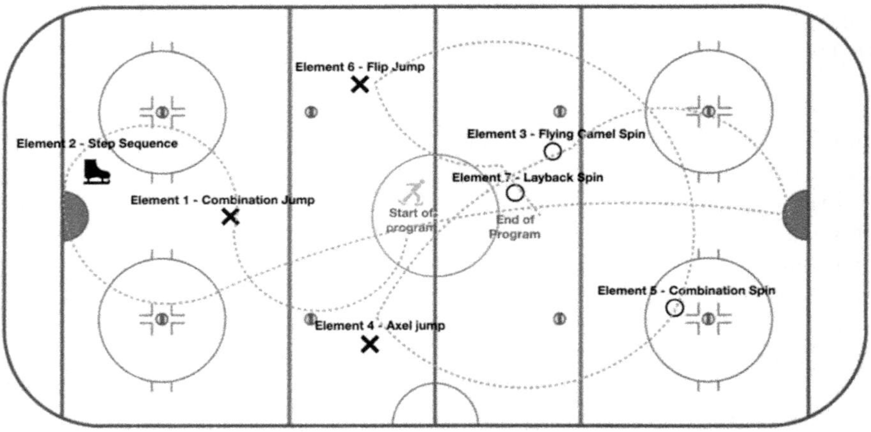

Fig. 2 Elements of a Junior Women Short program, Trajectorial Composition 2

Double or triple Flip jump, Jump combination[3], Flying camel spin, Layback/sideways leaning spin or camel spin without change of foot, Spin combination with only one change of foot, Step sequence fully utilising the ice surface (3 jump elements, 3 spin elements, 1 step sequence).

Each competitor together with their teams has chosen a different trajectory and composition, even though the program contents were the same (Figs. 1 and 2). As an example, through their execution the first competitor was able to obtain higher points and thus rank better than the second athlete. Hereby we are able to identify

[3] A jump combination is executed when a skater's landing foot of the first jump is also the takeoff foot of the following jump. All jumps are considered in the order they are completed.

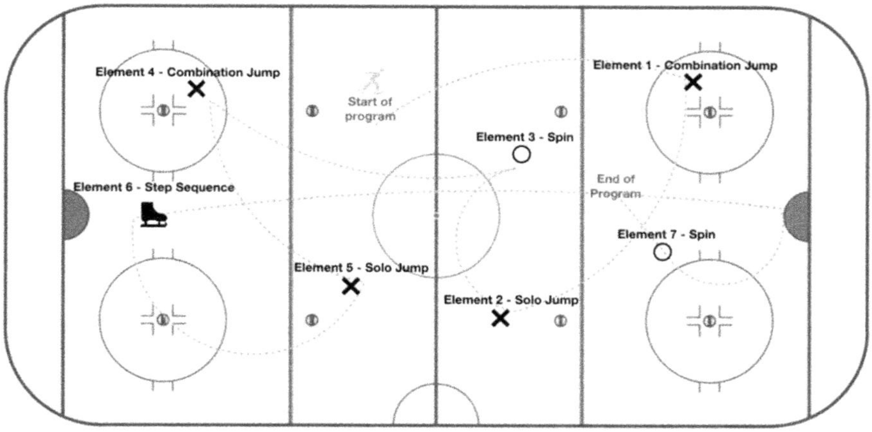

Fig. 3 Planned trajectories of a skating program

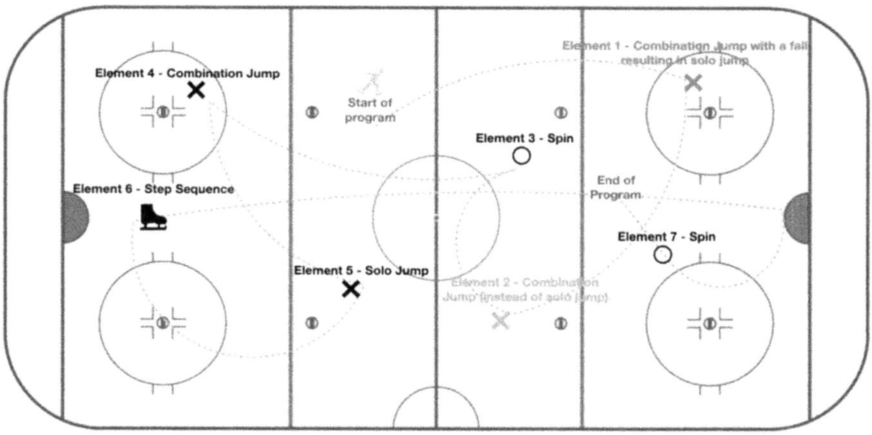

Fig. 4 Alternated program trajectory due to error on first jump combination

the important moments of figure skating routines, relevant for the perspective of the Trajectory Equifinality Approach (Sato et al., 2016)—Content, Composition, and Execution.

The program content can be understood as a constant variable in the figure skating program equation. For each figure skating category and age group, program contents are determined before the beginning of the season. Each year, based on the observations from competitions and performances of athletes from the last season, adjustments are taking place. These adjustments may concern the difficulty of the elements, length of the program, number of elements that need to be performed during the program or kind of element (e.g. jumps, lifts, choreographic elements, etc.). Together with the program contents, also the value of the performed elements may be changed as well as illegal elements.[4] One of such elements has, for many years, been a backflip. This highly dangerous element has been prohibited until season 2023/2024 when the ISU decided to open the possibility to skaters to perform this possibly dangerous jump and thereby showcase their extraordinary abilities and skills.

The value of each element determines how many points are awarded for the given movement if performed at each of the identified levels of difficulty.[5] Altogether, the changes of the program contents may be barely noticeable; however, at other times they make a vast difference that might even lead to skaters learning a new movement or skills that they did not master before.

Once the program contents for the season are determined, the skaters, together with their teams, might take on creating the program. The program composition in figure skating is a highly creative act taking place outside of the competitive season and serves as a preparation for the upcoming championships. This process is immensely time-consuming and consists of a music selection, choreography, drafting and perfecting the program contents, and choosing and creating costumes. This process, even though it is divided into multiple steps, needs to result in a holistic program. The holistic outcome of this creative journey is essential because of the artistic and aesthetic nature that figure skating programs have. All aspects must fit together resulting in a unity, which delivers an impressive experience to the spectators as well as the judges in competition. The wholeness and harmony of the program is an important factor considered in judges' scores and competitors who manage to deliver very good singular aspects, but fail to demonstrate a harmonic unison of all compositional moments during their programs, will not be perceived as positively as the ones who manage to fulfil this requirement. This is why, during the process of program creation, many ideas and alternatives are being tried and evaluated with the goal of finding the perfect combination that would deliver a holistic figure skating routine. Considering alternatives to create the perfect match results in the conception of a working Trajectory Equifinality Model (Sato et al., 2009) that represents the importance of excluding the necessary alternatives and at the same time, keep the correct options which need to fit together and thereby result in a holistic program.

Once the figure skating program has been created and perfected it shall be presented by skaters in competitions. In competitive moments, many psychological factors are influential on the performance of the program. Nervousness, anxiety, stress, exhaustion, as well as excitement, eagerness, determination, or motivation are intrinsic and extrinsic factors that immediately affect the figure skaters and highly influence their performance at the given event. If returning to the idea of viewing figure skating routines as equations, the component of performance is the most unstable and unpredictable one. There are, of course, individuals who cope with negative as well as positive stressors well and are quite consistent in delivering

[4] Movements that skaters are not allowed to perform in a program for reasons of safety or aesthetics.

[5] From basic level to level 4, in case of jumps the number of rotations determines the level of difficulty.

their programs. On others, however, the psychological factors might take a large toll resulting in a very poor performance or many errors. The performance, to a large extent, determines the score and further the final result of the authentic striving of the given champion. Yet, there have been many curious cases when even several falls or errors did not lead to a complete loss. Even so, during one competition, the skaters would allow for more than three of such falls or errors to happen, still, they would manage to win because of their qualitatively great program and demonstration of exceptional skills. A particular example of multiple errors and inconsistency in performance was seen in the ice dance couple Meryl Davis and Charlie White. During the Rostelecom cup,[6] one of the first competitions of the 2008/2009 season, Charlie White allowed for seven falls, which led the couple to lose their leading position and become third within the final result, which is still a great achievement. Later during that season, they managed to become US National champions and Four Continents champions with the same program, however then performed with no errors.

Spontaneously Changing Trajectories

Just like in any other athletic discipline, errors may happen during figure skating competitions, especially given the competitive setting and pressure that many athletes might experience during such a time. The errors that occur to professional figure skaters may be of different kinds—Falls or failure within the completion of an element, forgetting the routine, confusion due to the layout of the ice rink, or in couple's disciplines, asynchrony.

Falls or errors in the completion of elements happen the most frequently; a stumble or wrong take-off from a jump can cause skaters to lose balance easily. What may happen frequently as well is a mistake that does not cause the skater to lose their balance, but hinders them from completing the intended element successfully. Most frequently it is the case of performing a lower number of revolutions in jumps or not being able to complete an intended position within a spin.

Young skaters in particular are often subject to the problem of forgetting the routine midway through the program. This may happen to experienced skaters as well, those who might be able to improvise and pick up from a certain point within their music or movement. This mistake is perhaps the easiest to conceal in single skating, as the skater simply needs to keep the flow of the program and remember to do the required elements. In couple's disciplines, however, this might be a more serious problem, since synchronicity and unison is necessary to be kept. Still, through verbal or non-verbal communication of pair skaters or ice dancers the steady partner is able to help the one who is lost. This may lead to asynchrony, an error exclusive to a couple's disciplines. In such cases, the skaters are either not

[6] The interesting performance including errors can be watched here: https://www.youtube.com/watch?v=6BNqAUJK22A.

synchronised within their movements or their movements do not correspond to the beat and tempo of the music.

Confusion, most likely due to the layout of the ice rink, is once more a situation occurring more frequently to novice skaters. Even though most ice rinks have their standardised shape and measures, sometimes certain markers, like the position of the Zamboni entrance, the judges stand, spectators seat, or coaches' corner is in a different place than within the usual practice rink. Once such a confusion occurs, skaters either end up placing their elements in different points of the ice surface than intended or are unable to cover the entire surface of the ice rink with their movements and become rather static. Once more, this error is especially difficult in couple's disciplines, since two partners are performing a routine at the same time. In such situations, either the oriented partner needs to take the lead, or, in the worst case, the disoriented one confuses the other.

After the occurrence of any possible mistake, it is important for the competitors to pick up their routines and continue staying in the race. In order to maximise their chances of success even after the occurrence of an error, they might need to demonstrate very quick thinking and creativity in order to adjust to the particular situation. The result of this mental process is a spontaneous change of the succession of the program elements in order to achieve the maximum possible points for the given situation. An example of such a change shall be demonstrated on the following example of a short program:

For the purpose of this example seen in Fig. 3, the elements that the skater needs to perform in their program are as follows: Two solo jumps, two combination jumps, two spins, one step sequence. As we already discovered through the course of this chapter, the possibilities to lay out these required elements in a choreography are endless and up to the creativity of the skater and their coaching teams. For now, let's consider the following succession of the short program elements—combination jump, solo jump, spin, combination jump, solo jump, step sequence, spin. The trajectory of the program that is planned by this skater is demonstrated in the illustration below.

The error that happens to the competitor occurs in the first jump, which was supposed to be a jump combination of two subsequent jumps. The skater allows for an error during the take-off of the first jump resulting in a fall and thus, the inability to perform a subsequent jump. Through the quick reconsideration of possibilities, the skater may try to perform a jump combination as the next element in the program—instead of the solo jump. Since the fall occurred during the first jump of the intended combination, only the first jump (including the error) was counted. If the skater succeeds to do the combination jump later in the program, more points can be collected than by just performing a solo jump and receiving a fall for the combination. Thereby, the skater is able to partially compensate for the error and improve the initial situation which occurred after the first error. The spontaneously changed trajectory of the program may then look like visualised in Fig. 4.

The process within this specific action is very quick; however, its impact is crucial on the continuity of the performance of the athlete and of the outcome of the momentary competitive striving. Even if the skater is not able to achieve the full

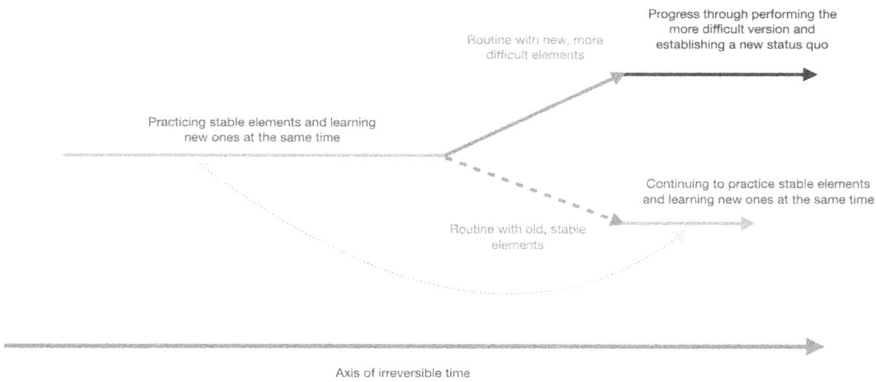

Fig. 5 The continuing process of improvement in figure skating practice and competition (by the author)

points for the program that contained an error, they are still able to avoid the worst possible consequence this error might have on their scores.

In some situations, especially if some elements are not performed consistently by a competitor yet, coaches may think of this strategy ahead of the competition and inform the skater about this "plan B" for situations if they experience a failure in one of the elements. In such cases, this alternative trajectory might even be practiced and prepared for ahead of time.

The consideration of trajectories and their alternatives in a competitive context is a very important moment leading to further personal development and change. It is not uncommon to consider different jumps or styles of other elements, such as spins or steps within figure skaters' programs during the practice and preparation process. This is most often the case once the athlete already feels comfortable enough in their program and has, besides the planned figures, mastered elements that are more difficult, and if executed without errors, they could bring the competitor more points than the ones that are currently included in the program. Sometimes, just for practice reasons, the competitors together with their teams could already integrate the more elaborate elements in the program and run through the routine during practice with these more difficult components, whereby the athletes are preparing for a next step within their progress. Then, in competitive setting, they might have a choice to perform the "old" routine with less difficult elements, as these are already mastered, aiming for good scores for the stable and outstanding performance of these.

This process of constant upgrade, improvement, and decision-making represents a very typical moment for the consideration of the Trajectory Equifinality Model.

As the competitors master a particular level of difficulty of their program, the aim is still a constant movement forward on the axis of irreversible time, as new and more difficult movements are then considered for further learning and development of the skill—as visualised in Fig. 5. At the same time, competitive abilities are being strengthened by the idea of mastery of a level. Thereby, once something the skater was unable to perform and what was practiced by them up until the skill was

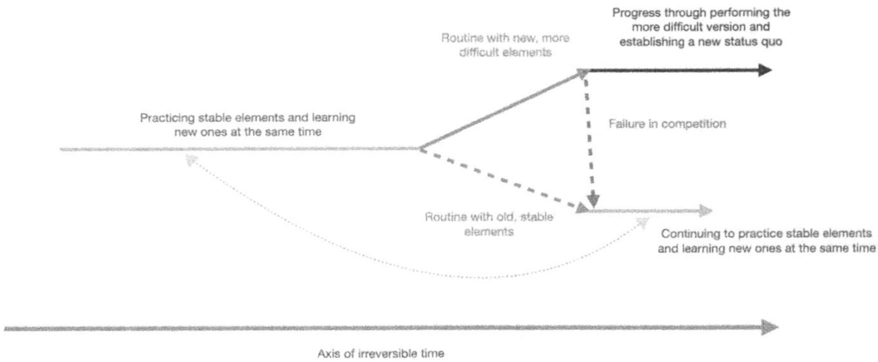

Fig. 6 The intended improvement, but discontinued progress due to failure in competition (by the author)

mastered, has become easy—easy, even up to the level when a new idea for further development could be opened up and strived for by the competitor and their team.

An interesting moment, however, arises in this model, once the competitor fails even with the so-called "safety program".

In this case as shown in Fig. 6, they do not manage to complete even the already mastered skills and perhaps struggle with the execution of movements that have been cleanly executed on many occasions before. Such may be the case after injuries or during times, when psychological aspects of the competitive mindset of professional athletes are particularly challenged. This set-back could be wrongly interpreted as a regression, thus, as a movement backwards on the axis of contingents of already learned skills and mastered elements. Nevertheless, it is impossible by the consideration of the Trajectory Equifinality Approach to move backwards in time, since the time axis is considered to be irreversible (Sato et al., 2009) as it is also true about the physical properties of time as such (Jancosek, 2023). How is it then that the athlete is regressing even though they are still moving forward in time? It is so, because of the athletes' development having reached an obstacle or perhaps a specific stage that hinders them in performance. This can be easily a bodily or mental change, such as growth or hormonal development, an injury, change in other aspects of life that psychologically transcends into athletic performance, or any other factor influential on skill and performance. In order to overcome the challenge, it is not necessary for the athlete to master the skill again. On the contrary, thanks to the important influence of muscle memory as well as understanding of the biomechanics of the motion it is, as it has been the case before the change, still comprehensible and within the athlete's abilities to perform the movements. What is necessary at this stage is psychological exploration of ways to overcome the change in the athlete's life in a positive way and thereby aid them in sustaining their athletic skills and abilities and move forward on the axis of irreversible time that is concerning their performance. Surpassing the obstacle results in overcoming the experienced retrogression and the ability to resume the previews skills. Such moments are very common throughout the career path of athletes and occur oftentimes due to a variety of reasons, as the bodily skill and performance cannot be isolated from psychological *Innenwelten* (Uexküll, 1909). of the athletes. The idea of the mind-body connection (Pickren & Rutherford, 2010) here gains particular meaning as the continuity of bodily performance is directly linked to the continuity of mental performance. Once a rupture on either side occurs, through the very strong interconnection of those two significant aspects, the changes in one area transcend to the other. This can be best demonstrated on the increased frequency of athletes suffering of depression during times of physical injuries (Smith, 1996) as it is known for regular physical movement to have a positive effect on the hormonal household of human beings, it is so that increases of serotonin and oxytocin levels are linked to times when people are engaged in athletic activities and also, to moments following this engagement. Professional athletes spend significant portions of their days engaged in movement and physical exercise which is why a sudden inability to continue doing so takes a particular toll on their mental wellbeing and thus, they perhaps suffer more visibly than individuals who sustained alike injuries but their profession and everyday life is not as closely linked to athletic activities. This also supports the importance of overcoming such ruptures or setbacks in the athletes' careers, as thereby their resilience skills become strengthened. This ability, again, has a positive impact on their future-oriented striving, as increased resilience abilities may help them deal with failure or further difficult situations.

Parallel Trajectories of Ice Dancers and Pair Skaters

As demonstrated in the examples of single skating, it is possible to already account for alternative trajectories during practice or spontaneously implement these in times of errors in competitive settings as strategies to maximise chances for success even if a mishap has occurred.

Even though ice dancers and pair skaters are supposed to be in perfect harmony, each of the partners still represents an individual that undergoes its own challenges and developmental steps in the ice rink as well as outside of the athletic setting. Within practice and competition, the choreography is composed in unison, so that all steps and movements are synchronised and harmonious. In case one of the skaters then allows for an error, there is very little to almost no chance for compensation later in the program, just as it would have been the case in single skating. Another reason for this is the different composition of pair and ice dance programs with almost no repetitions of elements. As described before, single skaters have several jumps incorporated in their programs, which can be altered or changed in placement. For pair skating, there are different types of jumps, such as throw jumps or parallel jumps, etc. that are either not repeated or there are important differences in the multiple jumps incorporated in a program that need to be obeyed. Thus, after a mistake on the first jump, the possibility to compensate for this error later during the program is almost non-existent. In this case, a much deeper psychological moment

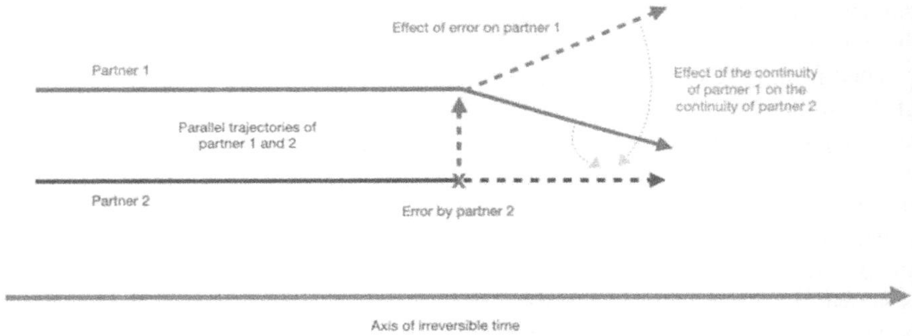

Fig. 7 Effect of error by one partner on the other

linked to the Trajectory Equifinality Approach is taking place, which connects to the continuity of the program for both partners after one of them allowed for a mistake to happen.

Sometimes, because of nervousness, pressure, and other psychological factors, after the first mistake happens, athletes let themselves go and spiral into a sequence of mistakes whereby the entire program and its continuity is affected. This might be the case regardless of the discipline—equally for single skaters as well as for couples. What is very interesting from the perspective of Trajectory Equifinality is how the continuity of the trajectory of the partner who did not make a mistake in the beginning may or may not become affected by the mistake done by the other partner.

In such instances, individual and collective aspects are crucial focus points. On one hand, the unison of both skaters is key for a successful performance, yet both partners also need to be good performers and athletes on their own. And once a mistake has happened by one partner the effect can then either transfer to the other one leading them to cause mistakes further during the course of the program, or, on the contrary, the other partner may not get affected by the mistake negatively and even perhaps bring up the ability to support the other partner throughout the progress of the routine in order to avoid further errors.

In this case as illustrated in Fig. 7, the other partner's trajectories depend much more on psychological properties and consistency than abilities related to bodily and athletic skill. This underlines the importance of aspects going beyond the athletic mastery of the given sport, which are particularly important when it comes to disciplines other than individuals. For ice dancers and pair skaters, mental strength and consistency that allows them to stay immune to errors of the other and overcome this moment without an interruption in their performance is something that may be a part of the practice routine. In this case, skaters would carry on their run-throughs during practice even if errors have happened with the goal of ex-post analysis together with their coaches in order to identify how to avoid these in the future as well as how to continue if such a mistake has happened without further impact on the performance.

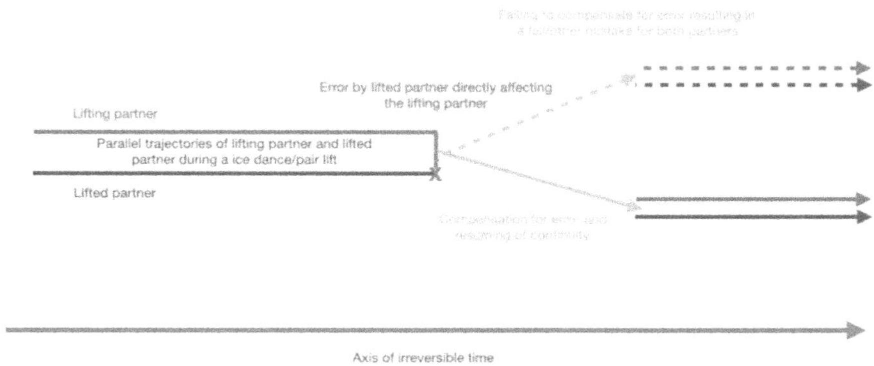

Fig. 8 Effect of error by one partner on both partners during elements performed in holds

Another specific aspect of errors that can only happen in couple's disciplines of figure skating are ones, where the problem on one partner's account directly affects the other partner of the pair. Such errors most frequently occur during lifts—here, either the lifted partner allows for an error in their movement which causes the lifting partner to lose balance or the lifting partner loses balance in the first place and thereby endangering the lifted partner as well. A similar situation can happen in couple's spins or steps that are performed in holds.[7] In such instances, it is particularly difficult for the partner who did not cause the error to maintain continuity as they are directly affected by the error caused by their partner.

A possible way of avoiding the worst possible outcome of such an error can be if one of the partners manages to directly compensate for the error of the other one. This may be the case during an error of the lifted partner where the lifting partner can perform an additional supporting move and thereby avoid losing balance and causing a fall. Whether the lift can then be performed on the level it was intended is not predictable; however, the alternative outcome of this compensation would not be directed towards completing the element as planned initially but merely towards keeping the integrity of the movement or even to one level further below, to avoid endangering oneself or the other partner.

Such compensatory behaviour, mapped out as in Fig. 8, can be observed in single skaters as well. An example could be during a failed entry into a jump, the skater may choose to take off but open the jump without performing any revolutions. This error will have a similar impact on their scores as a fall would have, however, their safety is much less at risk than it would be during a fall.

Decisions regarding contemplations of alternatives must be done incredibly quickly, in most cases within fractions of seconds. Mental processes during such

[7] In pairs, holds refer to the various ways partners connect while performing elements such as lifts, spins, and step sequences. These holds provide stability, control, and synchronisation. Common holds include hand-to-hand, waist hold, and lasso grip for lifts, etc.

In ice dance, holds are specific prescribed positions in which partners must maintain physical contact while skating. These include the closed hold, open hold, Kilian hold, etc.

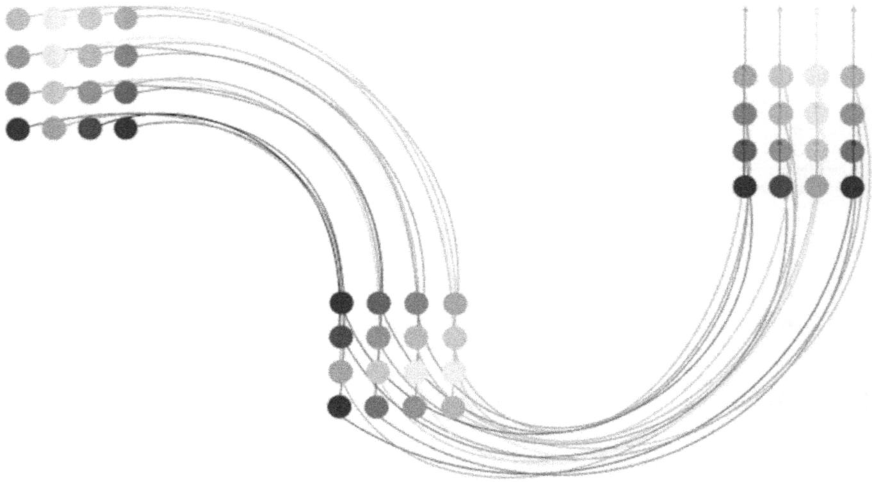

Fig. 9 Illustration of the trajectories of skaters in the Synchronised Skating element "Pivot Block"

moments are indeed incredibly complex, as the single skater first identifies the problem, evaluates their chances of completing the movement, then takes a decision on whether to risk a fall or to interrupt the performance of the movement for their own safety, and then they take the necessary actions to complete the trajectory their decision led them to. In a couple's disciplines, the sequence of decision making during errors is a bit more complex, since the process involves more than just one individual. In case the error is happening to one partner, the other partner must first register the error and see if they themselves are directly affected, and then they need to evaluate strategies to keep the continuity of the program as well as their own safety and the safety of the other one. If the mistake involves both partners simultaneously, the decision for the next movement needs to be on a common ground; however, oftentimes needs to happen within fractions of seconds and without the possibility of verbal communication or agreement on the next move. Such moments involve a very high incorporation of all senses and attention directed to the own body as well as to the body and movements of the other partner.

If looking beyond the borders of the four Olympic disciplines, in synchronised skating, the idea of unison and coordination of individual and collective trajectories becomes even more significant than in the instance of individual or couple's disciplines. Collective athletic striving, just as it is the case for synchronised skaters, may be viewed as a collection of individual trajectories from which such a program is composed.

These trajectories, visualised in Fig. 9, are highly dependent on the individual as well as the collective and can only cause the desired effect if all are fulfilled correctly and simultaneously. The aid for this is most instances the music which sets a certain beat that is followed by all skaters and thus, the individual steps are set on a specific count. However, errors in such a setting are of a very different magnitude than within single skating, pairs, and ice dance, as besides the competitor causing the error, the entire team is affected by the mistake. Here interestingly, the collective has sometimes the possibility to overpower the individual error and help the skater integrate quickly and resume the performance without further remorse, but in some cases, the error of one skater may have a domino effect which then strongly affects the entire team.

What the outcome of the error is strongly depends on the placement and the moment within the program when the failure has happened. In case of a simple stumble during a transition part or a moment when no hold is established between the individuals, the error has less of an effect on others than during the performance of an element or movement, requiring specific unison motion of the entire team, such as a pivot block. In this instance, the unity of the team reaches its peak as the acting of all skaters as one element makes it possible for the desired effect of the figure to take place.

Trajectories of Figure Skaters on the Axis of Irreversible Time

Independent of the kind of skating performance—collective or individual—one moment unifies them all within the position of Trajectory Equifinality, which is the axis of the irreversible time. The idea of irreversible time is crucial to athletes, especially figure skaters within all aspects of their career—whether it is their practice, competition, life course development, or any other moment affiliated with their athletic life and identity.

The axis of irreversible time is, however, particularly meaningful within the central topic of this chapter, which concerns errors and ruptures within planned trajectories and their further possible compensations. As demonstrated in the previous subchapter, once an error has occurred within a skating program, the skater(s) may compensate for it by changing the planned course of the program, but they cannot undo it. Therefore, if a mistake has happened and it was noticed by the panels of judges and technical specialists, the further striving of the athletes is only to prevent the worst possible outcome by trying to do everything within their power to achieve the best possible outcome given the condition that a deduction has already happened within their scores. This moment is particularly important, yet not unique to the figure skating world, as we find examples of such instances within our everyday life. For example, if a person misses the bus they need to catch to work, they know that they are already going to be late, but they can choose from a variety of alternative transportation options in order to decrease the amount of time by which they would be late if they simply waited for the next bus. In figure skating, such moments are a part of the competitive and athletic mastery and particularly interesting because of the aesthetic component of this sport. There is little to nothing aesthetic about waiting for the bus on the way to work. The aesthetic component contributes to the magnitude of inconsistencies and to the difficulty of compensating for these, as if a fall has already occurred during the routine, the perfectionist idea of an aesthetic program has already vanished, as falls are usually dangerous but seldom aesthetic.

Once the aesthetic integrity of the program is disrupted, a full compensation is impossible, given the idea of the irreversible time. The trajectories of figure skaters and their competitive routines are thus a very important matters for the investigation through the Trajectory Equifinality Approach as the modelling of these and ruptures occurring within them allow for the in-depth understanding of the amplification of the irreversibility by the aesthetic component of this sport.

Consciously, the idea of Trajectory Equifinality has not infiltrated the minds of sportspeople and their teams yet, nevertheless, unconsciously it has been carried out in practice ever since the invention of this sport, as an approach to keep the continuity and integrity of the routines in place no matter what the circumstances are. Further, conscious and targeted, consideration of Trajectory Equifinality in figure skating practice and competition could be beneficial to skaters and, perhaps, constitute a new approach to deal with ruptures in their planned trajectories. The possibilities of application in this context go, however, beyond the demonstrated examples—as creativity is given no borders here. Thus, I conclude this chapter with hopeful thoughts of future exciting explorations of the connections between sports and the Trajectory Equifinality Approach and Modelling.

References

International Skating Union (ISU). (2024). *ISU Figure Skating Media Guide 2024/25*. International Skating Union.

International Skating Union (ISU). (2024a). *Constitution and general regulations 2024*. International Skating Union.

Jancosek, N. (2023). Time as an organic metaphor. In M. A. Campill (Ed.), *Re-inventing organic metaphors for the social sciences* (pp. 15–31). Springer.

Pickren, W. E., & Rutherford, A. (2010). *A history of modern psychology in context*. John Wiley & Sons.

Sato, T., Hidaka, T., & Fukuda, M. (2009). Depicting the dynamics of living the life: The trajectory Equifinality model. In J. Valsiner, P. Molenaar, M. Lyra, & N. Chaudhary (Eds.), *Dynamic process methodology in the social and developmental sciences*. Springer. https://doi.org/10.1007/978-0-387-95922-1_10

Sato, T., Mori, N., & Valsiner, J. (Eds.). (2016). *Making of the future: The trajectory Equifinality approach in cultural psychology*. Information Age Publishers.

Sato, T., Tsuchimoto, T., Yasuda, Y., & Kido, A. (2021). Jaan Valsiner in Japan: The trajectory Equifinality approach (TEA). In B. Wagoner, B. A. Christensen, & C. Demuth (Eds.), *Culture as process*. Springer. https://doi.org/10.1007/978-3-030-77892-7_39

Smith, A. M. (1996). Psychological impact of injuries in athletes. *Sports Medicine, 22*(6), 391–405. https://doi.org/10.2165/00007256-199622060-00006

Uexküll, J. (1909). *Umwelten und Innenwelt der Tiere*. Verlag von Julius Springer.

Nursing Teacher's Ability Formation Process Using Trajectory Equifinality Approach: Narratives of a Nursing Teacher Who Has Been Reborn Through Various Encounters in the Face of Crisis

Chihiro Tanaka

Sunset on a Japanese beach (by the author)

C. Tanaka (✉)
Teikyo University, Tokyo, Japan

M. A. Campill et al. (eds.), *New Paths in Trajectory Equifinality Modelling*, Theory and History in the Human and Social Sciences,
https://doi.org/10.1007/978-3-032-25855-7_13

Introduction

Owing to changes in era and society, nursing discipline in Japan has undergone revisions in nursing education and training systems. With each revision, there has been an emphasis on improving the quality of nursing education and teaching of the nursing faculty. In its "First Report on the Examination of the Way of Educating Nursing Personnel at Universities (2019)," the Ministry of Education, Culture, Sports, Science, and Technology (MEXT) highlighted the importance of ensuring the quality of education. This was achieved through qualitative and quantitative enhancements of the faculty. This emphasizes the need to consider various measures to enhance the educational systems. Furthermore, in the "Report on the Future Role of Nursing Faculty" in 2010, the Ministry of Health, Labor and Welfare presented qualities that nursing faculty should strive to improve. These include human rights consciousness and an ethical perspective that respects diverse personalities, including possessing qualities such as individuals and nurses that can serve student goals.

In recent years, Japan has seen a rapid increase in the number of nursing universities, leading to diversification in the depth of experience among new nursing faculty, and advancements in the careers of nursing professionals (Japan Association of Nursing Colleges, 2011). Against this backdrop, efforts to enhance the capabilities of the nursing faculty involved in basic nursing education, including approaches to continuing education and self-improvement, are receiving increasing attention (Ministry of Health, Labour and Welfare, 2010). Previous research on the qualification and competency development of nursing faculty has often focused on specific aspects, such as the educational institutions and clinical settings of nursing faculty (Hirokawa & Hosokawa, 2021; Yamamoto, 2020), and factors influencing competency development (Ohtsu et al., 2006), resulting in partial and fragmented studies. Nursing faculty competencies refer to the knowledge, skills, and personalities that support educational practices. Previous research has not addressed the efforts to comprehensively and holistically understand competency development, including nursing faculty experiences and social backgrounds.

Tanaka and Okazaki (2016) focused on the experiences of nursing faculty and elucidated the competency development process among expert nursing faculty with over 10 years of educational practice experience. They revealed that the foundation of competency development among experienced nursing faculty members lies in their personal lives and a passionate commitment to education. They demonstrated that experienced nursing faculty members, as lifelong learners, continue to develop their competencies through their experiences, including life events. In studies concerning expert teachers, models suggest that competency increases with years of experience, and that expertise may entail losses and gains. Previous studies have clarified stage-like processes and pathways of competency development among nursing faculty (Tanaka & Sato, 2020).

However, perspectives concerning the evolution of the nursing faculty have been largely overlooked. It is necessary to elucidate the multifaceted and diverse nature of competency development over time, including the influence of society and culture. Therefore, this study focused on the experiential process of the nursing faculty, utilizing the foundation of cultural psychology. It was analyzed and examined using the Trajectory Equifinality Approach (TEA), which considers multiple trajectories and equifinality. Furthermore, this study aimed to identify pivotal points in the competency development process of nursing faculty and elucidate how nursing faculty use imagination to discover new dimensions.

Zittoun and Gillespie (2016) defined imagination as follows (see Fig. 1): Imagination refers to the freedom to explore alternative and distant experiences and envision one's way of being. This process allows individuals to explore different life possibilities and choices, and prepares them to take on social responsibilities in combination with TEA. Notably, even if not selected, choices envisioned through imagination persist as guides for future directions and aspirations. This process aids in analyzing the bifurcation points of the TEA and visualizing future possibilities. Assuming nursing educators use this process to visualize new options and approaches, it may lead to understanding their capacity-building process, depicting their growth within social and cultural contexts while creating meaning even in various crises. In particular, analyzing the branching points in the TEA using the Imagination Loop Model makes it possible to explore multiple options and visualize hopes and guidelines for the future, even for choices that were not selected.

Furthermore, Sato (2021) proposed connecting the concept of "Transduction" from the process philosophy of the French philosopher Simondon (2018) with TEA. In this study, "Transduction" refers to creating new choices by envisioning solutions through imagination in situations where multiple options exist, as addressed in TEA. Combining Transduction with Zittoun and Gillespie's (2016) Imagination Loop Model makes the explanation more concise. Therefore, this study analyzes the competency formation process, focusing on branching points from the perspectives of Imagination and Transduction. Using the Imagination Loop Model, we can explore how nursing faculty at critical branching points in the competency formation process use imagination to create new choices and envision future prospects and guidelines, even for options that have not been chosen. This approach enabled us to understand how nursing faculty continue their journey as educators, equipped with future prospects and guidelines, even for unselected options. This study discusses a nursing faculty member affiliated with a nursing vocational school who can visualize transductive resolutions at branching points during competency formation.

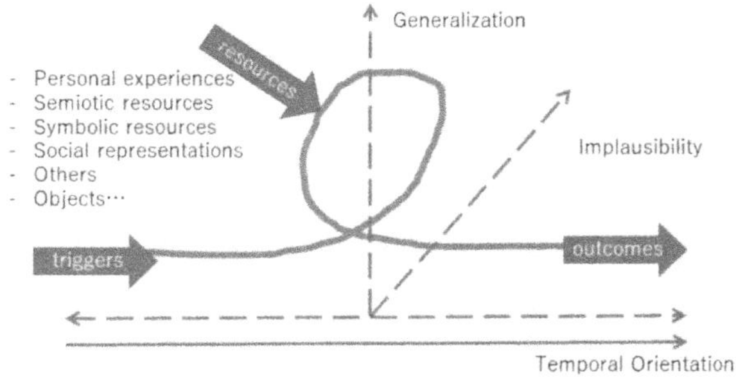

Fig. 1 Imagination loop model (based on Zittoun and Gillespie 2016)

Objective

This study analyzed how nursing faculty acquire and develop competencies as educators, including the necessary knowledge, skills, and personal qualities required for educational practice. It also examined the experiences through which students learn and shape their competencies.

Definitions of Terms

Nursing Faculty: This refers to the faculty members teaching nursing at universities, junior colleges, and vocational nursing schools. In this study, nursing faculty explicitly refers to faculty members at vocational nursing schools.

Experience: The definition of experience is based on Dewey's (1938) concept of "interaction between individuals and the external environment." It encompasses all the knowledge, skills, and emotions gained through past experiences in which educators are involved.

Competency of Nursing Faculty: The concept of competency is derived from the field of education, explicitly referring to the statement by Fujisawa (2004) that includes "knowledge and values that support teaching activities." Nursing faculty competencies encompass the knowledge, skills, and personal qualities that support educational practices.

Research Method

Research Design

This study employed a qualitative research design utilizing TEA as the analytical method.

Research Collaborators

Building on the work of Akita (2006) and Valsiner and Sato (2005), this study conducted a historical structured citation (HSI) targeting a nursing faculty member "A," with over 12 years of nursing education practice experience. HSI involves inviting individuals who have experienced events of interest to share their stories with researchers. This method differs from traditional random sampling, as advocated by conventional psychological research. Random sampling seeks to increase the generality of information obtained from samples by eliminating individual contexts or histories (Valsiner & Sato, 2005). However, experience is never solely internal. Individuals are inevitably influenced by the place, culture, and history in which they were born and raised (Sato, 2009). From this perspective, HSI invites collaborators, the protagonists of life, to describe their life processes through TEA rather than treating them as external samples, thus "inviting" them (Sato, 2015).

This study aimed to focus on the experiences of nursing faculty and explore the depth of experience in how competency is formed through interactions with the external world. It was necessary to adopt the perspective of the expertise gained through experience to reflect on and attribute meaning to the educational practices of the research collaborators. Therefore, nursing faculty member "A," with more than 10 years of teaching experience, was selected as the research collaborator. Regarding the number of research collaborators, according to the TEA, when the participant is a single case, the depth of individual experiences is explored. In contrast, four (±1) cases depict the diversity of experiences, and nine (±2) cases enable understanding of patterns of pathways (Sato, 2015). Based on these criteria, one research collaborator was selected for this study.

Data Collection Method

Semi-structured interviews were conducted between December 2020 and March 2021 to examine the experiences that led to competency formation through the narratives of nursing faculty members. The interview content was recorded with the consent of the participants using an IC recorder, and the interviews were transcribed verbatim. Each interview lasted approximately 60 minutes and was conducted individually in a quiet private room, to ensure confidentiality. Interviews were conducted according to the collaborators' situations. The central questions focused on three main areas: (1) the trajectory from completing the nursing education program to the present day, (2) motivation for aspiring to become a teacher, and (3) the experience accumulated as a teacher that contributes to competency formation. Specifically, inquiries were made about the experiences in which the interviewees felt that they had grown or encountered significant others.

Analysis Method

We used TEA to analyze the collected data by following the steps outlined below:

1. The audio data from the interviews were transcribed verbatim. Focusing on the narratives of experiences that led to the formation of competencies in the nursing faculty, transcripts were segmented into episodes. Each episode was labeled succinctly to represent the content and converted into cards. The cards were organized along a timeline and arranged in chronological order.
2. Based on the narratives of the research collaborator, the Equifinality Point (EFP) of this study was defined as "continuously maintaining the motivation for competency formation as a nursing faculty member." In TEA, Polarized Equifinality Points (P-EFPs) are set to expand researchers' understanding. In this study, "becoming a rigid veteran teacher" was set as the P-EFP because the interviewee

used such an expression. While the EFP is determined by the researchers' objectives in the TEA, setting the P-EFP clarifies the meaning of the EFP. In this case, while theoretically, the P-EFP for the EFP could indeed be "losing motivation for competency formation as a nursing faculty member," setting the P-EFP as "becoming a rigid veteran teacher" indicates that "continuously maintaining the motivation for competency formation as a nursing faculty member" is not simply the absence of losing motivation. By defining "becoming a rigid veteran teacher" as the P-EFP, it expresses a strong intention or desire to not become a rigid veteran teacher; thereby clarifying the meaning of the EFP. After setting the P-EFP, similar events, actions, choices, and feelings were compared to identify Obligatory Passage Points (OPP), which are the institutional, customary, or resulting essential passage points that most individuals experience, and Bifurcation Points (BFP), where behaviors diverge into various paths.

3. The process leading to the EFP was described, including BFP and OPP, as well as various pathways—behaviors or thoughts—and a Trajectory Equifinality Model (TEM)—diagram was created. In TEM, even if the participants did not discuss it, theoretically plausible meaningful pathways were included as dashed lines in the diagram to aim for reflective propositions about ways of living and to visualize supportive interventions.
4. In the TEM, the forces that propel progress toward the EFP are termed Social Guidance (SG), whereas inhibitory or restrictive forces are termed Social Direction (SD). It was considered which of these forces applied, and the factors leading to the choices made in each pathway were categorized based on the similarity of their meanings. A table outlining the conceptual explanation of TEM is presented (Table 1).
5. SG and SD, categorized in the TEM diagram, were added, completing the TEM diagram.
6. BFP in TEM was further analyzed using the Imagination Loop Model to visualize the transductive resolution.

Reliability of Analysis Results

Regarding the reliability of the analysis results, the researcher received advice from qualitative researchers to avoid common pitfalls during the interviews and to ensure that no biases were introduced to the participants. Additionally, TEA experts supervised each stage of the data analysis process.

Table 1 Explanation of the Trajectory Equifinality Model concept

Key concepts	Explanation of concepts
Equifinality Point; EFP	Concrete manifestations of equifinality
Polarized Equifinality Point; P-EFP	Situations contrary to equifinality
Bifurcation Point; BFP	Points where ambiguity or multiplicity arises
Obligatory Passage Point; OPP	Points where many people have similar experiences
Social Direction: SD	Forces that inhibit reaching equifinality
Social Guidance: SG	Forces that promote reaching equifinality

Results

Overview of Research Participant

Participants who consented to participate were female educators with 12 years of experience in educational practice. The interviews were conducted six times, with an average duration of approximately 90 minutes per session.

Trajectory Equifinality Model Diagram for Teacher "A"

The process of developing Teacher "A"'s competencies revealed eight branching points. In describing this process, " 《 》 " represents the BFP, "[]" indicates the context, " 《 》 " signifies the EFP, including the second EFP, "< >" denotes SD, "[]" denotes SG, and words underlined in bold represent transductive resolutions.

BFP 1: Taking the First Step as a Nursing Instructor

Teacher "A," who received guidance during their Master's program from their supervisor, took the first step as a nursing instructor, despite geographical distance. Engaging in the initial practicum course alongside their supervisors amid confusion and anxiety, they learned about chronic nursing through dialogue with them. Eventually, they continued to "conduct the practicum supervision alone."

> I was quite anxious about going straight into the practicum... my supervising professor guided the first course; thus, I was learning while following their lead. Whenever something came up, I could consult with them immediately, and I learned chronic nursing.

Teacher "A" received support from their supervising professor, as evidenced by their narrative of "learning while following their lead" as they took the first step as a nursing instructor.

BFP 2: Encountering the Complexity of Interpersonal Relationships Within University Organizations

Teacher "A" had been involved in practicum supervision with their supervising professor until then. However, as they began to take on supervision alone, they desperately studied the nursing of the assigned ward, including the care of high-risk patients and chronic nursing. During the practicum, when they encountered difficulties, they solved them with the help of their colleagues. Simultaneously, they encountered the complexity of interpersonal relationships within university organizations because of the hierarchy of positions and the closed workplace environment unique to university organizations.

> Once I started supervising the practicum alone, I was studying desperately, you know. I was questioning what the role of a practicum supervisor was, and when facing difficult problems, I consulted with my colleagues. Nonetheless, dealing with the complexities of

> relationships within my affiliation area, I witnessed a difficulty unique to university organizations.

As evidenced by the statement, "I studied desperately," Teacher "A" was studying diligently, mainly focusing on learning the nursing of the assigned ward. While being supported by the colleagues, they were experiencing the "difficulty of relationships" and were searching for the role of instructors within the unique challenges of university organizations.

BFP 3: Deepening Understanding of the Target Through Caring for Patients with Paralysis

Teacher "A" explored their daily role as an instructor, using images of educators encountered during their student days as clues. It is evident that they invested efforts in deepening their understanding of nursing from their focus on studying the specialization of the assigned ward while they were initially involved in practicum supervision. However, during this period, they understood the challenges and joys of teaching according to students' abilities and endeavored to understand students, as they did with nursing. In this process, there was an essential checkpoint of "consulting with superiors when troubled by student guidance." Through chronic nursing, superiors' educational views and clinical nursing practice experiences served as facilitative symbols. It became evident that the branching point of "deepening the understanding of the target through caring for patients with paralysis" held significant importance in the competency formation process.

> My superior is someone who can anticipate education... or rather, they often say things like, 'This student understands this much, so if we fill in the rest, the student can continue to grow on their own,' and I learned from their approach of guiding according to the students' abilities. Once, I encountered a patient with paralysis sitting in a wheelchair and their paralyzed arm drooping... I started thinking about how both the patient and student could recognize this danger, and what could be done so that the patient would become aware of it. I pondered how patients and students could value their arms, and engage in educational interactions. At that moment, I think I deeply pondered what the true understanding of the target meant.

Teacher "A" was contemplating "what true educational engagement means" and "true understanding of the target" through caring for patients with paralysis while learning "guidance tailored to students' abilities" from their superior.

BFP 4: Understanding That Nursing and Education Are Fundamentally Rooted in Understanding the Target

Teacher "A" discovered the students' strengths through their accumulated clinical nursing experience and understanding of human nature through chronic nursing. Instead of focusing solely on what they could not do, they emphasized their individuality by concentrating on what they could do while questioning their problem-solving thinking, thus deepening their understanding of the target. Eventually, while working at the university's graduate school preparation office, they learned about the importance of focusing on regional needs and understanding what it meant to establish graduate schools and meet community needs. Through daily educational practices and roles within the organization, they navigated the branching point of understanding that nursing and education are fundamentally rooted in understanding the target.

They were supported by forces, such as learning from practicum supervisors and their own clinical nursing practice experiences as well as research topics emerging from the field. However, they also faced challenges, such as an immense workload and a closed organizational culture, struggling between the expanding perspective of a nursing instructor and responsibilities they had to bear.

> When I think about understanding the target, I realize that I used to have a tendency to come up with answers quickly, and I do not think I could trust and wait for students or engage with as much patience as I should have had. However, while studying chronic nursing under my supervisor's guidance, I realized that as my understanding and perspective of patients deepened, so did my perspective toward the students. I was reminded that it was the same thing ... that realization was significant for me. Around that time, I believed that my involvement in the graduate school preparation office helped broaden my perspectives.

Teacher "A" was navigating a significant branching point in competency formation, understanding that "both nursing and education are fundamentally rooted in understanding the target" (BFP4). This is evidenced by the narrative, "the more my understanding and perspective of patients deepened, the more my perspective towards students did as well." For Teacher "A," it was not just about the patients or students; as indicated by the statement, "my involvement in the work of the graduate school preparation office helped broaden my perspective," they were also focusing on "addressing regional needs" and considering what universities are required to fulfill while deepening their understanding of the target.

BFP 5: Encountering Students Who Have Experienced and Been Wounded by a Disaster

By understanding the current situation of various practicum facilities and prioritizing bedside visits, Teacher "A" encountered diverse nursing perspectives among the bedside staff. Therefore, they strived to understand what it meant to establish a graduate school and what hospitals were seeking, and they made efforts as an instructor to ensure that students could conduct better practicums. They navigated the branching point of encountering students who had experienced and been wounded by a disaster. Superiors and colleagues supported them and were led to strive to protect students while hoping for and worrying about their safety in a safe environment. However, the forces of "devastating disaster conditions" and "physical distance from students" worked against them, leading to a struggle between these forces and the path of facing and confronting the fluctuating self.

"Understanding clinical instructors may sound simple, but it is not something that you can grasp until you step your foot at bedside. Nursing is not about having a single correct answer. There are various perspectives and values. Thus, I always emphasize the importance of being present in the field. While accumulating experience when a disaster struck, I was safe but could not grasp the extent of the disaster.

My superiors and colleagues expressed concern, suggesting that I return to my hometown because I was young. However, I had students here, and I felt there were things I needed to do here... I was wavering."

Teacher "A" found themselves "wavering" amidst the "devastating disaster conditions" and "physical distance from students" while experiencing the earthquake and worrying about the safety of the students.

BFP 6: I Want to Escape from Nursing

Teacher "A" encountered students practicing amidst fluctuations within extreme conditions of the earthquake and volunteering in the disaster-stricken area, experienced the nursing perspective crumbling under such extreme circumstances. Witnessing the reality of extremely unhealable conditions, Teacher "A" navigated the branching point of wanting to escape from nursing. While supported by caring families, vigilant colleagues, the presence of students, and their tenure as an instructor, they also faced the stark images of suffering residents and despair amidst the tragic environment of the disaster-stricken area.

"What I did as a volunteer in the disaster-stricken area was debris clearance. Although I went there as a nurse during the extreme conditions of the earthquake, I was deeply shaken by what it meant to protect my health. Until then, as a nurse specializing in rehabilitation nursing in chronic care, I had been accustomed to seeing people with disabilities strive to 'get better' .... However, in this crisis, I felt powerless, confronted with the limits of medicine, and questioned the meaning of life. I wanted to escape negatively. I was overwhelmed by feelings of despair as if there was nothing but hopelessness."

As a volunteer in the disaster-stricken area, Teacher "A" continued to question the meaning of "protecting health" amidst extreme conditions. As evident from the narrative of feeling powerless and confronted with the limits of medicine, feeling that there was nothing but despair, witnessing "unhealable extreme conditions" became a profoundly destabilizing experience for Teacher "A." Thus, challenging their previous values and beliefs.

BFP 7: Returning to the University and Engaging in Nursing Education

When various choices were presented, Teacher "A" worked as a nurse in a clinical setting, accumulating multiple encounters and experiences. At times, they worked as nurses involved in medical care in remote areas. At other times, they encounter numerous patients with illnesses and grapple with feelings of despair as they meet patients and staff. They affirm their existence alongside their vulnerabilities, contemplating life and health in a crisis, while searching for their way of being. Through this process, they transformed their values and believed that their limitations and strengths coexisted. This led them back to the branching point of engaging in university nursing education. While family circumstances acted as inhibiting factors, ongoing research and encounters with others promoted Teacher "A"'s return to education.

"Nurses are involved in maintaining and promoting individuals' health, and there is an image that they are all about improvement and hope. However, facing situations where things do not improve ... nothing changes ... it feels utterly powerless. Somehow, this is a setback. While returning to clinical practice as a nurse in various situations, I encountered nurses from rural areas. This made me profoundly reflect on the life I have lived so far and how privileged my environment is. I realized that being positive and hopeful was not the only correct way. We must understand that living means facing illness and aging, and that living has its strengths and limitations. I sincerely accept that my vulnerabilities and strengths, filled with hope, are part of who I am."

From the branching point of feeling the desire to escape from nursing, Teacher "A" chose to work as a nurse in clinical practice, experiencing various encounters and situations while carrying a sense of "powerlessness and, in a sense, a setback." Therefore, as reflected in the narrative of "being deeply introspective" and "understanding that always being positive and hopeful is not the only correct answer," Teacher "A" affirmed themselves, acknowledging their vulnerabilities while facing themselves.

BFP 8: Taking the First Step to Study in Graduate School

Teacher "A" again entered the nursing education field, encountering students who live complex human lives more deeply and broadly. Meanwhile, within the organization, they began to realize the necessity of articulating and conveying their thoughts to others through experiences in which values among educators clashed. With firm resolution and a sense of responsibility to see through the research that they had consistently pursued until the end, they took their first step into graduate school. Embracing living with conflicts, they followed the path of not giving up on thinking and reaching EFP as a nursing educator, where they maintained their motivation for professional growth and continued to face unanswered questions. Furthermore, they reached the Second Equifinality Point (S-EFP), where they continued to confront unanswered questions.

"Then, by chance, I had the opportunity to engage in nursing education and encounter students from various backgrounds. Looking back, I feel like I saw students but did not see them in the past. I neglected students. Perhaps I did not notice SOS signals from the students. I did not consider the basic premise that students are human beings before thinking about what they could or could not do. Perhaps I can realize that now, but only because it is now."

Teacher "A" again had the opportunity to engage in nursing education and returned to the university to become involved in nursing education. As seen in the narrative of "encountering students with various backgrounds," they encountered students living complex human lives and engaged with them as whole individuals. This attitude reveals Teacher "A"'s transition from valuing only strengths to affirming their existence with limitations and facing students as individuals who embody both limitations and strengths.

Imagination and Transduction

The imagination and resolution illustrated in Fig. 1 focus on the critical branching points important in Teacher "A"'s capacity-building process, depicting how they discovered new dimensions through their imagination. Teacher "A" found themselves at the branching point of wanting to escape from nursing (BFP6) while participating in volunteering activities in the disaster-struck areas. When facing nursing students who were wounded and shaken while engaging with patients and residents, Teacher "A" felt powerless as a healthcare professional. After stepping away from the educational field and standing in a clinical setting as a nurse, Teacher "A" encountered certain situations, such as interactions with nurses working in disaster-struck areas and women with disabilities. These experiences transformed them from valuing their strengths to affirming the co-existence of limitations and strengths. The path they follow upon returning to the educational field may be the same, but adorned with different values, acknowledging both limitations and strengths. This path represents a new dimension (Fig. 2).

Teacher "A," Who Faced a Crisis and Experienced a Rebirth Through Various Encounters

Teacher "A," specializing in chronic care nursing, was deeply committed to learning about their specialty through dialogue with superiors and a diligent study of nursing practices in their assigned wards. Through experiences, such as seeking advice from superiors when struggling to guide students, they reached a branching point where they deepened their understanding of their subject from the perspective of caring for patients with paralysis (BFP3). This turning point led them to consider the educational implications of the lives and experiences of patients, prompting them to

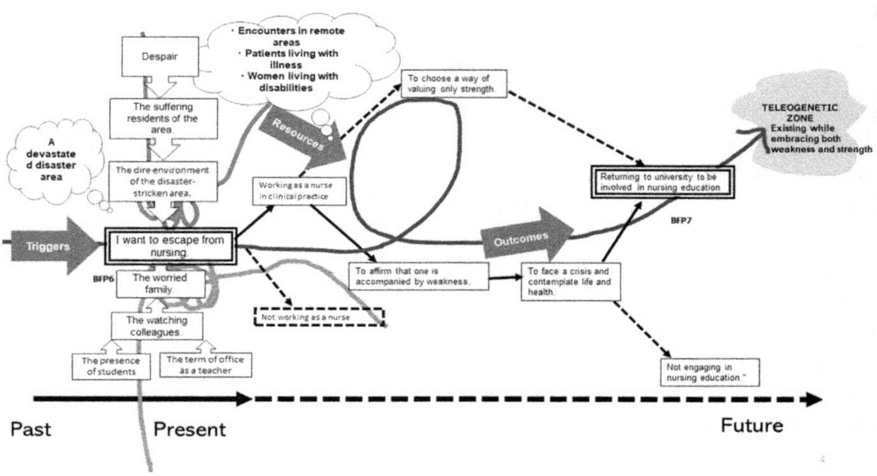

Fig. 2 Imagination and transduction (by the author)

rethink their role in patient care as a true novice. In their own words, "Encountering the phenomenon of the paralyzed arm of a patient... made me ponder how the patient could become aware of this danger, the student could realize the necessity of it, and both the patient and student could consider it as their arms ... I pondered what true educational involvement means." Through this narrative, Teacher "A"'s approach contrasted with attempts to change patients according to their own desires or simple problem-solving approaches, revealing a genuine effort to understand the subject and respond to others' needs.

We tend to unconsciously view things from our own perspective in daily life. However, true care can only be achieved by placing ourselves in the position of the patient and experiencing the world together. Florence Nightingale (2014) succinctly expressed this idea: "There is no other profession that requires the ability to immerse oneself amid another's emotions that one has never felt before. (Omission) If you do not possess this ability, you should retire. The essence of nursing is to understand patients' feelings and read every change in their expression without causing them to articulate their suffering." Teacher "A"'s gaze was directed toward the patients with paralysis and students facing them. Teacher "A" discovered each student's strengths through accumulated clinical nursing experience and an understanding of chronic care nursing. Instead of focusing solely on what they could not do, they emphasized their abilities and individuality, deepening their knowledge of the subject.

Furthermore, Teacher "A" encountered students practicing amid the turmoil during extreme disasters. While volunteering in the disaster-struck area, their nurtured nursing perspectives collapsed as they witnessed the reality of extreme unrecoverable conditions, leading them to the pivotal point of wanting to escape nursing (BFP6). While supported by concerned family members, attentive colleagues, presence of students, and their tenure as an educator, they were also confronted with the residents' suffering and a sense of despair in a disastrous environment. Teacher "A" pondered life and health while facing a crisis, searching for a path forward. When all the options were presented, they pursued the path of working as a nurse in a clinical setting through various encounters and experiences, such as working in medical care in disaster-struck areas and interacting with patients with illness. They encountered despair and affirmation while facing the limitations of the patients and staff members. They transformed their values, affirming the co-existence of limitations and strengths, and departing from their previous worldview. This journey ultimately led them to the pivotal point of returning to the university and engaging in nursing education (BFP7).

In a contemporary society grappling with issues that resonate with "limitations," the concept has often been portrayed as something to overcome. However, when facing the disaster crisis and encountering various individuals, Teacher "A" understood that in our lives and experiences, the seemingly contradictory notions of "limitations" and "strengths," as defined in dictionaries, are intimately intertwined and complement each other. Embracing this understanding, Teacher "A" returned to the educational arena as a nursing educator, embodying the idea of intertwining limitations and strengths as an integral part of their role.

Challenges in This Study

In this study, we visualized the competency development process of nursing instructors and focused on the pivotal moments to illustrate how they imagined and discovered new dimensions. Furthermore, by utilizing the TEA for the analysis, we uncovered the depth of experience of the nursing instructors. However, the study had certain limitations such as having only one participant and focusing on one instructor from a vocational school, leaving room for further development. In the future, it would be necessary to increase the number of participants, aiming for a more diverse range of experiences and typification of pathways to elucidate the competency development process of comprehensive nursing faculties.

Conclusion

Through an analysis conducted using TEA, the competency development process of the nursing instructor revealed a glimpse of educators who, despite facing crises, such as disasters, reflected on themselves through the lives of women with disabilities and patients with illnesses, and questioned their existence as human beings. Through a series of analyses, the image of the nursing instructor, who continued to grow through mutual engagement, became more apparent.

In society, "weakness" and "strength" are generally viewed dichotomously, with overcoming weakness and attaining strength regarded as virtuous. Confronted with the crisis of the earthquake disaster and various encounters, Teacher "A" understood that "weakness" and "strength," though defined as opposites, are in fact inseparably connected in life and mutually complementary. Returning to the educational field as a nursing educator, Teacher "A" embraced weakness and strength. Conceiving weakness and strength as complementary has the important implication of fostering an understanding of true strength that arises from sharing weakness with someone, and it provides opportunities to deepen reciprocal relationships with others (artistically visualized by the photography on the first page of the chapter).

The dimensions revealed through Teacher "A"'s account of living through crisis may not be novel. However, in nursing education, where the goal is to train healthcare professionals, genuine encounters begin when educators, as human beings, face their weaknesses while engaging with students as whole persons. It is through such interactions that care and education take shape.

With the spread of Crisis, nursing education faced abrupt changes. Traditional methods grounded in human-to-human engagement had to be altered, and clinical practicums, where students had learned the importance of nursing practice through direct interaction with patients, were suddenly moved online. The questions raised by this crisis such as "What is nursing?" and "What is care?" were opportunities to reconsider these fundamentals. The findings show that true care, and thus true education, begin when each of us involved in teaching, acknowledge our weakness and value students just as they are.

Acknowledgments We sincerely appreciate the cooperation of Teacher "A" who contributed immensely to this study.

Competing Interests The authors have no conflicts of interest to declare that are relevant to the content of this study.

Ethics Approval Ethical considerations were carefully adhered to during this study. Before seeking cooperation, the purpose of the study was explained to participants both orally and in writing. Participation in the study was voluntary, and participants were assured that they could withdraw without any disadvantages. Measures were taken to ensure that individuals and schools could not be identified. Audio recordings were permitted during the interviews, and digital data were securely stored in a designated memory and kept in a locked cabinet. After the conclusion of the study, data were retained for 3 years, after which audio recordings were deleted and physical records were shredded. The study was approved by the ethics committee of the researchers' institution prior to its commencement.

Authorship Credentials T. C. and T. S. contributed to the conception, design, analysis, and writing of the manuscript. All the authors have read and approved the final version of this manuscript.

Research Funding This research received support from the Japan Society for Nursing Education.

Appendix

This study is an extension and revision of a portion of the doctoral thesis submitted to the Graduate School of Human Sciences at Ritsumeikan University.

References

Akita, K. (2006). Life-long development of teachers and lesson creation. In K. Akita (Ed.), *Classroom research and discourse analysis* (pp. 217–227). Japan Broadcasting Corporation Educational Promotion Association.

Dewey, J. (1938). *Experience and education*. Ichimura N, translator. Kodansha.

Fujisawa, S. (2004). *The formation process of teaching and learning abilities as "reflective practitioners."*. Kazama Shobo.

Hirokawa, E., & Hosokawa, K. (2021). Process of starting to walk as a new teachers at nursing colleges as teaching instructors. *Journal of the Japanese Society of Nursing Education, 30*, 27–38.

Japan Association of Nursing Colleges. (2011). *FD guidelines for young nursing faculty members: Aiming for quality improvement in nursing education.*

Ministry of Health, Labour and Welfare. (2010). *Report of the study group on the future.* Roles of Nursing Instructors.

Ohtsu, H., Mochizuki, A., Adachi, M., & Watanabe, A. (2006). Analysis of factors influencing the formation of nursing instructors' abilities. *J Japan Soc Nurs Med Care, 8*, 21–30.

Sato, T. (2009). *Starting qualitative research with TEM: Aiming for research on time and process.* Seishin Shobo.

Sato, T. (2015). Saturation in TEM. In Y. Yasuda, A. Nameda, M. Fukuda, & T. Sato (Eds.), *Word map TEA theory section - learning the basics of multilinearity approach* (pp. 24–28). Shinyosha.

Satou, T. (2021). *About exhibition.* Exhibition Research Group.

Simondon, G. (2018). *On the mode of existence of technical objects*. Fujii C, Kondo K, Nakamura D, Stéfan L, Tachibana M, Yoneda T, translators. Hosei University Press.

Tanaka, C., & Okazaki, M. (2016). The formation process of developmental ability of expert nursing educator narratives about their experiences. *Journal of the Japanese Society of Nursing Education, 26*, 29–41.

Tanaka, C., & Sato, T. (2020). The structure of competence development in mid-level nursing teachers. *Journal of Academy of Nursing Education Research., 12*, 13–24.

Valsiner, J., & Sato, T. (2005). Historically structured sampling (HSS): How can psychology's methodology become tuned in to the reality of the historical nature of cultural psychology? In J. Straub, C. Kölbl, D. Weidemann, & B. Zielke (Eds.), *pursuit of meaning: Theoretical and methodological advances cultural and cross-cultural psychology* (pp. 215–252).

Yamamoto, M. (2020). Educational involvement of nursing school teachers toward students in clinical practice conferences. *Journal of the Japanese Society of Nursing Education, 29*, 43–56.

Zittoun, T., & Gillespie, A. (2016). *Imagination in human and cultural development*. Routledge.

Hidden Verticality in the Trajectory Equifinality Model? Theoretical Analysis in Relation to the Organization of School Services for Disabled and Handicapped Children

Dany Boulanger

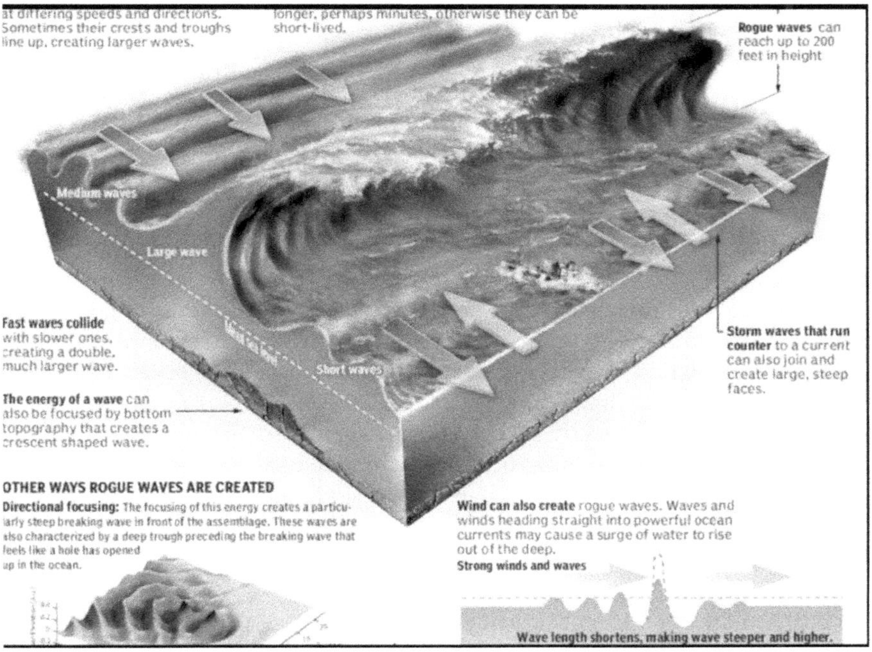

Rogue waves of the ocean (picture from the author)

D. Boulanger (✉)
Université du Québec en Outaouais, Outaouais, Canada

M. A. Campill et al. (eds.), *New Paths in Trajectory Equifinality Modelling*, Theory and History in the Human and Social Sciences,
https://doi.org/10.1007/978-3-032-25855-7_14

In this paper, I interrogate the relative absence or underdevelopment of "verticality"—that is, social stratification indicating people's positions and access to symbolic and material resources—in the Trajectory Equifinality Model (TEM), whose conceptual focus seems to fall primarily on the horizontal nature of people's trajectories. Adopting an abductive perspective, I draw on a specific case—the organization of service trajectories in elementary schools for disabled and handicapped children—to develop theoretical hypotheses about the absence of verticality in political and institutional discourses, as well as in dominant special-education models. I also suggest that these discourses and this model, by generating false impression, wrongly pretend that children's trajectories are horizontally framed. As a conceptual and methodological model, TEM can be used in micro-disciplinary fields like special education to understand trajectories of services. In this perspective, the hypothesis that I make about hidden verticality in special education will be further applied to TEM. On the other hand, I can think of how applying TEM to special education could reinforce the impression of horizontality, as verticality seems to be underdeveloped.

First, I discuss TEM's emphasis on horizontality over verticality. I do so by underscoring the importance of agency in people's trajectories and by presenting a culturalist (rather than structuralist) orientation toward constraints. I hypothesize that verticality, in terms of stratification, is horizontally refracted.

Second, I move to the special case of how trajectories of services are organized for disabled and handicapped children. After presenting the sociohistorical and political context underlying the emergence of a graduated and multilevel way of organizing services in schools, and particularly the Response to Intervention (RTI) model, I describe the principles of this model in relation to its promise of horizontality. I then deconstruct this promise by arguing for the manifestation of vertical structural dynamics that organize children's trajectories—which favor the educators' voices and aim at maintaining the functionality of the system—in the organization of services and that are masked. I'll conclude by arguing for the importance of epistemological rotation between verticality and horizontality and by proposing to tackle children's trajectories amidst dynamic tensions between these axes, in relation to TEM's epistemology.

Horizontality Versus Verticality in TEM

Agency in One's Trajectories in TEM

TEM is, above all, a horizontal model of trajectories. From a Bergsonian perspective (Bergson, 1998/1911), time is considered irreversible, meaning that it unfolds dynamically and unpredictably, like a river whose form is never the same. It is contextually and historically bounded, and it is strongly oriented by subject meaning-making processes. Trajectories can be schematized as "brooms" (Sato & Tanimura, 2016).

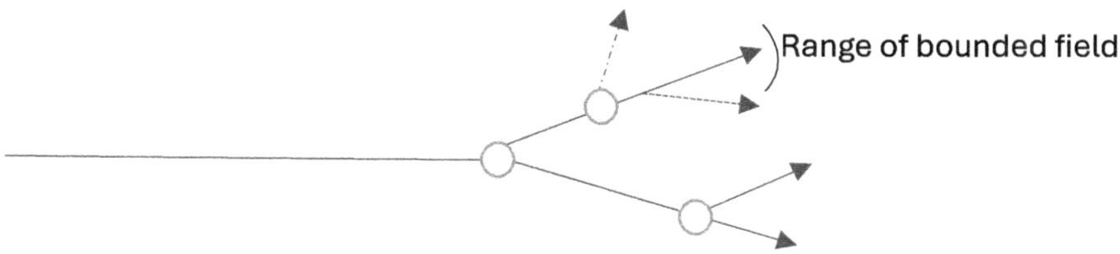

Fig. 1 Trajectories as brooms (by the author)

The different arrows (of Fig. 1) represent options that actualized themselves (the full arrows) or not (the dashed arrow) in the past or that could actualize themselves or not in the near future. For example, a woman could have invested in her career, but instead *decided* to give birth, or the opposite. A child who experienced school difficulties could have been integrated (or included) in a regular class, but it was instead decided that he or she would benefit from the services of a special education teacher in a special class.

The circles in Fig. 1 represent the bifurcation points at which people face options. Some options are privileged (e.g., the woman who gives birth) while others are put aside but remain "available" as possibilities for the near future.

The possibilities that are present in one's trajectory are "not closed points, but rather, orientations, or directions given to a field of options—they are what we are thinking 'about' in general terms, or they become the 'aboutness' of our 'actions' of our actions, that which they tend" (Zittoun & Valsiner, 2016, p. 9). This signals the person-centered nature of these general directions. In essence, TEM suggests that the person experiencing a trajectory (let us call it the moving person or the mover) actively makes a choice between options in a bifurcation zone, as in the case of the woman deciding to become a worker or a mother. The person constructs the zone of his or her journey. This occurs temporally—the person *re*imagines the past ("what could have been") and the future ("what could be") (Zittoun & Valsiner, 2016). Therefore, choice-makers are considered *autonomous and active authors* of their trajectories as well as agents of change. Yet, this happens in relation to others; no one is an autonomous subject acting in a vacuum. So, what are the constraints that the woman in our example may face (de Sousa Bastos, 2017)? And does the child in our previous example have a real impact—as an autonomous and active agent and author—on his or her school trajectory? Does he or she really have the choice among his or her options?

Constraints in TEM

Generally speaking, as *social* subjects, people are also "externally" guided:

> We propose two different social forces as Social Direction (SD) and Social Guidance (SG), which make trajectories diverge. Social Direction (SD) is the force that obstructs to go toward EFP [Equifinality Point] and Social Guidance (SG) is the force that helps to go

toward EFP. In many case, *either* SD *or* SG is *stronger than* the other is. *So, the person can make a choice* (Sato & Tanimura, 2016 p. 31; emphasis added).

In TEM, the constrained aspect of people's trajectories is regarded in terms of guidance related to forces, and this guidance is explained—in the previous quote—in terms of the strength of each of the forces. The external forces are then explained in terms of push—the stronger the push in a given direction, or the stronger the constraints that prevent something from happening, the more the person will be pushed in this direction or restrained from going there. This happens in a bounded environment that establishes limits (Fig. 1). In many papers, authors using TEM tend to make a complex analysis of the intricacy of different forces in terms of their holistic configuration. They are presented or *described* as complex fields of forces orienting the person in certain directions. The dynamics that *explain* these fields generally lie in their attractive properties or valences—their multidirectionality and the tensions—which could take the form of ambivalence—that they create.

The person faces opposite choices (a mother having to choose between going to university to get a better job or continuing to invest her time as a mother) that establish the range of possibilities—which is a quantitative notion—and form a tension-like field. In TEM, social forces are generally presented in terms of fields of tension between options and constraints. The latter are framed in terms of relations between enablers and blockers (the new job that the woman's husband gets "suggests" that she can stop working for a while to become a mother vs the societal discourses on productivity and individuality, along with government cuts in family support). The person experiencing ambivalence—when facing such "contradictions"—resignifies and negotiates (with others) the world through some signs and genres to generate some stability. In one of the previous examples, the woman's choice is mediated by the sense ascribed to maternity in political and institutional discourses as she ascribed some meaning to the latter in relation to her experience. The main focus for explaining the dynamic aspect lies in the subjective and intersubjective meaning-making processes. Ultimately, the person is the choice-maker; the tension enables or activates the person's sense-making process.

This person-centered conception of constraints makes sense because culture is considered deeply subjective: "[t]hrough the expression "Culture belongs to person" sounds a little strange, this is a central axiom of cultural psychology. Culture is not an external causal agent but a resource that persons utilize for their individual living" (Sato & Tanimura, 2016, p. 28). In relation to his or her environment, the person, as an open system, actively internalizes and externalizes the "voices" of his or her environment through multiple mediational processes. Subjectively and in relation to others, he or she actively *re*interprets the world to position and situate himself or herself (Sato, 2016; Valsiner & Sato, 2006).

The "outside" is made sense of in terms of the "inside" or of the transfer between the outside and the inside that the person masters (he or she has the key to managing it), and this happens horizontally. It would be more adequate to say that the boundary is quite flexible between the inside and the outside or that there is no boundary, depending on the authors' perspective (in TEM, the first one seems to be favorized).

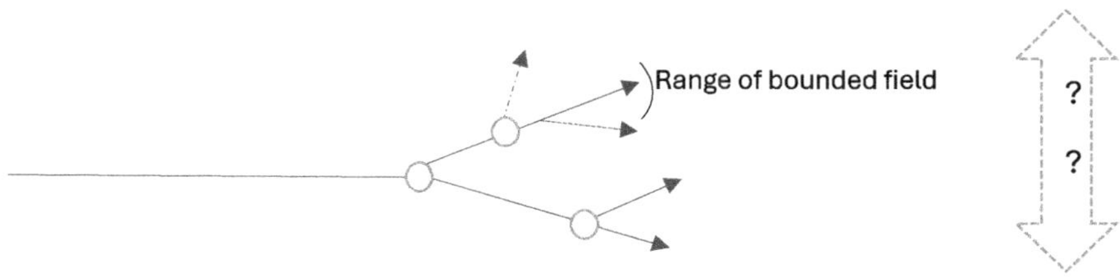

Fig. 2 Horizontality and verticality in trajectories (by the author)

The active and person-centered meaning-making process happens as the person moves in his or her environment through a series of transactions (e.g., a woman consulting a new doctor in a hospital). So, these moves or trajectories are both spatial—social transactions and meaning-making processes in and across ecological niches—and temporal (changing, developing oneself). These transactions are filled with obligations (obligatory passage points; Sato & Tanimura, 2016) of course—"a mother who wants a better job will have to go to the university" (p. 32). Yet, the explanation mainly lies at the level of the person's meaning-making processes through horizontal transactions.

In Fig. 2, we can see that this occurs horizontally in a culturally dynamic yet socially "flat" environment. Schematically, **verticality** is represented by the singularized relation between two kinds of options. The top signals actualized or "chosen" options and the bottom unactualized or "unchosen" options. The choice of top or bottom seems arbitrary—unactualized or "unchosen" options can be placed above too. The constrained nature of social guidance or regulation is part of this horizontal situation of the person advancing forward, both spatially and temporally.

TEM seems to be generally grounded in a culturalist frame of reference as compared to a structural paradigm (Grignon & Passeron, 1989; Bruner, 1996; Lessard, 2000; Jackson, 2011). In this framework, the symbolic aspect is developed in terms of dynamic processes. The latter are situated amidst ecological levels, both spatially (microsystem vs mesosystem) and temporally (microgenetic, for instance). These are cultural levels unfolding in a (relatively) non-stratified society. Notice that I do not refer here to the "linear" (static conception of culture) and deficit-based version of culturalism, which is related to the ideology of the culture of poverty (Forquin, 1979), but to a very dynamic version of culturalism that emphasizes symbolism in relation to singularity, processes, and ideological tensions (Bruner, 1996; Grignon & Passeron, 1996; Lessard, 2000).

A structuralist perspective, rather, entails considering hierarchy in terms of stratifications—the presence of strata signaling social inequalities and indicating symbolic positioning and access to material conditions for people (Forquin, 1979; Grignon & Passeron, 1989; Jackson, 2011). In this perspective, symbolic and material resources are therefore considered unequally distributed. From a culturalist perspective, the social forces are considered quite neutral (not considered in terms of inequalities of position and social domination), even if they are treated as part of cultural levels—spatiotemporal levels in people's niches and semiotic levels of generalization of meaning.

From a culturalist perspective, people's transactions and meaning-making processes happen in an *autonomous* way, that is relatively "detached" from the social strata; in this sense, this is related to cultural autonomy as opposed to *heteronomy* (Grignon & Passeron, 1989). For these authors, *culture* pertains to the symbolic aspect of life and society—which is stratified—and stratified *society* brings verticality into cultural processes. I have delved elsewhere into the tension between autonomy and heteronomy (Boulanger, 2026). I want here to highlight the fact that verticality, considered in stratified terms, seems to be relatively absent from TEM (and from other approaches in cultural psychology as well), running the risk of pushing aside or being partially blinded to— he vertical dimension of people's trajectories. Generally speaking, people are presented as (relatively) free movers in a relatively unstratified society, while "vertical" (stratified) mechanisms are still active.

A swimmer who looks at the wave—on the mere surface (Fig. 3)—to plan the environment he or she will swim in may fail to notice the presence of subcurrents vertically acting *under* his or her feet, currents that in fact could create further waves on the surface during his or her activity without him or her noticing, due to the blind spot created by not considering the vertical aspect of water's movements. A parent accepting school agents' prescription on children's transitions in school services trajectories tends to also be blurred by an *illusion of horizontality*. How can TEM account for the vertical nature of this kind of transition, and also of these very illusions, if it cannot fully account for verticality and therefore may itself participate in constructing such illusions?

In the next section, I show how services are horizontally presented to parents with reference to the main model that is being promoted primarily by researchers, politicians, and schools in North America (mainly), but also in other parts of the world, such as France. I then suggest some vertical dynamics that "guide" the

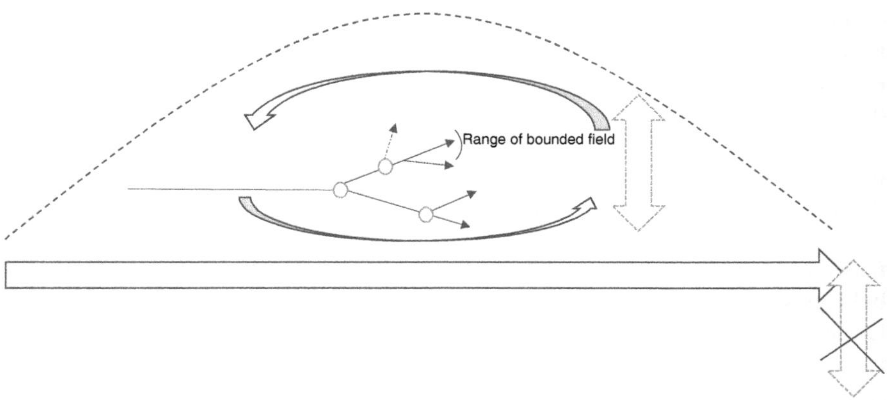

Fig. 3 Horizontal refraction of the verticality (by the author)

"horizontal" flow of children's placement in the organization of services in special education, without the actors noticing it.

Horizontality in Education: The Way Special Education Services Are Organized in Schools

Horizontally Distributed Services: Graduate and Multi-level Organization of Services and Its Context

In North America (mainly), but also in Europe (notably in France), a multilevel and graduated way of organizing services in school is privileged, by favorizing handicapped and disabled children's access to regular classes. In the United States, the Education for All Handicapped Children ACT adopted in 1975, and re-enacted in 1990 as the Individuals with Disabilities Act (IDEA) promoted the *right* of handicapped children to access school services in the most "normal" conditions possibles (Beauregard & Trépanier, 2010). In the United States, this logic is also anchored in the New Child Left Behind (NCLB) Act of 2001 as well as in the Individuals with Disabilities Education Act of 1975, and especially in its 2004's version (Aron & Loprest, 2012; Boily, 2020; Whitten et al., 2012). In France, the promotion of rights and the discourse on integration progressively emerged from the mid-1970s onward (Gris, 2014; Plaisance, 2013). In Quebec (Canada), since the mid-1970s, policies have promoted the idea of a graduated organization of services from the perspective of integration (Schimidt & Tardif, 2022; Plaisance & Schneider, 2013; Prudhomme, 2018).

Promoting the right of disabled and handicapped children to access school services provides the basis for the paradigm of *normalization,* defined as the "[u]tilization of means which are as culturally normative as possible, in order to establish and/or maintain personal behaviors and characteristics which are as culturally normative as possible" (Wolfensberg, 1972, in Gris, 2014, p. 15). In 1977, UNESCO promoted Wolfensberger's philosophy by emphasizing equality of opportunity in education and the right to education for every child. It was actualized through *mainstreaming*, meaning that every child must be integrated in the least restrictive and the most "natural" or normal environment possible. Schools have to create conditions for such an integration and for adapting disabled and handicapped children to the norms. This gave impetus to a movement of *integration*—meaning that school services must be organized in a way that prevents segregating disabled and handicapped children by automatically placing them in special schools or special classes in regular school. Rather, they have the right to be integrated, as much as possible, into regular classes where services must be adapted to their "needs" and in which they will be exposed to the norms that every citizen is expected to adhere to.

If children cannot be integrated into regular classes, they can benefit from specialized services outside of the classroom. The child's placement depends on his or her difficulties or needs. Sometimes, in this mainstream current, the word "need" is used, but in a more marginal way (compared the discourse on inclusion that emerged later on). The best option appears to be to frame the services in a graduated way, depending on the child's difficulties. The movement of integration—which emerges in opposition to segregation, manifested through a strict separation between specialized education (for disabled or handicapped children) and regular education—operationalized itself through a continuum of services (graduated), from regular classes to special classes (Schimidt & Tardif, 2022; Beauregard & Trépanier, 2010). It also implies possibilities for these children to progressively benefit from specialized and individualized services outside of regular class if the teachers' interventions (sometimes with the help of specialized educators in the classroom) appear not to be enough. This logic of placement has to be planned, hence the use of RTI models to rationalize the intervention.

At the beginning of the 2000s, we observed the emergence of multi-tier approaches in the United States. The intervention is framed around levels of educators' investment in children, depending on the severity and frequency of their problems (Trepanier, 2019). It is inspired by behaviorism and is implemented at the microsystemic level (interventions in and outside the classroom) and the mesosystemic level (the way school services are organized). Interventions are standardized and/or based on problem-solving methods (Trepanier, 2019). This logic is part of a special education policy adopted in Quebec in 1999. RTI is part of this trend. The latter is explicitly referred to in IDEA (2004) and NCLB (2002) (Aron & Loprest, 2012; Whitten et al., 2012) as well as in different governmental policy documents in Quebec (Boily, 2020).

For certain authors (c.f. Boily, 2020), RTI generally aligns with the paradigm of *inclusion* that emerges in the 1990s and 2000s in opposition to integration. The advocates of inclusion criticize the paradigm of normalization because it implies that children have to change themselves to fit the norms and it entails normative and behaviorist interventions to correct children's deficits (Gris, 2014; Trépanier et Paré, 2010).

Inclusion rather emphasizes the following principles (AuCoin et al., 2011; Gadbois, 2020; Schimidt & Tardif, 2022):

- Denormalizing interventions: children do not have to adapt to fit the school's norms; school services must be structurally adapted to fit children's needs by questioning the obstacles they create for them.
- Services must be flexible and comprehensive, and based on interprofessional collaboration.
- The continuum of services has either to be (a) completely eradicated or (b) rendered more flexible and continuous thanks to this collaboration and to the emphasis on children's diverse needs and capacities.

Adapting school services to children, depending on their needs and capabilities, through a comprehensive and flexible approach and by recognizing diversity as a resource, constitutes an alternative to mainstreaming. These principles are grounded in the general logic of horizontality I referred to in the previous section because they emphasize:

- The active participation of children considered as agents.
- The flow of these agents—as movers—within a flexible and continuum of services that are culturally comprehensive and oriented towards their basic needs in a collective and singular manner.
- The voices of children are supposed to guide their "placement," by educators listening to their needs and using diversity as a resource.

These same principles are promoted in policy discourses in which we can, for instance, notice the emphasis on school adapting services to children and a switch from referring to child's difficulties to the child's needs and capabilities. RTI, which is referred to in recent educational policies, as mentioned above, advocates a preventive approach. It entails a collaborative approach and the adaptation of services to children's "needs" and difficulties (Boily, 2020; Desrochers et al., 2015; Whitten et al., 2012; Trépanier, 2019).

In the aforementioned conditions, RTI—as it integrates some of the principles of integration inclusion and as it is aligned with a graduated, multilevel organization of services—is considered to enable the *horizontal flow* of services organization by creating collaborative conditions for continuity and flexibility, as well as epistemic conditions—emphasis respect for diversity and rights and emphasis on children's needs and capabilities—so as to make children's reality, as agents, the centerpiece of this organization (Desrochers et al., 2015; Whitten et al., 2012).

In the next section, I show how this approach is generally being implemented in Quebec (mainly), but also in the United States, by focusing on the reality of elementary schools. I will emphasize the promise of its horizontality (Glover & Vaughin, 2010) in teachers' discourses.

The Horizontal Way to Organize Services Figure 4 represents how services are (supposedly) "horizontally" organized through a graduated and multilevel continuum to orient child's "horizontal" placement.

The more intense the child's problem, the more resources are mobilized for handicapped and disabled children. The intensity of evidence-based interventions is adjusted to students' responsiveness. RTI, presented as a preventive framework, entails four general "processes":

1. Screening: identifying students with specific learning disabilities or other disabilities (NCRI, 2010) and students that are considered at risk of learning difficulties [RTI is also applied to behavioral problems] using tools "that are valid, reliable, and demonstrate diagnostic accuracy for *predicting* learning or behavioral problems" (NCRI, 2010, the emphasis is mine).
2. Progress monitoring: Monitor students' *responses to* educators' intervention "to estimate *rates of improvement*, identify students who are not demonstrating *adequate* progress" (NCRI, 2010, the emphasis is mine).
3. Data-Based decision making: Assessing student's progress based on "state and district benchmarks, level and/or rate" (NCRI, 2010) and using data "to compare

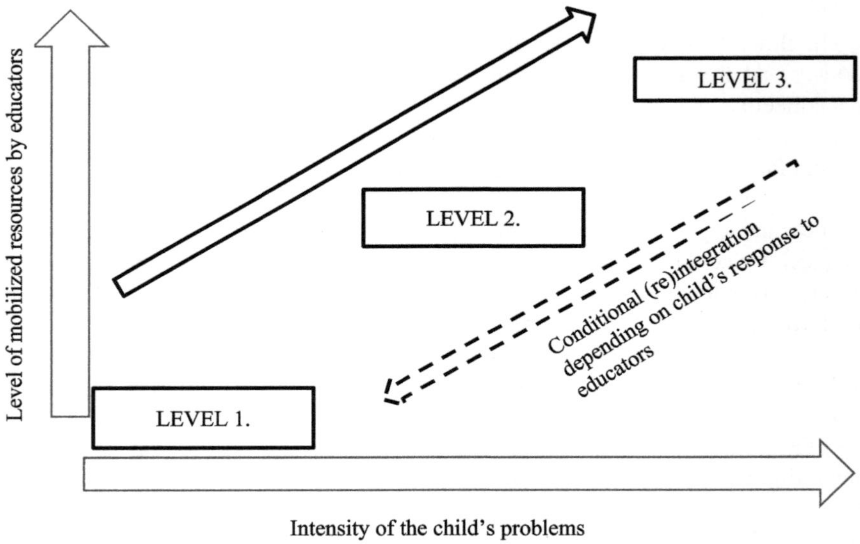

Fig. 4 The logic of child's placement in a graduated and multilevel continuum of services (by the author)

and contrast the adequacy of the core curriculum and the effectiveness of different instructional and behavioral strategies" (NCRI, 2010).

4. Implementing based on evidence-based practices and procedures referring to factors reflecting RTI framework.

What is monitored is the child's response to the intervention. "At-*risk* children *unresponsive* to classroom instruction" (Fuchs & Fuchs, 2006, p. 94; the emphasis is mine), which occurred at level 1 (more on this later), are given more intense and specialized measures. This enables "monitoring to identify students *in need of* more intense instruction" (Fuchs & Fuchs, 2006, p. 94; the emphasis is mine) based on "their degree of responsiveness" (Fuchs & Fuchs, 2006, p. 95).

Reflecting a fluid and horizontal trajectory process, RTI is considered "a form of *dynamic* assessment because its metric is change in student's level or rate of learning" (Fuchs et Fuchs, 2006, p. 94; emphasis from the authors) in that it "generates *diagnostic* information that helps practitioners make *classification* and program placement decisions (e.g., *moving* student from tier 1 to tier 2)" (Fuchs et Fuchs, 2006, p. 94; emphasis is mine). As we see in this excerpt, the mover (in a fluid trajectory) is the student. In graduated and multi-level interventions, the educator is considered the person "who 'followed' the children" (Plaisance and Schneider, 2013, p. 95, loose translation). This highlights the agency of children as movers within a fluid continuum in a horizontal fashion.

Because "inclusion" in regular classes, which are presented as a "natural" environment, is considered a right, this option is privileged. When they start schooling, all children are generally part of a regular class, except when major diagnoses have been detected. In the class, teachers implemented evidence-based practices that are *considered efficient* (generally, explicit methods that are situated in a behavioristic perspective) for the whole class (Desrochers et al., 2015).

In the first 2 years, teachers' focus is oriented toward the whole class, and they also have to detect the first signs of children's potential difficulties. In this so-called preventive approach, this can enable teachers to identify children who are at risk of developing problems. These children will be scrutinized further in the following years. Those whose problems are considered intense and stable will generally be reported to the school principal who will assign them to a special educator outside the regular class. At first, children with problems will be gathered in small groups—ideally homogeneous—for a few hours during the week outside the classroom (level 2). In the logic of the RTI approach (Whitten et al., 2012)—focusing on how children respond to educators' interventions—if children do not show significant improvement based on educators' expectations, more resources will be mobilized—and they will eventually benefit from individual and specialized services for many hours during the week.

At this point (or a bit earlier), an intervention plan is generally built for the child based on a formal diagnostic or on the way in which educators, mobilized as a team, frame the child's problems. If the problem gets worse, the child may be oriented toward a special class (level 3). In principle, if the child shows progress, as expected, he or she can progressively be reoriented toward the regular class, moving back in the distribution of services; the integration is therefore *conditional* on the child's adequacy of response to educators' interventions (the arrow oriented toward the first level in Fig. 5).

Despite the promise of horizontality associated with graduated and multilevel approaches like RTI, I hypothesize that it renders invisible vertical logic. I develop this hypothesis in the next section.

Vertical Distribution of Services

Vertical Labeling of Children and Exclusion

Generally speaking, interventions are still (and more than before) framed around the image of the typical and ideal child—a motivated, engaged, and stimulating child (especially a girl)—in relation to traditional school norms (Hansen et al., 2018; Plaisance & Schneider, 2013). Teachers feel more competent and at ease with children who fit this normative ideal; there is a "natural' flow between these teachers and children (Bergeron & St-Vincent, 2011; Tremblay, 2015). Implicitly, these children are those who embody teachers' privileged scholastic forms of socialization—ways of talking, thinking, moving and affectively regulating themselves—because of their parents' similar socioeconomic situation and other indicators of social position (Amirpur & Piérart, 2021; Black, 2011; Jackson, 2008; Kohout-Diaz, 2018; Ryan, 2006; Todd, 2012). Sharing these symbolic resources is associated with them also sharing the same (vertically) stratified social position in society. So, teachers

Multi-Level Prevention System

Primary Level

- **Focus:** All students
- **Instruction:** District curriculum and instructional practices that are evidence-based; aligned with state or district standards; incorporate differentiated instruction
- **Setting:** General education classroom
- **Assessments:** Screening, continuous progress monitoring, and outcome measures

Secondary Level

- **Focus:** Students identified through screening as at risk for poor learning outcomes
- **Instruction:** Targeted, supplemental instruction delivered to small groups
- **Setting:** General education classroom or other general education location within the school
- **Assessments:** Progress monitoring, diagnostic

Tertiary Level

- **Focus:** Students who have not responded to primary or secondary level prevention
- **Instruction:** Intensive, supplemental instruction delivered to small groups or individually
- **Setting:** General education classroom or other general education location within the school
- **Assessments:** Progress monitoring, diagnostic

Fig. 5 Multi-level intervention in RTI model (NCRI, 2010)

recognize themselves in children as the latter are representative of shared cultural resources and social positions. Under these conditions, the interaction *flows* and children *move* with ease in and across teachers' activities.

Inside the classroom, as a microsociety, *trajectories* of children's participation occur in a fluid and *horizontal* fashion, thanks to the cultural and structural alignment I have referred to. Yet, children who differ from the norms are still considered disturbing (for teachers), and difference is constructed as inferiority, despite political (and institutional) discourses' emphasis on inclusion and denormalization (Tuval & Orr, 2009).

Figure 6 presents the discrepancies between the types of children through processes of labelling and exclusion. By labeling children according to norms, mutually exclusive categories are created (good vs bad student, for example) and this leads to exclusion (Kohout-Diaz, 2018). This signals a logic of stratification:

> The attribution of lack of ability to some children and not to others is fundamental to representations of the school as structured hierarchically. Such stratification is pervasive [...] The process began with what was called "diagnosis". The formal aim of this procedure was to divide the new students (Tuval & Orr, 2009, p. 510).

The needs of handicapped and disabled children are framed in a very atomistic and deficit perspective—this is taken as a symbol of children's inferiority

Fig. 6 Child's level of unfit and exclusion (by the author)

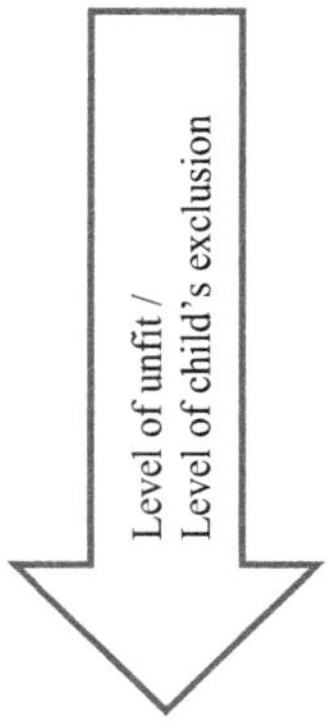

(Kohout-Diaz, 2018). Having needs is equated with having difficulties, which expresses internal and stable problematic traits. The same logic applies to the communicative capabilities which are constructed in terms of what children lack (Amirpur & Piérart, 2021). This is a negative term indicating the degree of discrepancy from a norm.

Because the disabled or handicapped child is different from teachers, he or she is perceived as frightening—this leads to erasing and negating child's difference by treating it as a deficiency, and therefore to excluding him or her (Gevrey, 2016). These children are generally silenced in by teachers and other educators and their voices are not considered when organization services and interventions for them (Mortier et al., 2011). Teachers' relation to disabled or handicapped child is mediated by their relation to child's parents' social positions (Collins & Borri-Anadon, 2021). From an intersectional perspective, disabled and handicapped children are often part of many minority groups (Collins & Borri-Anadon, 2021). This reflects a vertical logic of structural stratification.

Under these conditions, the child is leveled down through labeling processes that lead to exclusion (Fig. 6), which contrasts with the promise of horizontality (Glover & Vaughin, 2010) in a graduated and multilevel approach like RTI (Fig. 4).

Figure 7 presents this hidden verticality, which is projected into a third dimension of the initial schema (Fig. 4) of the graduated and multilevel continuum of services (such as RTI). Let me remind the reader of the "so-called" horizontal nature of this model of organization:

- Creating continuity and flexibility.
- Educators' collaboration.
- Epistemic conditions: respect for diversity and rights, emphasis on children's needs and capabilities, thereby promoting child's agency.

I have just demonstrated that these epistemic conditions are not respected in the current education system. This could have been anticipated by looking at some of the characteristics of RTI presented before. Screening children, rating their difficulties, and leveling them are intrinsically part of labeling processes that lead to

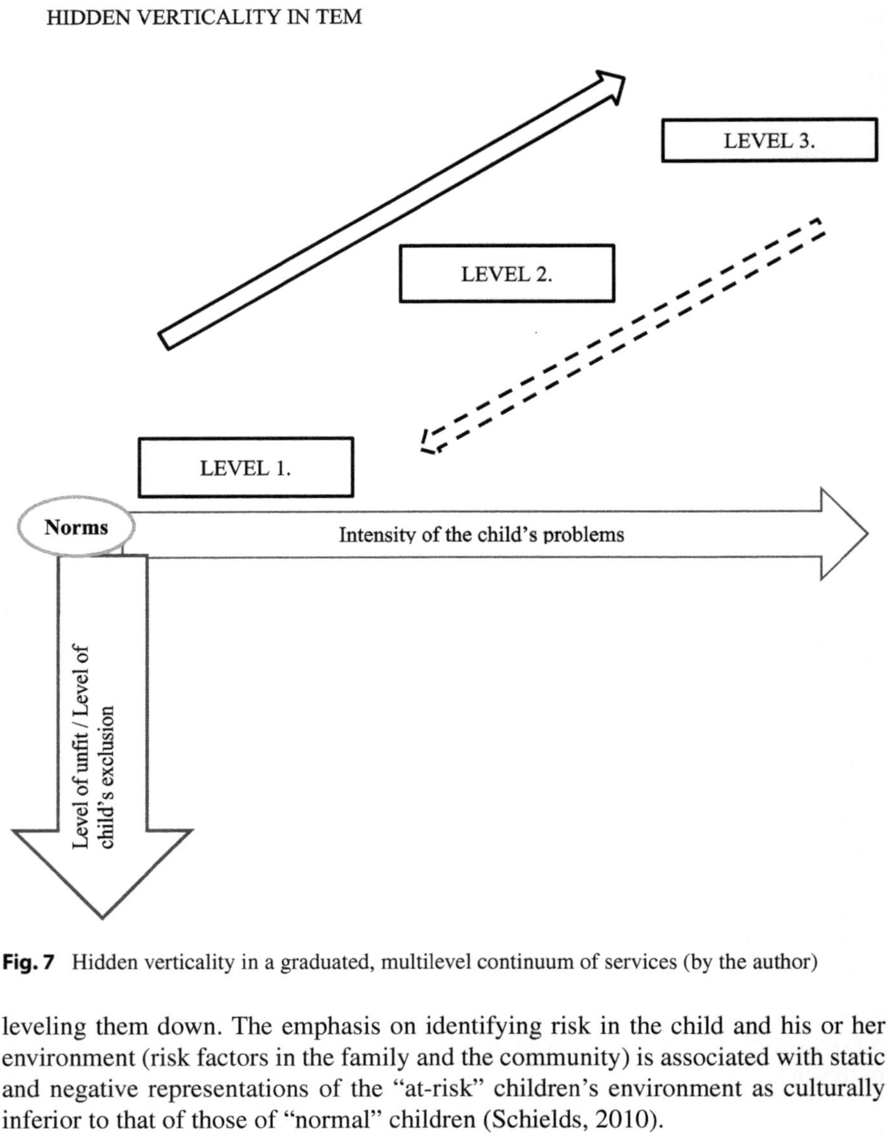

Fig. 7 Hidden verticality in a graduated, multilevel continuum of services (by the author)

leveling them down. The emphasis on identifying risk in the child and his or her environment (risk factors in the family and the community) is associated with static and negative representations of the "at-risk" children's environment as culturally inferior to that of those of "normal" children (Schields, 2010).

As mentioned before, a graduated, multilevel framework like RTI is supposed to guide educators in operationalizing an inclusion approach in which denormalization, rather than normalization, is central. As also indicated earlier, disabled or handicapped children are considered agents—that is, actors of their trajectories, their voices being heard and reflected in the organization of services—and horizontal movers. Yet, the promises of inclusion are generally unmet; services are typically framed in an integrative (the current of integration) and mainstream perspective associated with normalization rather than denormalization (Ryan, 2006). Labeling children according to a norm precisely corresponds to normalization. Horizontality applies to "normal" children, as mentioned before (more on this later).

The Educators: Horizontal Movers

Under these conditions, professionals frame and lead the intervention; they master the labeling process, thereby situating themselves in a vertical professional-client approach. In RTI, educators' own intervention is considered a test to determine children's needs (Fuchs & Fuchs, 2006). The same intervention is implemented:

> [It is] assumed that there is one appropriate method to teach such skills—as if all they needed to was find it. This approach ignores children's diversity or represents it negatively. A student who failed to acquire reading skill by the 'appropriate' teaching method within a set time limit was labeled slow or a failure (Tuval & Orr, 2009, p. 509).

As mentioned before, the RTI framework enables "monitoring to identify students *in need* of more intense instruction" (Fuchs & Fuchs, 2006, p. 94; the emphasis is mine). In this logic, special needs signal what children have to develop to meet teachers' expectations, based on school norms, as well as the measures implemented by teachers to facilitate children's adaptation (in terms of level of fit) to these norms and compensate for their deficiencies (Kohout-Diaz, 2018). To determine these needs, teachers have to monitor children, meaning identifying difficulties in children based on "their degree of responsiveness" (Fuchs & Fuchs, 2006, p. 95) to teachers' *own* interventions. Thus "different" children are in need of the teachers intervening more. Educators therefore have to monitor "At-*risk* children *unresponsive* to classroom instruction" (Fuchs & Fuchs, 2006, p. 94; the emphasis is mine). In an expert-client logic inherited from a positivist epistemology, the professional looks at how children, particularly those who are suspected of being at-risk, respond to them.

Teachers convey traditional norms that are considered universal and neutral and that are used as a tool to level down or level up children. Yet, they are attached to the symbolic universe of majority groups, like middle class families (Johannesson, 2006). In this logic, the practices in the classroom, and the expectations associated with them, are framed around the form of socialization of majority groups (Plaisance, 2013). Teachers favor children who are culturally aligned with them thanks to their families' social positions in a stratified society while leveling down and excluding the "different" children. The latter are considered in need of adults.

Teachers make minor adjustments for the "different" children—adjustments that tend to make these children's "particularities" more visible to the whole class and to exclude them by lowering their level of participation in classroom activities, conveying a restrictive conception of diversity (Nootens & Debeurme, 2010; Prud'homme et al., 2011). Teachers tend to loosen up the activities for "normal" children, by emphasizing their full participation. In this perspective, "the entire class became organized as a stratified hierarchy. This organization determined where each child was seated and what he or she would study and play with" (Tuval & Orr, 2009, p. 510).

"Normal" children's *rights* to participate in this society often manifest themselves through democratic and dialogical educational activities in which children are encouraged to express their opinions, bring their family's symbolic universe (Jackson, 2011; Todd, 2012) to the conversation by referring to quotidian family experiences and even to confront teachers' ideas. Yet, at-risk, disabled and handicapped children—integrated in the regular classroom—are generally restrictively monitored by the teacher who assigns them simple tasks in which their level of participation remains low, because they supposedly need the strict and directed framework of educators (Black, 2011). In this logic, educators' interventions have often a negative impact on children's well-being and needs and they tend to generate exclusion (Mortier et al., 2011).

I hypothesize that, at the moment when that children's cultural differences—as reflections of a social position in a stratified society—are perceived by teachers, through how children, speak, think, move, and regulate themselves differently, their difficulties become more apparent and are amplified. Then, in a monitoring process, teachers scrutinize these children by focusing on their negative responses to their interventions, on the basis of teachers' negative expectations. Children are not granted the right to participate actively, and therefore to demonstrate the variety of their competencies—which are generally situated in a cultural horizon that is kept invisible to teachers. How teachers react to these children and how they frame the intervention in a restrictive way orient teachers' representations in a way that validates their initial expectations and generates responses in children (demotivation, lack of engagement) that also validate these expectations. This is a typical Pygmalion dynamic. Minoring therefore leads to the management of specialized interventions outside the classroom, due to discrepancies that progressively accentuate, as a result of teachers' own interventions, and without them noticing their contribution to the problem that they considered internal to the child and intrinsic to his or her environment.

Figure 8 integrates the invisible horizontality of educators as movers and **presents** the hidden trajectories of disabled and handicapped children. The black dots are bifurcation points. The first bifurcation point (Level 1) is presented in three dimensions, the third dimension facing the reader's screen, to show that these children are leveled down at Level 1, when integrated in regular classroom. In two dimensions, it would give the impression that level 1 interventions place them at the top of the hierarchy, which is not the case.

Disabled and handicapped children are placed somewhere depending on:

(a) Labeling and monitoring processes—linear (children's response to educators' expectations and interventions) and *vertical* (levelling-down the "different" children) processes that are structurally and cultural grounded.
(b) The educators' interest and their (ascribed) role in maintaining a functional system through a smooth and horizontal organizational process.

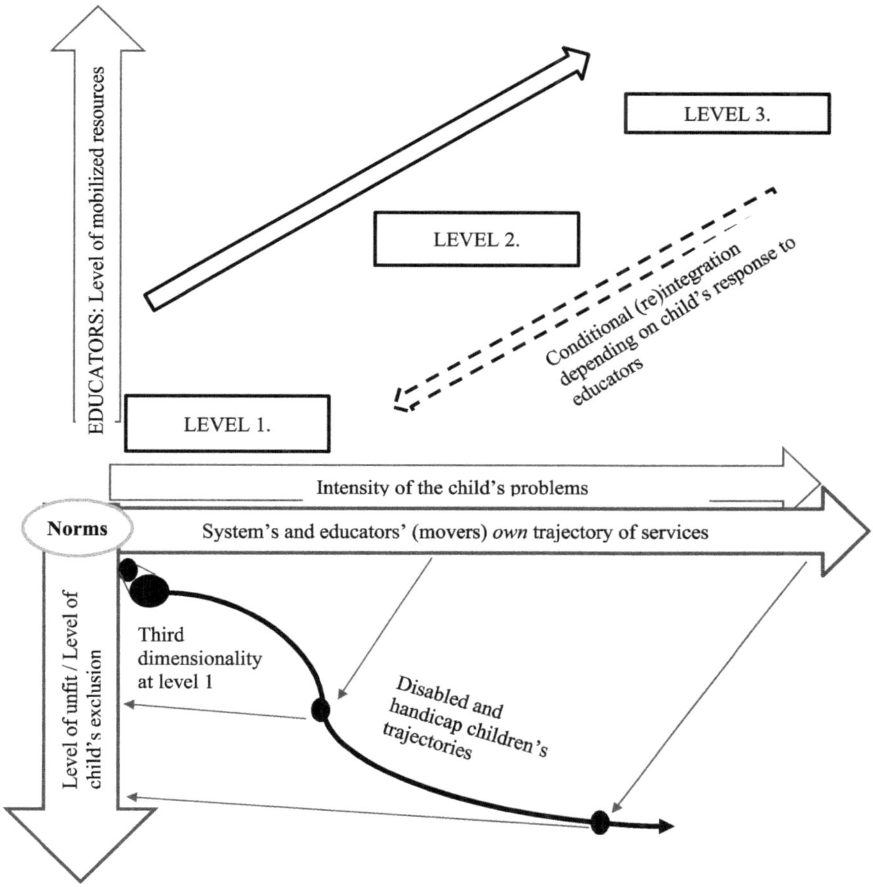

Fig. 8 The invisible dynamic of bifurcation management (by the author)

I have already addressed the first point (a). Let me add a few comments on that. When children are suspected of being "at-risk", they generally do not flow *horizontally* within classroom activities (Black, 2011) which tend to be framed in a restrictive way and used as a test (intervention as a test; NCRI, 2010) for further monitoring and exclusion. These children are generally excluded from fully participating in activities (Black, 2011). Their trajectories of participation inside the classroom therefore tend to be externally established and vertically constructed. Directing them to special services outside the classroom, and eventually to a special class, leads to more restrictive and "specialized" interventions addressing atomic and problematic aspects of learning in a restrictive frame of participation in which children apply what the experts convey and have to prove that they are progressing accordingly", in order to be eventually reintegrated full-time into "regular" classroom (Benoit, 2012, 2014; Noël, 2019; Plaisance & Schneider, 2013). Generally, the more the child progresses in this continuum, the less he or she can return, hence the unidirectional nature of his or her trajectory (Boily, 2020). The reintegration, which happens sometimes when children enter level 2 (spending a few hours outside of the classroom with a specialist in a punctual way; Beaulieu, 2016; Plaisance & Schneider, 2013; Boily, 2020), is *conditional* (rather than unconditional) to children's proving their right to benefit from this "normal" and democratic environment—normalization prevails here (Black, 2011).

Let me address now the second point (b). The placement of services is generally framed in a technicist perspective to maintain the school's social order and ensure the functionality and smooth flow of organization of school services (Black, 2011; Johannesson, 2006; Mortier et al., 2011). It is oriented by the functionalist ethos of school effectiveness/school improvement (SE/SI; Wrigley, 2013)—the goal is to make the system effective in its (linear) processes and its product, in terms of cost, academic performance, teachers' performance and school's positions with regard to national tests (Kohout-Diaz, 2018; Shields, 2010).

Within this logic, teachers and other educators use tools to preserve the equilibrium of the system, meaning that the services are allocated in a continuous fashion, like a train moving smoothly in the right direction, in order to make things work—that is, to be productive and generate high scores. Using best practices and tools in a technicist way to make things work is central to this approach. A graduated and multilevel approach like RTI, founded in evidence-based practices, appears to be an attractive option.

Thus, it is the *system's own needs* that are met in this falsely neutral approach that claims to be inclusive and universal. Intervention plans, for instance, are used to monitor children to place them in the right position in the system, to maintain order, and to serve the professional ethos. This means that professionals fight for *their right* to intervene with children with specific difficulties to delimit their zones of intervention (Prudhomme, 2018). Autistic children, for instance, are supposed to be reserved for certain specialists whose zones of intervention are outside of the regular class. Within the managerialist ideology associated with SE/SI, children are framed as clients of these services (Kohout-Diaz, 2018).

In these conditions, disabled and handicapped children follow teachers' expectations in the regular classroom, they follow the train of the system, and they follow the specialists outside the classroom. In this sense, the train *horizontally* moves and pulls the children (that are moved and pulled) as the latter are leveled down in a *vertical* continuum. Educators manage children's bifurcations by following the train—to ensure the system's functionality and maintain social order (keeping the excluded excluded)—in relation to a vertical positioning, from a top-down perspective (Fig. 8).

Yet this dynamic is hidden because political discourses, but also institutional discourses—as conveyed, for instance, in and through technicist tools—give the false impression that school is inclusive and favors equality and equity, while it generally produces the exact opposite. Neither the systemic functionality of school—how it operates to generate exclusion—nor the structural foundations of educators' representations and interventions are questioned (Vidal et al., 2021).

Thus, political and institutional discourses are ideological in the sense that they produce a false impression of democracy:

> The prevalent discourse of globalization describes young people as uniformly mobile, connected, articulate and agentic. [...] [Yet] these discourses "can create a utopian sense of open possibilities, generating new kinds of romantic constructions and youth and neglecting the materiality of lives".[1] The language of democratic participation does the same (Black, 2011, p. 468).

Social inequalities are masked by these discourses (Goyer & Borri-Anadon, 2019). Hence the tendency to hide verticality behind a discourse emphasizing horizontality. This masking effect happened in political and institutional discourses, but also in scientific discourses (Soared & Borri-Anadon, 2025) which are not so separate from policies' ideological dynamics (Valsiner, 2012). When referring to inclusion, authors often mask its vertical and structural aspect (Vidal et al., 2021). So what solution would TEM provide, as it seems to partially mask this verticality?

Concluding Remarks: The Importance of Epistemological Rotations and Tensions

In this paper, I shed light on the false impression of horizontality—as a "promise"—in the trajectories of educational services for disabled and handicapped children as a reflection of TEM's main emphasis on horizontality as well. TEM appears to be a theoretical and methodological model to conceptualize people's trajectories. As such it can be used in microdisciplinary fields like special education to understand the cultural dynamics related to the trajectories of services. In this perspective and in an abductive logic, I referred to the trajectories of services as a special case to generate theoretical hypotheses pertaining to the hidden vertical dimension of trajectories in special education and beyond that, to generalize about TEM. On the other hand, it seems that applying TEM to special education could reinforce the impression of horizontality as verticality seems to be underdeveloped in TEM.

This special case renders obvious the display of vertical dynamics that researchers often mask for ideological reasons or because they are not sufficiently highlighted enough in their theoretical models. While political and institutional discourses mask the stratified dynamics of services trajectories by creating false impression of horizontality—emphasizing the flow of children considered as active agents in the perspective of denormalization and inclusion—, researchers must be critical of their own possible blind spots. This is why I propose that readers further develop the societal aspect of TEM, considered in terms of stratification. In this respect, I propose an epistemological rotation from horizontality to verticality to shed light on the principle of heteronomy—meaning making processes are structured by vertical processes (e.g., teachers' differentiated relation to children based on the affinity of social position).

[1] This author quotes McLeod (2009, p. 280).

By creating such a rotation in relation to the specific case of special education, I have tried to highlight the other side of the coin and the operation by which horizontality is masked. This sheds light on the stratified nature of trajectories and, more specifically, bifurcations (Grossetti et al., 2009). Yet your role is to switch my analysis back to horizontality, revendicating the flow and the horizontality of the agents who can (de)construct meaning, switching from a structuralist to a post-structuralist logic.

In this logic, an agentic approach has been emerging since the 1990s in the field of special education, emphasizing the voices of disabled and handicapped children, their meaning-making processes, and their attempt, as epistemic agents, at social recognition (Schneider, 2007)—that is, how they mobilized symbolic resources to make sense of their identity in relation to others (Gevrey, 2016; Montandon, 2021). Their liminal situation—a central angle for many authors referring to TEM—is central to the (re)positioning dynamics of children who constructively manage ambivalence amidst the tensions between different values and ideologies in school (Plaisance & Schneider, 2013), that is, the same position teachers are positioned in (Boulanger & Dionne, 2019; Schields, 2010).

In this regard, teachers are not truly horizontal movers, since their actions are framed by the technicist ethos of SE/SI in a system that tends to become more centralized around governmental orientations around certain standards (Boulanger & Dionne, 2019; Schields, 2010; Thomazet, 2008). Political-ideological discourses convey a false impression of horizontality to teachers, just as teachers do with children (Gonçalves & Lessard, 2013).

Considering the agentic perspective that I just presented, *children are also horizontal movers*, in that they try to resist the imposition of meaning by educators who attempt to vertically framed children's trajectories while also trying to resist political pressure in this direction and revendicate their professional position (Atkinson, 2004; Boulanger & Dionne, 2019; Prud'homme, 2018; Hansen et al., 2018).

Thus, trajectories emerge across different ecological (cultural) layers—as advocated by TEM—and at the dynamic border of horizontality (with regard to the principle of autonomy, as opposed to heteronomy, with actors claiming their right to produce meaning) and verticality. While some recent approaches in sociology (Bauman, 2000) refer to the fluidity of forms and trajectories, new forms of hidden stratification are being highlighted in relation to the neoliberal (invisible, because ideological) structuration of public and institutional interventions (Beck, 1992). In this perspective, cultures are considered flexible and fluid while being structured by societal forces that also manifest themselves through a plurality of options and positions (Lahire, 1998, 2002, 2004). This is reflected in the study of trajectories in special education through a dynamic tension between dynamic of inclusion and exclusion (Tateo, 2025; Valenzuela, 2025) with different options being constructed by actors positioning themselves with regard to their stratified situation in schools and in relation to ideologies (Atkinson, 2004; Mauricio et al., 2025; Plaisance & Schneider, 2013). Here, *we return to the actual principles of TEM*. Yet I still integrate the vertical aspect a bit more as one part of a dynamic tension (tensegrity; Tateo & Marsico, 2013). In this respect, I frame—as meta-theoretical level—the integration of verticality in the epistemological ethos of TEM. I think that some theoretical work needs to be done in this direction.

References

Amirpur, D., & Piérart, G. (2021). « Peut-être que mon fils aurait pu rester là-bas »—Un collage ethnographique sur l'altérisation dans les parcours scolaires « singuliers ». *Alterstice, 10*(2), 33–44.

Aron, L., & Loprest, P. (2012). Disability and the education system. *The Future of Children*, 97–122.

Atkinson, D. (2004). Research and empowerment: Involving people with learning difficulties in oral and life history research. In: *Disability & Society, 19*(7), 691–702

AuCoin, A., Goguen, L., & Vienneau, R. (2011). Pas plus spécial que nécessaire: analyse des politiques scolaires de la Nouvelle-Écosse à l'égard de l'inclusion scolaire des élèves avec handicaps. *Éducation & francophonie, 39*(2), 23–49.

Bauman, Z. (2000). Living in the era of liquid modernity. *Cambridge Anthropology*, 1–19.

Beaulieu, J. (2016). Intensification des modalités de services orthopédagogiques selon les difficultés des élèves ?: La réalité d'une commission scolaire. *Revue de l'Association des Orthopédagogues du Québec, 2*, 10–17.

Beauregard, F. & Trépanier, N. S. (2010). Le concept de l'intégration scolaire...mais où donc se situe l'inclusion? D. N. Trépanier, & M. Paré (dirs.), *Des modèles de service pour favoriser l'intégration scolaire* (p. 31–56). Presses de l'Université du Québec.

Beck, U. (1992). From industrial society to the risk society: Questions of survival, social structure and ecological enlightenment. *Theory, Culture & Society, 9*(1), 97–123.

Benoit, H. (2012). Un enjeu de l'inclusion scolaire: du discours du trouble au discours du besoin. *Actes du XIIe Congrès—AIRHM Québec*, 47–53.

Benoit, H. (2014). Les dispositifs inclusifs: freins ou leviers pour l'évolution des pratiques. *La nouvelle revue de l'adaptation et de la scolarisation, 65*(1), 189–204.

Bergeron, G., & St-Vincent, L. A. (2011). L'intégration scolaire au Québec: regard exploratoire sur les défis de la formation à l'enseignement au primaire et préscolaire. *Éducation et francophonie, 39*(2), 272–295.

Bergson, H. (1998/1911). *Creative evolution*. (A. Mitchell Mineola, Trans.). Dover.

Black, R. (2011). Student participation and disadvantage: Limitations in policy and practice. *Journal of Youth Studies, 14*(4), 463–474.

Boily, É. (2020). *Étude des rôles des enseignantes, des orthopédagogues et de leur collaboration en contexte d'implantation du modèle de réponse à l'intervention en lecture au premier cycle du primaire*. [Thèse de doctorat, Université du Québec à Montréal].

Boulanger, D. (2026, in press). *Rethinking the field of school-family-community partnership in the light of the tension between autonomy and heteronomy.* Human Arenas.

Boulanger, D. & Dionne, P. (2019). Mobilisation of adult learners: Bergson, Vygotsky and beyond. Dans P. Bendassolli (Dir.), *Culture, work and psychology: Invitations to dialogue Advances in Cultural Psychology: Constructing Human Development* (pp. 199–221. Information Age Publishing.

Bruner, J. S. (1996). *L'éducation, entrée dans la culture: les problèmes de l'école à la lumière de la psychologie culturelle*..

Collins, T., & Borri-Anadon, C. (2021). Capacitisme et (néo)racisme au sein des processus de classement scolaires au Québec: Interprétations par les intervenants des difficultés des élèves issus de l'immigration. *Recherches en éducation, 44*. https://doi.org/10.4000/ree.3337

de Sousa Bastos, A. C. (2017). Shadow trajectories: The poetic motion of motherhood meanings through the lens of lived temporality. *Culture & Psychology, 23*(3), 408–422.

Desrochers, A., Laplante, L. & Brodeur, M. (2015). Le modèle de réponse à l'intervention et la prévention des difficultés d'apprentissage de la lecture au préscolaire et au primaire. Dans

M.-F. Morin, D. Alamargot, & C. Gonçalves (dirs.), *Perspectives actuelles sur l'apprentissage de la lecture et de l'écriture* (p. 290–314). Les éditions de l'Université de Sherbrooke.
Forquin, J. C. (1979). Note de synthèse—La sociologie des inégalités d'éducation: principales orientations, principaux résultats depuis 1965—2e Partie: Inégalités d'éducation et disparités socio-culturelles. *Revue française de pédagogie, 49*, 87–99.
Fuchs, D., & Fuchs, L. S. (2006). Introduction to response to intervention: What, why, and how valid is it? *Reading Research Quarterly, 41*(1), 93–99.
Gadbois, M.-È. (2020). *De l'intégration à l'inclusion : analyse de dispositifs soutenant la scolarisation d'élèves ayant des besoins particuliers* (Doctoral dissertation, Université du Québec à Montréal).
Gevrey, V. (2016). Une expérience de chercheur clinicien. Cliopsy, 15, 73–85.
Glover, T. A., & Vaughn, S. (2010). *The promise of response to intervention: Evaluating current science and practice*. The Guilford Press.
Gonçalves, G., & Lessard, C. (2013). L'évolution du champ de l'adaptation scolaire au Québec: Politiques, savoir légitimes et enjeux actuels. *Canadian Journal of Education/Revue canadienne de l'éducation, 36*(4), 327–373.
Goyer, R., & Bori-Anadon, C. (2019). Le paradigme inclusif à travers le prisme des rapports sociaux inégalitaires. *Revue des sciences de l'éducation de McGill, 54*(2), 194–205.
Gris, S. (2014). *Mouvement vers l'inclusion et évolution de la politique d'intégration scolaire au Québec: entre permanence et changement, une difficile légitimation de la mise en œuvre*. [Mémoire de maîtrise, Université de Montréal].
Grignon, C., & Passeron, J.-C. (1996). *Le savant et le populaire: Misérabilisme et populisme en sociologie et en littérature*. Gallimard/Seuil. No Child Left Behind Act of 2001, Pub. L. No. 107–110, 115 Stat. 1425 (2002).
Grossetti, M., Bessin, M., & Bidart, C. (2009). *Bifurcations: Les sciences sociales face aux ruptures et à l'événement*. La Découverte.
Hansen, J. H., Molbæk, M., Schmidt, M. C. S., Jensen, C. R., & Lassen, M. C. (2018). Approaching inclusion as social practice: Processes of inclusion and exclusion. *Journal of Educational and Social Research, 8*(2), 9–19.
Jackson, L. (2008). Dialogic pedagogy for social justice: A critical examination. *Studies in Philosophy and Education, 27*(2), 137–148.
Jackson, T. (2011). From Cultural Values to Cross-cultural Interfaces: Hofstede Goes to Africa. *Journal of Organization Change Management, 24*(4), 532–558.
Jóhannesson, I. Á. (2006). "Strong, Independent, Able to Learn More…": Inclusion and the construction of school students in Iceland as diagnosable subjects. *Discourse: Studies in the Cultural Politics of Education, 27*(1), 103–119.
Kohout-Diaz, M. (2018). *L'éducation inclusive: un processus en cours*. Éditions Erès.
Lahire, B. (1998). *L'homme pluriel. Les ressorts de l'action*.
Lahire, B. (2002). *Portraits sociologiques: dispositions et variations*. Nathan.
Lahire, B. (2004). *La culture des individus. Dissonances culturelles et distinctions*. La Découverte.
Lessard, C. (2000). Évolution du métier d'enseignant et nouvelle régulation de l'éducation. *Recherche et Formation, 35*, 91–116.
Mauricio, C., Boulanger, D., Tateo, L. & Beaulieu, J. (2025, mai 7–8). *Coloniser la voix: variation stylistique et injustice épistémique d'élèves considérés à besoins spéciaux*. [Communication présentée au *Colloque de la Chaire UNESCO DCMÉT*, ACFAS, Université Concordia, Montréal, Québec].
McLeod, J. (2009). *An Introduction to Counselling* (4th ed.). Open University Press.
Montandon, C. (2021). Formes du négatif et altérité lors d'interactions entre élèves et enseignants dans des situations d'apprentissage contextualisées. *La nouvelle revue-Éducation et société inclusives, 91*(5), 13–29.
Mortier, K., Desimpel, L., De Schauwer, E., & Van Hove, G. (2011). 'I want support, not comments': Children's perspectives on supports in their life. *Disability & Society, 26*(2), 207–221.

National Center on Response to Intervention (NCRI). (2010). *What is response to intervention (RTI)*. U.S. Department of Education, Office of Special Education Programs. https://files.eric.ed.gov/fulltext/ED526859.pdf
No Child Left Behind Act of 2001. (2002). Pub. L. No. 107–110, 115 Stat. 1425. congress.gov
Noël, I. (2019). Signaler un élève pour répondre à ses besoins particuliers ou soulager le système? *McGill Journal of Education, 54*(2), 226–244.
Nootens, P., & Debeurme, G. (2010). L'enseignement en contexte d'inclusion: proposition d'un modèle d'analyse des pratiques d'adaptation. *Nouveaux cahiers de la recherche en éducation, 13*(2), 127–144.
Plaisance, É., & Schneider, C. (2013). L'inclusion scolaire des enfants handicapés comme révélateur des tensions éducatives. *Phronesis, 2*(2–3), 87–96.
Prud'homme, L. (2018). *Instruire, corriger, guérir? L'orthopédagogie, l'adaptation scolaire et les difficultés d'apprentissage au Québec, 1950–2017*. Presses de l'Université du Québec.
Prud'homme, L., Dolbec, A., & Guay, M.-H. (2011). Le sens construit autour de la différenciation pédagogique dans le cadre d'une recherche-action-formation. *Éducation et francophonie, 39*(2), 165–188.
Ryan, J. (2006). Inclusive leadership and social justice for schools. *Leadership and Policy in Schools, 5(1)*, 3–17.
Sato, T. (2016). Introduction. From TEM to TEA: The making of a new approach. Dans T. Sato, N. Nori, & J. Valsiner (Dirs.), *Making of the future: The trajectory equifinality approach in cultural psychology* (p. 7–12). Information Age Publishing.
Sato, T. & Tanimura, H. (2016). The trajectory equifinality model (TEM). As a general tool for understanding human life course within irreversible time. In Dans T. Sato, N. Nori, & J. Valsiner (Dirs.), *Making of the future: The trajectory equifinality approach in cultural psychology* (p.21–42). Information Age Publishing.
Schimidt, D. A. T., & Tardif, M. (2022). Les valeurs de justice et d'égalité à la base de la scolarisation des EHDAA au Québec (Canada). *Periferia, 14*(2), 89–114.
Schneider, C. (2007). Être intégré, être en marge, être reconnu ? L'enfant en situation de handicap et son statut social dans une classe ordinaire. *Éducation et sociétés, 20*(2), 149–164. https://doi.org/10.3917/es.020.0149
Shields, C. M. (2010). *Transformative leadership in education: Equitable and socially just change in an uncertain and complex world*. Routledge.
Soares, R. & Borri-Anadon, C. (2025, Septembre). Willful ignorance as a lens to understand the denial of inequalities in inclusion Research. [Communication présentée à la *Conference internationale Beyond binaries. Advancing inclusion and social justice through decolonizing and critical global citizenship in education*, Allemagne].
Tateo, L. (2025, Septembre). Cultural psychology of inclusion. [Communication présentée à la Conférence internationale *Beyond Binaries. Advancing inclusion and social justice through decolonizing and critical global citizenship in education*, Allemagne].
Tateo, L., & Marsico, G. (2013). The self as tension of wholeness and emptiness. *Interacções, 24*, 1–19.
Thomazet, S. (2008). L'intégration a des limites, pas l'école inclusive ! *Revue des sciences de l'éducation, 34*(1), 123–139.
Todd, C. A. (2012). *The role of communication partners in conversations with people with learning difficulties*. [Thèse de doctorat, University of Exeter, United Kingdom].
Tremblay, P. (2015). Les attitudes d'enseignants du secondaire envers la Politique québécoise de l'adaptation scolaire. *Canadian Journal of Education/Revue canadienne de l'éducation, 38*(3), 1–29.
Trépanier, N. S. (2019). L'organisation de services multipaliers et la réponse à l'intervention: quels liens avec les modèles de services d'orthopédagogie? In Trépanier, D. N. S. (dir.), *Des modèles de service d'orthopédagogie. Une typologie et des considérations pour l'organisation des services et des interventions en contexte d'inclusion scolaire* (3e éd.), (pp. 101–118). JFD Éditions.
Tuval, S., & Orr, E. (2009). Social representations of inclusion and stratification: ethnographic research within two Israeli elementary schools. *Disability & Society, 24*(4), 503–516.

Valenzuela-Ramírez, P. (2025). Unity of opposites: an old philosophical notion for addressing contemporary problems. [Communication présentée à la Conférence internationale *Beyond binaries. Advancing inclusion and social justice through decolonizing and critical global citizenship in education*, Allemagne].

Valsiner, J. (2012). *A guided science: History of psychology in the mirror of its making*. Transaction Publishers.

Valsiner, J. & Sato, T. (2006). Historically Structured Sampling (HSS): How can psychology's methodology become tuned in to the reality of the historical nature of cultural psychology? In Straub, D. J., Kölbl, C., Weidemann, D., & Zielke, E. (Dirs.), *Pursuit of meaning. Advances in cultural and cross-cultural psychology* (p. 215–252). Transcript Verlag.

Vidal, M., Boisvert, M., Murahara, F., Borri-Anadon, C., & Beauregard, F. (2021). Les angles morts des travaux sur l'inclusion scolaire à la lumière de la théorie de la justice sociale de Nancy Fraser. *L'éducation en débats: analyse comparée, 11*(1), 7–23.

Whitten, E., Esteves, K. J., & Woodrow, A. (2012). *La réponse à l'intervention: Un modèle efficace de différenciation*. Traduit par D.D Demers. Chenelière Éducation.

Wolfensberger, W. (1972). *The Principle of Normalization in Human Services*. National Institute on Mental Retardation.

Wrigley, T. (2013). Rethinking school effectiveness and improvement: A question of paradigms. *Discourse: Studies in the Cultural Politics of Education, 34*(1), 31–47.

Zittoun, T. & Valsiner, J. (2016). Imagining the past and remembering the future: How the unreal defines the real. Dans T. Sato, N. Nori and J. Valsiner (Dirs.), *Making of the future: The trajectory equifinality approach in cultural psychology* (p.3–20). Information Age Publishing.

Imagination's Role in TEA

Music and Me: Borders, Equifinalities, and Bifurcations in the Life Trajectories of Young Musicians

Crisleane de Araújo Silva and Giuseppina Marsico

The orchestra of life (by Crisleane de Araúja Silva)

Music and Me: Borders, Equifinalities, and Bifurcations in the Life Trajectories of Young Musicians

Analogous to a piece of music, formed by notes and rests, human trajectories are composed of elements of continuity and discontinuity. The borders between these elements, whether in a musical score or in human life, integrate and provide movement to the parts of a larger systemic unit (Valsiner, 2020). This systemic unit can be understood, respectively, as music or human development.

C. de Araújo Silva (✉)
Federal University of Bahia, Salvador, Brazil

G. Marsico
University of Salerno, Fisciano, Italy

M. A. Campill et al. (eds.), *New Paths in Trajectory Equifinality Modelling*, Theory and History in the Human and Social Sciences,
https://doi.org/10.1007/978-3-032-25855-7_15

By considering borders a fundamental element of human psychological life, we question how they are embedded in a life trajectory, especially regarding decisive moments. This work analyzes the psychological repercussions of a government music program for the personal trajectories of young Brazilians.

First, we present an overview of the Brazilian Núcleos Estaduais de Orquestras Infantis e Juvenis da Bahia [State Nuclei for Youth and Children's Orchestras of Bahia; NEOJIBA] program and highlight the role of music as a catalyst for personal and social change among young musicians and the broader community. Next, we address the elements that compose different life trajectories, considering both shared and individual aspects. For this purpose, we introduce conceptual foundations such as equifinality points (EFPs), bifurcation points (BFPs), and borders to aid in understanding the present work's empirical findings and theoretical discussion.

Subsequently, we present the cases of three young participants who became musicians in the NEOJIBA program's most advanced ensemble, the youth orchestra. We discuss each participant's trajectory in an idiographic manner, drawing on the study's central concepts. Finally, we present a model that illustrates the insertion of borders as a potentially collaborative element for the trajectory equifinality model (TEM), contributing to the microgenetic analysis of BFPs.

Music as Social Development and Human Development

Music education projects have established a link between music and social development across various countries (Coppi, 2018; Costa et al., 2017; Costa et al., 2019; Hopkins et al., 2017). In Brazil, NEOJIBA aligns with this perspective by linking the teaching and practice of music to the development and social inclusion of children and adolescents facing conditions of socioeconomic vulnerability.

Considering access to musical practice as a strategy for social development, NEOJIBA is founded upon the five fundamental principles of El Sistema (Govias, 2011). These include social development, group musical activity, frequent meetings, non-selective access, and network connectivity. This means that, from the moment of their enrollment in the program (which is free of charge), the child or adolescent will find opportunities to develop musically through group or individual lessons, mentoring activities, and participation in orchestras, rehearsals, and public performances.

Transcending the social sphere, programs such as NEOJIBA offer the potential for personal transformation, contributing to the development of motor, social, educational, intellectual, and emotional skills (Cuadrado, 2019; Martins & Messias, 2018; McFerran, 2016; Varner, 2019, 2020). Conversely, the demands of building and maintaining a musical career, which requires significant dedication and sacrifice, can lead to the neglect of social and affective experiences in the life of a music professional, to the detriment of musical excellence (Richerme, 2015).

Building a musical career, therefore, requires continuous sacrifice for the sake of performance quality. This and other factors, such as constant exposure to a demanding public, increase the risk of mental illness within this professional category, particularly the development of anxiety and depression (Vaag et al., 2016). Tensions related to the profession or to other spheres of life become part of a person's narratives about themselves. These narratives tend to encompass aspects that are both mutually condescending and dissenting, constituting a heterogeneous unit (Sato et al., 2014) called the self (Marsico & Tateo, 2017).

These heterogeneous aspects of the self constitute a larger, continuous, and dynamic systemic unit (Valsiner, 2020). Human development integrates maturational, experiential, and cultural changes (Magnusson & Cairns, 1996), and our ability to attribute meaning to such events allows our life trajectories to be characterized by nonlinear narratives that express the choices we make across various situations and moments. Narrating these processes of continuity or change is, therefore, a constitutive part of human development, forming an important component of a cultural order. Culture, in turn, allows us to integrate elements such as language, beliefs, and customs that develop and change at specific times and spaces.

Human Experiences in the Face of Similar Event

It is common for human groups to experience similar events, such as marriage, paternity, and maternity, among others. These events are denominated EFPs (Sato et al., 2014) and are present in the trajectories of groups located in a specific space and time. While individuals may share a collective event, each person experiences affections and narrates their own life story based on singular records. Facing the same collective event, each individual may experience doubts or motivations related to their life history and future expectations, meaning that the possible choices or BFPs are unique and emerge from the particularities of each trajectory.

The choices that emerge from these BFPs can result in trajectory EFPs, which, in turn, can point toward new bifurcations. The narratives arising from these experiences can encompass contradictions or ambivalences, which are typical of border experiences (Marsico & Tateo, 2017).

Human experiences and their diverse meanings are organized by culture (Sato et al., 2014). Culture is formed bidirectionally through the human–world relationship. The exchange between person and environment is mediated by signs the person creates along their life trajectory (Sato et al., 2014; Valsiner, 2012). The trajectory equifinality approach (TEA) seeks to understand a complete life trajectory based on two principles: a) examining broad units, rather than isolated elements out of context; b) taking into account the tensions between past and future (Sato et al., 2014). Methodologically, the trajectory equifinality model (TEM) assists in understanding the diverse elements of continuity and discontinuity in a life cycle. This theoretical–methodological process supports the analysis of the EFPs and BFPs present in human trajectories.

Singular Events, Choices, and Tensions

Presenting themselves in an individualized manner within a trajectory, BFPs represent the possibilities the subject can visualize as potential choices for a specific moment. For example, upon finishing high school, a young person might visualize two possibilities: (1) working in a shoe store, or (2) taking a university entrance exam to get into a Music college. The elements they visualize restrict the possibilities and make them explicit, and their choice is guided by various factors, including affections, community or family expectations, and personal desires, among others.

Human choices are situated in irreversible time (Sato et al., 2014), forming a trajectory marked by decisions that may later be evaluated as either adequate or erroneous. The irreversibility of time favors the emergence of affections or tensions. Tensions are demarcated, emphasized, and encouraged by borders (Marsico, 2011, 2013, 2016), which connect and separate experiences, affections, and possibilities, among other elements of psychic life.

Marsico (2011) contends that the border space should not be understood as a conceptual void. The border that emerges in a dilemmatic situation is a field of possibilities, in which the diverse elements constituting the "inside" and the "outside" can be analyzed. The dynamism of the border, however, reminds us that these elements are not rigidly located but can shift, at times belonging to one field, at other times to another. The border space is, therefore, a perspective that connects elements from both fields, bringing them closer and, paradoxically, making them more ambiguous.

The tensions that emerge from decisive moments constitute human experience and cannot be completely extirpated. Since the human trajectory is marked by dynamic events, choices are part of everyday life, making a fertile ground for affections such as joy or regret. Furthermore, if tensions take on forms that contradict the picture the subject has constructed about themselves, they will require new significations. The emergence of new meanings in the face of tensions does not eliminate the tension but is fundamental for maintaining the integrity of the self (Marsico & Tateo, 2017).

Embedded in the human life trajectory and its psychic organization, borders can be analyzed as part of narratives that address EFPs and BFPs, offering the potential for a better understanding of emerging tensional aspects.

Method

This exploratory, idiographic, and interpretative qualitative study focuses on three young musicians from a Brazilian symphonic orchestra. The orchestra has approximately 115 members, including the woodwind, string, and percussion sections. Narrative interviews, conducted individually with each participant, were employed for data collection. Each interview was initiated by the following prompt: "Narrate your story with music, from your first contact with this art form until today."

The three young musicians chose their own pseudonyms for the purposes of this research: Salatiel, 22 years old, oboist, male; Maria, 23 years old, oboist, female; and Matryovsk, 25 years old, violinist, male. The narrative interviews were recorded in audio format and subsequently transcribed for analysis.

Analysis Procedures

The results were analyzed and interpreted from the perspective of Cultural Semiotic Psychology, utilizing the TEA (Sato et al., 2014). We established an approximation between theoretical aspects of the TEA and the concept of psychological borders in cultural psychology (Marsico, 2011, 2013, 2016; Marsico & Tateo, 2017; Valsiner, 2020).

First, the researchers defined the participants' entry into the youth symphonic orchestra as the trajectory EFP. The analysis addressed events that occurred prior to joining the orchestra, as well as those that occurred thereafter. The participants' statements were transcribed and transformed into individual maps or timelines, which demarcated the main events and statements from the participants' narratives. The data were subsequently analyzed, considering the following:

a) BFPs in the trajectories of young orchestra musicians regarding their experiences with their community of origin, with music, and with the orchestra.
b) The types of borders through which young musicians transit following their enrollment in the music education program and, more specifically, their experience as an orchestra musician.
c) Borders relationships between the various spheres of their lives.

Results and Discussion

Case 1 Salatiel—The Loneliness of Discovering the Notes and Oneself

Salatiel is a 22-year-old undergraduate student in Music, who plays wind instruments such as the oboe and the transverse flute. Born in a small town in the Brazilian state of Bahia, at the age of 15, he moved to the state capital alone after passing a selection process for the NEOJIBA youth orchestra. Salatiel has undertaken numerous tours with the orchestra in both Brazil and Europe. His weekly activities include taking university classes, performing his duties as an educational monitor at NEOJIBA, and participating in orchestra rehearsals.

Salatiel first encountered orchestral music at the age of eight, which is when he began to envision a future as a musician. He reports that, even then, there were family expectations that he would become a doctor. During this period, Salatiel began participating in a local music education project. He learned to play the transverse flute with the help of a teenage flutist, as there was no teacher for the instrument in his town.

At the age of 14, Salatiel received an oboe from the project. This presented him with the challenge of figuring out how to produce sounds and learn the notes, as there was also no local oboe teacher. Alone, Salatiel adopted the strategy of randomly experimenting with the sounds produced, identifying them as musical notes, and recording them. Six months later, he received an invitation to perform an oboe solo on a television program, accompanied by a renowned national orchestra.

At the age of 15, Salatiel moved alone to the state capital to join NEOJIBA's most advanced orchestra, despite his family's appeals for him to remain in his hometown. Upon moving to the capital to pursue a career as a musician, his relationship with his family became more distant. Loneliness emerges as a central theme in Salatiel's narrative, encompassing both the experience of living alone and the lack of familial support or recognition regarding his chosen profession, as shown by the following statement:

> It is even somewhat sad, because every time we leave the concert, there at the Theater, all the family members and friends who have come to honor you are there, you know? Then you go, greet everyone... And I... I have always been left alone.

When he was 18, Salatiel enrolled at the University to pursue a degree in Music, balancing his undergraduate studies with his responsibilities at NEOJIBA. During the interview (Fig. 1), he expressed the desire to, in the future, pursue a master's degree in the United States of America (USA). Figure 1 illustrates the main events in Salatiel's trajectory, emphasizing his relationship with music.

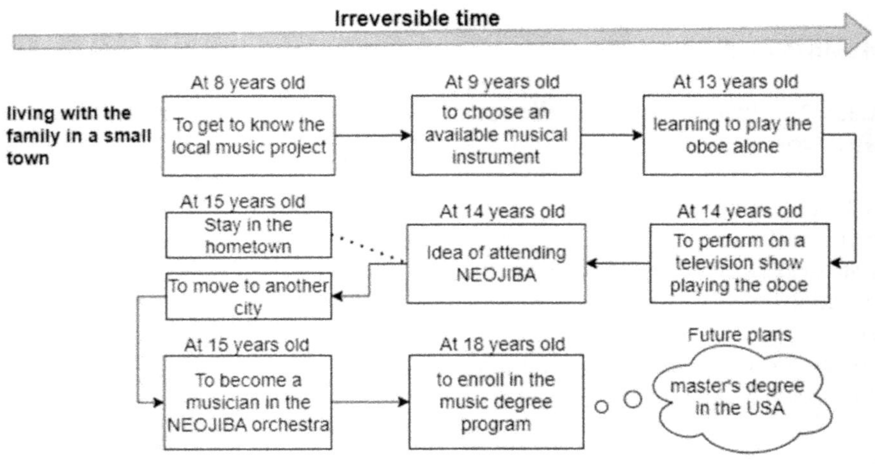

Fig. 1 Salatiel's trajectory (by the authors)

Case 2 Maria—The Happiest Person in the Orchestra

Maria is a 23-year-old pursuing a degree in Music at the university, who lives with her mother and brother. She plays the oboe, an instrument she learned through the NEOJIBA program at the age of 14. She joined the NEOJIBA youth orchestra at 19. Her weekly activities include taking university classes, working as a monitor at NEOJIBA, participating in orchestra-related rehearsals and classes, and offering free music lessons as part of an international program for low-income individuals. Maria also emphasizes her musical practice at home, with periods where she will practice for up to 12 hours daily.

Maria chose the oboe when, upon hearing it for the first time, she encountered what she called "the most beautiful sound in the orchestra." During adolescence, Maria had to balance her activities at NEOJIBA with her high school studies, while also dividing her attention between the challenges of choosing a future profession and her parents' divorce. At NEOJIBA, Maria first faced the reality of social vulnerability in Brazil when she encountered "people who were starving." The following statement illustrates Maria's surprise upon discovering this new context: "I remember that there were people who would wait for everyone to eat their snack, to see if there would be leftovers, so they could eat what remained or take it home."

Maria also had other unprecedented experiences at NEOJIBA, such as traveling around the city by herself and to other countries on her own merit. The latter was so remarkable to her that, even while unwell during a European tour, she was elected "the happiest person in the orchestra."

As she approaches the end of her undergraduate degree, Maria expresses her expectations of obtaining an international scholarship or pursuing a master's degree in Music. Figure 2 depicts the main events in her trajectory with music.

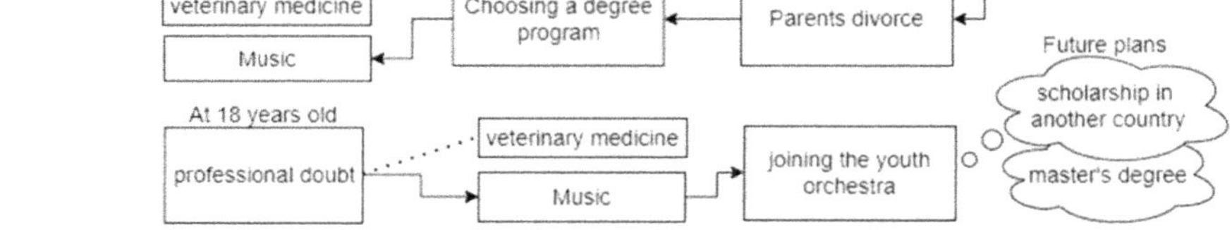

Fig. 2 Maria's trajectory (by the authors)

Case 3 Matryovsk—That Old Dream...

Matryovsk, a 25-year-old, is pursuing a degree in Music at the university, specializing in composition and conducting. He was born and raised in a small town in the state of Bahia, and moved to the state capital at the age of 21, after simultaneously passing the selection processes for both the university and the NEOJIBA youth orchestra. At NEOJIBA, he works as a violinist and a monitor. In addition to the violin, Matryovsk also plays the cello and the piano.

When he was 6 years old, Matryovsk expressed interest in a keyboard, which led his family to form a popular music band that gave public performances. Matryovsk did not like these performances but felt pressured to participate. To avoid these moments and, concurrently, tensions with his parents, he would frequently pretend to fall asleep right before the performances were about to start.

During his childhood, Matryovsk heard a violin and became enchanted with the possibility of learning that instrument. However, he could not find any violin lessons in his town, so the desire faded and was replaced by another interest: digital games. During his adolescence, Matryovsk held various jobs, including bagging at a supermarket. At 18, he had to complete compulsory military service, a period that was significant in shaping his identity as a "serious and stern" person. During this time, he remembered his old interest in the violin. In his words, he felt the awakening of "that old dream," which led him to discover the NEOJIBA program.

Despite performing publicly with the orchestra, Matryovsk reports preferring the behind-the-scenes work. Therefore, he intends to work in the future as a teacher and as a composer of soundtracks for digital games, uniting multiple areas of interest. Figure 3 illustrates the main elements of his trajectory.

Borders and Bifurcations Found in the Trajectories

It is possible to identify the coexistence of different types of borders in the trajectories of the three musicians participating in this study. These borders can intertwine in multiple situations; for example, the crossing of a geographical border can also trigger the overcoming of cultural, cognitive, and psychological borders. Next, we will analyze each of these border elements in the trajectories of the three participants, considering their potential intersection and interdependence.

Geographical borders appear numerous times in the three participants' trajectories, through migratory phenomena, movement within the city, or national and international travel. For Salatiel, traveling to another Brazilian state for the first time to perform on a television program was a decisive moment in his trajectory, as we can observe in the following statement:

> After this door that opened for me, I said: "This is really what I want, look what I achieved in such a short time! I am certain that I can achieve more; I am certain that I can dedicate myself, and I can reach where I want to be!"

On a smaller geographical scale, yet with a strong psychological impact, Maria also highlighted the experience of moving unaccompanied through the capital city where

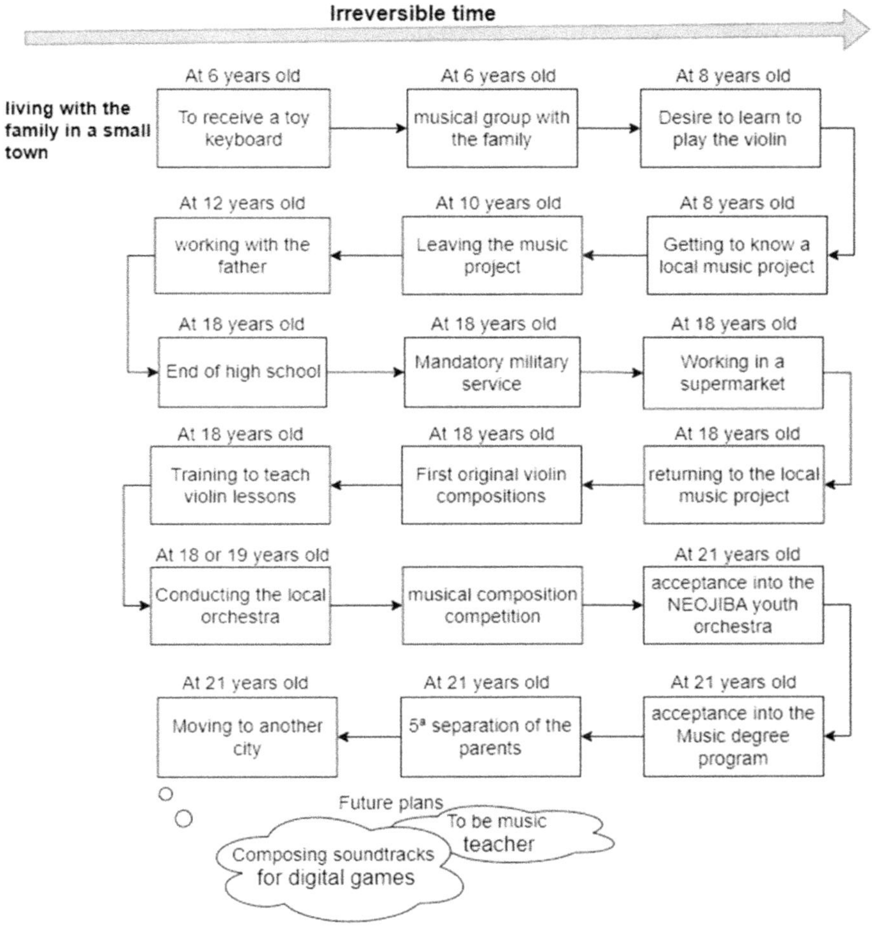

Fig. 3 Matryovsk's trajectory (by the authors)

she had always lived. Before attending NEOJIBA, she was not allowed to ride the bus alone or to travel in the city without an adult family member. Her first solo outing through the city was necessitated by her attendance at rehearsals and performances at the Castro Alves Theater, one of the country's most important theaters. The unprecedented nature of this experience is captured in the following statement:

> It was the first time I had left my familiar surroundings, you know? Because I lived right next to the school, I didn't have this issue with transportation, so it was the first time I had to leave my house, take a bus to go to a place... To perform in a theater I had never been to in my life... I was 15, 16 years old... It was impactful.

In the sphere of migratory phenomena, the narratives of Salatiel and Matryovsk converged, revealing both their similarities and their particularities. For Salatiel, his move to a different city represents an explicit connection between geographical borders and other, relational and psychological borders. For Salatiel, the crossing of geographical borders impacted the social and cultural spheres, resulting in ambiguous experiences within himself.

Thus, although he was moving closer to his dream of being a musician, Salatiel felt increasingly distant from his family, who did not value his achievements. The happiness he finds in music contrasts with the sadness he feels due to the lack of familial recognition. Despite the cultural difficulties he faces in contradicting his family's values, such as pursuing a career in medicine, Salatiel feels satisfied with his choice and dedicates himself to it fully.

The geographical distance from his family therefore also meant distancing himself from family expectations, provoking significant relational discontinuities in Salatiel's life. In turn, deciding to move to follow his great dream—and to persist with it despite the distance from his family—strengthens the view of himself that Salatiel constructs, contributing to his integrity of self.

This moment in Salatiel's trajectory yields the following BFP: "Remaining in the city of origin" versus "Moving to the capital." This BFP is located at the music/non-music border in his trajectory. In Fig. 4, the (p) music/non-music border encompasses visible possibilities of paths to be considered, in the form of a BFP.

A few years later, when old enough to take university entrance exams, Salatiel could have followed his family's expectations and chosen to pursue a degree in medicine, or he could have chosen a profession other than medicine or music. Had this moment appeared in his trajectory as a period of doubt, it could have potentially presented itself as a BFP. Although medicine appears in Salatiel's narrative as his family's desire for his professional life, he never considered this profession a real possibility, so it never materialized as a component of a BFP. In other words, the choice to become a doctor or not could have constituted a BFP at some moment in Salatiel's trajectory, had it become a personal doubt when he was choosing his profession.

In all three cases, the border that separates and unites professional possibilities includes the profession of musician and, on the other hand, professional fields such as being a doctor, a supermarket bagger, a soldier, or any other area that emerged in the "non-music" field. In the cases of Salatiel and Matryovsk, however, there were no BFPs associated with the moment of decision regarding the professional sphere.

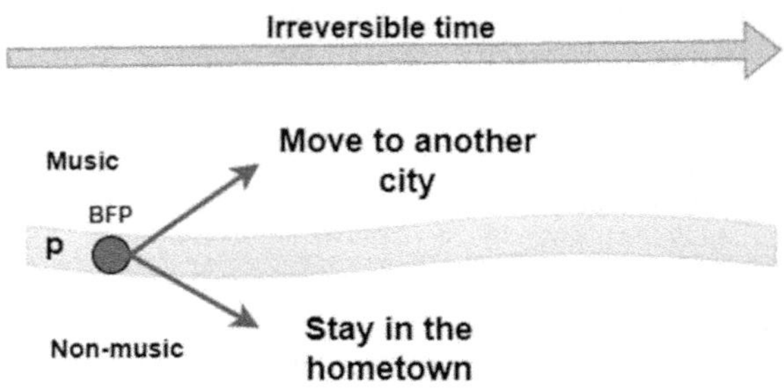

Fig. 4 Bifurcation point in Salatiel's trajectory (by the authors)

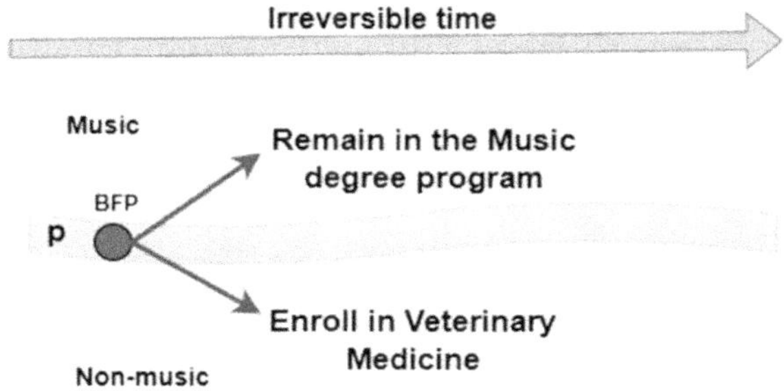

Fig. 5 Bifurcation point in Maria's trajectory (by the authors)

Both participants chose music, calling it "a dream" and expressing no doubt about their choice.

In Maria's case, however, the border that connects and unites professional possibilities revealed the following BFP: "remaining in the music program" versus "pursuing a degree in veterinary medicine." In this context, the open field of professional possibilities presented itself as a concrete doubt between two university programs, revealing a significant BFP at the music/non-music border, as illustrated in Fig. 5.

As we have seen, borders can highlight tensions that evoke suffering and conflicts, but they can also present themselves as pacified, expanding possibilities for a trajectory. This is what we observe in Matryovsk's trajectory regarding the change of city. For Salatiel, migration intensified conflicts with his family; in contrast, for Matryovsk, the geographical change alleviated his suffering related to family conflicts. Since proximity to his family caused him to suffer from arguments and separations, geographical distance helped reduce this tension.

Furthermore, Matryovsk's move to a new city occurred at a propitious moment for him to build and strengthen his autonomy, which had been so fragile during his childhood and adolescence. Having grown up under his father's impositions, Matryovsk spent his childhood and adolescence seeking ways to express his feelings, but he was neither truly welcomed nor heard. Leaving the city in adulthood or pretending to sleep as a child are events that share a common characteristic in Matryovsk's trajectory: the function of peacefully freeing him from great discomfort.

Emergent psychological changes resulting from the change of city are also observed in Matryovsk's trajectory. With imperative cultural references, such as an imposing father and military experience as a soldier, Matryovsk saw himself as an introspective and shy young man who strove to "appear serious," which led to a generalized, severe, and stern countenance. Thus, Matryovsk's demeanor hindered the possibility of communication and friendship between him and other young people while he was still in his hometown.

After moving to a new city and integrating into the NEOJIBA program, Matryovsk met people whom he judged to be serious and, simultaneously, kind. Upon realizing that it was possible to reconcile professional seriousness with friendships and kindness, he began developing new forms of interaction. Having made the

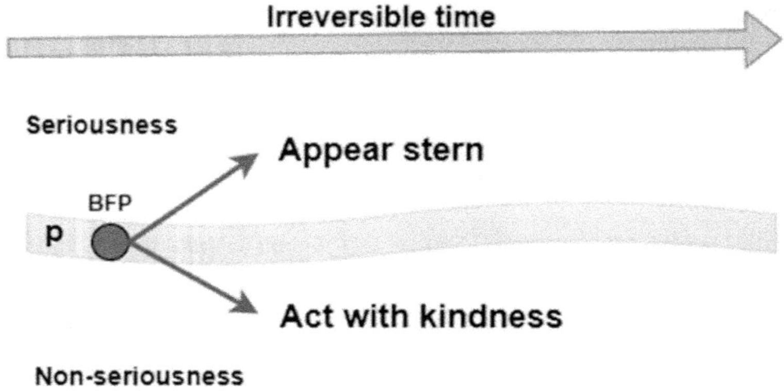

Fig. 6 Bifurcation point in Matryovsk's trajectory

decision to be kinder, he began making friends and feeling calmer and more fulfilled. The moment of doubt about how to behave toward other people reveals a significant BFP in Matryovsk's trajectory: "To present oneself as serious" versus "to act with kindness," within the "being serious"/"not being serious" border, as illustrated in Fig. 6.

The border that appears in this case could encompass various possibilities associated with both fields of seriousness and non-seriousness. Depending on the individual's significations and the culture that shapes their worldview, they might associate seriousness with sternness, but could also associate it with other behaviors, such as being punctual or responding diligently to emails related to their monitoring duties.

By moving away from the military culture and drawing closer to the emerging culture among NEOJIBA participants, Matryovsk began creating new meanings that maintained the characteristic of professional seriousness while simultaneously smiling and joking with orchestra colleagues and students. In conjunction with the cultural and contextual change, the emergent tension at the "being serious"/"not being serious" border, marked by the distancing from people, contributed to the emergence of new perspectives and significations.

As we have seen, moving between diverse spaces and cultures fosters psychological changes that facilitate new developments in a person's actions. As observed in the three cases, crossing borders can contribute to the autonomous constitution of the subject, representing a significant step for their development. Within the same border field, distinct BFPs can emerge, marked by movements of tension and relief. This dynamic and ambiguous process demands the emergence of new meanings, which must be integrated into the self (Marsico & Tateo, 2017).

Reconciling opposing spheres and relinquishing some available options at a bifurcation may result in intra- or interpersonal conflicts. The choices and meanings emerging from these conflicts can paradoxically generate both joy and sadness, as we observed in Salatiel's case. On the other hand, creating new meanings to reconcile apparently opposing poles can also contribute to the reduction of tension. This is exemplified by Matryovsk's reconciliation of his interest in digital games (which, during adolescence, opposed musical practice) with the profession of musician/composer. He brings these spheres closer by envisioning composing soundtracks for computer games.

The crossing of geographical, social, and cultural borders is therefore intertwined with numerous other aspects of life, such as relationships with music, family, and elements of a city, among others. Contact with cities, monuments, museums, or theaters of historical importance, as well as interacting with different cultures, expands possibilities and makes borders in other dimensions, such as the sociocultural and psychological fields, more flexible. Dynamically, BFPs can emerge at these borders, increasing or decreasing tensions, representing choices and experiences that are irreversibly situated in time.

Bifurcation Points and Borders: Theoretical Approaches

In the TEM, an EFP can be defined before data collection, but this does not suggest that new EFPs cannot emerge during the course of the research. On the contrary, the emergence of new EFPs is expected during data analysis, as occurred in this study. In this work, we predefined the EFP as "entry into the orchestra," but also identified other EFPs during the analysis. For example, the EFPs of family conflicts (appearing in all three narratives) and migration (appearing in the trajectories of Salatiel and Matryovsk).

BFPs are singular periods that appear as decisive moments for an individual. When faced with specific options, such as moving to another city or remaining in their city of origin, a person feels pressured to make a decision, often amid inter- and intrapersonal tensions.

Intensifying and alleviating tensions, borders encompass these specific possibilities of choice but are not restricted to them. Borders represent open fields where innumerable possibilities can emerge. Stated differently, BFPs are restricted and delimited areas of choice, with clear options, whereas borders are dynamic zones with diverse possibilities for bifurcation. Various specific BFPs can therefore emerge within a border, potentially presenting greater or lesser tension in the pre- and post-decision periods.

Figure 7 presents our proposed model, illustrating the insertion of borders as areas of tension within a human trajectory, making them an element associated with the analysis of results extracted and analyzed using the TEM. As borders are dynamic, the tension within them fosters the emergence of various BFPs, which can guide the formation of new meanings. The tension of border elements is intensified by the emergence of a BFP, the resolution of which either increases or decreases tension. The resolution of these tensions generally requires the subject to create new meanings (Marsico, 2024; Marsico & Tateo, 2017; Mele et al., 2021), thereby contributing to the permeability of the border and the integrity of the system.

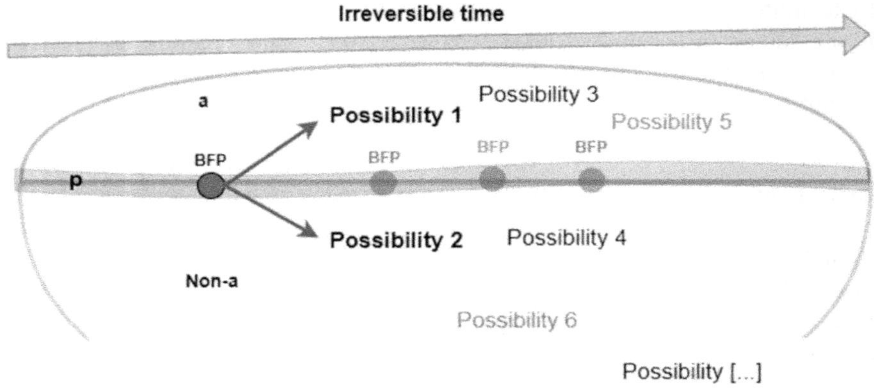

Fig. 7 Borders and bifurcations in a life trajectory (by the authors)

When borders are included in the analysis of a human trajectory, they add to the elements of bifurcation, equifinality, and irreversible time, thereby enhancing the analytical possibility of understanding the tensions that precede or follow the emergence of EFPs. As dynamic and open fields of possibilities, borders can be understood as zones of tension, from which various possibilities for choices or bifurcations can arise. In this way, they contribute to the microgenetic analysis of processes of tension, bifurcation, signification, and consequently, of human development.

Final Considerations

While the trajectories of young people engaging with music may start with a similar element, other EFPs emerge throughout the narratives and become evident from the detailed analysis of each trajectory. In this study, in addition to the EFP initially defined by the researchers (entry into the orchestra), we observed other events shared by the participants.

We observed several EFPs in the trajectories of Salatiel and Matryovsk, such as: a) originating from small towns in the interior of the state; b) having participated in local music projects in their hometowns; c) the need to live alone in the state capital to participate in the NEOJIBA orchestras; d) sharing housing with other students they met in the capital. Despite these convergences, as advocated by Sato et al. (2014), the analysis also revealed that their narratives present singular characteristics.

Another element that emerged from the trajectories of the three participants is that of geographical borders, which appear to facilitate important psychological processes. Geographical borders mobilize the emergence and expansion of processes of discovering new social and cultural contexts or strengthening autonomy.

In all three narratives, geographical borders appeared as migratory phenomena, as movement within the same city, and as national or international travel.

Regarding shared elements, the NEOJIBA scholarship appears in all three narratives. In the trajectories of Salatiel and Matryovsk, the stipend they received from the program made moving to and staying in the state capital possible, thereby enabling the young men to dedicate themselves to the program and the university. In Maria's case, the scholarship also proved significant, yielding a satisfying professional return even during adolescence. Associated with this, participants shared elements of autonomy, represented by aspects such as having their own work, their own dreams, and their own choices.

On a more singular register, tensions, doubts, and decisions are crucial elements for understanding an individual's psychological dynamics. In this sense, narratives about the same EFP can present distinct—perhaps opposite—affections and meanings. Stated differently, a teenager who chose to be a musician against his parents' wishes and a teenager whose mother suggested she enroll in a music project share an evident EFP (having been selected for the youth symphonic orchestra), but they may present very different affections and narratives about "becoming a musician."

The differences between narratives express the contextual and psychological distinctions between people, and can also represent differences between moments within the same trajectory. Becoming acquainted with other sociocultural contexts through new environments or perspectives can give rise to new borders, especially those of a psychological nature. In this way, psychological processes of signification or of creating autonomy can be visualized within a trajectory. By delimiting and expanding possibilities, the tension arising from border elements can be crucial for the emergence of new perspectives on oneself and the world (Marsico & Tateo, 2017).

The model we propose in this chapter highlights borders as a field to be considered in the emergence of BFPs within a trajectory. Integrating the border fields approach with the TEM can assist us in the microgenetic comprehension of a trajectory, especially regarding the emergence of bifurcation processes. Possessing an ambiguous and paradoxical nature (Marsico & Tateo, 2017), borders have the potential to bifurcate in distinct directions, thereby increasing or attenuating tension within the self.

The consideration of a life trajectory as a dynamic and irreversible process in time—where contexts and people modify themselves bidirectionally—highlights changes and psychological elements as key points for understanding human development. Combining the concept of borders (Marsico, 2011, 2013, 2016, 2024) with the TEA and the TEM provides adequate theoretical and methodological resources for a research and analysis process that addresses psychological aspects in a profound and contextualized manner.

Acknowledgments Giuseppina Marsico acknowledges Federal University of Bahia, Brazil (Edital Professor Visitante/PVB/UFBA and CAPES-PRINT for the financial support).

References

Coppi, A. (2018). "El Sistema" e il "Coro de manos blancas": Modelli educativo-musicali tra realtà consolidate e scenari futuri. *Musica Docta, 8*(1), 81–100. https://doi.org/10.6092/issn.2039-9715/8840

Costa, J. A., Mota, G., & Cruz, A. I. (2017). O Projeto Orquestra Geração: A duplicidade de um evento musical/social. *Sociologia, 33*, 135–154.

Costa, J. A., Cruz, A. I., & Mota, G. (2019). Between adoption and adaptation: Unveiling the complexity of the Orquestra Geração. *Research Studies in Music Education, 41*(3), 293–309. https://doi.org/10.1177/1321103X18773824

Cuadrado, F. (2019). Music and Talent: An experimental project for personal development and well-being through music. *International Journal of Music Education, 37*(1), 156–174. https://doi.org/10.1177/0255761418794720

Govias, J. A. (2011). The five fundamentals of El Sistema. *Canadian Music Educator, 53*(1), 21–23.

Hopkins, M., Provenzano, A. M., & Spencer, M. S. (2017). Benefits, challenges, characteristics and instructional approaches in an El Sistema inspired after-school string program developed as a university–school partnership in the United States. *International Journal of Music Education, 35*(2), 239-258. https://doi.org/10.1177/0255761416659509

Magnusson, D., & Cairns, R. (1996). Developmental science: Toward a unified framework. In R. B. Cairns, G. H. Elder, & E. J. Costello (Eds.), *Developmental science* (pp. 7–30). Cambridge University Press. https://doi.org/10.1017/CBO9780511571114.003

Marsico, G. (2011). The "non-cuttable" space in between: Context, borders and their natural fluidity. *IPBS. Integrative Psychological and Behavioral Science, 45*(2), 185–193. https://doi.org/10.1177/1354067X15623020

Marsico, G. (2013). Moving between the social spaces: Conditions for borders crossing. In G. Marsico, K. Komatsu, & A. Iannaccone (Eds.), *Crossing borders: Intercontextual dynamics between family and school* (pp. 361–374). Information Age Publishing.

Marsico, G. (2016). The borderland. *Culture & Psychology, 22*(2), 206–215. https://doi.org/10.1177/1354067X15601199

Marsico, G. (2024). *Cultural psychology of bordering process*. In J. Valsiner & M. Tamm (Eds.), *Breakthroughs in cultural psychology* (pp. 229–249). Tallinn University Press.

Marsico, G., & Tateo, L. (2017). Borders, tensegrity and development in dialogue. *Integrative Psychological and Behavioral Science, 51*(4), 536–556. https://doi.org/10.1007/s12124-017-9398-2

Martins, D. A. F., & Messias, P. Q. (2018). Motricidade humana na educação musical. *ouvirOUver, 14*(1), 168–180. https://doi.org/10.14393/OUV22-v14n1a2018-12

McFerran, K. S. (2016). Contextualising the relationship between music, emotions and the well-being of young people: A critical interpretive synthesis. *Musicae Scientiae, 20*(1), 103–121. https://doi.org/10.1177/1029864915626968

Mele, E., Español, A., Carvalho, B., & Marsico, G. (2021). Beyond technical learning: internship as a liminal zone on the way to become a psychologist. *Learning, Cultural and Social Interaction, 28*(1). https://doi.org/10.1016/j.lcsi.2020.100487

Richerme, L. K. (2015). Who Are Musickers? *Philosophy of Music Education Review, 23*(1), 82–101. https://eric.ed.gov/?id=EJ1066102

Sato, T., Yasuda, Y., Kanzaki, M., & Valsiner, J. (2014). From describing to reconstructing life trajectories: How the TEA (trajectory equifinality approach) explicates context-dependent human phenomena. In B. Wagoner, N. Chaudhary, & P. Hviid (Eds.), *Cultural psychology and its future: Complementarity in a new key* (pp. 93–105). Information Age Publishing. http://www.infoagepub.com/products/Cultural-Psychology-and-Its-Future

Vaag, J., Bjørngaard, J. H., & Bjerkeset, O. (2016). Symptoms of anxiety and depression among Norwegian musicians compared to the general workforce. *Psychology of Music, 44*(2), 234–248. https://doi.org/10.1177/0305735614564910

Valsiner, J. (2020). Where occidental science went wrong: failing to see systemic unity in diversity. *Psychology and Developing Societies, 32*(1), 7–14. https://doi.org/10.1177/0971333620903880

Valsiner, J. (2012). *Fundamentos da psicologia cultural: mundos da mente, mundos da vida. Artmed Editora.*

Varner, E. (2019). Holistic development and music education: Research for educators and community stakeholders. *General Music Today, 32*(2), 5–11. https://doi.org/10.1177/1048371318798829

Varner, E. (2020). General music learning is also social and emotional learning. *General Music Today, 33*(2), 74–78. https://doi.org/10.1177/1048371319891421

Mirror Pathways: Life Trajectories in Research and Fiction

Namrataa Mamgai, Punya Pillai, and Mila Tuli

> *"Gaut (Gohat), tor dal chula maan dhairik,*
> *Kuterī khuldī chhuyon kī,*
> *Dagda baithīk, lambī rāti kī,*
> *Katdī chhuyon mān, tū bhī ai jā kachhiṛī mān,*
> *Hyund mainon mān merā gaon mān."*
> *Chamola,* 2013, *p. 15*

Devprayag confluence (Source: https://himalayashelter.com/rivers-of-uttarakhand)

N. Mamgai (✉) · P. Pillai
Department of Human Development and Childhood Studies, Lady Irwin College, University of Delhi, Delhi, India

M. Tuli
Institute of Home Economics, University of Delhi, Delhi, India

M. A. Campill et al. (eds.), *New Paths in Trajectory Equifinality Modelling*, Theory and History in the Human and Social Sciences,
https://doi.org/10.1007/978-3-032-25855-7_16

Introduction

Chamola's (2013) couplet vividly encapsulates the deeply nostalgic essence of Uttarakhand's rural winter traditions and storytelling culture invoking communal warmth. Though not confined to any particular season, storytelling remains an enduring cultural root of the region woven through centuries and decades, and shared by people of all ages, genders, and castes. The couplet describes a quintessential scene from rural Uttarakhand which can be translated as local lentils like gaut (horsegram) and tor dal simmering patiently on the chulha (wood-fired stove), the rhythmic grinding of spices in a kuterī (stone grinder), and people of my village are seated by the hearth through the long, quiet nights of Hyund (the cold season). The folk stories involved in such gatherings are not just solitary monologues but communal performances, with every listener contributing *hungra* (interjections) to steer the storyteller further into the story. Each tale ends with the soothing refrain: *"Kaath kaani, raat byaanee"* (With tales and stories, the night slips away). Regardless of the place these folk stories are told (indoors or under open skies by the fire), they help in preserving memory, laughter, sorrow, and deep-seated wisdom acting as, in the language of Trajectory Equifinality Approach (TEA), the equifinality points in Uttarakhand's cultural psychology. The shared tradition of folk storytelling highlights how despite the historical, social, generational, and environmental diversities communities somehow arrive at shared cultural expressions and values. The Devprayag confluence of rivers is a symbolic embodiment of collective trajectories of the people of Uttarakhand; their histories, identities, cultural understandings, and sacred rituals finding common ground.

Folklore is distinguishable from other literatures as a form of oral performance in an intimate face-to-face setting for a communal event (Arpad, 1975). It is prone to re-creation and variations, yet it takes into its fold a certain unconscious collective structure, and representations publicly owned, diffused with memory, and constructed in the moment. Bascom (1953; 1965) describes folklore as a form of collective consciousness transmitted across generations in diverse forms like stories, songs, dance, or poems often accompanied by gestures or assistive instruments. More formally speaking, folk literature is a historical phenomenon comprising intrinsic and essential content with a shared origin or experiential structure, passed down through informal channels and continuously evolving over time (Stavrou, 2015).

Folk tales as a narrative subset of folk literature are not mere reflections of events but vessels of raw truth, embodying the rhythms of fear, joy, faith, and values that follow the trajectories of real lives. Like many indigenous groups of India, the people of Uttarakhand possess a collective intellect and identity shaped not only by visible realities but also by intuitive memory and feeling. Their folk narratives preserve unrecorded emotions, events, lives, and communal lessons, offering a vital lens for cultural exploration. As Pant (2024) explains, *lok*, the Hindi translation for the word "folk", refers not only to people in a demographic sense but to their lived experiences, beliefs, and philosophies. Thus, as represented in Fig. 1, folk narratives serve both as historical archives and the evolving mirrors expressed in the form of performances or art in generational transmission translating with collective identity.

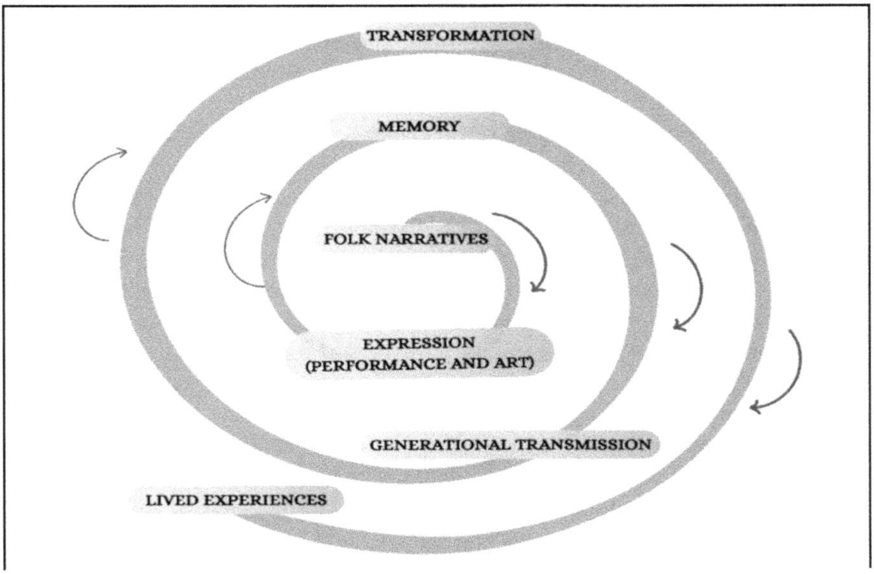

Fig. 1 Spiral trajectory of Folklore transmission and equifinality (by the authors)

Hence, it can be asserted that a people's history resides in their folk narratives (Woodson, 2012) which simulates into real life scenarios. We attempt to open realms of folk indigenous narratives from the state of Uttarakhand by situating it within its cultural antiquities and evolving modes of knowledge transmission. This analysis is a result of deep engagement with several vernacular texts, oral recitations, and regionally embedded idioms of storytelling, often preserved in Hindi and local dialects. The wide insights presented by these narratives foster their continued transmission in domestic, communal, and ritual contexts presenting nuanced textures of regional epistemologies that remains selectively explored in current scholarship. This foundation facilitates not just ethnographic depth but also culturally assimilated paradigms for assessing life trajectories, particularly when analyzed through frameworks such as the Trajectory Equifinality Approach (TEA).

Folk Culture of Uttarakhand: Historical Roots and Regional Identity

Uttarakhand's cultural identity is layered and dynamic with roots in the ancient treatises of *Haimavat or Madhya Haimavat* (Vedic period), Uttarkuru (Aitareya Brahmana), *Uttarpanchal* (Upanishadic Period), and *Uttarapath* and *Karupath* (Panini's Ashtadhyayi), marking centuries of evolution (Hāṇḍā, 2002; Sati & Litt, 2023; Pokhariya, 2021). The identity of the inhabitants is shaped by the historic transformation due to cultural exchanges and migrant practices from various regions over centuries, Punjab, Rajasthan, Kannauj, and South India, among others. This results in a folk scenario that is not static at all but a living, evolving continuum (Pokhariya, 2021).

Along with geographic division, Uttarakhand is linguistically divided into different regions as well, each with its own dialectal variations. Few of those dialects being Kumaoni, Garhwali, Jaunsari, and Rongpa, each embedded with unique oral traditions and socio-cultural metaphors (Channa, 2005; Rani & Sharma, 2007; Sahu, 2023). These widely used oral instruments are not formulated from a well-organized or structured system; they rather possess unique phonetics, words, and expressions for each emotion, experience, and observation. Linguistic devices such as idioms and proverbs are so seamlessly woven into daily speech that they spontaneously emerge in conversations navigating several contemporary challenges such as migration, education, social mobility, and so on.

For instance, a commonly used proverb "*Maduvak jas balaud chha, mains kain dhanauk jas balaud hun chha*" (One should not be like the panicles of finger millet, but like the drooping panicle of ripened rice) signifies the value of softness, malleability, and adaptation. Another one "*Jyaath jyu boli ke maarni, kamarai todni*" (An elder doesn't merely scold; their words can be harsh enough to break one's back) emphasizes the critical role of empathy and responsibility in nurturing the next generation (Pant, 2024). Similarly "*Raaj karan aapan des, bheekh maangan pardes*" (to rule in one's own country and beg in a foreign land) represents the emotional dilemma of migration, where simple living in a familiar place is more dignified than prosperity in a foreign land; and "*Jhak maar jhoongar khai, saaj ni khai, baasi khai*" (Out of sheer helplessness, one ends up eating coarse barnyard millet, not when it's fresh, but when it's stale) critiques delayed wisdom and false pride often surfacing at the cost of dignity and well-being (Pokhariya, 2021). All such customarily invoked proverbs reflect shared intergenerational experiences culminating in wisdom passed down to this day serving as the equifinality points where individual and collective histories converge. Through such sayings, folk communities articulate internal conflicts, moral choices, and resilience in adversities, making these folk expressions crucial bifurcation points within personal trajectories.

While Uttarakhand possesses a rich linguistic and cultural heritage, any comprehensive exploration would be incomplete without addressing its vibrant spiritual epoch. This landscape is marked by a deeply reciprocal relationship between devotees and local deities (*devtas*). Often referred to as *gram* (village) or *kul* (intergenerational-familial) or *isht* (revered and loved personal god or chosen deity) *devta*, these deities permeate within the natural landscape of the state (Sati & Sati, 2020). Devtas such as *Nanda Devi* (Goddess of a mountain by the same name), *Haru Saim* (village guardian deity), *Gwél* (God of Justice), and *Bholanath* (an incarnation of Lord Shiova), are not distant cosmological entities for the devotees but the central power beings governing their everyday life.

Locally they are perceived in forms of Devangi (divine figures like Shiva and Vishnu), and *Bhootangi* (spirits, ancestors, and local supernatural beings)

(Pokhariya, 2021). Where many of them, once human figures, are now revered as divine entities due to bifurcation points (BFPs) in their life trajectories involving rigorous discipline or spiritual quests symbolizing obligatory passage points (OPP) that ultimately leads to Equifinality Points (EEPs) of divinity (Arya & Mehta, 2019; Bisht, 2013; Budhwar, 2010; Kumar, 2023; Lohani, 2019). Apart from classical gods, many deities are reimagined Vedic gods like *Nāga* (serpent God), and *Yaksha* (male guardian spirit) in paintings with solar motifs, pointing us towards the direction of ancient traditional tantric influences, later further enriched by Buddhist aspects of worship (Barthwal, 2018). Mystical rituals like *Jaagar* are used to create a living interface between the human and these divine counterparts through drumming and folk chantings (Sati & Litt, 2023). Such rituals are comparable to similar global traditions like *Bhuta Kola* (Karnataka), *Zar* (Africa and other Middle East), *Sanghyang Dedari* (Indonesia and Bali), and *Wáátawa / Wáánaanú* (Chukk, Micronesia) underscoring the universality of these narrative trajectories (Al-Shahi, 1984; Dobbin & Hezel, 2011; Prasad, 2024; Putri, 2017). The TEA analysis proves useful, as these vibrant tales, deeply integrated into the environment and everyday lives of the people and can be employed to identify both similarities and differences. The Trajectory Equifinality Approach (TEA), first proposed in 2004 (Sato et al., 2009, 2016), provides a robust framework for analyzing how such narrative maps offer varied entry points in the interplay of real and imagined life (Masaki, 2025). TEA's Trajectory Equifinality Model (TEM) distinguishes between actual life courses (representing lived pathways "what happened") and imagined or counter possibilities ("what could have also happened"). The model further helps identify Equifinality Points (EFPs) where different trajectories converge, Bifurcation Points (BFPs) where they diverge, and Obligatory Passage Points (OPP) marking the culturally mandated rites and transitions. Historically Structured Sampling (HSS) marks the diversity of pathways of individuals and groups over time, and the Three Layer Model of Genesis (TLMG) scaffolds the common beliefs with the multiplicity of influence on psychological phenomena over time, further allow explorations on the grounds of plurality and mirrored realities embedded in these narratives (Masaki, 2025).

Many such mirrored realities integrating the pluralities of the relationship between folk beliefs and real life are further illustrated in the form of vivid tales of deities. Apart from the abstract conceptualization the deities are treated more like family members bestowing blessings on respect and punishment on neglect. One such instance being, the 2013 floods of Uttarakhand, which are popularly attributed to the relocation of the Dhari Devi idol. The relocation created a bifurcation point (BFP) within the assimilated respect among the community members about devi's chosen place of worship. This resulted in communal misfortune, only rectified by returning the idol to its original place (an EFP restoring cosmic order) (Berti, 2024). Situated along the Alaknanda River in Dhari village, the goddess is believed to represent the upper torso of Kali, while her lower half resides in Kalimath, another revered Shakti Peeth or Seat of Power, signifying the cosmological duality of the divine. The trajectory towards communal reverence when TEAfied (Fig. 2) is similar to many divine figures all over India. It follows a pathway of mystic origin, hard

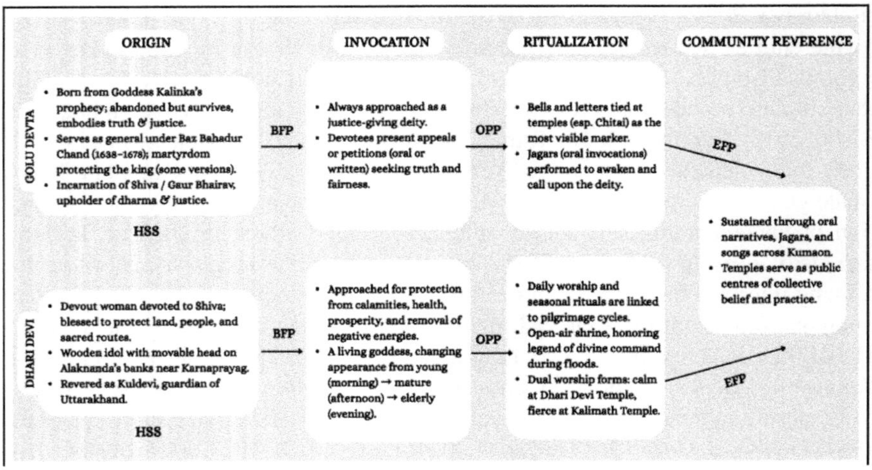

Fig. 2 Three-layer model of genesis of two deity tales of Uttarakhand (by the authors)

penance, communal invocation, and ritualization ultimately leading to divine acceptance within communities. Her dual nature depiction in Dhari, and esoteric persona in Kalimath mirror the tantric and maternal aspects of Kali, another divine figure embedded in Indian mythology (Ramani & Alekya, 2019).

Some might dismiss the incident as mere coincidence but in a time of climate crises, the Dhari Devi narrative acts as a symbolic protest, asserting the sanctity of cultural landscapes against the forces of unchecked modernization. Such folk narratives surrounding deities have a crucial role to play within the mental and emotional wellbeing of the people as well. As Kharkwal (2023) argues, indigenous practices, which are often marginalized in mainstream psychiatry, serve as crucial tools for culturally grounded responses against emotional and psychological distress (Kafal tree live, 2025a, b). Temples such as that of Golu Devta (Gwel, a prominent local deity) act as sacred loci where followers appeal to intertwine distress with the pursuit of wellbeing among devotees. Much like the tales of collective faith surrounding Dhari Devi, the mystical birth of Gwel, his invocation within community, the ritualization of his worship and eventual elevation to cosmic divinity follows a similar pattern. The genesis of both of their tales and ultimate collective folk identity can be understood by Fig. 2. Often revered as the god of justice, Golu devta's temple draws thousands each day, where devotees submit written petitions and even legal documents, in hopes of divine adjudication and redress. Upon fulfillment, they offer gratitude with religious processions, brass bells, and embellished red veils. It is believed however the negligence of such acts of gratitude attracts legal or domestic troubles as a reminder to complete the progression to restore order (EFP) (Budhwar, 2010; Kumar, 2023; Malik, 2016).

Even several of the shared cultural accounts associated with supernatural entities like spirits (*Masaan, bayaal, or Upari hawa*), witches (*chudails*), and fairies (*anchari*, *kinchari*) follow trajectories marked by multiple BFPs such as premature death leading to a restless existence (EFPs) and emotional tragedies.

An illustrative folk tale in this context is of *Jeetu Bagadwal*, who was believed to be claimed by Anchari (forest fairies). The narrative follows a typical trajectory: Jeetu, despite being warned by elders to not play flute atop a mountain (BFP), draws the attention of the *Anchari* and is chosen by them. With respectful acknowledgment yet he calls upon his patron deity, Bhairav devta (OPP) for help. However, unable to escape his fate (irreversibility of actions), on the sixth day of Ashaaadh (June–July), he bids farewell to his loved ones and vanishes (EFP). In many versions, Jeetu later becomes a local protective spirit (referred to as "ksehtrapal") revered during Asaadh (similar to Gwel & Dhari devi) also known as *Ropai* (paddy planting) season through rituals and dance (Khanna & Bhairav, 2023). Even though somewhat primitive such tales give rise to precautionary practices like avoiding certain colors in isolated areas and inform rituals like exorcisms through mantras, sacred threads, and samshan (cremation ground) poojas which are enacted in everyday life to restore balance (Pande, 1993). Narratives as such, are not merely bedtime stories for children, but foundational pillars of diverse belief systems that flourish in the Himalayan state of Uttarakhand.

Folkloric Expression and Transmission

Folkloric expressions embedded in narratives and art forms function both as mode of transmission for generational wisdom and creative reimagining of collective memories. Through the lens of TEA, Uttarakhand's folk tales can be perceived as more than entertainment or moral instructions, but as avenues of restoration for traditions for continual renewal. Rituals, songs, narratives, and symbols are the embodiment of both fear and respect toward unseen forces. Uttarakhand's spiritual world is mirrored in its oral epics presenting the real paths of farmers, pilgrims, warriors, and healers, identifying strategies for resistance against caste hierarchies, gender norms, and ecological challenges. Although a precise classification would be insufficient but for the sake of general understanding the nuanced folkloric traditions, expressions of local wisdom, and collective imagination can be elaborated as per their medium and nature of transmission (Fig. 3) (Pant, 2024; Pokhariya, 2021; Rawat, 2023).

1. **Oral-Verbal Expression (Vāṇīvilās-parak)**

Original forms preserved and shared through oral traditions, oral-verbal expressions. These were later collected and documented in narrative, lyrical, and musical forms.

A. **Narrative (Kāthātmaka):** Includes structured tales passed down through storytelling, often with moral, mythological, or emotional significance such as:

- **Dharmakathā:** Tales of cosmology, nature, moral order, human civilization, and divinities.

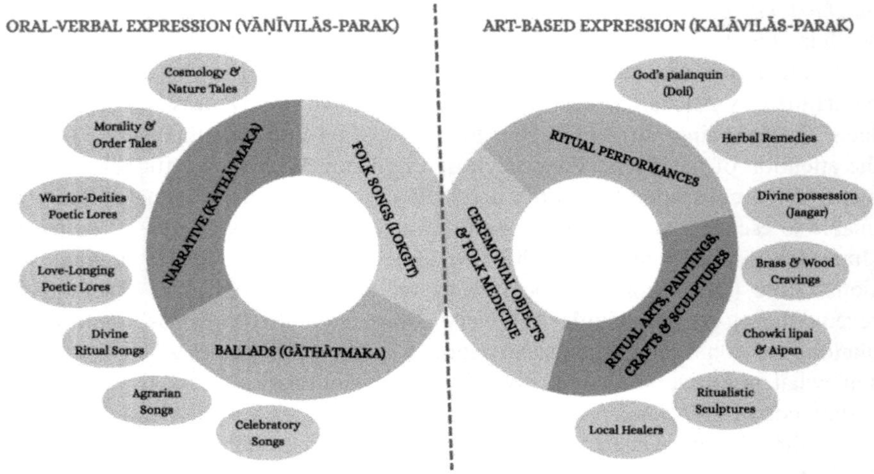

Fig. 3 Classification of folkloric expressions by transmission mode (by the authors)

- **Lokkathā:** Stories of gods, demons, folk heroes, and lovers.
- **Lokkahānī:** Didactic tales, humorous narratives, ghost stories, children's tales, and lyrical storytelling, for entertainment combined with moral instruction. These reflect both everyday wisdom and supernatural imagination.

B. **Ballads (Gāthātmaka):** Lyrical, poetic compositions sung in rhythm and often recount heroic, romantic, or religious sagas. They are deeply emotive and rich in metaphor like:
   - **Heroic and Religious Ballads**: *Haru Heet,* Ballads written and sung to praise warrior-deities of the region holding ancestral and divine reverence.
   - **Romantic Ballads**: Tales of longing, strength, and social defiance often performed in communal spaces, especially during festivals or ritual gatherings.

C. **Folk Songs (Lokgīt)** Community-based lyrical expressions deeply tied to ritual, seasonal, agricultural, and celebratory life:
   - **Ritual Songs**: Associated with *rites of passage* such as birth, marriage, and death. For example, lullabies, wedding songs, and funeral chants.
   - **Seasonal Songs**: Celebrates changes in weather and natural cycles. For example, *Phooldei* songs during spring; *Khatduwa* songs for agricultural rituals; *Harela* songs for prosperity and sowing.
   - **Agricultural Songs**: Sung while sowing, harvesting, or threshing crops. Reflect agrarian identity.
   - **Devotional and Celebratory Songs**: Include rhythmic, choral, or dialogic forms: *Jhora* group dance songs; *Chanchari*, festive and communal singing; *Bhagnoul*, seasonal migration and fertility; *Nyauli*, melancholic,

Fig. 4 Aipan art drawn on walls, wooden stools entry points of houses (by the authors)

solo female song, often a lament; *Pandav leela*, acts with rhythmic music as tributes to ancestors; Dialogic songs, call-and-response structures between genders or characters. These songs are often accompanied by dance, gesture, and spontaneous interjections (*hungra*), making them highly participatory and performative.

2. **Art-Based Expression (Kalāvilās-parak):** These include visual, ritualistic, and symbolic forms of folklore, embodying aesthetics, spirituality, and protection.
   - **Wall Paintings and Ritual Arts**: *Chowki lipai and Aipan* (Fig. 4) drawn on walls, wooden stools entry points of houses called as dheli, invoking prosperity and protection. Sacred motifs like Lakshmi's feet, sun symbols, are drawn using geru and rice paste in more contemporary form using red and white paint.
   - **Sculptures and Crafts**: Wooden carvings in temples and homes (Fig. 5); brass and stone iconography of local deities.
   - **Ceremonial Objects and Folk Medicine**: *Yantras* and talismans made from *tejpatta*, iron, or sacred ash (*booj*); use of temple flowers, vermilion, and threads in healing rituals; herbal remedies based on local knowledge systems.
   - **Ritual Performances**: *Jagar*, spirit-invoking rituals with music, trance, and possession (Fig. 6); *Yatras,* marked by devotees journeying on foot bearing palanquins of deities in solemn procession across sacred landscapes (Fig. 7)*;* *Bhāna*, *Nyoli*, solo or dramatic enactments reflecting spiritual or social concerns.

Far beyond preserving memory and myth, all of these and many other forms of living evolving folkloric expressions are cultural blueprints of existence of people "*lok*" of Uttarakhand. Ritual arts, wall paintings or the performative stories andsongs tracing life's pathways contours ecological, gendered, and moral constraints. In this way they stand as active frameworks through which communities negotiate identity continuity and change, mirroring folk fictions and serving as converging locus (EFP) of lived realities.

Fig. 5 Wood carvings in traditional house (Source:https://travelindevbhoomi.in/2022/03/20/likhai-the-wood-work-of-kumaon/)

TEAfication of the Himalayan Tales

Elaborating on the folkloric landscape of Uttarakhand and intricate life trajectories shaped by personal agency, societal norms, and cosmic beliefs provide a fertile ground for a TEA analysis. Trajectory Equifinality Approach (TEA) helps us understand how traditional indigenous stories encode life strategies, coping mechanisms, moral negotiations, and turning points relevant to a community's worldview. As discussed formerly folk narratives from different regions of Uttarakhand do more than entertain, they serve as potent life maps to steer across grief, love, duty, sacrifice, and transcendence.

Each tale reflects a developmental journey defined by critical Bifurcation Points (BPS), Obligatory Passage Points (OPPs), and shifting Social Directions (SDs) (bent trajectories, detours, collapse, or even ascents) reshaping their trajectory. Their eventual ethnographically nuanced Equifinality (whether tragic, redemptive, or spiritual) reflects the core cultural values like honor, devotion, and liberation of that region. The folklore lives through various stages of human development (illustrated in Fig. 8) from animals and animistic tales in childhood to wisdom tales of old

Fig. 6 Divine Possession: Jaagar (Source:https://www.timesnowhindi.com/spirituality/article/jagar-pooja-of-uttarakhand-through-which-ancestors-and-local-deity-is-called-interesting-facts/378563)

Fig. 7 The Nanda Devi Raj Jat Yatra: A 280-km Pilgrimage to Roopkund Held Once Every 12 Years (Source:https://www.peakadventuretour.com/nanda-devi-raj-jat-yatra.html

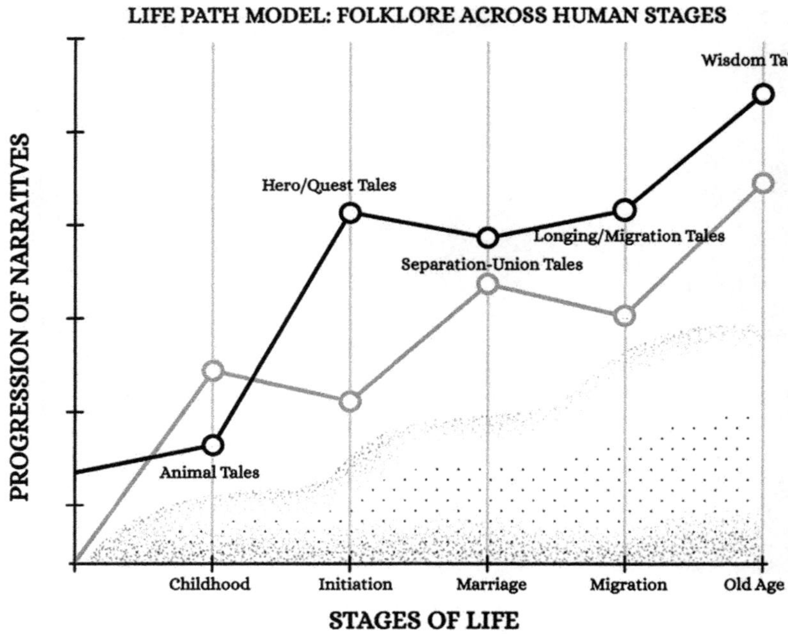

Fig. 8 Life path model in folk narratives (by the authors)

age giving a delightful lens for every age group. To facilitate a structured discussion, these folklores can be explored through separate thematic lenses.

A. **Tales of Divine Justice and Interventions**

While many of these tales have echoes across the State, several of them remain static to a region or specific season, such as *Nirawali Jaita* and *Birūṛ Panchamī aur Sātū Aṭhū* (Pant, 2024; Pokhariya, 2021). These lesser-known tales serve as testaments to the faith in cosmic justice stating significance of discipline, resilience, and the lived experiences of women across Uttarakhand. Both the narratives poignantly mirror female experiences where they have to go through suffering and endure in hopes of eventual divine justice. In *Nirawali Jaita*, the struggle of surviving in harsh hilly terrains is located in spending nights in rain-soaked cowsheds, walking long distances through dense forests to collect grass and fuel, or facing exclusion in the cold circumstantial hardship. These acts become symbolic agents within narratives' spiritual logic presenting critical BFP that test human dignity. Similarly, often termed as a *"Vrata Katha"* (customary tale retold during a fasting procession), *Birūṛ Panchamī* and *Sātū Aṭhū* reflect on a story about a childless household transitioning into socioemotional urgency rooted in cultural imperative for a male heir. The daughter-in-law's rit-

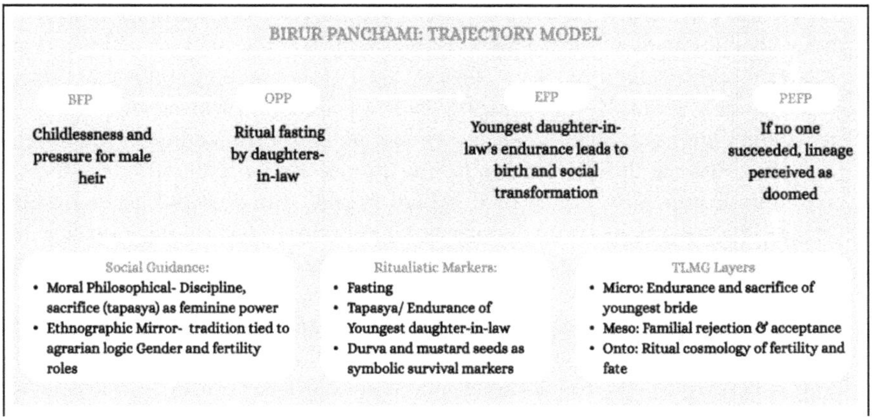

Fig. 9 Birur Panchami: Trajectory analysis model (by the authors)

ual fasting during *Birur Panchami* becomes an Obligatory Passage Point (OPP), symbolizing discipline and spiritual investment. Her silent resilience and tenacity ultimately lead to EFP, redemption through divine intervention, communal validation, and transformation of patriarchal norms (Fig. 9). Both of the pathways highlight striving against these oppressive hierarchies, often through subtle defiance rather than outright rebellion. Social Guidance (SG) in these tales emerges from gendered norms and domestic expectations that normalize suffering within domestic roles, while Equifinality Points (EFPs) are facilitated by divine forces. Elements such as sparrows pecking rice, divine rainfall, the whispered dream, or saving the child serve as narrative catalysts that restore moral balance. Furthermore, ecological elements not only shape the storytelling environment but act as moral witnesses and collaborators, reinforcing the Himalayan cosmology wherein spirituality is deeply embedded in the natural world.

Other than the subtle hierarchical battles, the tales within these undulating terrains are imbued with livelihood interactions, social stratification, and caste-based dynamics. The tale of *Sidhuva Bidhuva*, rooted in the Ramola caste of Uttarakhand, intricately blends divine intervention, pastoral livelihood, social dynamics, and spiritual legacy (Alter, 2012; Budhwar, 2010; Kafal Tree Live, 2025a, b; Pokhariya, 2021). Gangu Ramola's life trajectory, marked by affluence, ego, ruin, and partial redemption, unfolds through a series of significant bifurcation points. His refusal to share land, driven by anger and pride toward a divine figure (Lord Krishna), initiates his moral collapse, resulting in loss of social status and material wealth. Yet divine intercessions such as encounter with Rukamani in Dwarka and miraculous birth of the twins Sidhuva and Bidhuva despite Gangu's celibacy vow create restorative points pivotal to his trajectory. The twin's birth under socially ambiguous circumstances leads to their abandonment in a cave making a critical BFP in their own trajectories. Rescued and nurtured by Sage *Neelpal*, they experience temporary ascension through their acquisition of tantric *vidya* or training. However, their desire to leave the sage's care invokes a curse of eternal unrest, reflecting an irreversible outcome. Despite this, they attain lasting admiration within tantric traditions, a symbolic Equifinality Point (EFP) where tragedy and spiritual elevation converge. The tale has its own versions as it moves more toward the Nepalese terrains with linguistic differences rooted in their culture (Singh, 1989). This tale reflects the dynamic interplay of human agency, divine will, and ecological forces, with nature operating not as a passive backdrop but as an active moral agent. Reinstating the fact how folk traditions transform personal misfortunes into collective rituals and spiritual inheritance, where sorrow becomes sacred and socially redemptive.

B. **Animal and Bird Tales**

Social redemptions and resolutions through communities are often preserved in the linguistic repository of the region in union with ecological elements such as bird calls. Based on converging themes, two tales namely *"Bhāi bhūkko, maiṁ sitti"* (Brother died of hunger while I was asleep) and "*Kafal Pako Mail Ni Chakho"* (Kafal is ripe, but I have not tasted it) refer to few bird calls as moral instruments of resolution. Beginning with the seasonal festivals and practices, familial relations transition to delayed recognition and ultimately tragic ends (Agarwal, 2008, Gururani, 1996; Pant, 2024; Pokhariya, 2021). The first tale is set around the festival of *Bhitauli*, a seasonal reunion tradition wherein parents visit their married daughters during the *Chaitra* month (March–April) to present gifts and blessings. It follows a young boy's resolve to reunite with his sister shaped by Social Guidance (SG) rooted in familial tradition, which is disrupted by social directions (SD) embedded in patriarchal norms that physically and emotionally separate daughters from their natal homes. The denial of shelter to the brother by his sister-in-law marks a tragic BFP, leading to his untimely death. The sister's delayed recognition of his presence, realized only after his passing, culminates into her own tragic end. Her cry over her brother's lifeless body *"Bhāi bhūkko, maiṁ sitti"* (Brother died of hunger while I was asleep) becomes a cultural equifinality point, immortalized through the belief that she reincarnates as the *Ghuguti* bird. The belief persists that the bird echoes the same lament in her call of *"Bhāi bhūkko, maiṁ sitti,"* where the moral and emotional core of kinship becomes a lasting voice in the natural world.

Likewise, *Kafal Pako Mail Ni Chakho* further explores the irreversible loss, within the tone of maternal grief and moral ambiguity. Set during *Chaitra* month, the time when Kafal (Himalayan bayberries) ripen, the story follows a mother and daughter in a remote Kumaoni village. The narrative's bifurcation begins when the mother leaves her daughter to guard a full basket of Kafal, instructing her not to eat any, while she goes to fetch cattle fodder. Despite the overwhelming temp-

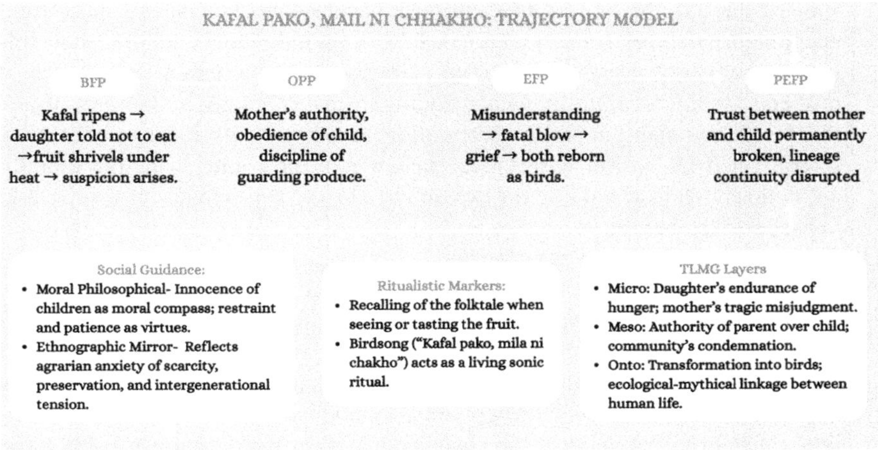

Fig. 10 Kafal Pako, Mail Ni Chakho: Trajectory analysis model (by the authors)

tation, the daughter refrains from touching berries and falls asleep while waiting. However, when mother returns, she finds the basket half eaten and, in a fit of rage, severely beats the daughter causing her tragic death. As the sun sets the shrunken berries regain their shape due to cold evening air making the basket full again. Overcome by grief and guilt the mother realizes her mistake, but emotional weight proves too much and she too dies from sorrow. The narrative reaches its sorrowful EFP in folkloric transformation of their grief into birds like in the previous tale (Fig. 10).

It is still widely assumed that whenever Kafal ripen, two birds sing: one laments (the daughter), "*Kafal Pako Mail Ni Chakho*" (Kafal is ripe, but I have not tasted it), and the other replies (The mother) "*Pur Putai Pur Pur*" (They are all there, my daughter, they are all there). The two narratives, while holding a certain level of moral accountability, critique the interplay of relationships with established societal, patriarchal, and economic norms.

C. **Tales of Mythical Beings**

Beyond their spiritual depth, Uttarakhand's folk narratives are richly interwoven with supernatural influences. The tale of *Jeetu Bagadwal*, for instance, features the *Anacharis* (forest fairies), while another compelling story titled *Dyot* (Pant, 2006) centers around a spirit dwelling at a *Naula* (water source). In *Dyot*, an innocent woman is tormented by a *Masaan* (malevolent spirit), who coerces her into performing his chores each time she visits the *Naula*, threatening dire consequences if she reveals his presence. Eventually, the woman confides in her husband. In a clever move, the husband dons his wife's attire and visits *Naula* in her place. There he confronts the spirit, teaches him a lesson, and compels him to vow never to trouble anyone, rather acting as a guardian spirit from now on.

Viewed through the lens of TEA, the tale encapsulates how such supernatural encounters catalyzes communal renewal, shifting individual hauntings into collective wellbeing. Despite the initial pathways of exploitation and silence, it reorients toward a culturally valued equifinal state (not only in the form of justice for the woman but in the reformation of the spirit itself into a protective force). Such tales offer descriptive frameworks for coping with the morally ambiguous, while upholding the possibility of expected transformation even in the supernatural realm.

D. **Tales of Cosmological Frameworks**

Another cosmogonic tale is the Ātmik Nandā Gāthā sung by Bhīmrām of Chāni (Pokhariya, 2021), serving not just as the origin story of the universe but as a dynamic cosmological framework. According to this ballad, the Earth emerged from a primordial churning of waters, a concept mirrored in many pan-Indian myths, yet uniquely echoed through local symbolisms. The emergence of equifinal trajectories beginning from chaos and void, proceeding toward structured order via organic metamorphosis, a bubble becoming a stalk, a fruit, then a red lump, and ultimately, a golden bird. The golden bird's solitude catalyzes creation, establishing a pivotal bifurcation. The rupture of the female bird's womb and the resultant sacred rivers mark another TEA node of transformation through sacrifice. The eventual churning events produce deities, cosmological entities, and mythic figures like *Ajīt* that represent successive socio-cosmic turning points. The four cardinal pillars erected by gods parallel the moral structuring of the world, introducing weight, balance, and human responsibility. Such motifs are recurring themes in diverse traditions, from the Vedic *Purusha Sukta* where the cosmic man is sacrificed to give birth to the social and cosmic order (Pskhu, 2019), to the Norse myth of *Ymir* whose body forms the world (Kure, 2003), and creates the cosmos through sacrifice. This structural mirroring of creation, sacrifice, and stabilization sequence forms a shared archetype in origin myths across cultures.

More folk narratives delve into these geological processes as cosmic events, such as etiologies of eclipses, reflecting the generational repository and social memory encoded as shared myths and legends. The blemished moon spattered by dung or cursed by sages or the moon's waxing and waning emerge as narrative symbols of regulated emotional expressions, a TEA-aligned idea of cyclical divergence and reintegration. Their existence underlines a realm of reality for the inhabitants where nature is sentient and interaction with the supernatural is a fundamental component of personal and communal trajectories.

E. **Ballads of Love**

In Uttarakhand, there is no exclusive term or literary form dedicated solely to love stories. Instead, the emotion of love particularly of romantic and devotional kinds is subtly presented through powerful expression within a variety of traditional folk genres such as *Chaiti* ballads (seasonal folk songs), heroic epics (*veer gatha*), and religious narratives. These forms reflect layered and intersecting trajectories of life paths shaped by sociocultural norms, divine intervention, and human agency central to the Trajectory Equifinality Approach (TEA).

Perhaps the most celebrated love ballad of Kumaon, *Rajula-Malushahi* presents the majestic tale of romance, societal constraint, valor, and spiritual persistence (Budhwar, 2010; Pande, 2018; Pant, 2024; Pokhariya, 2021). The story narrates the love between Malushahi, son of the Katyuri king Dulashah and Queen Dharmadevi of Bairath, and Rajula, daughter of the Bhotiya trader Sunpati and his wife Ganguli. Bound by a prenatal promise, where the two childless couples vow at Bagnath Temple (or in some versions, Haridwar or Chitrashila) to marry their children, if born (a trajectory of fate is already set). Years later, Rajula and Malushahi meet at the Agneri Temple by the banks of the western Ramganga, and with a single glance they fall deeply in love. But this love has to meet the harsh reality of socio-political interests, where Rajula's father arranges her marriage to an aged king, Bikhai Pal of the Hun dynasty, for wealth and political gain. As Rajula gets acknowledged with truth she embarks on the journey to Malushahi's palace in Bairath to disclose her pain. Yet once again, fate intervenes, and due to mystical sleep both of them are unable to communicate, a fictional event probably equivalent to the silencing of young love due to social dynamics. Upon waking up Malusahi reads the letter left behind by her, discussing the whole scenario, making him renounce his throne and setting off to reclaim Rajula in a *yogi's* disguise. He reaches the Bhotiya region, but is discovered and poisoned by the father. His mother, Dharmadevi, sees this in a dream and sends a rescue force. Meanwhile, Rajula is married off forcibly and held captive by Rishipal. Eventually, through magical intervention by the royal guru, Malushahi is revived and succeeds in rescuing Rajula.

This epic love story with a grand narrative includes classical elements such as predestined dreams, temple encounters, heroic disguise, mystical experiences, and ultimate reunion. The tale reflects divergent yet converging life paths (Fig. 11), a hallmark of TEA, where social institutions, personal choices, and spiritual

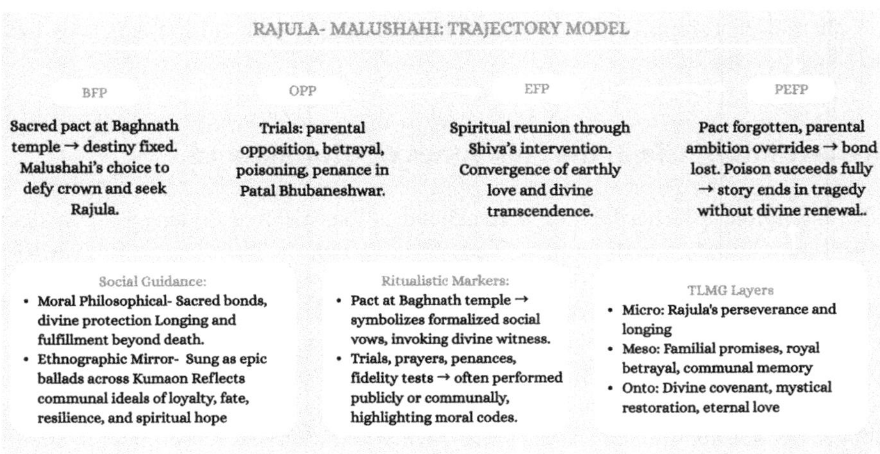

Fig. 11 Rajula Malushahi: Trajectory analysis model (by the authors)

forces all shape the trajectory toward equifinality, that is, the realization of love, through suffering, resistance, and transformation. Royal lineage, the promise made at the temple, societal expectations of arranged marriage, and the valorization of sacrifice act as clear Obligatory Passage Points (OPPs), which get bifurcated by Rajula's decision to defy her father and Malushahi's choice to renounce kingship, and the betrayal by society that leads to his poisoning. Rajula's solitary night journey, her silent letter, and Malushahi's yogi disguise represent individual agency and rebellion, revealing how alternative paths emerge when dominant social scripts are disrupted. The revival of Malushahi via tantric intervention also introduces supernatural legitimacy to their bond, merging spiritual and social trajectories. The tale has found its due recognition through modern glimpses in visual platforms such as Coke Studio India (Coke Studio India, 2024; Meher, 2024).

Another tale of love with not so happy ending is of Tiloga and Amardev illustrating how love, though transcendent, can be inevitably constrained by the socio-cultural structures of its time (Chamola, 2013). Tiloga, a Suryavanshi princess, and Amardev, a warrior renowned for his martial valor, embody forbidden love in its most tragic form. Their secret meetings, done under the cloak of the night across the Alaknanda, represent a critical turning point where personal desire collides with communal expectation. The lovers' fate is sealed when Amardev is murdered and Tiloga, in a dramatic act of bodily protest, severs her breasts before ending her life. This represents TEA's assertion that critical events, however tragic, create a pathway toward a predetermined moral resolution. A cursed well at Amshera, with Tiloga's ominous declaration, "Whoever drinks from this well shall become the morsel of kaal (time)," acts as a tangible mirror of their doomed union. Both narratives of Rajula Malushahi and Tiloga Amardev, have resemblance to contemporary archetypal tales of Romeo Juliette (Kottman, 2012), Dhola Maru (Dholi, 2023), and Moirang-Sai (Yumnam, 2020). Though tragic in some aspects, the tales signify sacralization of loyalty and love, making their stories eternal through remembrance, aligning with cultural ideals of self-sacrifice and destiny.

Reflections of Life in the Folk Tunes of Uttarakhand

The intangible folk heritage of Uttarakhand is like the free-flowing river system dwelling within its harsh terrains. They have variant origins ranging from heroic ballads, miraculous births, shapeshifting deities to tragic love legends, which ripples into the breathing echoes of experience. The collective culture depicts the central elements through critical turning points, ritual obstacles, and moral negotiations mirroring the concepts of TEA. Regardless, their abstract and mythical genesis villagers continue to chant mantras, wear sacred threads, and preserve temple ash or flowers as spiritual talismans, acts embodying perpetuity of these belief systems. Scholars such as Jung and Frazer have argued that concepts often labeled as magical thinking and animistic belief are not irrational but represent a coherent worldview rooted in intuition, archetypes, and collective memory (Oesterdiekhoff, 2008). While none of it could be confirmative to a scientific discovery, they carry profound healing powers and deep emotional resonance, shaping responses to uncertainty, adversity, and transformation.

The sentient coherence of these narratives is also preserved and renewed through regional songs with festivals acting as the affective equifinality points for real-life implications and symbolic interpretations of natural phenomena. For instance, the arrival of *Basanta Ritu* (spring) is viewed as the profound awakening of body, land, and spirit reflected in the burst of colors from *burāns (Rhododendron)* and mustard blooms, across the Himalayan landscape. The springtime hums of "*Mera dandi kathiyun ka muluk jailu basant ritu ma jai*" (Should you ever visit my homeland of undulating hills, let it be in the season of spring) sung by a known folk singer Narendra Singh Negi (T-Series Regional, 2014) are not just invitation for someone to visit hills in a specific season (T- Series, 2014). They are metaphors for emotional homecoming expressing how their homeland is best experienced when it's alive and blooming. Similarly, "*Phool dei, Chamma dei*" is a springtime chant associated with the festival on arrival of the season led by young children blessing neighboring houses by sprinkling fresh flowers and rice in their courtyards (Joshi & Bhardwaj, 2016). This act of singing door to door invokes abundance, reinforces ecological vitality and social integration. Additionally, the evocative lines from a few more folk songs such as "*Sāt Samundar Pār cha Jānā*" (C.S. Rahi Foundation, 2009; Kafal Tree, 2020) and "*Chhāna Bilorī*" (Baramasa, 2022) subtly encode the historical reality and pain of displacement due to male out-migration and daily struggles of domestic chores in hilly areas and offer quiet yet powerful resistance against patriarchal constraints. While on surface they reflect economic displacement, a more nuanced vision subtly unravels the emotional bifurcation between rooted love and forced aspirations. Grounded in observations Uttarakhand's folk traditions preserve and transmit existential trajectories, encapsulating the joys, sorrows, and resilience of everyday life turning into a mirrored and dynamic legacy.

Conclusion

Elaborate and vivid mosaics of Uttarakhand's folk culture as established act as both a mirror and a pathway for comprehending the embodied trajectories and imagined possibilities of its inhabitants. The cultural forms (oral narratives, proverbs, rituals, and ballads) are far from being remnants of the past; these traditions are dynamic, evolving with each retelling and performance. They function as living architectures of experience, tracing trajectories that mirror both fictional and research pathways converging at equifinality points where narrative, practice, and social reality intersect. Trajectory Equifinality Approach (TEA) serves as a most potent epistemological framework to study how these cultural expressions map the intersection of individual and collective life courses, accentuating points of convergence, divergence, and transformation molded by history, environment, and belief systems.

Apart from documenting the Himalayan folk heritage, this paper emphasizes the potential of theoretical engagement with multiple indigenous folk cultures in integration with suitable theoretical paradigms globally. This helps identify the need for illuminating the broader questions of continuity, adaptation, and creativity in human existence. Drawing on Jung's concepts of archetypes, these expressions are not unidimensional, but manifest universal symbolic patterns that resonate in both individual and collective unconscious (Walters, 1994). Halbwach's theoretical perspective on collective memory underscores the significance of these traditions in encoding social knowledge, moral frameworks, and ecological awareness ensuring their perpetual transmission across generations (Assmann & Czaplicka, 1995). Warburg's *Mnemosyne Atlas and Visual Memory* provide a unique phenomenon associated with these folk images, symbols, and rituals, acting as mnemonic devices that bridge past and present, linking landscape, community, and sacred imagination (Badea, 2021). Furthermore, Turner's (2002) discussion on the performative roles of folklore and rituals as building blocks to collective identity and continuity of communities. When viewed through the integrative lens of these scholarly analytical orientations, communal engagement with such practices reveals the intricate processes through which belonging is articulated and communities negotiate the entwined dynamics of gender, caste, and environmental changes.

Further research avenues could examine the interplay of oral, performative, and visual traditions, in response to ecological imperatives, ritual practices, technological transformations, migration, and broader spectrum of sociocultural issues. By synthesizing perspectives on collective memory, performative enactment, and symbolic expressions, these academic insights can enhance the complexity and richness of cross-cultural discourses. Scholars can identify a myriad of perceptions on sustained communal reproduction, reinterpretation, and innovation in the folk world in response to social, environmental, and historical pressures. Myriad folk narratives have also served as anchors to several revolutions of freedom and rights. Additional discussion on the role of cultural elements in communal unity against common usurpers of the people's land heritage provides the groundwork for another subsequent, more detailed intellectual discourse within the field. The enquiries as such not only promise to enrich our understanding of mechanisms of indigenous culture and contemporary social dilemmas, but also identify the generative potential of folk traditions in fostering innovation, resilience, cross-cultural perspectives, and symbolic cognition in human society.

Uttarakhand's folk culture exemplifies how narratives, performances, and rituals are central to meaning-making, identity formation, and psychological well-being. By engaging with these living traditions through interdisciplinary frameworks such as TEA, researchers and storytellers alike can appreciate the multiplicity of pathways that shape human experience.

As Girish Tiwari "Girda", a celebrated Kumaoni poet, reflects:

Chahe hum ni lye saku (Maybe we might not be able to bring it),
Chahe tum ni lya sako (Maybe you won't be able to bring it either),
Magar kwe na kwe to lyalo udin yo duni ma (But somebody, someday, will bring that day into this world).
Vi din hum ni hulo lekin (That day we won't be here, but)

Picture 1 Small local temples in stone (by the authors) (In Uttarakhand, in many places, small shrines are there in rock crevices made with small stones in the name of the patron gods of its people) Photo courtesy: Namrataa Mamgai

Picture 2 Aipan art. This is a form of what may be called evolved folk art drawn on the entry point of the house called *dheli*. It is usually made during Diwali, the festival of lights. Tiny feet of the Goddess of Wealth, Lakshmi, are depicted. It is an invitation for her to visit the house and bring abundance. The art form is sometimes made on wooden stools (*chowkis*) placed in the temple area of the house where the idols and pictures of Gods are displayed. The chowkis are also used during auspicious occasions of significant religious ceremonies or marriage rituals. Originally the traditional *pahadi* (mountainous) houses were coated with mud and cow dung, and the same folk art was done using a base coat of red clay (*geru mitti*) and a thin slurry of soaked rice, hence it used much simpler motifs. As the housing design changed people began using red and white paint which allowed more intricate patterns. (Hand drawn by Namrataa Mamgai)

> Hum lai vi din hulo (We will also be present that day)
> Jaita ek din to aalo u din yo duni mein (When that day comes, it will surely arrive in this world).
> (ETV Bharat, 2020; Khanna, 2023)

Even if we are unable to witness certain days ourselves, and even if others may not, the continuity of culture, memory, and tradition ensures that these living expressions of Uttarakhand will persist, shaping futures yet to come. In this enduring rhythm of narrative, song, and ritual, the land and its people write a shared story that transcends generations, affirming that what begins as a small ripple today can create transformative waves tomorrow (Pictures 1, 2, 3, and 4).

Picture 3 Shiv Archan (The worship of Lord Shiva) Using ingredients such as soil and cow dung, 108 *shivlings* (*Shiva's* sign or symbol; 108 is a sacred number in Hindu tradition signifying cosmic unity) are made and worshipped over a 5–6 hours procession/ceremony. (Photo courtesy: Namrata Mamgai)

Picture 4 This is a picture from the first author's house, of the *pooja* (worship) area. The idol of goddess *Kali* representing the cycle of life, and a decorated *chowki* (wooden stool) are placed (Photo courtesy: Namrataa Mamgai). Golu devta: 1) Golu Devata: The God of Justice of Kumaun Himalayas by C. M. Agrawal, Published 1992, Shree Almora Book Depot Almora. 2) Nadi nani Stritva (Marathi) by Anne Feldhaus, translated by Vijaya Dev, Published 2014, Padmagandha Prakashan, Pune. Kumar (2023)

References

Agarwal, D. (2008). *Folk tales of Uttarakhand*. Children's Book Trust.

Al-Shahi, A. (1984). Spirit possession and healing: The zar among the Shaygiyya of the Northern Sudan. *British Journal of Middle Eastern Studies, **11***(1), 28–44.

Alter, A. (2012). Himalayan flutes, sprites and mountainous geographies. *European Bulletin of Himalayan Research, **40***, 9–26.

Arpad, J. J. (1975). Between folklore and literature: Popular culture as anomaly. *The Journal of Popular Culture, **9***(2), 403–422.

Arya, P., & Mehta, J. P. (2019). A review on traditional health care system of Uttarakhand. *Environment and Ecology, **37***(2), 582–588.

Assmann, J., & Czaplicka, J. (1995). Collective memory and cultural identity. *New German Critique, 65*, 125–133.

Badea, G. (2021). Aby Warburg: The collective memory as a medium for art. *Anastasis Research in Medieval Culture and Art, 8*(1), 244–254.

Baramasa. (2022). *Channa Billauri: Pahadi Mahilaon ka Dukh Ukerte Geet ki Kahani. Gaane ke Bahane.* Baramasa [Video]. YouTube. https://www.youtube.com/watch?v=KiggAJY-mmc

Barthwal, A. (2018). Buddhism in Uttarakhand: Monuments from past and present. *Journal of the Centre for Heritage Studies, **1***, 67–75.

Bascom, W. R. (1953). Folklore and anthropology. *The Journal of American Folklore, **66***(262), 283–290.

Bascom, W. (1965). The forms of folklore: Prose narratives. *The Journal of American Folklore, 78*(307), 3–20.

Berti, D. (2024). Gods and rivers as legal persons in India. In Encounters with the invisible (pp. 211–227). Routledge India.

Bisht, B. (2013). *Nanda ke Jaagar: Sufal Hwe Jaya Tumari Jatra. Culture Department, Uttarakhand*. Vinsar Publishing Company.

Budhwar, K. (2010). *Where Gods dwell: Central Himalayan folktales and legends*. Penguin Books.

C.S. Rahi Foundation. (2009). *Garhwali Lokgeet Chandra Singh Rahi. Saat Samodar Paar ch Jaanu bwe.* Garhwali geet. [Video]. YouTube. https://www.youtube.com/watch?v=a-QKy-MU6-0

Chamola, S. (2013). *Uttarakhand ki Lokkathaein (Kaat Kaani, Raat Byaani)*. Vinsar Publishing Company.

Channa, S. M. (2005). The "descent of the pandavas": ritual and cosmology of the Jads of Garhwal. *European Bulletin of Himalayan Research, **28***, 67–87.

Coke Studio India. (2024). *Sonchadi. Neha Kakkar x digV x Kamala Devi* [Video]. YouTube. https://youtu.be/L9CfCjedhPE?si=siPgl3rLAAK1CGS4

Dholi, S. L. (2023). Dhola Maru: Mystique symbols of love. *Journal of Rajasthan Association for Studies in English, **19***, 85–94.

Dobbin, J., & Hezel, F. X. (2011). *Summoning the powers beyond: Traditional religions in Micronesia*. University of Hawaii Press.

ETV Bharat. (2020). आज भी देवभूमि की फजिा में गूंजती हैं "गर्दिा" की परिोई कवताएं, हम लड़ते रैया भुला हम लड़ते रूंला. ETV Bharat News. https://www.etvbharat.com/hindi/uttarakhand/state/nainital/people-tribute-to-girish-chandra-tiwari-on-10th-death-anniversary-in-nainital/uttarakhand20200822205547538

Gururani, S. (1996). *Fuel, fodder, and forests: Politics of forest use and abuse in Uttarakhand Himalaya, India*. Syracuse University.

Hāṇḍā, O. (2002). History of Uttaranchal. Indus Publishing.

Joshi, K., & Bhardwaj, N. (2016). Ancient practices for water and forest conservation followed by women in lesser Himalayan region of Nainital, Uttarakhand, India. *Asian Agri-History, **20***(3).

Kafal Tree. (2020). Pratham Vishwayuddh ke Anubhavo par Uttarakhand ke Agyaat Sainik ka Racha Lokgeet. *Kafal Tree*. https://kafaltree.com/folk-song-sath-samunder-par-ch-janu/

Kafal Tree Live. (2025a). Jee reya, Jaagi reya (Dr. Meena Kharkwal, Psychologist Health Talk). Episode-2 [Video]. YouTube. https://www.youtube.com/watch?v=mWQIe-Hwpe0

Kafal Tree Live. (2025b). Sidhuva Biduva ki Lokgatha. Dr Prayag Joshi. Lok Khojyar "Dr. Prayag Joshi".[Video]. YouTube. https://www.youtube.com/watch?v=t9ncgU-dEDo

Khanna, R. (2023). The Citizen—Independent Journalism | Indian News | The Citizen. *The Citizen—Independent Journalism | Indian News | the Citizen.* https://www.thecitizen.in/life/peoples-poet-girda-today-after-the-final-journey-958190

Kottman, P. A. (2012). Defying the stars: tragic love as the struggle for freedom in Romeo and Juliet. *Shakespeare Quarterly, **63***(1), 1–38.

Kumar, A. (2023). Lore, legends, and landscape of Uttarakhand: Exploring the socio-religious significance of golu devta-god of justice. *International Journal for Multidisciplinary Research., **5***(5), 1–8.

Kure, H. (2003). In the beginning was the scream. *Scandinavia and Christian Europe in the Middle Ages*, 311–319.

Lohani, G. (2019). Samridhi aur Seema ke Rakshak Devta Haru Saim ke Janm ki Katha. [The story of the birth of Haru-Saim Devta]. *Kafal Tree.* https://kafaltree.com/story-birth-of-haru-saim-devta/Kafal Tree+2Kafal Tree+2Kafal Tree+2

Malik, A. (2016). *Tales of justice and rituals of divine embodiment: oral narratives from the Central Himalayas. Oxford University Press.*

Masaki, F. (2025). Self-regulated learning from a cultural psychology perspective: shifting from strategy to process with the trajectory Equifinality approach. *Human Arenas, **8***(1), 131–149.

Meher, P. (2024). *Rajula Malushahi. Priyanka Meher. Kamla Devi. Mac Dhami. Nikhil. Swapnil.* [Video]. YouTube. https://youtu.be/MXCfPcSE5Fw?si=XgkgKn1e7p_2pa-6

Oesterdiekhoff, G. W. (2008). Magic and animism in old religions: The relevance of sun cults in the world-view of traditional societies. *Croatian Journal of Ethnology and Folklore Research, **45***(1), 43–66.

Pande, B. D. (1993). *History of Kumaun* (C. M. Agarwal, Trans.). Shyam Prakashan Shri/Almora Book Depot. 2.

Pande, V. (2018). The making of a 'Kumauni' artifact: The epic Malushahi, HIMALAYA. *The Journal of the Association for Nepal and Himalayan Studies, **38***(1), 17.

Pant, P. (2006). *Purvajo ki sunai kahaniyaan*. Goljyu Publishers and Distributors.

Pant, P. (2024). *Hum aur hamara kumaon*. Ankit publishers.

Pokhariya, D. S. (2021). *Uttarakhand ki Lok Sanskriti aur Sahitya*. National Book Trust.

Prasad, H. (2024). A comparative analysis of cultural perspectives: Kantara's Bhuta Kola and Nigeria's Ijele Masquerade. *Shaping Narratives: Tamil Cinema and its Rendition of Women's Empowerment-An Avenue for Social Change, 2*, 186–192.

Pskhu, R. (2019). Role of Purusha-sukta in Philosophy of Vishishtadvaita. In *4th international conference on contemporary education, social sciences and humanities* (Vol. 329, pp. 200–202).

Putri, L. G. (2017). The revival of Sang Hyang Dedari dance: a phenomenological approach to social-ecological reconstruction in Bali. *ASEAN Journal of Community Engagement, **1***(1), 72–82.

Ramani, B. V., & Alekya, C. (2019). A narrative of Uttarakhand disaster shaped by cultural politics. *IOSR Journal of Humanities and Social Science, **24***(7), 43–47.

Rani, M., & Sharma, R. K. (2007). Socioeconomic and demographic characteristics of tribes of Uttarakhand, India. *Tribal Health Bulletin., **13***(1&2), 23–41.

Rawat, C. (2023). Folklore studies in Uttarakhand. *Folklore Studies in India: Critical Regional Responses, 76.*

Sahu, P. (2023). Language and linguistics. *Indian Journal of Language and Linguistics, 4*(2), 32–41.

Sati, V. P., & Litt, D. (2023). *Uttarakhand: Society, culture, and pilgrimages*. Today & Tomorrow's Printers and Publishers.

Sati, V. P., & Sati, V. P. (2020). Change in culture and custom. *Himalaya on the Threshold of Change*, 103–111.

Sato, T., Hidaka, T., & Fukuda, M. (2009). Depicting the dynamics of living the life: The trajectory equifinality model. In *Dynamic process methodology in the social and developmental sciences* (pp. 217–240). Springer US.

Sato, T., Mori, N., & Valsiner, J. (2016). *Making of the future the trajectory equifinality approach in cultural psychology*. Information Age Publishing.
Singh, S. C. (1989). Some characteristics of migration in mountain society: Case studies from Garhwal Himalaya. *Economic Journal of Nepal, **12***(3), 49–61.
Stavrou, E. P. (2015). Determining the cultural identity of a child through folk literature. *American Journal of Educational Research, **3***(4), 527–534.
T-Series Regional. (2014). *Basant Ritu Maa Jaiyee—Garhwali Song Narendra Singh Negi—Chali Bhai Motar Chali* [Video]. YouTube. https://youtu.be/aU-2XjLTSWw?si=7PF-5gTId-8YZs5h
Turner, V. (2002). Performance theory in an anthropology program. *Teaching Performance Studies, 85*.
Walters, S. (1994). Algorithms and archetypes: evolutionary psychology and Carl Jung's theory of the collective unconscious. *Journal of social and evolutionary systems, 17*(3), 287–306.
Woodson, C. G. (2012). *African Mythsn and FolkTales. Courier Corporation.*
Yumnam, S. (2020). The maibi phenomenon: A site of crisis and resolution. *Quest Journals, **8***(12), 59–68.

The Multidimensional Trajectory Equifinality Model in the Context of Sleep, Dreams, and Emotional Well-Being

Aniko Szeko

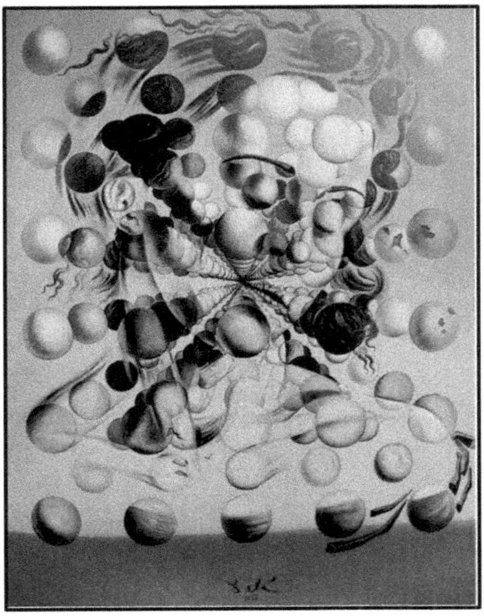

Galatea of the Spheres, Salvador Dali, 1952

A. Szeko (✉)
Sigmund Freud University Vienna, Vienna, Austria
e-mail: aniko.szeko@mail.sfu.ac.at

M. A. Campill et al. (eds.), *New Paths in Trajectory Equifinality Modelling*, Theory and History in the Human and Social Sciences,
https://doi.org/10.1007/978-3-032-25855-7_17

Figure presented on the first page of the chapter, an Artwork form Dali (Galatea of the spheres) supporting the 3D TEM concept.

The Guest House

This being human is a guest house.

Every morning a new arrival.

A joy, a depression, a meanness

some momentary awareness comes

as an unexpected visitor.

Welcome and entertain them all!

Even if they're a crowd of sorrows,

who violently sweep your house

empty of its furniture,

still, treat each guest honorably.

He may be clearing you out

for some new delight.

The dark thought, the shame, the malice,

meet them at the door laughing,

and invite them in.

Be grateful for whoever comes,

because each has been sent

as a guide from beyond.

(Rumi, n.d. in Jalāl al-Dīn Rūmī. & Washington, 2006)

Introduction

We spend approximately one-third of our life sleeping (Harley, 2021), out of which we possibly spend almost half of it in the REM phase of sleeping, where majority of dreams occur (Walker, 2017). Dream recall is affected by various factors, such as the timing of awakening, personal sleep architecture, and neurophysiological activation levels during REM sleep (Eichenlaub et al., 2014). Consequently, even when we forget about our dreams, they still affect our waking lives.

Since the human lifespan nowadays is around 80 years long on average (Kumar, 2021), and as we potentially spend time sleeping 25% of our time—around 20 years –, it leads to around 10 years of dreaming during an average human lifespan (Harley, 2021). This amount of time can be considered significant enough to be seen as important in an individual's life.

Consciousness, while integral to our human experience, remains largely a mystery. According to a few, it is an epiphenomenon that lacks proper causality between body and brain states (Chalmers, 1996; Kim, 2005). Consciousness consists of varying levels and states, which are determined by a combination of awareness and wakefulness. These levels range from basic life animation to higher self-awareness and a sense of uniqueness. Our conscious function enables us to have individual experiences of qualia (Jackson, 1982), and controlled hallucinations driven by a desire to survive (Seth, 2017).

Consciousness pervades our daily life, also manifesting in altered states such as sleep and dreams. The altered states of consciousness help to integrate unconscious information into the conscious, while working at the edge of awareness. This can be exploited well in psychotherapy or mindfulness practices, where unconscious positive neuroplasticity (Hanson et al., 2023), the rewiring of negative biases, thoughts, or habits can emerge from.

The relationship between sleep and emotions is not merely correlative but fundamentally reciprocal. Emotional events that occur during the day have the potential to alter sleep quality and dream content at night, while poor sleep and distressing dreams influence how one feels and functions the next day. This cyclical interaction has significant implications for understanding affective disorders, stress regulation, cognitive performance, and psychological well-being more broadly (Goldstein & Walker, 2014; Tempesta et al., 2018). The scientific investigation of this bidirectional relationship has expanded significantly in the last two decades, moving beyond surface associations to uncover causal pathways and mechanistic insights through methods such as actigraphy, polysomnography, electrophysiology, and neuroimaging.

The emotion-sleep-dream nexus does not occur in a vacuum. It is embedded in social, developmental, and cultural contexts that shape how individuals perceive, interpret, and regulate emotional experiences across waking and dreaming states. Thus, a comprehensive understanding of this cycle must go beyond neurocognitive models and include symbolic, cultural, and experiential dimensions. The continuity hypothesis of dreaming (Bell & Hall, 1971), Hartmann's theory of emotional contextualization in dreams (1996), and Revonsuo's threat simulation theory (2000) all point towards a central role for dreams in affect regulation, mediating, reinforcing, or transforming emotional content through metaphor and narrative.

To map the complexity of this relationship, the current chapter introduces and applies the further extended Trajectory Equifinality Model (TEM) (Sato, 2009; Valsiner, 2000) as a conceptual tool. Originally developed in cultural psychology, TEM provided a temporal-spatial framework for visualizing how individuals as open systems navigate life-course trajectories over time through key decision points—bifurcations—and along multilinear possible trajectories passing through

Obligatory Passage Points to reach equifinal states finally. In this context, this chapter extends TEM to endless numbers of three-dimensional mental spaces, leading to a multidimensional model in the end by incorporating sleep quality, dream content, and symbolism—originated by altered states of consciousness—as an interactive axis that reflects the influence of both prior emotional states and future emotional possibilities.

Dreams are not only expressions of emotional residue but also potential mechanisms of adaptation, exploration, and emotional reprocessing. In the following, this chapter will examine empirical evidence for the connectedness of sleep quality and dreams to emotional functioning from day-to-night and night-to-day directions of the feedback loop.

Furthermore, a theoretical elaboration will follow on intercultural differences in dream interpretation, sleep practices, and emotional outcomes before turning to the three-dimensional TEM itself. The chapter concludes with a theoretical synthesis that positions emotion, sleep, and dreams within a bio-cultural feedback system.

Day-to-Night Effects: How Daytime Emotions Influence Sleep and Dreams

Emotional experiences during the day—particularly those involving stress, anxiety, or unresolved affect—can significantly alter the architecture of sleep and the emotional tone of dreams (Vandekerckhove & Cluydts, 2010; Palmer & Alfano, 2017). This relationship operates through both physiological and psychological mechanisms. Physiologically, stress activates the hypothalamic-pituitary-adrenal (HPA) axis, resulting in elevated cortisol levels that can delay sleep onset, reduce sleep efficiency, and fragment rapid eye movement (REM) sleep, the stage most strongly associated with dreaming (Meerlo et al., 2008; Grafe et al., 2023). Psychologically, unprocessed emotional concerns may manifest in heightened cognitive and affective arousal at bedtime, making initiating and maintaining sleep more difficult and increasing the likelihood of emotionally intense or negative dream content (Espie, 2002; Zhang et al. 2024).

One factor mediating this effect is individual sleep reactivity, or the tendency for a person's sleep to become disrupted in response to stress (Kalmbach et al., 2018). Individuals with high sleep reactivity are more prone to insomnia on stressful days and are more likely to experience nightmares or emotionally dysphoric dreams. Kalmbach et al. (2018) found that elevated daily stress predicted reduced sleep efficiency and longer sleep onset latency on the same night, with particularly strong effects in individuals high in neuroticism and low in emotional resilience.

In parallel, the concept of affect load and affect distress has been proposed as a model for understanding dream reactivity. Levin and Nielsen (2009) suggested that individuals with a high accumulation of emotional stress (affect load) and poor affect regulation (affect distress) are more vulnerable to experiencing negative and intense dream content. This vulnerability may explain why some individuals are more likely to suffer from recurrent nightmares following acute or chronic stress.

Support for these models comes from both laboratory and naturalistic studies. Cartwright et al. (2006) demonstrated that individuals who experienced interpersonal conflict during the day were significantly more likely to have negative dreams that night, particularly if the conflict remained unresolved. Schredl and Reinhard (2010), in a diary study, confirmed that participants' self-reported mood in the evening predicted the emotional tone of their dreams, with negative moods associated with more unpleasant and anxiety-laden dreams.

Further support comes from the continuity hypothesis of dreaming, which posits that dream content reflects waking-life concerns, emotions, and experiences (Bell & Hall, 1971). Schredl (2025) confirmed the emotional continuity in a mixed questionnaire and dream diary study. While specific activities and people might or might not appear in dreams, emotional themes are highly likely to carry over (Malinowski & Horton, 2014).

Building on the continuity hypothesis, Hartmann (1996) proposed that dreams serve not merely to replicate waking experience but to contextualize dominant emotional concerns. According to his theory, emotionally salient experiences—especially traumatic ones—are reprocessed during dreaming through symbolic imagery. For example, someone feeling overwhelmed might dream of being swept away by a tidal wave. These images, while not literal representations of waking events, embody the core emotion and help the brain file the experience into existing memory networks in a less distressing form.

This theory aligns with findings that trauma survivors initially dream about the event itself, but over time, their dreams shift towards metaphorical representations of emotion (Chen & Nehrig, 2024). Hartmann (1998) described that such symbolic dreams often precede emotional improvement, suggesting that dreaming contributes to psychological recovery. These findings imply that emotional experiences during the day—especially those that remain unprocessed—can be woven into the narrative of the night, guiding dream content and influencing the trajectory of emotional adaptation.

Understanding the influence of daytime emotion on sleep and dreams has important implications for mental health and therapy. Emotional dysregulation during the day, if left unresolved, can result in sleep disturbances and distressing dreams, which in turn impair the capacity for emotion regulation the next day (Walker & van der Helm, 2009).

In sum, the day-to-night influence is supported by robust evidence from sleep and dream content studies. Stress, unresolved affect, and negative emotional states during the day influence both the quantity and quality of sleep and the affective tone of dreams. These findings provide a critical foundation for understanding how emotion regulation is a 24-hour process, not confined to waking life.

Night-to-Day Effects: How Sleep and Dreams Influence Next-Day Emotions

The influence of sleep quality and dream content on emotional states the following day has gained increasing empirical and clinical attention. Emerging research shows that poor sleep quality, especially fragmented or insufficient REM sleep, negatively impacts next-day emotional regulation, mood, and cognitive flexibility. Conversely, restorative sleep and emotionally positive dreams appear to facilitate emotional stability and resilience upon waking (Goldstein & Walker, 2014; van der Helm et al., 2011).

A foundational body of work by Walker and colleagues (Walker & van der Helm, 2009; Goldstein & Walker, 2014) demonstrates that REM sleep plays a critical role in the overnight modulation of emotional experiences. During REM, memories are reactivated in a neurochemically distinct environment that allows emotional memories to be reprocessed with reduced physiological reactivity. This leads to the decoupling of emotional tone from memory content, allowing individuals to recall events with less distress (van der Helm et al., 2011). This is often metaphorically described as REM sleep functioning as overnight therapy.

Yoo et al. (2007) found in their fMRI study that sleep deprivation leads to increased amygdala reactivity and decreased connectivity between the amygdala and medial prefrontal cortex-structures involved in the regulation of emotion. This neurobiological profile mirrors what is seen in anxiety and mood disorders, suggesting that a single night of poor sleep can produce temporary, disorder-like impairments in emotional functioning.

One of the clearest pathways by which dreams influence next-day mood is through nightmares and emotionally negative dream content. Individuals who experience nightmares, even in non-clinical populations, report higher levels of anxiety, and irritability the following day (Levin & Nielsen, 2009; Schredl, 2009). In clinical populations, such as those with PTSD, nightmares are a core symptom that contributes significantly to daytime distress, hyperarousal, and avoidance behaviours (Germain, 2013).

Schredl (2009), in a large-scale study, found that about 18% of all dreams reported by participants influenced their next-day mood, with nightmares being far more likely to leave a negative emotional residue than neutral or pleasant dreams. This carryover effect was not random. It was predicted by factors such as dream recall frequency, personality traits (e.g., thin boundaries, neuroticism), and levels of current life stress. In regression models, nightmare frequency partially mediated the relationship between stress and next-day mood, suggesting that stress-related dreams are a key mechanism through which emotional disturbances persist across the sleep-wake boundary (Schredl, 2009).

Schredl and Reinhard (2010) found that emotionally positive dreams had a statistically significant (though smaller) positive effect on morning mood, compared to the negative effects of nightmares. While nightmares are more salient, the emotional effects of positive dreams should not be underestimated. Dreams involving reunion with loved ones, success, or healing can generate a lingering positive affect, often described by dreamers as feeling comforted, joyful, or hopeful upon waking. This suggests that dream sleep can serve not only as a processing system for distress but also as a source of emotional reinforcement and motivation.

Malinowski and Horton (2014) found that participants reported increased motivation, creativity, or feelings of connectedness after positive dreams, findings that align with theories of dreaming as not merely replay but reconstruction or simulation of emotional states. The affective tone of a dream, therefore, may influence waking behaviour, even when the specific content is forgotten.

Dreams also appear to simulate social and emotional experiences, offering a safe space for encountering fears, desires, and conflicts. The threat simulation theory proposed by Revonsuo (2000) argues that dreaming evolved to simulate dangerous scenarios and thereby enhance waking preparedness. However, this theory can be expanded to include simulations of social scenarios, as many dreams involve emotionally charged interactions with familiar others (Nielsen & Lara-Carrasco, 2007). These simulations may allow the dreamer to mentally rehearse emotional responses, potentially improving emotional intelligence or resilience the next day.

Lucid dreaming and dream awareness may amplify this effect. Individuals trained in lucid dream techniques often report using their dreams to confront fears, rehearse difficult conversations, or seek creative insight—interventions that have been shown to have measurable effects on next-day emotional state and behaviour (Stumbrys et al., 2014; Maciejewicz, 2022).

In sum, the night-to-day influence of sleep and dreams on emotion is multilayered, involving both neurobiological and symbolic mechanisms. Disturbances in sleep—particularly those involving nightmares or REM fragmentation—amplify negative emotion and weaken the ability to self-regulate. Conversely, restorative sleep with emotionally positive dreams can promote resilience, clarity, and motivation. As we shall see in the next section, this dynamic interaction forms a continuous, bidirectional loop of emotional processing across day and night.

The Bidirectional Feedback Loop of Emotional Processing

While numerous studies discussed above have independently investigated how daytime emotions affect sleep and how sleep influences next-day mood, recent advances in longitudinal data analysis and multilevel modelling have enabled researchers to quantify the bidirectional nature of these relationships more precisely. This section synthesizes key findings that support the existence of a continuous emotional feedback loop linking day and night.

Daily diary studies offer a naturalistic approach to understand the day-night emotional cycle. In a six-week study, Triantafillou et al. (2019) used smartphone-based assessments to track daily mood and self-reported sleep quality across a large adult sample. Using hierarchical linear modelling, they found significant within-person associations between sleep quality and next-day emotional valence. Specifically, when individuals slept better than their personal average, they reported higher positive affect and lower negative affect the next day. Interestingly, the

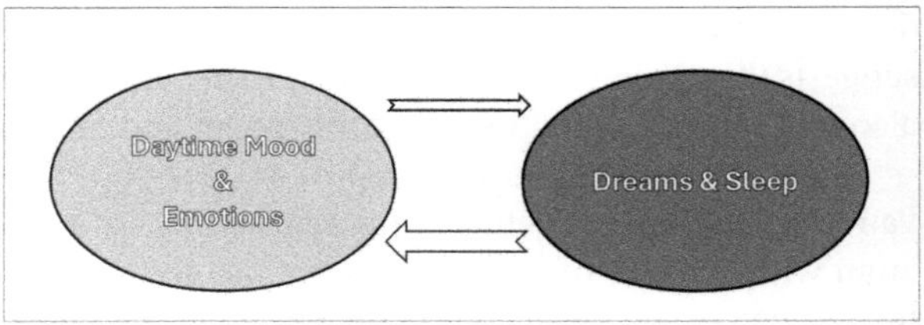

Fig. 1 The bidirectional feedback loop between dreams & sleep and emotions (by the author)

reverse association—daytime mood predicting subsequent sleep—was also significant, but weaker, suggesting an asymmetry in the strength of the bidirectional loop (Fig. 1). These findings suggest that although both directions matter, sleep has a stronger effect on next-day emotion than vice versa.

Multivariate models also point to mediating and moderating variables that shape the sleep-emotion relationship. Wang et al. (2024) found that rumination mediates the relationship between negative dream content and next-day anxiety. Along this model, a nightmare does not inherently cause daytime distress, rather, it is the post-sleep cognitive elaboration—the tendency to replay, interpret, or worry about the dream—that maintains emotional arousal.

The effect of daytime mood and emotions on sleep quality and dream affect is mutual, nevertheless dreams and sleep have higher effect on daytime moods and emotionality than the opposite.

Personality traits also moderate the bidirectional effect. Individuals high in neuroticism or with thin boundaries (i.e., those prone to heightened emotional sensitivity and fantasy) tend to experience greater carryover effects between dream and waking emotion (Schredl, 2009). Moreover, nightmare frequency has a mutual interaction with chronic daytime stress—i.e. anxiety—and reduced emotional resilience, indicating that emotionally disturbing dreams can serve as a pathway through which anxiety is internalized and re-expressed (Remedios et al., 2023; Townsend et al., 2016; Zhang et al., 2024).

Poor sleep on one night significantly predicts lower positive affect and higher irritability the next day (Soffer-Dudek et al., 2011; Palmer et al., 2024). Higher irritability in turn predicts longer sleep latency and more disturbed dreams the following night, and these translate as a self-perpetuating loop of emotion and sleep disruption (Vandekerckhove & Wang, 2018; Yap et al., 2020).

All in all, the pattern is consistent: (i) daytime stress and emotional intensity lead to poorer sleep and more negative dream content, (ii) in turn, poor sleep quality and emotionally dysphoric dreams predict worse emotional functioning the next day, (iii) these effects are partially mediated by cognitive-emotional factors such as rumination, and moderated by personality traits and nightmare frequency.

Cultural Perspectives on Sleep, Dreams, and Emotion Regulation Practices across Cultures

Emotion, sleep, and dreams are universal human experiences, but they are embedded in culturally specific frameworks that shape how these phenomena are understood, valued, and acted upon. Cross-cultural studies have shown that cultural norms and beliefs significantly affect dream interpretation, sleep practices, and the emotional salience of dream experiences (Lohmann, 2000; Mageo, 2011; Domhoff, 1996). Integrating these cultural dimensions into the sleep-dream-emotions model enhances our understanding of individual differences in emotional regulation and highlights the limitations of one-size-fits-all psychological theories.

One of the clearest cultural distinctions lies in the interpretive framework surrounding dreams (Domhoff, 1996). In many Western, industrialized societies, dreams are often dismissed as meaningless mental byproducts—*just dreams.* This viewpoint reduces dreams to an epiphenomenon without agency or impact. As a result, the emotional influence of dreams is often ignored or pathologized, particularly when individuals experience distressing or intrusive dream content (Faccini & Del-Monte, 2024).

In contrast, indigenous and non-Western cultures often pair dreams with spiritual, moral, or communal significance. Among the Asabano people of Papua New Guinea, for example, dreams are seen as important sources of knowledge and emotional insight, directly influencing waking decisions and rituals (Lohmann, 2000). A frightening dream may be interpreted as a warning from ancestors, triggering community-based responses such as storytelling or ritual cleansing. These practices provide collective frameworks for emotional processing, validating dream-related anxiety and offering culturally embedded mechanisms for resolution (Samson et al., 2023).

Similarly, in Tibetan Buddhist traditions, dreams are not only symbolic but are deliberately cultivated through practices such as dream yoga, aimed at achieving heightened awareness and emotional transcendence (Knauft, 2020). Here, dreams are tools for self-regulation, moral instruction, and spiritual progress. Such cultural frameworks drastically alter how emotional residue from dreams is carried into the next day, either as a burden, a message, or an opportunity for transformation.

Culture shapes not only the interpretation of dreams but also their content. A comparative study by Samson et al. (2023) found that forager communities in Tanzania and the Congo had more threatening dream themes, but those threats were often resolved collectively: the dreamer was rescued by the group or overcame danger with help. In contrast, Western dreamers often reported unresolved threats, experienced in isolation. This suggests that collectivist cultures may simulate emotional mastery through dreams, whereas individualist cultures simulate personal struggle, possibly leading to morning anxiety.

In summary, different cultures differ in how they regulate emotional expression, which in turn affects the emotional content of dreams. In societies where anger or fear is suppressed, those emotions often surface in dreams, resulting in elevated distress. Conversely, cultures that encourage open emotional expression may offload some emotional tension during waking hours, resulting in less emotionally intense dreams.

All in all, dreams are more likely to exert a positive influence on emotional well-being when embedded in a supportive interpretive community. In some Indigenous American traditions, dreams are shared during morning rituals, where elders or spiritual guides offer interpretations and coping strategies. This communal reframing not only validates emotional responses but also reduces distress through symbolic transformation. A nightmare, for example, may be understood as a spiritual message rather than a sign of pathology, enabling the dreamer to regain agency. This interaction supports a bio-cultural model of emotional regulation across the sleep-wake cycle. The same neural mechanisms of REM processing may be operating across all humans, but their outputs and meanings are shaped by cultural narrative, ritual, and belief.

The growing body of work arguing for the bidirectional sleep & dream versus emotion feedback loop, and the diverse approaches of the culturally embedded ways of the interpretation of dreams are setting the stage for integrative conceptual models that explain how individuals navigate emotional adaptation over time. The next section introduces one such model: the three-dimensional Trajectory Equifinality Model (TEM), which provides a powerful tool for visualizing how emotional experiences, sleep, and dreams shape one another.

The Trajectory Equifinality Model (TEM): A 3D Framework Interpretation of the Role of Sleep and Dreams for Emotion Regulation

To conceptually integrate the temporal, psychological, and cultural dynamics of the sleep-dreams-emotion relationship, the Trajectory Equifinality Model (TEM) offers a highly suitable framework. Originating from developmental and cultural psychology (Sato, 2009; Valsiner, 2000), the TEM emphasizes the interplay of time, choice, and context in shaping human development. It proposes that people move through trajectories—pathways shaped by both internal and external influences—which may lead to similar outcomes (equifinality)—even if with differences in the degree of manifestation—while diverging at critical decision points known as bifurcations. The inclusion of both "real" (lived) and "ir-real" (imagined or simulated) pathways makes it particularly apt for application to dreaming.

I argue for TEM to be extended into a three-dimensional (3D) model by adding a third axis, representing dreaming and nighttime emotional processing, – thus transforming the whole model into a sphere shape—allowing us to model how day-to-day emotional states interact with symbolic, and unconscious experiences during sleep, and how those influence the emotional states of the next day (Fig. 2).

The TEM extended to the three-dimensional sphere, creating the 3D TEM. The yellow asterisk illustrates a recurring dream leading to two different emotional manifestations at different times/occurrences.

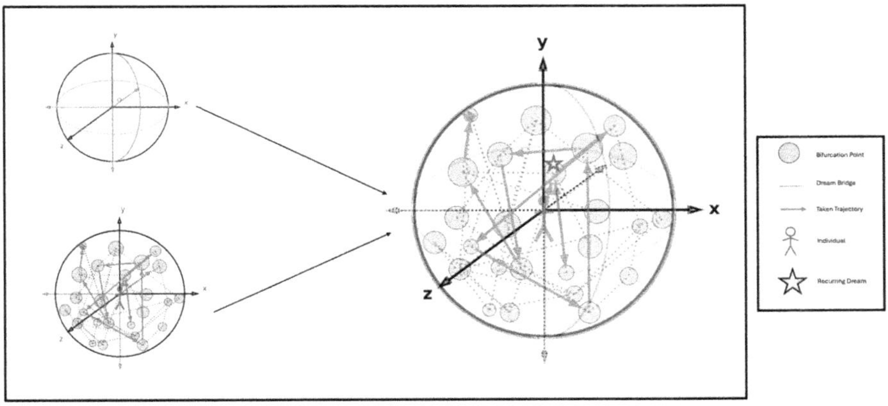

Fig. 2 The TEM merging into the three-dimensional sphere (by the author)

Real and Ir-Real Trajectories: The Role of Dreams

TEM is unique in its inclusion of "ir-real" trajectories that were not taken in real life but exist in memory, imagination, or cultural narrative. This feature aligns well with the function of dreams, which are inherently simulations: they incorporate emotional residues from past experiences and project possible future scenarios (Simor et al., 2023), often metaphorically or symbolically (Hartmann, 1996). In this context, dreams serve as narrative bridges opening up multilayered possible trajectories—through Bifurcation Points—offering to connect lived emotional states to imagined possibilities, reinforcing or altering one's emotional trajectory.

For instance, someone who experiences workplace humiliation might dream of public embarrassment (a metaphorical continuation of the emotional experience) or triumph (a symbolic counter-narrative). Regardless of its "reality", the dream itself can influence the dreamer's next-day emotions and sense of agency.

In TEM language, these are emotional Bifurcation Points (BFPs), where the life trajectories shaped by the Y axis—lived experiences and personality traits, i.e. nature and nurture axis—along the irreversible time—X axis—are multiplied into a three dimensional space—thus the third, Z axis—where one BFP in the intersection of the X and Y axis will be present in endless variations along the Z axis influenced by sleep and dreams.

To put it into mathematical context for illustrations sake: in the original model one point was characterized by two coordinates (X, Y), here this very same point will be characterized by three coordinates (X,Y,Z), and endless number of points will exist in the space where the X and Y coordinates are identical, only the value of Z can take up endless possibilities. The individual will then choose a trajectory in one direction or another, depending on the content and their interpretation of their dream. At this first virtual step in the 3D TEM space at least the value of one coordinate must change; nevertheless, it is possible that all three values of all three coordinates represent a new value.

To visualize this simply from the perspective of emotional processing and dreams: imagine a 3D graph with three intersecting axes: (i) the X-axis representing the Irreversible Time (past -› present -› future), (ii) the Y-axis standing for the Environment or Waking Experiences in a certain sociocultural environment, i.e. the actual emotional trajectory (declining, stable, improving mood), and (iii) introducing the Z-axis, opening up the Dream dimension (symbolic detours, interruptions, or integrations).

A Bifurcation Point (BFP) is a node where present decisions—such as whether to engage in emotion regulation strategies or maladaptive behaviours—determine the trajectory's next direction. Each point in the intersection of the three axes represents a possible state of emotional being in irreversible time (X axis), influenced by the day's stress level and nighttime sleep quality (Y axis), and the dream's emotional tone (Z axis). Meanwhile, dreams act as tunnels or bridges—between the endless number of BFPs—that either reinforce the previous trajectory or enable a shift towards a new emotional state.

For instance, a nightmare following a stressful day may reinforce the decline in emotional trajectory, while a positive dream or cathartic dream reinterpretation may lift the trajectory. A neutral or mundane dream may stabilize the emotional trajectory already taken (lateral continuation).

Free Will and Symbolic Bifurcations, from 3D TEM to Multidimensional TEM

A critical innovation of the 3D TEM model is the broadening of agency through dreams. The presence of endless number of BFPs in the original TEM enables that people are not passively carried along their trajectories but can intervene through endless number of possible choices, routines, and cognitive reframing. In the three-dimensional TEM these BFPs are spread in the spheric space, along all possible positions of the Z axis.

Additionally, dreams themselves may act as symbolic bifurcations within the original BFPs,—i.e. dream within a dream, or new system of 3D TEMs within each BFS (Fig. 3)—the moments where imagined possibilities shift how the individual feels or interprets waking life, thus extending the BFPs themselves to a three-dimensional TEM sphere. This connects to the idea of lucid dreaming, where the dreamer is aware of dreaming and may consciously guide the dream, practicing agency even in symbolic space (Stumbrys et al., 2014), i.e. testing out and deciding to choose from possible symbolic or dream BFPs influencing the position of the BFP of the life course TEM along the Z axis, and by intervening consciously editing those.

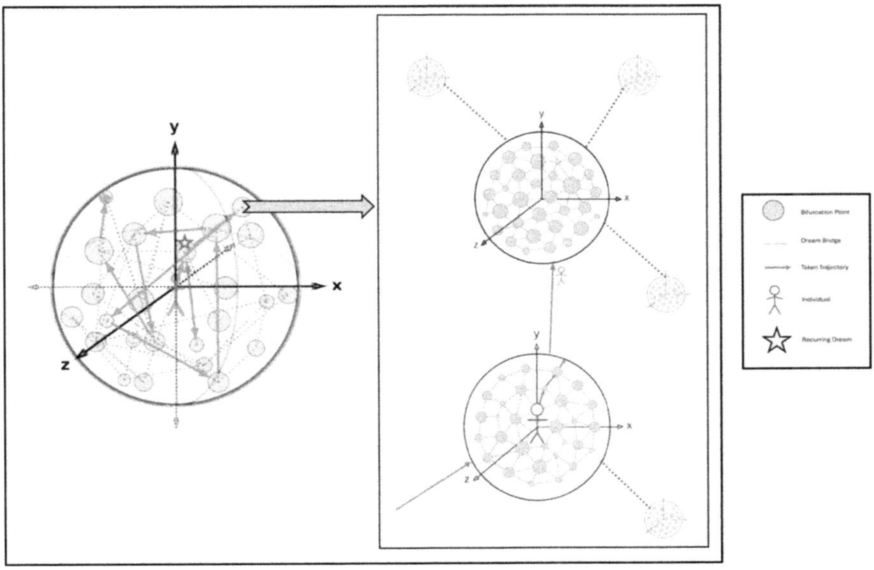

Fig. 3 From three-dimensional to multidimensional TEM (by the author)

This capacity for symbolic revision suggests that not only are dreams shaped by past experience, but they can also influence future mood, choices, and meaning-making, providing equifinal paths to emotional resolution.

The manifestation of the dream bridge—what became the taken trajectory—arriving from the previous BF—i.e. emotional manifestation of the previous dream—within the particular BF (zoomed into), incorporating endless numbers of symbolic Bifurcation Points (again)—i.e. possible taken trajectories within the dream scenario—within the individual life trajectory's Bifurcation Points. The three-dimensional model repeats itself endlessly within the main three-dimensional model (aka 3D TEM), building up the multidimensional TEM.

Obligatory Passage Points and Cultural Embedding

The TEM originally incorporates Obligatory Passage Points (OPPs), stages or conditions that all individuals pass through, but the experience and outcome vary (Sato, 2009; Valsiner, 2000). In the multidimensional model, sleep serves as OPP which every individual passes through the night, but the quality of that night (restful or disturbed, dreamless or vivid, symbolic or chaotic) determines where one lands on the emotional spectrum the next morning. Sleep—and accompanying dreams—is thus a universal, yet variable force in shaping emotional affect.

Discussion

The findings across empirical literature, theoretical models, and cultural insights converge on a consistent conclusion: emotion, dreams, and sleep are entangled in a dynamic, bidirectional relationship, mediated by dream experiences, sleep quality, and modulated by cultural frameworks.

The evidence is robust that emotional states during the day, especially stress, anxiety, and dysregulation, alter sleep quality and increase the probability of emotionally negative dreams (Kalmbach et al., 2018; Schredl & Reinhard, 2010; Vandekerckhove & Cluydts, 2010; Palmer & Alfano, 2017; Espie, 2002; Zhang et al. 2024; Triantafillou et al., 2019; Cartwright et al., 2006; Schredl, 2025; Malinowski & Horton, 2014; Walker & van der Helm, 2009). In turn, disturbed sleep and nightmares impair next-day mood regulation, executive functioning, and stress tolerance (Goldstein & Walker, 2014; van der Helm et al., 2011; Walker & van der Helm, 2009; Yoo et al., 2007; Levin & Nielsen, 2009; Schredl, 2009; Germain, 2013; Malinowski & Horton, 2014). The result is a vicious cycle, in which the aftershocks of 1 day echo into the next through the night.

Adequate sleep, emotionally neutral or positive dreams, and effective emotion regulation during the day foster improved emotional resilience and sleep continuity. Small positive interventions in one part of the cycle—mindfulness during the day, or cognitive-behavioural techniques for sleep, especially paired with Imagery Rehearsal Therapy (IRT)—can ripple into long-term emotional well-being.

The Trajectory Equifinality Model (TEM) provides a powerful integrative lens to conceptualize this process. By extending the model first into a three-dimensional space (irreversible time x waking emotional trajectory (shaped by the sociocultural space and personal attributes) x dream dimension) we can capture how the past (yesterday's stress and last night's sleep and dreams) influences the present emotional state, through the shaping of a Point (BFP)—with countless ir-real BFPs s in parallel—which offers choices (e.g., coping strategies, rumination, habits), and influence the manifestation of a particular future trajectory. Dreams basically act as symbolic tunnels or bridges, redirecting emotional trajectories by simulating alternative futures or recontextualizing past events. Manifestation of a certain emotional state, here a BFP in the life trajectory open up the multidimensional aspect of TEM by offering endless number of possibilities within a dream to choose from (Fig. 4).

In this model, sleep is the Obligatory Passage Point (OPP) that every individual must traverse nightly, but the quality and symbolism of that passage vary and influence the outcome. Emotional trajectories are not fixed, but rather plastic and influenced by narrative, agency, and culture. As discussed above, incorporation of cultural frameworks reveals how meaning-making around sleep and dreams differs vastly. In some traditions, dreams are seen as messages, warnings, or spiritual interventions, and are processed communally, while in others, dreams are trivialized or pathologized, often leading to isolation and emotional repression.

Summary of the multidimensional TEM concept: the traditional two-dimensional TEM is further extended to a three-dimensional sphere, as sleep as an OPP opened up the countless numbers of BFPs connected by dream bridges, leading to possible

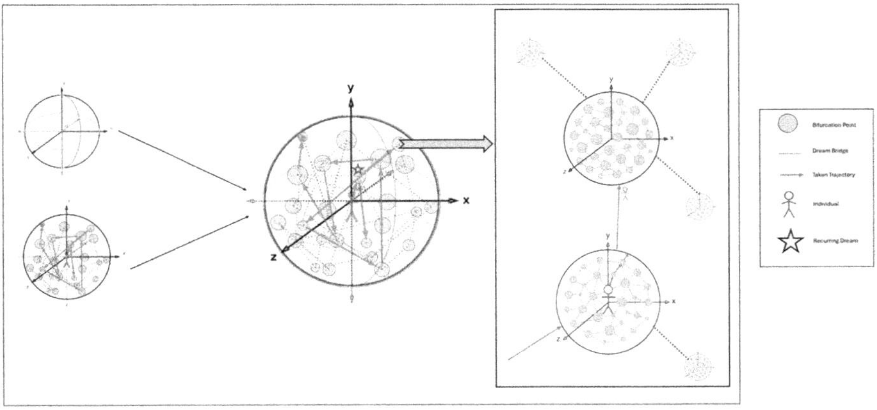

Fig. 4 The multidimensional TEM (by the author)

manifestation of emotional states. The whole model extends into multidimensional layers when endless possible dream scenarios are offered within each three-dimensional TEM BFP. The dreamer chooses a dream scenario from the multidimensional TEM, within the three-dimensional BFP, which stands for the previous day emotionality, and the bidirectional interaction between the three-dimensional and multidimensional TEM then manifests a dream as new bridge towards the next chosen, manifesting BFP, i.e. the next day emotionality.

Conclusion

This chapter attempted to apply the TEM to investigate the role of sleep and dreams on mood and emotional processing. This led to the extension of the model to a three-dimensional sphere where the individual is born in the middle of the sphere and arrives at the surface of that sphere—at the end of the lifespan—along an endless number of possible trajectories, and multidimensional possible dreams within dreams.

By extending the TEM into the three-dimensional space as one's life course, imagine the sphere as a huge ball full of several tiny balls within, where each tiny ball represents a Bifurcation Point in one's life, out of which few must be—Obligatory Passage Points –, and out of the rest numerous Bifurcation Points few needs to be passed through by the individual. Moreover, this huge ball—as the individual—is moving in space and time influenced by the environment as well as colliding with endless number of other huge balls, i.e. other individuals (Y axis) in the irreversible time and space (X axis), while it mixes the tiny balls—Bifurcation Points (i.e. possibilities), as well as the Obligatory Passage Points (for instance, if it happens that an individual completely skips sleep frequently for a certain amount of time, so the odds for an Obligatory Passage Point for sleep deprivation and its biological effects will and have to manifest)—within the huge ball (the individual life course). Nevertheless, the individual has agency over the choice of the trajectories as the possibilities are dynamically changing around the individual as a consequence of the previous trajectory chosen from the previous Bifurcation Point on, including the effect of altered states of consciousness, like sleep and dreams (Z axis).

Emotions and sleep & dreams are dynamically intertwined across a continuous 24-hour cycle. The findings reviewed in this article demonstrate that the relationship between daytime emotional states and nighttime sleep and dreaming is bidirectional, recurrent, and modulated by cognitive, physiological, symbolic, and cultural variables. As discussed above, empirical studies across diverse methods, ranging from diary studies to fMRI-reveal robust, predictive associations: stress and emotional volatility disrupt sleep and increase dream negativity, while poor sleep and distressing dreams exacerbate next-day mood disturbances, reduce resilience, and impair executive function.

This interaction is not symmetrical, sleep quality and dreams more strongly influence next-day emotion than the reverse (Schredl & Reinhard, 2010; Triantafillou et al., 2019; Newman et al., 2022). This finding positions sleep and dreams as a potent regulatory mechanism, a nightly opportunity to reset, reorganize, or reinforce emotional states. When that mechanism fails (e.g., via insomnia, nightmares, or emotional overload), it sets in motion a downward spiral of psychological distress.

The Trajectory Equifinality Model (TEM), adapted into a three-dimensional framework that incorporates additional endless number of ir-real Bifurcation Points in a sphere and their endless possible trajectories, helps to visualize how emotional trajectories unfold over time, shaped by past experiences, Bifurcation Points in the present, and the multidimensional symbolic detours provided by dreaming. This model integrates insights from affective neuroscience, developmental psychology, and cultural anthropology, emphasizing the importance of both agency and symbolic imagination in emotional navigation. Dreams are not only reflections of waking concerns but are active agents in emotional reprocessing, potentially opening new pathways or solidifying emotional recovery.

Cultural perspectives reveal that the meaning and emotional impact of dreams are profoundly shaped by social context, belief systems, and ritual practices. Cultures that treat dreams as meaningful and communally interpreted may enhance their healing potential, while those that pathologize or trivialize dreams may inadvertently suppress a valuable tool for emotional regulation. Incorporating these cultural frameworks into clinical settings offers new opportunities for personalized and holistic therapeutic strategies.

In conclusion, I argue for an interdisciplinary collaboration among clinical and cultural psychologists, psychotherapists, cultural and medical anthropologists, and sleep scientists. Ultimately, understanding the complexity of the feedback loop between emotion, sleep, and dreams may offer one of the most integrative pathways towards enhancing mental health, emotional resilience, and personal growth. By addressing both daytime emotional regulation and nighttime symbolic processing, mental health interventions can become more holistic and sustainable.

References

Bell, A., & Hall, C. (1971). *The personality of a child molester: An analysis of dreams*. Aldine.
Cartwright, R., Agargun, M. Y., Kirkby, J., & Friedman, J. K. (2006). Relation of dreams to waking concerns. *Psychiatry Research, 141*(3), 261–270. https://doi.org/10.1016/j.psychres.2005.05.013
Chalmers, D. J. (1996). *The conscious mind*. Oxford University Press.
Chen, C. K., & Nehrig, N. (2024). Trauma and dream work: Mending tears in the fabric of time. *American Journal of Psychotherapy, 77*(3), 129–134. https://doi.org/10.1176/appi.psychotherapy.20230051
Domhoff, G. W. (1996). Cross-cultural studies of dream content. In *Finding meaning in dreams. Emotions, personality, and psychotherapy*. Springer. https://doi.org/10.1007/978-1-4899-0298-6_6
Eichenlaub, J., Bertrand, O., Morlet, D., & Ruby, P. (2014). Brain reactivity differentiates subjects with high and low dream recall frequencies during both sleep and wakefulness. *Cerebral Cortex, 24*(5), 1206–1215. https://doi.org/10.1093/cercor/bhs388
Espie, C. A. (2002). Insomnia: Conceptual issues in the development, persistence, and treatment of sleep disorder in adults. *Annual Review of Psychology, 53*(1), 215–243. https://doi.org/10.1146/annurev.psych.53.100901.135243
Faccini, J., & Del-Monte, J. (2024). Bad dream, nightmares and psychopathology: A systematic review. *Frontiers in Psychiatry, 15*, 1461495. https://doi.org/10.3389/fpsyt.2024.1461495
Germain, A. (2013). Sleep disturbances as the hallmark of PTSD: Where are we now? *The American Journal of Psychiatry, 170*(4), 372–382. https://doi.org/10.1176/appi.ajp.2012.12040432
Goldstein, A. N., & Walker, M. P. (2014). The role of sleep in emotional brain function. *Annual Review of Clinical Psychology, 10*, 679–708. https://doi.org/10.1146/annurev-clinpsy-032813-153716
Grafe, L., Miller, K. E., Ross, R. J., & Bhatnagar, S. (2023). The importance of REM sleep fragmentation in the effects of stress on sleep: Perspectives from preclinical studies. *Neurobiology of Stress, 28*, 100588. https://doi.org/10.1016/j.ynstr.2023.100588
Hanson, R., Shapiro, S., Hutton-Thamm, E., Hagerty, M. R., & Sullivan, K. P. (2023). Learning to learn from positive experiences. *The Journal of Positive Psychology, 18*(1), 142–153. https://doi.org/10.1080/17439760.2021.2006759
Harley, T. A. (2021). *The science of consciousness*. Cambridge University Press.
Hartmann, E. (1996). Outline for a theory on the nature and functions of dreaming. *Dreaming, 6*(2), 147–170. https://doi.org/10.1037/h0094452
Hartmann, E. (1998). *Dreams and nightmares: The new theory on the origin and meaning of dreams*. Plenum Trade.
Jackson, F. (1982). Epiphenomenal Qualia. *The Philosophical Quarterly, 32*(127), 127–136. https://doi.org/10.2307/2960077
Jalāl al-Dīn, R., & Washington, P. (2006). *Rumi: poems*. Alfred A. Knopf.
Kalmbach, D. A., Anderson, J. R., & Drake, C. L. (2018). The impact of stress on sleep: Pathogenic sleep reactivity as a vulnerability to insomnia and circadian disorders. *Journal of Sleep Research, 27*(6), e12710. https://doi.org/10.1111/jsr.12710
Kim, J. (2005). *Physicalism, or something near enough*. Princeton University Press.
Knauft, B. M. (2020). Life is but a dream: Culture and science in the study of Tibetan dream yoga and lucid dreaming. In K. Mageo & C. Lutkehaus (Eds.), *New directions in the anthropology of dreaming* (pp. 255–275). Routledge. https://doi.org/10.4324/9781003037330-13
Kumar, K. (2021). *What is the life expectancy today?*. https://www.medicinenet.com/what_is_the_life_expectancy_today/article.htm
Levin, R., & Nielsen, T. A. (2009). Nightmares, bad dreams, and emotion dysregulation. *Current Directions in Psychological Science, 18*(2), 84–88. https://doi.org/10.1111/j.1467-8721.2009.01614.x

Lohmann, R. I. (2000). The role of dreams in religious enculturation among the Asabano of Papua New Guinea. *Ethos, 28*(1), 75–102. https://doi.org/10.1525/eth.2000.28.1.75

Maciejewicz, B. (2022). Impact of sleep and brain science of lucid dreaming: Insights into therapeutic applications. *Journal of Neuro and Oncology Research., 2*(3), 1–7. https://doi.org/10.46889/JNOR.2022.3303

Mageo, J. M. (2011). *Dreaming culture: Meanings, models, and power in U.S. American Dreams*. Palgrave Macmillan.

Malinowski, J., & Horton, C. L. (2014). Evidence for the preferential incorporation of emotional waking-life experiences into dreams. *Dreaming, 24*(1), 18–31. https://doi.org/10.1037/a0036017

Meerlo, P., Sgoifo, A., & Suchecki, D. (2008). Restricted and disrupted sleep: Effects on autonomic function, neuroendocrine stress systems and stress responsivity. *Sleep Medicine Reviews, 12*(3), 197–210. https://doi.org/10.1016/j.smrv.2007.07.007

Newman, D. B., Epel, E. S., Coccia, M., Puterman, E., & Prather, A. A. (2022). Asymmetrical effects of sleep and emotions in daily life. *Affecetive Science, 3*, 307–317. https://doi.org/10.1007/s42761-022-00112-x

Nielsen, T., & Lara-Carrasco, J. (2007). Nightmares, dreaming, and emotion regulation: A review. In D. Barrett & P. McNamara (Eds.), *The new science of dreaming: Vol. 2. Content, recall, and personality correlates* (pp. 253–284). Praeger Publishers/Greenwood Publishing Group.

Palmer, C. A., & Alfano, C. A. (2017). Sleep and emotion regulation: An organizing, integrative review. *Sleep Medicine Reviews, 31*, 6–16. https://doi.org/10.1016/j.smrv.2015.12.006

Palmer, C. A., Bower, J. L., Cho, K. W., Clementi, M. A., Lau, S., Oosterhoff, B., & Alfano, C. A. (2024). Sleep loss and emotion: A systematic review and meta-analysis of over 50 years of experimental research. *Psychological Bulletin, 150*(4), 440–463. https://doi.org/10.1037/bul0000410

Remedios, A., Marin-Dragu, S., Routledge, F., Hamm, S., Iyer, R. S., Orr, M., Meier, S., & Schredl, M. (2023). Nightmare frequency and nightmare distress during the COVID-19 pandemic. *Journal of Clinical Sleep Medicine., 19*(1), 163–169.

Revonsuo, A. (2000). The reinterpretation of dreams: An evolutionary hypothesis of the function of dreaming. *Behavioral and Brain Sciences, 23*(6), 877–901. https://doi.org/10.1017/S0140525X00004015

Samson, D. R., Clerget, A., Abbas, N., Senese, J., Sarma, M. S., Lew-Levy, S., Mabulla, I. A., Mabulla, A. Z. P., Miegakanda, V., Borghese, F., Henckaerts, P., Schwartz, S., Sterpenich, V., Gettler, L. T., Boyette, A., Crittenden, A. N., & Perogamvros, L. (2023). Evidence for an emotional adaptive function of dreams: A cross-cultural study. *Scientific Reports, 13*(1), 16530. https://doi.org/10.1038/s41598-023-43319-z

Sato, T. (2009). Developmental transformation in cultural psychology: An introduction to the trajectory equifinality model. *Integrative Psychological and Behavioral Science, 43*(3), 338–352. https://doi.org/10.1007/s12124-009-9095-0

Schredl, M. (2009). Effect of dreams on daytime mood: The effects of gender and personality. *Sleep and Hypnosis, 11*(2), 51–57.

Schredl, M. (2025). Are dream emotions shifted towards more negativity compared to waking -life emotions? An empirical study. *International Journal of dream Research., 18*(2).

Schredl, M., & Reinhard, I. (2010). The continuity between waking mood and dream emotions: Direct and second-order effects. *Imagination, Cognition and Personality, 27*(3), 271–282.

Seth, A. (2017, July). *Your brain hallucinates your conscious reality* [video]. TED conferences. https://www.ted.com/talks/anil_seth_your_brain_hallucinates_your_conscious_reality

Simor, P., Peigneux, P., & Bódizs, R. (2023). Sleep and dreaming in the light of reactive and predictive homeostasis. *Neuroscience & Biobehavioral Reviews, 147*, 105104. https://doi.org/10.1016/j.neubiorev.2023.105104

Soffer-Dudek, N., Sadeh, A., Dahl, R. E., & Rosenblat-Stein, S. (2011). Poor sleep quality predicts deficient emotion information processing over time in early adolescence. *Sleep, 34*(11), 1499–1508. https://doi.org/10.5665/sleep.1386

Stumbrys, T., Erlacher, D., Johnson, M., & Schredl, M. (2014). The phenomenology of lucid dreaming: An online survey. *The American Journal of Psychology, 127*(2), 191–204. https://doi.org/10.5406/amerjpsyc.127.2.0191

Tempesta, D., Socci, V., De Gennaro, L., & Ferrara, M. (2018). Sleep and emotional processing. *Sleep Medicine Reviews, 40*, 183–195. https://doi.org/10.1016/j.smrv.2017.12.005

Townsend, E., Heym, N., & Hochard, K. (2016). The behavioral effects of frequent nightmares on objective stress tolerance. *Dreaming, 26*(1), 42–49. https://doi.org/10.1037/drm0000013

Triantafillou, S., Saeb, S., Lattie, E. G., Mohr, D. C., & Kording, K. P. (2019). Relationship between sleep quality and mood: Ecological momentary assessment study. *JMIR Mental Health, 6*(3), e12613. https://doi.org/10.2196/12613

Valsiner, J. (2000). *Culture and human development: An introduction*. SAGE.

van der Helm, E., Yao, J., Dutt, S., Rao, V., Saletin, J. M., & Walker, M. P. (2011). REM sleep depotentiates amygdala activity to previous emotional experiences. *Current Biology, 21*(23), 2029–2032. https://doi.org/10.1016/j.cub.2011.10.052

Vandekerckhove, M., & Cluydts, R. (2010). The emotional brain and sleep: An intimate relationship. *Sleep Medicine Reviews, 14*(4), 219–226. https://doi.org/10.1016/j.smrv.2010.01.002

Vandekerckhove, M., & Wang, Y. L. (2018). Emotion, emotion regulation and sleep: An intimate relationship. *AIMS Neuroscience, 5*(1), 1–17. https://doi.org/10.3934/Neuroscience.2018.1.1

Walker, M. (2017). *Why we sleep*. Penguin.

Walker, M. P., & van der Helm, E. (2009). Overnight therapy? The role of sleep in emotional brain processing. *Psychological Bulletin, 135*(5), 731–748. https://doi.org/10.1037/a0016570

Wang, X., Soondrum, T., & Dai, L. (2024). Neuroticism affects nightmare distress through rumination. *Sleep and Breathing, 28*, 2629–2637. https://doi.org/10.1007/s11325-024-03135-9

Yap, Y., Slavish, D. C., Taylor, D. J., Bei, B., & Wiley, J. F. (2020). Bi-directional relations between stress and self-reported and actigraphy-assessed sleep: A daily intensive longitudinal study. *Sleep, 43*(3), zsz250. https://doi.org/10.1093/sleep/zsz250

Yoo, S.-S., Gujar, N., Hu, P., Jolesz, F. A., & Walker, M. P. (2007). The human emotional brain without sleep-a prefrontal amygdala disconnect. *Current Biology, 17*(20), R877–R878. https://doi.org/10.1016/j.cub.2007.08.007

Zhang, J., Pena, A., Delano, N., Sattari, N., Shuster, A. E., Baker, F. C., Simon, K., & Mednick, S. C. (2024). Evidence of an active role of dreaming in emotional memory processing shows that we dream to forget. *Scientific Reports, 14*(1), 8722. https://doi.org/10.1038/s41598-024-58170-z

The Outbreaking Self from Arts into TEA

Potential of Comics to Reflect Future and Trajectory Equifinality Approach in Psychology: Initial Ideas

Rebecca Moura de Almeida Ferreira Carvalho
and Vera Lucia Trevisan de Souza

Inner-Out Wonderland, Painting by the first author using acrylic and collage, 21 × 29.7 cm

R. M. d. A. F. Carvalho (✉)
PUC-Campinas Investigates the potential of comics and animations within the field of Psychology, São Paulo, Brazil

V. L. T. de Souza
Stricto Sensu Graduate Program in Psychology, Pontifical Catholic University of Campinas (PUC-Campinas), São Paulo, Brazil
e-mail: vtrevisan@puc-campinas.edu.br

M. A. Campill et al. (eds.), *New Paths in Trajectory Equifinality Modelling*, Theory and History in the Human and Social Sciences,
https://doi.org/10.1007/978-3-032-25855-7_18

Introduction

Comics can be understood as an art form in which figures work together to create a complete whole. However, if we consider them simply as a combination of text and images, we might erroneously believe that comics are simple. This would be a mistake, as this art form has a unique narrative style that no artistic or linguistic form can reproduce.

Unlike cinema and theater, comics do not force the audience to follow a pre-set timeline. Readers can appreciate each panel at their own pace, progressing through the story. Comics, unlike photography or painting, are not static. They have a fluid narrative conveyed through panels and speech balloons, allowing the story to be constructed by the reader's interpretation. At the same time, the timing is not indefinite. The artist designs the size, composition of panels, character expressions, dialogues, settings, and colors, considering the reading order, intended meanings, and the reader's thought process. It is an art that achieves its full potential through the appreciation of its audience.

Comic Books' Characteristics

Comic books' main characteristic is that they are a form of communication based on the fragmentation of narrative linearity by the reader. This linearity must be recomposed when the reader produces meaning. In comics, more than any other language, there is no reading possible without reader participation (Vergueiro, 2018, p. 7, Translation ours).

The comprehension of a comic reflects not only the artist, their work, and their worldview but also the reader, who fills the gaps between panels with their subjectivity. The language of comics relies on the power of its gaps where the specificity of comics as an artistic language and their potential for psychology resides.

This chapter begins by presenting this dimension, followed by examples of empirical research in the school context that used comics as a mediator of practices. Then, we propose observing the potential of comics to rethink the concept of time along with the Trajectory Equifinality Approach (TEA).

To transform comics into a mediation tool it is necessary understand comics structures. Thus, the division and nomenclature of the three subtopics of this chapter represent some of comics'classic structures, inviting the reader to approach this form of art by linking our constructed proposals. The technical definitions and theoretical contributions will be presented, interweaving our perceptions and analysis.

The Origins

Researchers and theorists do not seem to reach a consensus on the origins of comics. Some trace the roots of comics back to prehistory, suggesting that cave paintings represented a sequence of actions narrated to the rest of the tribe. Others associate

Egyptian paintings with the early forms of comics, considering them a series of successive images containing narratives (McCloud, 2005; Luyten, 1987).

Other origins relate to illustrated storytellers in fifth-century India, known as the *bhopas*. *Bhopas* were priests who traveled through villages carrying rolls of cloth, called *phad* or *par*, which depicted characters and scenes from regional epic myths. These nomadic storytellers spread worldwide, acquiring different names in various countries (Campos, 2022). This technique also advanced Buddhism in East Asia, with monks using image rolls to explain Buddhist stories. In China, the government encouraged the production of comic versions of classic Chinese literature to provide access to education for the entire Chinese population. In contrast, other researchers observe pre-Columbian picture manuscripts from 1519, which possess characteristics later adopted by modern comics (McCloud, 2005).

Regardless of their origins, comics are understood as an ancient form of expression that evolved over decades. They inherit the millennia-old art of narrating myths, fables, and stories through sequential images. Comics are a unique vehicle of creative expression, combining artistic and literary forms to narrate a story or dramatize an idea using figures, images, and words (Campos, 2022; Eisner, 2010). These stories are constructed within one or more panels.

Panels

A panel is an illustration typically bordered by lines. Each panel advances the story by linking scenes with figures, settings, and speech, thought, or narration balloons. Eisner (2010) believes the fundamental function of panels is to communicate ideas and/or stories through words and images. According to him, the actual task of the artist is to arrange the sequence of events so that the gaps in the action are filled. "Once the sequence is known, the reader can provide the intermediate elements based on their own experiences" (Eisner, 2010, p. 46). This highlights the artist's ability to select essential elements that can be "frozen" within the frame of a panel, the border. Beyond its primary function as a frame, the border can be part of nonverbal language, creating new possibilities for setting, action, and emotional support. The artist's stroke can be crafted to suggest specific actions or responses from the reader or to engage them emotionally with the narrative (Einer, 2010).

It is important to note that this emotional engagement with the reader is not exclusive to comics. It is a powerful and humanizing dimension inherent in the arts. Any form of art has the potential to affect individuals by fostering the development of more elaborate ways of being, existing, thinking, and acting in the world (Souza et al., 2018). Vigotski (1998) highlights the power of this language to evoke emotions, reflections, and contradictions in his work "Psychology of Art." Art enables meanings related to individuals' various roles and interactions with their context, promoting imagination and the expression of emotions.

In all works of art, we observe elements that reflect our subjectivity. However, the specificity of comics lies in the gaps that create a "void." This void compels the reader to use their imagination to anticipate what comes next and to complete what is unfinished. Unlike other forms of art, which we perceive as "finished" syntheses, comics require us to engage with each panel, integrating what appears as the materiality of the production with what we imagine and anticipate as events, situations, or possibilities. We deal with both realized and unrealized elements.

Beyond Panels

Another interesting point is that art can affect individuals because of its open nature, which promotes a defamiliarization of reality (Souza et al., 2018). This defamiliarization is essential for generating new meanings and senses related to lived experiences. As an artistic form, comics also exhibit this trait. However, due to their descriptive nature, which connects expressive images and words, this surprise occurs more literally and causes less defamiliarization depending on the narrative. The panel composition created by the artist, the plot choice, the character expressions, and even the style of the panels and void allow us to fill them with our own experiences in different ways, fostering the development of more complex relationships between the individual and the world.

In comics, the reader is guided through the paintings in a reading that reflects the reading process of a culture itself. In a Western culture, reading goes from right to left while in manga (comics of Japanese origin) reading goes from left to right. This format does not change even when importing or exporting comics around the world. Through the reading process in a way that "no other form of language can emulate, engaging them in a uniquely participatory construction of meaning" (Vergueiro, 2018, p. 6). This is particularly interesting for Cultural Psychology when we consider the possibility that the artist's narratives are constructed to reach readers and involve them in deeper meanings related to the complexities of human experience. That is, considering the artist's intentionality with their cultural production. This construction can be viewed from a dialectical perspective, as it is created by the artist and the reader, who attributes meanings and senses to the production.

Valsiner (2004) introduced the concept of the "promoter sign." A sign becomes a promoter sign by channeling future actions and internalizing them as feelings. In cultural psychology, signs are a key concept for integrating cultural phenomena from a psychological perspective. The "promoter sign" is the sign that guides and orients a person (Valsiner, 2004; Sato & Tanimura, 2016).

In the case of comics, their system of codes can be viewed as signs. The various systems in comics come together in narratives as a code system. Comics produce numerous codes in constructing meanings; reading them creates them by evoking different codes (Postema, 2018). Collections of codes, individually, can be unequal and may convey meanings differently. However, in comics, these codes begin to interact and make sense with each other. Magnussen (2000) refers to this process as a "complex sign." According to her, the signs of a panel are not interpreted individually but within the context of other panels. The interpretation of a comic panel is formed by different interacting signs, not only due to the panels themselves but also the spaces between them, enabling "creating a bigger, more complex sign than the panel itself" (Magnussen, 2000, p. 195).

For example, considering the aesthetics chosen by artists, we can observe that panels can be highly vague, showing little or nothing of a specific scene and offering only clues. Often, the artist may not seek realistic human images but cartoonish ones to resonate with the reader's meanings. Highly realistic art represents an external world, while cartoonish art can access the reader's internal world. This type of art can attempt to align with readers' concepts, experiences, and interpretations. If an artist wants to represent the beauty and complexity of a physical world, some degree of realism might be necessary. The narrative clues and seemingly simple appearances chosen by the artist can evoke myriad images in the reader's mind, filling in these created panels with their experiences (McCloud, 2005).

This underscores the potential of using comics to think critically and broadly about social and collective issues, involving the reader and their experiences. We can observe how this relates to psychological practice more clearly in the following subtopic, where we will exemplify professional practices and present another interaction that we believe exists between artists and readers in the space between panels, specifically in the gutter.

Gutter

Although we explored the millennial roots of comic history in the previous subtopic, Western modernity was not as welcoming to this powerful art form. McCloud (2005, p. 3) points out the erroneous societal view that comics are "for children, poorly drawn, cheap, and disposable," a misconception perpetuated by the collective. This perception even influenced artists' views of themselves for many years. The term "comic book" had such negative connotations that many professionals preferred to be known as "illustrators" or "commercial artists."

For Eisner (2010), McCloud (2000, 2005), and their followers, comics are a potent sequential art form that mobilizes imagination and expression and must be taken seriously by critics and professionals. Extending this thought to Psychology, we also understand that this art form has been perceived negatively, undermining its potential use in the field. In an integrative review (Carvalho & Souza, 2023) examining studies in psychology and education between 2012 and 2022, it was observed that the use of anime and manga (Japanese-style animation and comics) could foster the elaboration and reflection on essential issues in the developmental process of children and adolescents, both in educational and psychological fields. However, the number of findings in psychology is still scarce compared to education.

Beyond the Gutter

This chapter aims to continue breaking prejudices and misconceptions Psychology might have regarding comics. We believe they are essential material for Psychology, particularly in allowing readers to fill in the gaps of the work with their subjectivity. Just as Gutter appears in comics, Psychology emerges as a reflective and collective possibility when using comics in practice.

The Gutter is the white space that separates panels and conveys a movement of time and/or space in the narrative. A gutter " transforms two separate images into a single idea" (McCloud, 2005, p. 66). From a psychological perspective, the Gutter plays a fundamental role in expressing human subjectivity through imagination and emotion. The contained space and the "non-space" are significant in the narrative structure, inviting the reader to "fill in the gaps." According to McCloud (2005), the reader looks at two disconnected images, two separate Panels, and transforms them into a single idea, a continuous reality, challenging our imagination to complete the entire scene. Nothing is seen between the two panels, but our imagination suggests a flow of time and space. We mentally conclude a continuous, unified reality by connecting the Panels and constructing meaning in the narrative. "Within these panels, we can only convey information visually. But between panels, none of our senses are required at all. Which is why all of our senses are engaged!" (1994, p. 89).

This expressiveness of human subjectivity in using comics appears in our research and psychological practices. In the school context, Carvalho (2023) observed the potential of Japanese comics (and animations) to mobilize the emotions and imagination of adolescents in Brazil. On the other hand, Pantaleo (2023) observed the potential of American, British, and Australian comics (and illustrations) to stimulate students' critical and creative thinking in Canada. Although both studies focused on Education and Psychology, the different types of comics, intervention proposals, audiences, and locations demonstrate the diversity and potential of using these tools in the field.

Using comics as mediators in psychological practices enables a critical, welcoming, and transformative approach to individuals' living conditions. Carvalho and Souza (2024) observe the potential of these media to access emotions and stimulate adolescents' imagination. They also highlight the power of comics as mediators of actions against prejudice in the school context. This reinforces how comics can be used to think critically and broadly about social and collective issues involving individuals, as presented in the previous subtopic.

We agree with Lopes (2021) that the various forms of using comics in practice allow for employing this tool as a space for "listening and speaking, producing subjectivity, and collective self-construction, viewing the comic book as a means rather than an end in itself, and as unfinished, open to reinvention in the work with the diverse and infinite youth" (Lopes, 2021, p. 15).

Open Panel

When we read a comic for the first time, we might think that panels show a single moment in time and that between these "frozen" moments, our mind creates an illusion of time and movement linearly. However, this definition is incorrect since comic time is far more complex. Figure 1 illustrates this complexity.

Notice that the panel in Fig. 1 does not represent a "single moment" like a photograph. Figures and intervals within the same panel create a different illusion of time when associated with words. The various actions and reactions of characters, onomatopoeias, and speech bubbles construct a sense of time that does not fit the definition of a "frozen panel" like in photography. They are not photos, static frames, or single images, as a single panel can indicate a passage of time through the reading sequence combined with the pictures. In this example, the onomatopoeia "flash" creates a specific camera sound in our minds and gives us a notion of a particular duration. The figures, balloons, and intervals between them create the illusion of time, constructed with the reader, and are reinforced by words representing something that can only exist in time: sound (McCloud, 2005).

A film is projected in the same space (the screen), while different spaces are occupied in comics. These different spaces in comics are what time is to cinema. However, the way we understand this "time" differs. When reading comics, we begin to understand time spatially since, in comics, time and space are one entity (McCloud, 2005). For example, if the artist wants to increase the sensation of time, they can repeat the same static panel, enlarge the panel size, or widen the gutter between panels. Due to the panel and gutter sizes, these spaces affect the reader's sense of duration and, thus, the narrative's time.

Fig. 1 Extracted from McCloud (2005, p. 95)

> With comics, the frame ceases to represent an instant and becomes the representation of a duration. […] The key point is, precisely, the signs of movement, the lines that express the displacement of the figures. […] These lines do not represent any object but precisely movement and, therefore, duration; they are the temporal connector that holds together a series of still figures, each captured at a crucial moment. Thanks to these lines, the image not only counts but also represents duration, even though each of the figures that appear is reproduced in a unique instant. […] Through the exponent of the movement signs that represent time within the image and suggest the correct succession of events, the time used in reading is transformed into the duration of the image (Barbieri 1993, pp. 225–229, Translation ours).

The temporal aspect of comics seems potent for fostering reflection, warranting more studies on time and its relationship with comics. However, other artists and appreciators often overlook the importance of time. Similarly, the notion of time is also neglected in Psychology.

Beyond Open Panels

In Psychology, the concept of time is dominated by notions of linear, chronological, and pre-determined time. However, a person is not a collection of moments, and their life trajectory is not a single line connecting points in time arbitrarily defined by investigators and psychologists (Sato et al., 2009). We cannot study an individual's life trajectory without an appropriate time understanding. However, much like in comics, the significance of time seems to be underestimated in Psychology.

One reason psychologists disregard time, as presented by Sato et al. (2009), relates to the desire for representations that focus on false stability through data analyses blind to variability and dynamics. This aspiration leads to studies seeking, for example, correlations between biological factors and personality, ignoring cultural factors.

The Trajectory Equifinality Model (TEM), part of the Trajectory Equifinality Approach (TEA), is an interesting methodological proposal for considering time in our practices. TEM is one way to understand the flow and continuity of life from the perspective of the agent whose life course is being studied (Sato et al., 2009).

Similarly, comics can contribute to reflecting on the importance of time. In comics, the "past," present, and future can be seen and are highly regarded in the narrative trajectory. Each panel we read is the present moment, the panels we have read are the past, and those we are yet to read are the future (McCloud, 2005). In films and television, it is always the "now." The narrative construction does not allow for smooth back-and-forth movement. In comics, however, time has potential in the future, which we have yet to read through the interpretations and subjectivity we add, as well as the time we delve into between and within panels. As mentioned in the previous subtopic, all are constructed from our subjectivity and collectively with the artist.

If we consider TEA like comics, we can understand that by considering time, we highlight points of equifinality by observing a person's real and possible trajectories. Unlike longitudinal studies that use psychological scales, these repetitions interpret only numbers, ignoring the uniqueness of each person's trajectory (similar to how our eyes interpret only frames and not the unique time of each frame). The vector model does not offer a developmental or historical view of life satisfaction, as it consists of the temporal sequence of results (Sato et al., 2009). In TEA, however, we assume that each individual's trajectory must be validated, recognized, and valued, reflecting their unique process, while numbers represent only the outcome. Understanding the process allows for a broader understanding of the generated results, much like in comics, where time is viewed broadly, and the gaps between panels, the journey from one panel to another, are as significant (or more so) than the panel itself.

The power of the TEA, like that of comics, is accentuated when we observe the subjectivity of individuals and their trajectories. In comics, even using various framing strategies and techniques, these artistic works help us create and imagine the narrative in our own time. The artist guides and constructs the work, while comics allow readers to appreciate the story in their unique time. A reader may rush through dialogues without focusing much on the images or spend several minutes on each panel, reflecting on the form or content and revisiting previous panels to contemplate them more closely.

Similarly, the TEA focuses on transforming individual and singular human experiences within an irreversible time in their life trajectory. Individuals choose one at a time from various possibilities; these transactions between the human and their environment (Sato et al., 2014).

This effect becomes even more potent if we advance our analysis and consider the Open Panels (panels beyond the page's margin). The time contained by the familiar icon of a closed panel escapes into infinite space. This technique can sometimes establish the mood and a sense of place or create a timeless sensation (McCloud, 2005). What is interesting about Open Panels is that what the reader imagines outside the panel can have more impact than what the artist explicitly shows. The artist invites readers to expand imaginative possibilities and venture into infinite spaces. The reader, in turn, accepts this invitation, further expanding reflective possibilities by introducing their own experiences.

Similarly, the concept of Irreversible Time used in the TEA characterizes real-time by never repeating events from the previous period, flowing from an infinite past toward an endless future. There is no timeless repetition because things, even if they happen again, will never be the same and will never happen in the same way (Sato et al., 2009). This infinity of future possibilities, like in the Open Panels in comics, can have more impact than what is shown in results from longitudinal studies using psychological scales.

To understand all these notions of time better, let us observe Fig. 1.

In this comic (Fig. 2), using the Japanese reading (right to left, arrows were added to facilitate understanding), we observe panels of different sizes focusing on different parts of the characters. Gutters (the spaces between panels) also appear, composing the scene. If we continue examining the work, we might ask about the setting, the characters' positions, the wind, the tears, and even the characters'

Fig. 2 Made by the first author based on Otomo (2023)

shadows. Combining these elements gives the impression that time, especially in the smaller panels, seems to move more slowly, while the larger panel appears to have "more time." However, the artist does not specify how much time passes between one panel and another. It is merely our perception, based on our experience, of the events and the work's narrative.

We can still imagine the two characters looking at each other and, from their expressions, infer what they might be thinking or feeling. You might want to return to a previous panel, move forward, or pause for a few seconds on a panel that caught your attention. You might remember something you saw, read, or experienced as you look. Perhaps the tears falling or the characters' clothing remind you of a moment in your life or someone you know. This can make you read the comics in 2, 3 seconds or more. Alternatively, maybe you are tired, wanting to move through the text quickly, paying little attention to the images, and reading the panels in less than a second. Here, we observe how the reading time of each panel is unique to each reader, based on their experience at the moment of reading (which changes every time they re-read it as their experiences also change). How you read the panels or relate to them is a mark of your history and reveals your trajectory—faster or slower, more indecisive, insecure, or focused—constituting specificities of a constitution related to the environment in which you develop.

This is similar to TEA, which considers that an individual's trajectory reflects their unique process, which is recognized and valued. The path you took before reading the panels, your impressions, and what you reflected on afterward (as well as the gaps in between, the voids, and the times) are important and validated. An example is Yasuda's (2005) research, which interviewed couples who could not have children and who, even after fertility treatment, decided to adopt. The study observed how different experiences with infertility resulted in life decisions intertwined with the subjects' social, cultural, ethical, and interpersonal processes, manifesting over time. Yasuda did not just ask, "Why are you considering adoption?" but investigated their trajectories, choices, and the society they are part of, relating to these experiences to answer their questions.

Returning to the comic presented, if I had shown you, the reader, a few previous pages, you would understand that the scene had been destroyed by a bomb that devastated the city, killing thousands of people. A composition of scenes showing dead people calling for help, buildings in ruins, sometimes occupying entire pages, other times short, flowing in a quick time of despair and death. The city is drawn realistically to associate the reader with their reality and humanity's history, sometimes using the Open Panel technique—wars and bombs decimating towns and people in seconds. If you, the reader, had read these previous pages, the impact and perceptions of the panels in Fig. 1 would change. We would better understand the spatial location of the two characters amidst the destruction and construct the "space" (setting and time) of the work in our minds. And if we go even further back, knowing the work from the beginning, we could understand, for example, who the characters are, the location, how they reached this point, why the destruction occurred, and imagine why the characters have these expressions. All this expands our perceptions and constructs the work's narrative. Thus, like the TEA, observing and understanding the subject's past and individual experiences is essential to consider new possibilities.

Now, imagine that I have shown you only the first panel. This static panel cannot convey the fluid narrative of time slowing down or the focus on the characters' faces, making us pay more attention to their expressions and imagine them looking at each other intensely. We cannot consider the time you take between one panel and the next (because there is no next panel). The vector model in Psychology does something similar. It does not offer a developmental or historical view, considering this temporal sequence of results or the movement between them. It does not account for the gaps, the panels, and the time. It makes static cuts and derives results from them without observing the time and subjectivity of its subjects.

However, we need to rethink this perspective. Psychology, especially in areas focused on Development, needs a trajectory model that expands the opportunity to explore the complexity of an individual's life stories. The TEA allows us to observe potential and/or unrealized past and possible future trajectories and conceptualize how trajectories are in the construction process (Sato et al., 2009).

Conclusion

Western comics have faced misconceptions and prejudices created by society. They are viewed as children's consumption, cheap, disposable, and undeserving of importance in research or professional practice. Over the years, current research has shown the potency of this artistic form for psychological practices by enabling the expression of emotions and elaborating on essential themes in human life.

However, beyond practical possibilities, comics also help us understand the importance of considering time in our field, which is neglected in Psychology due to the dominance of a linear, chronological, and pre-determined notion of time. We cannot study an individual's life trajectory without an appropriate understanding of time, and comics help us grasp this different perspective, primarily when related to the TEA.

Looking at time differently from the traditional psychological model is essential for the field's growth as both a science and a profession. This time, addressed in the TEA, is similar to the time in comics, considering the reader's subjectivity, trajectories, and choices. Along with this subjectivity, the narrative of comics is constructed just as an individual's life trajectory is for the TEA. We believe that the ideas, relationships, and reflections presented in this chapter can inspire new elaborations in practices and research, advancing the field of Psychology. More than just a practical tool, comics provide Psychology with a crucial theoretical lesson: a model of subjective, non-linear time that is essential for moving beyond outdated chronological views and truly understanding the construction of a human life.

Acknowledgments Our gratitude to the National Council for Scientific and Technological Development (CNPq) for the scholarships that provided partial funding for this research, particularly the doctoral scholarship granted to the first author.

References

Barbieri, D. (1993). *Los lenguajes del comic*. Paidós Ibérica.

Campos, R. (2022). *HQ uma pequena história dos quadrinhos Para uso das novas gerações*. Edições Sesc.

Carvalho, R. M. de A. F. (2023). Animes e Mangás mobilizando Afetos e Imaginação na Escola. [Dissertação de Mestrado, Pontifícia Universidade Católica de Campinas] https://repositorio.sis.puc-campinas.edu.br/bitstream/handle/123456789/17121/ccv_ppgpsico_dissertacao_carvalho_rmaf.pdf?sequence=1&isAllowed=y

Carvalho, R. M. de A. F., & Souza, V. L. T. (2023). Animes, mangás, psicologia e educação: Uma revisão integrativa. *Rev. Psicopedagogia, 40*(123), 394–402. https://doi.org/10.51207/2179-4057.20230036

Carvalho, R. M. de A. F., & Souza, V. L. T. (2024). Reflexões sobre as violências e as diferenças no contexto escolar utilizando animes. *Revista Debates Insubmissos. 7*(24). https://doi.org/10.32359/debin2024.v7.n24.p196-212

Eisner, W. (2010). *Quadrinhos e arte sequencial*. Martins Fontes.

Lopes, D. E. N. (2021) "Nós" entre rabiscos e palavras: a construção de uma HQ para políticas públicas com jovens em vulnerabilidade. [Dissertação de Mestrado Profissional em Psicologia e Políticas Públicas] https://repositorio.ufc.br/handle/riufc/63054

Luyten, S. (1987). O que é Histórias em Quadrinhos. *Brasiliense, 1987.*
Magnussen, A. (2000). The semiotics of C. S. Peirce as a theoretical framework for the understanding of comics. In A. Magnussen & H. Christiansen (Eds.), *Comics and culture analytical and theoretical approaches* (pp. 193–207). Museum Tusculanum Press.
McCloud, S. (2000). Reinventando os Quadrinhos. MBooks [Brazilian's Edition].
McCloud, S. (2005). Desvendando os Quadrinhos. 2ªed. MBooks [Brazilian's Edition].
Otomo, K. (2023). Akira [Originally Published in Japan between Dec. 20 (1982) to 25 de Jun. (1990) by Young Magazine].
Pantaleo, S. (2023). Elementary students' engagement in transduction and creative and critical thinking. *Literacy UKLA, 58*(1), 58–71. https://doi.org/10.1111/lit.12350
Postema, B. (2018). *Estrutura Narrativa nos Quadrinhos: Construindo sentido a partir de fragmentos*. Editora Peirópolis.
Sato, T., Hidaka, T., & Fukuda, M. (2009). Depicting the dynamics of living the life: The trajectory equifinality model. In J. Valsiner, P. Molenaar, M. Lyra, & N. Chaudhary (Eds.), *Dynamic process methodology in the social and developmental sciences* (pp. 217–240). Springer.
Sato, T., & Tanimura, H. (2016). The trajectory Equifinality model (TEM) as a general tool for understanding human life course within irreversible. In T. N. Sato, N. Mori, & J. Valsiner (Eds.), *Making of the future: The trajectory equifinality approach in cultural psychology* (pp. 21–42). IAP Information Age Publishing.
Sato, T., Yasuda, Y., Kanzaki, M., & Valsiner, J. (2014). From describing to reconstructing life trajectories: How the TEA (trajectory Equifinality approach) explicates context-dependent human phenomena. In B. Wagoner, N. Chaudhary, & P. Hviid (Eds.), *Cultural psychology and its future: Complementarity in a new key* (pp. 93–105). Information Age Publishing.
Souza, V. L. T., Dugnani, L. A. C., & Reis, E. C. G. (2018). Open-access Psicologia da arte: fundamentos e práticas para uma ação transformadora. Estudos de Psicologia. https://doi.org/10.1590/1982-02752018000400005
Valsiner, J. (2004). The promoter sign: Developmental transformation within stricture of dialogical self. Paper present at the symposium Developmental aspects od the dialogial self. Gent. https://vbn.aau.dk/en/publications/the-promoter-sign-developmental-transformation-within-the-structu
Vergueiro, W. (2018). Prefácio à Edição Brasileira. In B. Postema (Ed.), *Estrutura Narrativa nos Quadrinhos: Construindo sentido a partir de fragmentos*. Editora Peirópolis.
Vigotski, L. S. (1998). *Psicologia da Arte*. Martins Fontes.
Yasuda, Y. (2005). Self-reassessment following infertility: Branching selection by couples unable to have children after infertility treatment. *Qualitative Research in Psychology, 4*, 201–226. https://www.jstage.jst.go.jp/article/jaqp/4/1/4_201/_pdf/-char/ja

To Sing or Not to Sing?

The Potential and Use of the Trajectory Equifinality Approach in Practice

Anna Fedorova

Introduction

The following chapter is written employing autoethnography methodology: a reflexive, story-driven inquiry that situates my lived experience within wider cultural and institutional contexts. Following Ellis and Bochner's framing of autoethnography as both evocative and analytic, using "thick" personal narrative to illuminate social processes, I adopt a first-person voice to examine how I have been working towards becoming an opera singer, as well as exploring through Trajectory Equifinality Approach (TEA) if it ended up being successful. This methodological choice allows me to evaluate that my rehearsal room, and performance stage are not merely backdrops for my individual ambition. Rather, they are sites where norms, power, pedagogy, and aesthetics intersect with a body and a voice in training.

I align with contemporary developments that integrate personal narrative with process-relational models of development (Ellis & Bochner, 2000), committing to a transparent position of vulnerability, and stakes of writing about teachers, competitors, family members, repertoires, and institutions.

To make sense of my journey, I use the TEA as an analytic prism. TEA treats development as a guided trajectory through sociocultural time, divided into bifurcation points (critical choices or chance events), obligatory passage points (assessments, competitions), and fields of social guidance (teachers, coaches, directors, scores, traditions). I thought that my story of opera singing and everything it involves, aligns with this approach well, and as I go on and share it, I make sure to pseudonymize the identities of individuals involved.

The decision to sign as a mezzo soprano, the pivot from Italian, French, German, and Russian repertoire, the common stage fright, slight anxiety before an audition,

A. Fedorova (✉)
Sigmund Freud PrivatUniversity, Vienna, Austria

M. A. Campill et al. (eds.), *New Paths in Trajectory Equifinality Modelling*, Theory and History in the Human and Social Sciences,
https://doi.org/10.1007/978-3-032-25855-7_19

or the participation in a masterclass—each function as a bifurcation that redirects momentum. Entrance exams, auditions—each operate as mechanisms of progress. TEA's central claim of equifinality is that multiple, non-identical paths can lead to similar endpoints. Thus, allowing me to embark on divergent routes (late starters, cross-disciplinary movers, singers who pause for various reasons, etc.) as legitimate pathways towards professional artistry rather than deviations from a single norm.

In what is about to be read, I shed light on scenes from practice rooms, lessons, and stages with a TEA-informed reading of how my voice, body, and identity are co-shaped by institutions and traditions. The aim is not to generalize from one life, but to show, through one life—my life, how the becoming of an opera singer is a culturally organized, contingently guided trajectory with more than one possible finale.

The Beginning of an Opera Journey

Ever since I was 16 years old, I remember sitting down with my mother at around January's time and thoroughly going over numerous music academies that offered a few-month-long opera masterclasses abroad, over the summer. I've been singing since I was seven (Fig. 1), and whether I was singing on stage in Riga, Austria, Italy, or anywhere else in the world, it didn't intimidate me too much. On the contrary, I loved singing, and even more so, I loved to perform. In a way, I would even draw a connection between the entire scene of opera performance, anything related to the act of opera in the connection to the Trajectory Equifinality Approach (Sato, 2017). TEA "focuses on the longitudinal changes in individual trajectories" (Hirose & Creswell, 2025, p. 4), meaning that during my teenage years, achieving the end goal of becoming an opera singer was associated with happiness; however, the trajectories or the paths towards such states have changed over time.

To begin with, I think it's important to point out that seeing someone perform looks way easier than it is for the one performing. It's not just a mere performance

Fig. 1 Performing on stage at the age of seven (by the author)

of singing, acting, and wearing a costume – behind are long and never-ending hours of practice. Each practice includes a warm-up, which is crucial, as it is worth 50% of the final performance outcome. Warm-ups include more than humming and singing through the repertoire multiple times. It consists of breathing exercises, and activation of different body parts (even those that don't appear as utilized): neck, jaw, headspace, shoulders, legs, diaphragm, chest, and abdominals. The warm-up includes sirens and glide exercises, vowel exercises and scale work, staccato and legato exercises, arpeggios and dynamic control, resonance and placement, to name a few. During each aspect of the warm-up, my vocal coach, Svetlana, would draw analogies of who or what I was supposed to imagine myself as to get a better outcome from the exercise. For example, "Anya, each time we change from vowel 'a to 'o when singing intervals, you need to imagine a hot potato in your mouth to make it airy and allow for the space in your throat". Another example, which I remember very clearly, was pretending to be a "tractor with a loader". I had to pretend to have a loader behind my head, which would throw the high notes away, the same way the normal loader tractor throws dirt. In contrast to the high tonality, whenever I had to sing to activate my lows, Svetlana would ask me to imagine myself as a tree with roots deeply planted in the ground for support—it is in a Russian school of opera to ground yourself and find support in the lower body.

Bifurcation Point

That is how each time I had to choose to transform into a deep-rooted tree (Fig. 2) or a loader tractor, I'd reach the Bifurcation Point (BFP) (Sato et al., 2009). In relation to TEA, BFP occurs at a moment when a system's trajectory can "branch" into several potential directions, often due to an internal or external change in conditions. In other words, it's the point where a single trajectory splits into multiple possible future outcomes, and small variations or decisions can lead to significantly different results. For instance, if I choose to be a tree when going to the higher vocal register, it will make the sound very pressured and stiff, whereas the intention is to always have high notes airy, round, and precise. This way it would shift the entire technique of the chosen piece, resulting in a completely different sound quality. This could be dangerous for both the singer, in terms of the vocal cords' health, as well as for the audience—it is hard to conceal wrong technique from the knowledgeable audience.

As a singer, I'd stumble on BFP again, but this time on the stage instead of the practice room. On the stage, I had to get into character. It was time to put on a show. As an artist, there is always a choice of whether to get in the role and identify with the storyline of the character you are playing or to be yourself, standing and singing. The first choice is always preferable because you want to engage the audience in the story, for them to actively be part of it, instead of you being a storyteller and them passively listening. Staying in character can also be tough, due to the ease of falling out of it. There are numerous reasons behind it. In my childhood, I forgot the lyrics,

Fig. 2 "Deep-rooted tree" metaphor (by the author)

froze on stage, and ran off the stage, instead of choosing to stay in the role of the shepherd girl from "The Aria of the Shepherd" by Francesca Caccini until the end.

Social Direction

I was told by both my mother and Svetlana, that when acting out a certain character, there is always a need for social referencing—someone to set an example of. This is when Social Direction (SD) (Sato et al., 2009, p. 15) comes into play. SD is concerned with the ways in which social influences—in this case, composers' description of the character in the context of the aria/story; previous performances with this role; Svetlana's interpretation of the fictional character—directly or indirectly influence the possible trajectories an individual might follow. In a trajectory equifinality framework, SD helps explain how social systems or contexts can direct people's choices and life courses, steering them towards certain outcomes.

To take off from where I began this chapter, in one of such music academies where I spent the summer of 2018, I spent the entire month polishing the character of Giovanni Paisiello "Chi Vuol La Zingarella", which translates, "who desires the gypsy girl?". "Chi Vuol La Zingarella" is an aria that is sung by an older gypsy woman in the story and portrays her desire for companionship. She may be old, but she has a lot to offer. The English translation spells it out, "Who'll the gypsy pick, so winning wise and pretty. As one and all may see, for ladies at their window, their fortune I can tell; the ladies indoors, too, I can amuse as well. When old men feel love burning, I set their heads a turning." It's clear to see that the role requires confidence and charisma. To get into this role properly, I had to do my fair share of thorough research on the customs and social norms at that age in Italy, and what did it mean to be an attractive gypsy woman in terms of behaviour and self-presentability. All those aspects were deducted based on Social Direction (SD), which I gathered from previous performances, based on the comments of Svetlana, based on my mother's interpretation and the literature. I remember locking myself in the practice room with my laptop in front of me, analysing every move across the stage of Cecilia Bartoli, who is a mezzo-soprano opera diva. As an aspiring mezzo-soprano, Cecilia Bartoli's velvet voice, smooth as butter, would set the example for me in a technical and acting sense. She would be the first singer I would turn to for a reference on how to present myself on stage in a certain role, regardless of whether it's Italian, as Cecilia Bartoli is Italian. I recall being so fascinated by the lightness and flirtatious temper of her voice that whenever practicing the role, I would visualize her movements across the stage, her facial features, her accenting on certain words and her overall grace. Social Direction is a very powerful tool in the world of opera, as everything is based on creativity and on putting on a good show, which, from the amateur perspective, are set as examples from previous, iconic performances.

Social Guidance

Something also to bring to the attention is that my passion for opera wouldn't have emerged without my parents taking me to live performances in operas and theatres. I've been exposed to such entertainment first-hand since a very young age. Thus, my mother took me from concert to concert, from theatre to theatre, and from opera house to another, even more so when we travelled, and this created a degree of Social Guidance (SG) (Sato et al., 2009). As we know, SD and SG are the two peas of the same pod; however, in the bigger picture, my mother's SG left a bigger impact than solely absorbing what was happening on stage. Each classical concert that my mother chose for us to attend left an impression beyond explanation. I remember watching "The Nutcracker" ballet in the Bolshoi Theatre back in Moscow at around New Years' time and leaving the theatre with a magical, glowing feeling in my chest, as if it was full of shimmering sparkles. I also remember attending Georges Bizet's 1875 opera comique "Carmen" in Verona's open-air arena on a hot summer evening with my parents and tearing up from how passionate the performance was. This time, the shimmering sparkles stayed. I was growing impatient to also 1 day stand on the stage of the Arena di Verona performing in the role of Carmen in a long

Fig. 3 "Carmen" performance on the Arena di Verona (contributed by the author)

white, layered dress, barefoot, jumping around, illuminated with the stage lights (Fig. 3).

Without these experiences, I wouldn't have even thought about pursuing the path of an opera singer if it weren't for my mom introducing me to this world, for my mom granting me these experiences. This is how her SG set the building blocks of my passion for both being in the audience of a good opera/ballet/classical concert performance and a performer. First, there was exposure, then there was motivation to enter the field of opera, then came the turn for the practicality approach, which my mother also guided me through. With her help, I went through the trial-and-error stage of finding the best suitable vocal coach. Three vocal coaches later, I met Svetlana, who then took over the SG process by taking me to various singing competitions, concerts and pushing me to social exposure. It was a wonderful experience of meeting like-minded, talented individuals, sharing a love for classical music, however, it also had its dark side. Little did I know that the second I began singing on a more professional level and competing, it wouldn't always stay friendly and empowering of each other's talents. There were a lot of moments of jealousy, unhealthy competitiveness and even back-stabbing. As I was applying for the music academies to continue singing but on a more serious level after graduating high school, I caught myself in a loop of doubt. All the years of singing classes, intensive summer courses in the music academies, competitions, and concerts – it was all being undermined by the world I was so desperately trying to be part of. The application to such musical higher institutions consisted of four stages:

1) Interview and a speech.
2) Auditioning part where I performed three pieces.
3) Music theory, also known as solfeggio, knowledge.
4) Another final performance and acting.

In order to continue to the next stage, the acceptance committee had to accept the results of the previous stage. After each stage, the responsible person for evaluating that specific part would get back to me with feedback.

Equifinality Point

As one might have noticed, this part of the chapter is slowly approaching the Equifinality Point (EFP) (Sato et al., 2009). In TEA, EFP refers to the outcome that multiple diverse trajectories can converge upon, illustrating the flexibility and multiple pathways that can lead to a similar result.

To return to the selection process for a music higher institution, the responsible person providing me with feedback after each stage wouldn't miss the opportunity of undermining and belittling my capabilities. For example, after the second stage, I was told all the areas for improvement and at the end he told me, "It is very unlikely for someone to be accepted from the first time, especially at such a young age as yours". I was eighteen years old then. It was the right age to start applying everywhere and putting in the work to develop new vocal techniques. Surprisingly, I passed through the third round after hearing such an "encouraging" reflection. I did not make it through the fourth round, though. By the time I booked my flight to Vienna, the COVID-19 pandemic had broken out. This took a very big toll on the entire in-person activities, including in-person auditioning and performances. Such an unfortunate turn of events shifted the entire industry upside down, forcing professors and juries to work from home via ZOOM, which is very unthinkable for evaluation of vocal capacities and music theory knowledge. The entire experience was surreal for everyone. Everyone involved in the evaluation process was overwhelmed by the rapid technical switch to ZOOM and Skype calls. Something that can be portrayed and presented best in person would lose its fragile pieces and nuances, which could only touch the soul in a face-to-face setting. I had to go start from the beginning, this time, with more challenges coming from the new reality, not only from the world that I was so desperately trying to enter. For the entire year of COVID-19, I was recklessly applying everywhere: Vienna, Graz, Salzburg, Berlin, and Verona. Whether those were conservatories, academies, or music schools, I knew I had to make it work. Despite all my hard work and attempts, I would fall behind. In Verona, the newly included rule of having to speak Italian, although education was in English, was an instant "no". Berlin restricted itself to candidates who graduated from formal music-related institutions, such as music schools, which I, sadly, could not relate to, as I only had individual vocal and piano classes. Austria was the last resort. I believe, in the Trajectory Equifinality Approach (TEA, Sato, 2017), it's called taking on multiple paths to reach the final goal, also known as the Equifinality Point (EFP). The Equifinality Point I had in mind was to be *successful in my career*, which, at that time, I could seemingly come closer to by accessing the field of classical music and becoming an opera singer. During COVID-19, I was spending days in our basement warming up my voice, going over my repertoire, running through scales, and practicing piano. COVID-19 left me all alone, but thanks to Svetlana, well equipped. She and I put together a weekly schedule to compensate for the lack of in-person classes, being of vast importance in the opera world, as represented in Table 1.

To call my pandemic days intense would be an understatement. Although the plan was followed as intended, there were days when I felt low on battery or simply

Table 1 Weekly schedule

Monday	Tuesday	Wednesday	Thursday	Friday	Saturday	Sunday
Vocal practice: 1 h.	Breathing exercises	Piano: 1.5 h. of training: Left and right hands	Vocal practice: 1 h.	Breathing exercises	Piano: 1.5 h. of training: Left and right hands	Presenting the newly learned aria (by heart)
Going over the repertoire	Working on a new aria & piano	Music theory: 1 h.	Going over the old repertoire	Working on a new aria & piano	Music theory: 1 h.	N/A
Cool down	Cool down	N/A	Cool down	Cool down	Cool down	Cool down

demotivated. This mental state was a very common one during the pandemic, therefore, I thought that keeping myself focused on a goal (EFP) and organized would both increase my chances of getting in and would keep me away from falling into the lockdown melancholy. I was not a robot, nor unbreakable, so, of course, there were days when I felt low, demotivated and simply tired of doing the same routine over and over again. This is when the first thoughts about pursuing another career began to crawl into my mind. This was the first time I thought, "maybe opera was not the only path that I would take to lead me to happiness".

Polarized Equifinality Point

This is when I first encountered Polarized-EFP. As Tatsuya Sato et al. claimed in the research paper on Depicting the Dynamics of Living the Life: The Trajectory Equifinality Model, "a person is not the pile of traits and a life trajectory is not a single line connecting the discrete time points which researchers arbitrarily set" (Sato et al., 2009, p. 22). The solid aspect in reaching whatever outcome, whether the EFP or the Polarized-EFP, would be the irrevocability of time. So, what is the Polarized-EFP, and what did it mean for me in the context of singing? A Polarized-EFP occurs when diverse and opposing trajectories or pathways lead to the same result. While traditional equifinality focuses on multiple paths leading to a common outcome, polarized EFP emphasizes that these paths can be starkly different or even contradictory. This concept points to the flexibility and complexity in reaching a goal, suggesting that varied and sometimes opposite approaches can be equally valid in achieving the same outcome. In the context of singing, the pandemic shifted my perception of how I'd get into the conservatory. Who would've thought that in the span of a few months, life wouldn't be the way we're all used to living it? The concept of planning was no longer relevant. Never could I imagine myself sitting locked in my house, spending hours after online school in the basement, sweating over my music sheets and rehearsing new repertoire with Svetlana on the other side of my computer screen. I thought this was the new reality, which was a very devastating thought, considering all the plans I had going for my future opera career, but I had no other choice other than to adapt to the new reality. For that reason, keeping in mind all the nuances of Italian music institutions and German music, I began to apply the Austrian technique of singing and performance. On top of having to substitute the technique engraved in me since a young age, I had to make sure it all gets translated through the camera lens. It was still COVID-19, after all, and all auditions were virtual and pre-recorded. The difference between the Russian school of opera and the Austrian is that the Russian tends to favour a deep, rich, and resonant vocal timbre. The Russian school emphasizes a more robust, darker tone, which is especially suited to the dramatic and emotional depth of Russian operas. The tone often has a heavier, more grounded quality, which is particularly noticeable in the lower registers. Whereas, Austrian opera singing, particularly in the tradition of *Wagner* and *Mozart*, tends to focus on clarity, lightness, and flexibility in the voice. While a rich timbre is still valued, the overall tone is typically brighter and lighter compared to the Russian operatic singing. Austrian singers often emphasize precision and agility, especially for roles in composers like *Mozart* or *Strauss*.

In addition to all the time pressure, peer pressure, new singing technique, changes in the entire application process, and living in the unknown, I began to seriously consider going into psychology. I began to see myself in the role of a university student more vividly than in the role of an opera singer, which I wanted to be so desperately for as long as I can remember. I think all I wanted was stability, as it was the most unstable time of my life. It was my final year in high school, and my classmates were sending in applications to various international universities for all kinds of qualifications. Whereas I began to feel silly for helplessly trying to get into the field, which was built on presence, in the moment, the audience was sharing in the auditorium, the magic of here and now. But then, everything becoming virtual took away the magic from the art of singing completely. It was very difficult not to compare myself with the others; it was very difficult to continuously tell my mother that opera is still exactly what I am after, although deep down inside I felt terrible for lying. Again, the moment for rounds of applications was approaching. I was preparing everything virtually:

1) An interview and a speech, which had to be pre-recorded and uploaded to the application portal.
2) Auditioning part where I performed three pieces, which were also pre-recorded and uploaded.
3) Music theory, also known as solfeggio, was tested via an online platform.
4) Improvised final performance and acting translated virtually.

All of this seemed like a nightmare to me right now. I began to go through the round without the slightest bit of enthusiasm. I began to feel fed up with my own dream. This time, I applied to all three conservatories and music academies in Austria twice. The first time I failed on the second round, the second time I failed on the third. The positive emails that came after each round were giving me hope and motivation again but failing for the second year in a row felt like backstabbing. After the final, third application to the music academy in Vienna, I got a conditional acceptance, which stated that I could only get a chance of securing a spot if I completed a foundational year. I remember thinking to myself, "Finally some progress". And even though, in 2021, no one still knew the format of classes and courses, if they were to be held online, in-person or 50/50, it felt good that the change was happening. I got out of the locked house, the draining routine in the basement, I graduated from high school and moved to Vienna. I moved closer to my EFP *to being happy*.

Upon my arrival in Vienna, the courses were structured 50/50. Music theory and individual vocal classes were in person, language, acting, and classical music history were held virtually. For the first 2 months, I had a stable academic schedule. After my classes, I rented out a music room to improve in the areas that my new vocal coach, Katarina, advised me to work on. Katarina was a professional and a perfectionist. She has a perfect approach to my voice and how to refine it according to the Austrian school of opera; however, on a personal level, her and I never clicked. In opera, especially in a private setting, personal connection is of extreme importance. However, Katarina only saw me as a mechanical doll, something that I really didn't like. In the third month of my courses, another wave of COVID-19 began, involving more challenges and difficulties. QR codes, 100% virtual classes, no option of renting out a practice room, without even mentioning competing and performing. Yet again, life froze before even getting the chance to defrost after the first lockdown.

At that time, I had arrived at a point where I decided to get out of my comfort zone and materialize the thoughts I had during COVID-19 at home – apply for a bachelor's in psychology. I was always interested in psychology, especially in the changes a human goes to under stress, the behavioural patterns and the influence of the environment the person grew up in on their development. I read lots of books, both psychological and self-help, listened to various podcasts, analysed people and their behaviour, consequently questioning it. I also really enjoyed sharing my observations with my mother, since she was also quite a fan of psychology as a discipline. It just never occurred to her that I could be interested in something other than opera. That's why, when I revealed the news to her, the first reaction was expected. My mother was in denial. She refused to acknowledge my reasons for putting opera on hold and me trying out something new, something that felt more right for me to pursue at that time. I remember her not believing what I was saying, completely minimizing the situation, claiming, "you are just demotivated again, it will go away". But it didn't feel like another wave of demotivation, it felt like the actual change was needed. If I completely wanted to be happy, I needed to enjoy what I was doing, and opera wasn't cutting it for me then. As much as Vienna is the capital of classical music, it was also the origin of psychoanalysis. From there on, I began my research, but this time alone, as my mother refused to help me, she said, "In that case, figure it out on your own what you want and where you want to be, and once you do, we will see". Therefore, I came up with a new action plan. The first step was to create a list of potential universities in Austria where I saw myself studying psychology. The program had to be held in English, since my command of the German language was not enough for studying psychology in academic German. This is how

I ended up at my current university. Nonetheless, finding it was not enough, as there was also an application process to be completed. As this may be the new trajectory, the goal or the BFP remained the same, and I was motivated all over again. I felt the thrill of excitement. I felt unstoppable, even though the challenge was to get accepted in the first place. After submitting my application, I remember receiving an email where I'm being asked to provide grades in my high school transcript for biology and statistics – the two courses I never took. The university offered intensive summer courses in both biology and statistics to prepare the prospective students for the entry exam. The challenge was scaring me a little, but paradoxically, making the program even more desirable. I was in for the ride. I remember reading the textbook provided for the two subjects in the spring, taking notes and running mock tests at the end of each chapter. I am an advocate that hard work always pays off. I also remember updating my father (since my mom wasn't yet ready to know about the status of my newly chosen path) and him saying, "Anya, I'm not sure you will be able to acquire 2 years' worth of material in a few months, but you can try". For some reason, it had the opposite effect on feeling discouraged. Now I felt like I needed and wanted to prove to myself I can overcome all the challenges on the way, I can get into the program and be one of the most driven students in class, making the most of the education I will be provided with. I am a visual learner, which means that if I can imagine myself doing something, I am certainly getting it. I could clearly see myself studying at my current university and being one of the nerdiest students, which I am now.

Up until the summer intensive courses, I was very dedicated to catching up on the material that would be taught to us. I wanted to be prepared. By the time the courses began, I had read the two textbooks and worked through numerous exercises, so the content taught to us in the classroom wasn't new to me. Two intense weeks later, I successfully wrote the exams and was admitted to the bachelor's in psychology degree.

Reaching BFP

In the following September, the first lectures began. I remember how great a feeling it was—I felt stable, my mother was finally realizing that this was the best choice I could've made for myself, my father was impressed with the hard work, but most importantly, I loved studying psychology. I could finally feel good about being consistent with my new goal. Or my adjusted goal. Now, I am in my last year of bachelor's degree, doing an exchange year in Italy with a clear vision of what I want to do after I graduate. I think that this chapter, in the context of TEA, is to highlight that there is no single "correct" path to a given outcome or goal. People may experience different challenges, different trajectories from what they initially thought, or, on the contrary, follow distinct trajectories, still ending up achieving the same result. This is the chapter where I break down the reason why the chosen trajectory was not to sing, but rather to go after my genuine desire—studying psychology, and thus, to be happy in my life.

Conclusion

Tracing my path through the Trajectory Equifinality Approach (Sato et al., 2009), clarifies that the question was never simply *to sing or not to sing*, but how a life becomes oriented towards a meaningful end goal under shifting and changing paths. My opera journey unfolded through repeated Bifurcation Points- technical choices, auditions, masterclasses; within fields of Social Direction and Social Guidance shaped by teachers, family, and famous opera divas serving as role models. The pandemic redirecting my route through a Polarized Equifinality Point: diverging practices (at-home rehearsals, virtual auditions, adopting a completely foreign singing technique) and then a decisive, yet unexpected turn towards psychology. TEA's insistence on the irreversibility of time helps explain why "starting over" was not crossing over the past, but continuation. It was another trajectory towards the same Equifinality Point I ultimately sought: a sustainable form of fulfilment and growth—to be happy. Autoethnographically (Ellis & Bochner, 2000), this chapter shows how personal narrative is not anecdote but evidence of culturally patterned development. Opera did not disappear from my life; it simply took a different meaning, a different form in my life. The journey demonstrates that there are many legitimate paths to artistry and the personal end destination, and that choosing differently can still mean arriving, fully, at one's chosen end.

Appendix

Figure 3 *"Carmen" performance on the Arena di Verona* was generated using an AI tool OpenArt.ai

Additionally, ChatGPT 5.0 version was implemented in creation and alphabetical sorting of APA 7 style citations.

References

Ellis, C., & Bochner, A. P. (2000). Autoethnography, personal narrative, reflexivity: Researcher as subject. In N. K. Denzin & Y. S. Lincoln (Eds.), *Handbook of qualitative research* 2nd ed. pp. 733–768. Sage.

Hirose, M., & Creswell, J. W. (2025). An intersected mixed methods design: Using the Trajectory Equifinality Approach as a qualitative methodology in mixed methods research. *Annals of Mixed Methods Research, 4*(2), 469–484. https://doi.org/10.51108/ammr.4.2_469

Sato, T., Hidaka, T., & Fukuda, M. (2009). Depicting the dynamics of living the life: The Trajectory Equifinality Model. In J. Valsiner, P. C. M. C. Molenaar, M. C. D. P. Lyra, & N. Chaudhary (Eds.), *Dynamic process methodology in the social and developmental sciences* (pp. 217–240). Springer.

Sato, T. (2017). *Collected Papers on Trajectory Equifinality Approach.* Chitose Press.

hana-TEM, Exploring Life Trajectories Beyond Verbalization: Expansion of Trajectory Equifinality Modeling and Development of a New Method Using Natural Objects

Taeko Kamikawa, Teppei Tsuchimoto, Nozomi Kato, Akiyo Nakamoto, and Fuminori Nakatsubo

Hana-TEM Hana-TEM expressing a general life trajectory (by the authors)

T. Kamikawa (✉)
Soka University, Tokyo, Japan

T. Tsuchimoto
Eminent Associate Professor, Research Organization of Open Innovation & Collaboration, Ritsumeikan University, Kyoto, Japan

N. Kato
Fukuyama City University, Hiroshima, Japan

A. Nakamoto
Konan Women's University, Hyogo, Japan

F. Nakatsubo
Hiroshima University, Hiroshima, Japan

M. A. Campill et al. (eds.), *New Paths in Trajectory Equifinality Modelling*, Theory and History in the Human and Social Sciences,
https://doi.org/10.1007/978-3-032-25855-7_20

Introduction

Understanding human development and life trajectories is a crucial challenge in various academic fields, including psychology, sociology, and education. Trajectory Equifinality Modeling (TEM) has evolved as a qualitative research method to address this challenge (Yasuda & Sato, 2023). TEM is characterized by its ability to depict multilinear pathways leading to Equifinality Points (EFP) while considering individual choices and social influences.

TEA (Trajectory Equifinality Approach) is a qualitative research method that "depicts the process by which individuals who have received life maintain their lives within their environment, live their daily lives, and fulfill their life journeys while incorporating signs (Sato, 2015)." TEA is composed of three methodologies. Firstly, "Historically Structured Inviting (HSI)" for selecting research collaborators. Secondly, "Trajectory Equifinality Modeling (TEM)"which visualizes life pathways based on irreversible time. Thirdly, "Three Layers Model of Genesis (TLMG)" which understands individual internal transformation processes through three layers: the "action level," "signs level," and "values/beliefs level."

While conventional TEM relies primarily on verbal expressions to describe life trajectories, hana-TEM aims to transcend the limitations of verbalization by utilizing natural objects (such as flowers and stones). This method is designed to enable richer expression of the "ambiguity" and "complexity" inherent in life trajectories, making it accessible even to those who struggle with verbal expression. Furthermore, artistic expressions are expected to promote self-reflection and deepen dialogue between oneself and others.

Flowers are important objects that embody both symbolic and aesthetic meanings, possessing deeply personal as well as social characteristics. In Japanese culture particularly, while cherry blossoms are often said to represent ephemeral beauty and the impermanence of life, there is a widely shared view that cherry blossoms have been associated with "feminine" imagery since ancient times (Nakamoto, 2023). Additionally, the word "kachōfūgetsu" (花鳥風月), which encapsulates ways of appreciating and enjoying landscapes, incorporates "flower" (花), making it a familiar term that evokes Japan's natural aesthetic sensibilities.

On a personal level, specific flowers create emotional connections through memory. For example, flowers that bloomed in one's mother's garden, bouquets received from a first love, or flowers offered at funerals form each individual's unique world of meaning. On a social level, flowers function as shared symbols in gift-giving, celebrations, and ceremonies, serving as media used in people's shared communication. In this way, flowers can be considered special entities that bridge both extremely private experiences and culturally shared meaning systems. In other words, hana-TEM represents a significant methodological advancement in understanding and reconstructing individual subjective experiences.

The hana-TEM was initiated through workshops titled "hana-TEM: Drawing My Trajectory Through Art" conducted at TEA and the Japanese Association of TEA for Qualitative Inquiry in June 2023 and May 2024, where its potential has been explored. Therefore, this study proposes hana-TEM as a new method that incorporates non-verbal expressions while maintaining the foundational concepts of TEM. The objectives of this study are twofold.

1. To explore the experiential processes and insights generated through hana-TEM.
2. To explore the potential academic contributions of hana-TEM.

Theoretical Background

Tsuchimoto et al. (2024) identified four theoretical foundations for hana-TEM. To begin with, the theoretical foundation of hana-TEM lies in understanding and expressing experiences that are difficult to verbalize during development. The concept of "hyper-generalized affective semiotic field" proposed by Valsiner (Valsiner 2014; Valsiner et al. 2023) demonstrates that such "beyond language" domains are critically important in shaping the future. This semiotic field encompasses sensory and emotional experiences prior to verbalization and serves as a crucial driving force in human development.

Secondly, to overcome the limitations of conventional TEM, which relies primarily on linguistic data, hana-TEM integrates multiple theoretical approaches. Among these, it adopts the expression method using natural objects, drawing inspiration from the "lifeline" concept of Narrative Exposure Therapy (NET; Schauer et al., 2011/2023). In NET, a single string represents the flow of life, with flowers (representing happy events and good times) and stones (representing traumatic events) placed along it to visualize important life-turning points and changes. However, hana-TEM develops this further, maintaining TEM's concept of multilinearity while enabling freer expression.

Thirdly, a characteristic feature is the adoption of Composition Work theory (Konopka & van Beers, 2014), leaving the meaning-making of materials to the participants' subjectivity. While Composition Work expresses self-identity using multiple stones based on dialogical self theory, hana-TEM expands this idea, enabling a richer depiction of individual experiential worlds through the broader use of natural objects. Through this process, participants could reinterpret their experiences and discover new meanings.

Finally, the theoretical framework of the intermodal pre-construction (IMPreC) method proposed by Valsiner et al. (2023) clarifies hana-TEM's methodological positioning. IMPreC Methods emphasize avoiding excessive generalization and simplification through language, while maintaining the multilayered nature and richness of experience. Based on this theoretical position, hana-TEM enables the visual and tactile expression of existential experiences and emotions that are difficult to verbalize using concrete materials such as natural objects.

In addition to these references, this study suggests that Obeyesekere's concept of symbolic relocation provides important insights into the theoretical characteristics of hana-TEM. This concept represents a set of infinite possibilities for symbolic substitution, creating a foundation for flexible adaptation to new contexts (Valsiner, 2014). In hana-TEM, participants expressed their experiences using natural and artificial objects, a process that can be understood as symbolic relocation. Materials such as flowers and stones are flexibly assigned meanings as symbols expressing individual experiences and emotions and are interpreted in new contexts. Related to this point, Valsiner (2014) notes that culturally functional spaces are characterized by hypergeneralized signs that anchor the sensations of people in those spaces in identifiable ways. The expressive space created by hana-TEM functions as a culturally functional space. The materials placed by the participants generate layered meanings that, while invisible in the environment itself, are retained in the memories of both creators and observers. Thus, hana-TEM can be positioned as a methodology that goes beyond mere visual expression, providing a space for new meaning generation through symbolic relocation and enabling the expression and understanding of experiences in hypergeneralized semiotic fields.

Method of hana-TEM Analysis in this Study

This study analyzed hana-TEM creation process and completed works of four participants (Akiyo, Nozomi, Taeko, and Teppei). These participants, all members of the Research Exchange Committee of TEA and the Japanese Association of TEA for Qualitative Inquiry, visualized their life trajectories through hana-TEM, focusing on themes such as “recent concerns” or “sources of conflict” in their daily lives. The creation process was carried out privately by each participant, who used natural objects such as flowers and stones to represent their experiences. Upon completion, participants shared explanations of their works and engaged in discussions on the insights and reflections gained through the hana-TEM process. We position the four cases presented here as demonstrations. Moreover, providing examples of workshop creators’ personal experiential expressions helps participants grasp the atmosphere of hana-TEM and understand our original intentions.

Case Studies of hana-TEM

This section examines the “Reason for the selection” of materials and the “Overview of the Trajectory“through both the creation process and completed works of hana-TEM by four participants (Akiyo, Nozomi, Taeko, and Teppei).

Akiyo’s Example

This hana-TEM represents my process of coming to terms with my father’s passing (see Fig. 1).

In early February, my father was hospitalized due to deteriorating health. The stone in my hana-TEM symbolizes the anxiety I felt about his hospitalization. A detailed examination later confirmed that he had stage 3 pancreatic cancer. While my mother was deeply distressed by the sudden diagnosis, my instincts as a nursing

Fig. 1 Akiyo's hana-TEM (April 29th, 2024)

professional (SD) made me anticipate the challenges ahead. However, recent advancements in chemotherapy had given me both hope and apprehension regarding his treatment (SG).

After a period of stability, my father was discharged in mid-March to continue outpatient anticancer therapy. I felt relieved that he could return home, yet my professional judgment (SG) told me that this discharge was only temporary. While I intellectually understood that this was not a discharge to be celebrated, the fact that I instinctively chose a red flower to represent this moment in my hana-TEM suggests that, deep down, I felt a sense of unexpected joy and relief.

A week after his discharge, my father developed a high fever and was urgently hospitalized. The sudden deterioration in his condition was deeply distressing for our family. He was diagnosed with a severe infection, and given the circumstances, we had to consider a Do Not Resuscitate (DNR) order. Respecting his previously expressed wish not to undergo cardiopulmonary resuscitation (SG), we made the difficult decision to allow a natural passing. Ultimately, he spent his final moments in a family-oriented end-of-life environment (SG).

Although I remained professionally composed as a nursing specialist (SG), my father's sudden passing left me emotionally numb. The preparations made at home for his return (SD), his untouched car and cell phone (SD), and his workspace, still filled with his belongings (SD), all seemed to deny his absence. However, as I learned of the many acquaintances who mourned him, I began to fully grasp the profound impact of his presence. Through this realization, I was finally able to acknowledge the reality of his passing.

For my hana-TEM, I selected flowers and stones from our garden. While stones represented moments of shock and grief, I used flowers to symbolize my father's death as an Equifinality Point (EFP), conveying both gratitude and remembrance. Initially, I was overwhelmed by regret and sorrow over his unexpected passing. However, incorporating elements from our garden—where he had spent so much of his time—helped me feel a continued connection to him.

Nozomi's Example

My daughter voluntarily expressed her desire to take an entrance examination for a private junior high school and had been studying for the entrance examination since the end of her fourth year of elementary school. However, she was unable to obtain admission to a private junior high school of her choice. This hana-TEM was created with my daughter 1 month after she entered junior high school (Fig. 2, 3).

My daughter and I drove a little further out of the ocean to obtain materials for hana-TEM. We walked side by side along the spring beach, picking up shells, sea-glass, and driftwood. In the past, we went to the seaside to refresh ourselves from our negative experiences. Flowers were collected from flowerbeds at home.

We placed materials in which we thought our states of mind belonged. The flower at the beginning represents my daughter's rejection of a private school. The blue line following this is my daughter's TEM, and the green line is my TEM; her flower is facing down because we created it facing each other. My daughter managed to find positive aspects while attending public school. For example, the second

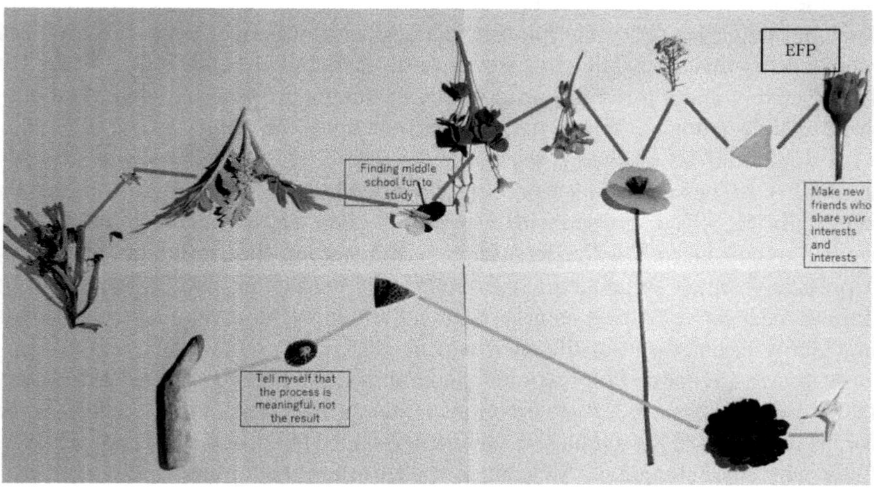

Fig. 2 Nozomi and the daugter's hana-TEM1 (April 28th, 2024)

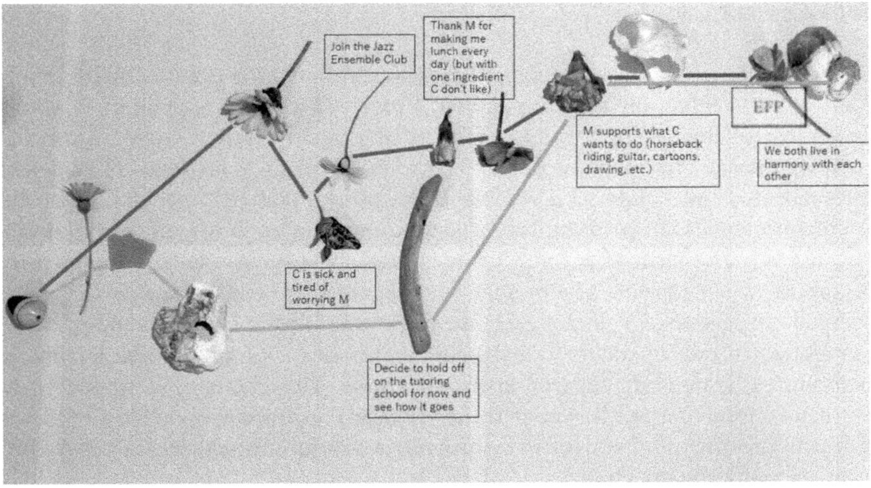

Fig. 3 Nozomi and the daughter's hana-TEM2 (April 28th, 2024)

little yellow flower represents her joy at being able to attend the same middle school as her friends in elementary school. While she tries to find joy in her studies in middle school and obtains a horseback riding license, she has been wanting to try and take trips as a distraction, and the location of the flower indicates that her daughter's state of mind is going up and down in small increments.

On the other hand, I am bothered by the enormous amount of money I paid for the tutoring school and its results, but I am trying to somehow lift my spirit by telling myself that the process is more important than the results. However, I cannot express this sinking feeling with flowers, so I expressed the enormous amount of money I paid for the tutoring school with driftwood drifting in the dark sea, and the feeling that the process is more important than the result with plain-colored shells, which can be found on any beach and which I would not normally pick up. During the junior high school preparation period, I placed a sharply pointed ceramic piece that was probably washed away many times and was not yet in its finished form. In hindsight, I feel that these sharp ceramics that had not yet become seaglass represented our disappointment that our efforts were insufficient.

Finally, when connected by a line, the same events were experienced and the materials that were initially placed separately overlapped near the equal final point. The daughter decided to immerse herself in hobbies in which she had not been able to devote time to studying for exams. For example, she learns to play in the garden and takes care of her hamsters. I tell myself that my role is to support my daughter by allowing her to do what she wants. And I have realized that in order for the two of us to continue to live well together, my daughter is trying to act like an adult in her own way, that the lunches I make for her help us communicate, and that it is important to strike a balance between what she wants to do and what I expect of her.

Taeko's Example

During my doctoral program, I experienced the profound life event of childbirth. In connection to this transformative period, I received a teddy bear adorned with a flower as a celebration of my child's birth, which subsequently became a symbol of great significance for me. This flower later found its place in my hana-TEM, where it represented my family as a notable Equifinality Point (EFP), highlighting the interconnectedness of personal and academic experiences in my scholarly journey (see Fig. 4). The birth of my child was by caesarean section (BFP), marking the beginning of my journey as a mother while navigating post-surgical anxiety. As I pursued my academic path alongside the responsibilities of childcare and research, I grappled with the challenge of balancing these roles. To represent these complex experiences, I primarily selected artificial flowers. This choice was influenced by two key factors: first, the flower on the teddy bear I received at my child's birth was artificial, and second, I sought to incorporate a playful element into my daily life, growing alongside my child.

The people who supported me, as well as my own emotions, were symbolically expressed through various artificial flowers (SG), leaves (SG), and beads (SD/SG). Each material represented specific experiences and emotions within different contexts. For example, the sparkling blue beads cascading along my life trajectory resembled raindrops, metaphorically embodying both the anxieties I faced and the nourishing rainfall essential for my personal and professional growth (SD/SG). Through this process of visualizing my experiences in hana-TEM, initial perceptions of hardship and anxiety transformed into sources of new meaning and insight.

Upon completing my composition, I made an unexpected discovery—I had incorporated more flowers than stones, contrary to my initial expectations. This realization, which emerged organically through the hana-TEM process, profoundly

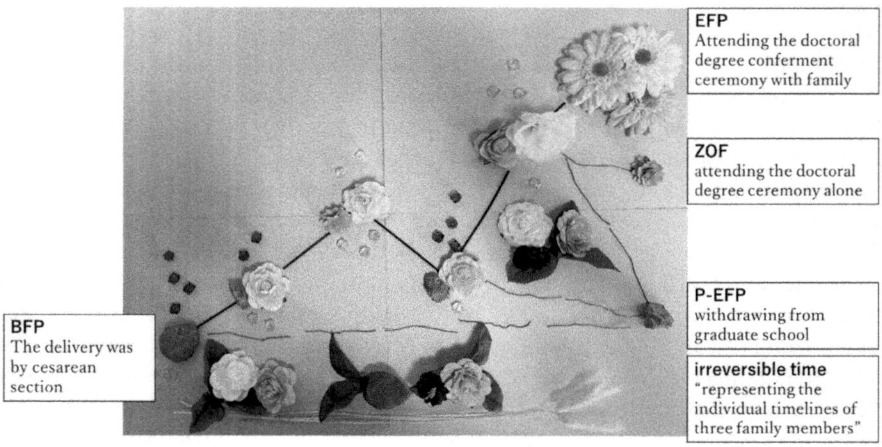

Fig. 4 Taeko's hana-TEM (March 21st, 2024)

impacted me. I could visually confirm that experiences I had once perceived as overwhelming challenges also encompassed numerous opportunities for joy and personal development. This newfound perspective reinforced my confidence in the choices I made during my doctoral studies while simultaneously navigating childbirth and parenthood. It also deepened my gratitude toward those who supported me. Among the possible paths—attending my doctoral degree ceremony alone (ZOF) or withdrawing from graduate school (P-EFP)—I ultimately achieved my most deeply desired outcome: attending the ceremony with my family (EFP). This realization brought me profound joy and fulfilment.

My hana-TEM encapsulated the complexity and richness of life trajectories through the soft medium of artificial flowers—originating from the teddy bear gifted to me upon my child's birth. It vividly expressed the dual challenges of doctoral research and childcare, paralleling a child's development through both play and learning while navigating difficulties along the way. Rather than merely narrating a story of overcoming adversity, this composition embodied a narrative of growth and gratitude, woven from the interplay of multiple roles and lived experiences.

Teppei's Example

The hana-TEM shows strong feelings connected to life. The purple pattern at the bottom left represents my experience with my pet dog, Marron, who lived with my family until he died. In his final years, Marron loses his back legs, becomes blind, and often cries aloud (see Fig. 5). Living far from my parents, I worried about their burden. To mourn his death, I added flowers to hana-TEM in his memory.

The light-blue pattern reflects my complexity and discomfort with certain students. These students did irrelevant things during class or talked to the rear of the room. The shiny stones collected from the sea represent important lessons that I have learned as a teacher through interactions with students. However, the path to these students is hidden by the leaves, symbolizing a path that I might choose to ignore.

The green pattern represents my feelings toward my 90-year-old grandfather whose health has recently deteriorated. I hope that he will recover. I always want him to meet my daughter, Ayaka, who loved picking dandelions in the park. To express this, I added a pink pattern to the dandelion symbolizing the Ayaka. This dandelion carries her message to my grandfather: "Here is a flower for you.

The future extends beyond the leaf path. Different paths were surrounded by dense plants. As an EFP, an orange gerbera flower represents the happiness that one wants to achieve. This finding suggests that another challenge may exist. The rose at the top of the mountain (chosen by Ayaka) represents this journey. This part of the hana-TEM expresses my belief that although my family and I face hardships, our fears and worries will drift away 1 day like dandelion seeds in the wind. My joy is represented by a chain of small flowers. They symbolized that raising children, although difficult, is deeply connected to happiness.

Fig. 5 Teppei's hana-TEM (May 28th, 2024)

Consideration

Significance of Narrative and Reflection through Materials in hana-TEM

The hana-TEM can be expected to contribute to clinical and educational fields as a method for understanding experiences that are difficult to narrate or that have not yet been verbalized by oneself. In this regard, we discuss the significance of the hana-TEM using natural and artificial objects.

When we talk about ourselves, especially if it is a difficult subject, we can gradually prepare our hearts while preparing materials. The hana-TEM can be gradually performed after the preparation of the materials. In addition to hana (real flowers), various materials such as artificial flowers and stones can be used to create hana-TEMs. Therefore, the materials must be selected independently. In other words, we are already facing hana-TEM at the preparatory stage of creating hana-TEM. The hana-TEM created by Akiyo uses flowers and stones from her father's garden at home, which one might infer brings important meaning to the EFP, as it allows her to feel her father's presence close to her. Nozomi goes to the beach with her daughter to collect materials, and Tephti uses the flowers that her daughter finds. In both cases, the creation of hana-TEM through dialogue with the family began with the preparation of materials. In contrast, Taeko's hana-TEM uses processed materials such as artificial flowers and beads. This was chosen as to "add a sense of fun," and it is thought that artificial materials lead to rich creativity.

Next, materials can express feelings in the moment that cannot be expressed only in linguistic notation. Non-verbal expressions include physical, musical, and figurative expressions. However, by using material, we are not required to have any skills related to the method of expression. Of course, even if several materials are prepared, not all may be used, and some may be damaged during the creation process. It is possible that we did not have the correct material to match the image. None of the two objects, especially the natural objects, had exactly the same shape. However, we can create a hana-TEM by simply arranging the materials we have and selecting those that best match the events we have experienced and our feelings at that time. If someone is not comfortable with language notation or is not confident in their own skills regarding other representation methods, the material will help create hana-TEM. Taeko used "A teddy bear's flower given to celebrate the birth of a child" for the EFP. Tephythmia depicts the "act" of flowers passing from his daughter to his grandfather. Thus, each hana-TEM is an original expression of the creator's own feelings because the materials used are assigned meanings based on the creator's feelings. We create objects of hypergeneralized value throughout our life course (Valsiner, 2014, 2024). Natural and artificial objects with no special meaning became valuable objects for each individual in the process of creating hana-TEM, and we thought we could express the complexity and richness of the hypergeneralized affective semiotic field depending on the material in which they were placed.

Additionally, reflection through hana-TEM allows one to become aware of one's own emotions, even if they are chaotic, by arranging materials. The hana-TEM is not created with an image of its final form in mind from the beginning but is formed through self-reflection during the creative process. In the process of creating Akiyo's hana-TEM, she was aware of feelings she was not aware of by "suddenly picking up a flower in her hand." Taeko also explained that her feelings changed due to "new discoveries" when she completed hana-TEM. We presume that this occurs often during the process of creating a hana-TEM. The process of finding new meanings can be seen as a dynamic movement in which nonverbal symbols generate new emotions from a hypergeneralized affective semiotic field (Valsiner, 2014, 2024). In addition, it would be captured through reflections.

Thus, hana-TEM is expected to contribute to the clinical and educational fields. For example, in the field of early childhood education and care, it may be possible to listen to a subject who is too young to speak fluent or who does not want to speak by understanding her feelings through hana-TEM. In the field of nursing, we also thought that it could be used as a care activity for the elderly and mentally ill subjects. Furthermore, as a research method, the hana-TEM would be beneficial as an interview technique for participants who have difficulty with verbal communication.

Natural Objects as Gegenstand for Depicting Past Experiences

Theoretically, hana-TEM can be understood as an individual's act of creating a new *Umwelt*. Umwelt refers to the subjective semiotic world of meaning for an organism (Uexküll, 2010; Kull, 1998). Each of us constructs its own subjective environment, *Umwelt*. The experience of hana-TEM can be considered an act of creating a new *Umwelt* that is similar to, yet distinct from, past *Umwelten*. Here, the similarity between past experiences and those depicted in the hana-TEM is crucial (Fig. 6).

Such similarities include emotional (qualities of joy, anxiety, etc.), physical (bodily movements, postures, and physical memories), relational (patterns of interaction with others), and meaning-making (interpretations and valuations of experience). These similarities function as a scaffold for reinterpreting past experiences and discovering new meanings. This similarity is also reflected in the selection and arrangement of the materials. Richer expression becomes possible when the quality of experience resonates with the physical properties of materials such as stones and flowers.

The small semiotic world constructed as a hana-TEM naturally differs from its actual experience. While subjects can directly access the experience itself, when expressing it using signs like flowers and stones, these objects are not "the past events themselves." Furthermore, when attempting to express an event, it can be depicted using multiple symbols (symbolic removal). Nevertheless, in the hana-TEM process, when someone sensually selects a flower, that flower becomes a

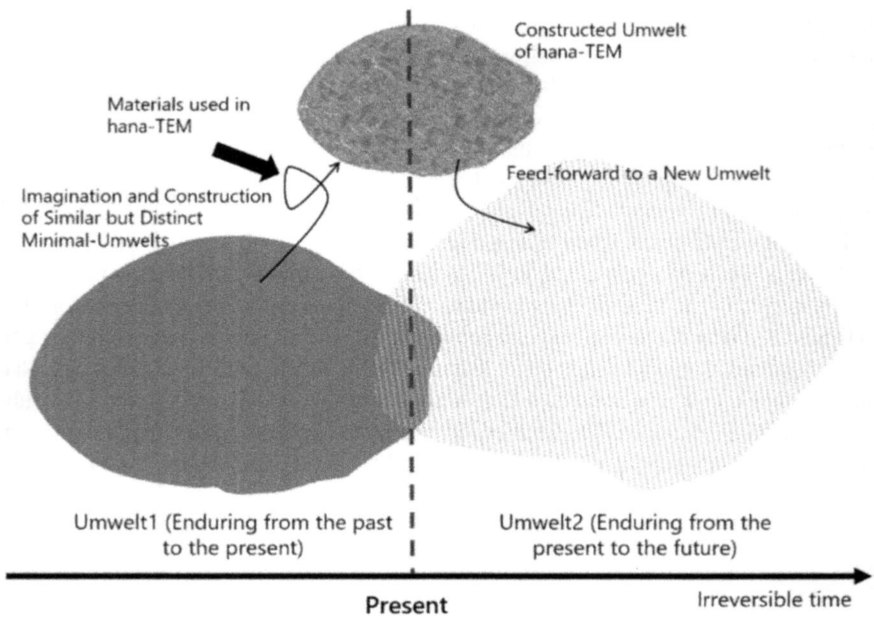

Fig. 6 Mutual-feeding between hana-TEM and past Umwelt

unique object with an affective flavor representing "my experience at that time, in that place."

Moreover, such sensations arise not only from individual living processes, but also from historical and collective contexts. For instance, the act of arranging stones in hana-TEM may evoke the historical context of Japanese garden designs. When selecting an object from among several natural objects, the object's symbolic meaning and history emerge. This was clearly demonstrated in the present study. In Teppei's case, roses were placed in areas related to loved ones (grandfather and daughter) because they symbolize "love." In Akiyo's case, the collective context of "stones in father's garden" was significant. These examples show that although hana-TEM uses natural objects, these objects become deeply meaningful to individuals.

How does the use of common industrial products (buttons, counters, and small figurines) instead of natural objects differ from hana-TEM? An interesting example is Taeko's hana-TEM creation using artificial flowers. Here, although the objects are industrial products, their special meanings create a deeply emotional atmosphere throughout the pathway. Thus, even industrial products, if they hold personally significant uniqueness in one's life, can enrich the description of experiences in the hana-TEM. The use of industrial products instead of natural objects is related to processing. Gardening is a notable example of cultivated nature that is deeply connected to human development, where the tension between personal and collective cultures is regulated by transforming natural objects for specific purposes (Tsuchimoto, 2024). In gardens, the acts of miniaturizing natural landscapes or recreating "nature-like" scenery are similar to the process of abstracting and reconstructing experiences.

However, industrial products often have standardized shapes and colors, which makes it difficult to find "one-of-a-kind" items. Considering hana-TEM's function of re-presenting life, natural objects that have no identical copies—or more specifically, objects that allow for "unique" encounters like everyday flowers or roadside stones—might better resonate with the actual reality of our experiences' uniqueness. In Akiyo's hana-TEM, a randomly picked red flower emerged as a sign of a personally meaningful moment. This is the significance of using natural objects in hana-TEM: in the "modeling" process, we encounter materials with various shapes, colors, scents, and textures, and such bodily engagement with materials creates "unexpected" encounters. If contingent encounters with meaningful objects can be created in the context of hana-TEM, the construction will become pleromatic.

From this perspective, the resonant relationship that develops between materials and individual experiences is important in hana-TEM. Whether natural or artificial, the essential question is whether the material connects deeply with individual experiences and catalyzes the generation of new meanings. Therefore, material selection in hana-TEM should not be viewed as a simple dichotomy between natural and artificial objects but rather examined from the perspective of how materials resonate with individual experiences and what new meanings they can generate. The processes of selection and use become crucial for reinterpreting experiences and discovering new meanings.

Methodologically, hana-TEM enables direct expression from levels 3 and 4 of Valsiner's "language generalization" levels. Verbal narratives can reduce the inherent richness of an experience by framing it categorically. Valsiner et al. (2023) proposed intermodal pre-construction (IMPreC) methods as a class of methods, emphasizing the importance of expressing and thinking about experiences at the thresholds of levels 3 and 4, while avoiding convergence into point-like signs through language (over-determination). The hana-TEM enables the expression of individual subjective meaning worlds using concrete materials such as natural objects (or one-time artificial objects), allowing visual and tactile expressions of existential experiences and emotions that are difficult to verbalize. These characteristics position it as an IMPreC method for depicting existentially important individual experiences.

So far, we have dealt with cases in which past umwelts are depicted through hana-TEM. Another important aspect is the generation of a new reality during the hana-TEM creation process. Individuals express their past experiences on a sheet of paper. However, the resulting hana-TEM exists in a different phase from their original experience. Such a hana-TEM becomes a minimal Umwelt that resembles the original experience and serves as a sign that resonates with it.

The importance of this minimal umwelt lies in its function of reinterpreting past experiences and engaging in future relationships with others. While this is evident in all the hana-TEM cases in this study, let us focus on Nozomi's hana-TEM. Through constructing hana-TEM using materials collected with her daughter, Nozomi deepened her understanding of their future relationship dynamics, including "exploring one's own way of being adult-like" (daughter) and "recognizing the role as a mother" (parent). Thus, the significance of hana-TEM as "action" or "praxis" lies in how the newly established Umwelt mutually feeds with other (existing) Umwelts, enriching both.

In summary, hana-TEM is a method for reconstructing a minimal Umwelt that is similar to past Umwelts. Natural objects are meaningful analogies that depict life through their one-time nature. Furthermore, hana-TEM is significant in that it generates future possibilities based on past experiences.

Conclusion

The hana-TEM, grounded in the theoretical framework of Trajectory Equifinality Modeling (TEM), introduces a new approach to understanding life trajectories through non-verbal expression using natural objects. This study reveals that hana-TEM can be positioned as a method for reconstructing a minimal Umwelt, similar to yet distinct from past Umwelts. The unique aspect of this method lies in the resonant relationship that develops between materials and individual experiences, allowing for the visual and tactile expression of existential experiences and emotions that are difficult to verbalize.

Theoretically, as one of the Inter-Modal Pre-Construction (IMPreC) Methods, hana-TEM facilitates expression that preserves the richness of experience while avoiding excessive linguistic generalization. Additionally, it offers significant contributions to the development of qualitative research methods by generating new meanings through contingent encounters with materials and by linking individual experiences with historical and collective contexts.

Practically, hana-TEM has potential applications in various fields related to human development, including clinical psychology, education, and nursing. It is expected to be particularly effective in engaging with individuals who struggle with verbal communication and in promoting self-awareness. Moving forward, through methodological refinement and strengthening of theoretical foundations, hana-TEM is anticipated to provide new perspectives for understanding human development and experience, offering an innovative approach in life trajectory research.

References

Konopka, A., & Van Beers, W. (2014). Compositionwork: A method for self-investigation. *Journal of Constructivist Psychology, 27*(3), 194–210.

Kull, K. (1998). On semiosis, umwelt, and semiosphere. *Semiotica, 120*(3–4), 299–310.

Nakamoto, M. (2023). SAKURA and 'nation' [桜と「国民」]. *The Ritsumeikan Bungaku, 681*, 193–210.

Sato, T. (2015). Trajectory Equifinality Approach (TEA): TEM, HSI, TLMG [複線径路等至性アプローチ(TEA)TEM、HSI、TLMG]. In Y. Yasuda, A. Nameta, M. Fukuda, & T. Sato, TEA理論編 複線径路等至性アプローチの基礎を学ぶ [TEA Theory Volume: Learning the basics of the Trajectory Equifinality Approach] (pp. 4–8). Shinyosha.

Schauer, M., Neuner, F., & Elbert, T. (2023). Narrative exposure therapy: A short-term treatment for traumatic stress disorders (2nd ed.) [ナラティブ・エクスポージャー・セラピー[第2版]] (S. Mori & T. Mori, Trans.). Kongo Shuppan. (Original work published 2011)

Tsuchimoto, T. (2024). *The semiotic field of the garden: Personal culture and collective culture*. Information Age Publishing (Emerald Publishing).

Tsuchimoto, T., Kamikawa, T., Nakamoto, A., Kato, N., & Nakatsubo, F. (2024). hana-TEM: Drawing my path through art [hana-TEM:アートで描くわたしの径路]. *Qualitative Research and Social Implementation, 1*, 66–77.

Valsiner, J. (2014). *An invitation to cultural psychology*. SAGE.

Valsiner, J., Tsuchimoto, T., Ozawa, I., Chen, X., & Horie, K. (2023). The inter-modal pre-construction method (IMPreC): Exploring hyper-generalization. *Human Arenas, 6*, 580–598.

von Uexküll, J. (2010). *A foray into the worlds of animals and humans: With a theory of meaning*. University of Minnesota Press.

Valsiner, J. (2024). An invitation to cultural psychology: A semiotic approach [文化心理学への招待:記号論的アプローチ] (T. Sato, A. Nameta, T. Tsuchimoto, & T. Miyashita, Trans.). Seishin Shobo. (Original work published 2014).

Yasuda, Y. & Sato, T. (2023). TEA at 17 years old: Its trajectory and future prospects [満17歳を迎えたTEA その径路と未来展望]. In T. Sato & Y. Yasuda (Supervising Eds.) & T. Kamikawa, T. Miyashita, M. Ito, & I. Ozawa (Eds.), カタログTEA: 図で響き合う [Catalog TEA: Resonating through diagrams] (pp. 76–90). Shinyosha.

References

Conclusion

The Vision of TEA

Concluding Thoughts

Teppei Tsuchimoto, Marc Antoine Campill,
and Natalie Jancosek

A mythical atmosphere of someone's daily life, made in Kyoto by Campill (August 2025)

T. Tsuchimoto (✉)
Eminent Associate Professor, Research Organization of Open Innovation & Collaboration, Ritsumeikan University, Kyoto, Japan

M. A. Campill
Department of Humanities, Philosophical and Training, University of Salerno, Fisciano, Italy

N. Jancosek
Senior Researcher, Fondazione Jaan Valsiner: University for the Future, Salerno, Italy

M. A. Campill et al. (eds.), *New Paths in Trajectory Equifinality Modelling*, Theory and History in the Human and Social Sciences,
https://doi.org/10.1007/978-3-032-25855-7_21

Introduction

Trajectories, although each one of them is unique and different from others, have one common aspect—their continuity directed toward the future on the axis of irreversible time. With respect for all their aspects, such as emergence, continuity, direction, and purpose, further possibilities lie ahead of this approach.

The vision of TEA is a projection into the potential of methodological value of the trajectory equifinality approach for future use. It is in itself a trajectory with multiple potential outcomes and crossing-points that are filled with Bifurcation and Equifinality Points.

Throughout this book, many ways of emergent trajectories and their outcomes for a variety of instances were explored, allowing for a start of the exploration of this approach and all its nuances. Yet, even at the end of this volume, still the questions regarding the future of TEA remain open:

> What can the potential future of TEA bring us as humans and researchers?

and

> How can TEA grow beyond its current restrictions?

Just like the possibilities and trajectories of TEMs remain open and their directions without restrictions, so does the future of TEA. However, at the present moment already, it is possible to explore visions of new trajectories for this approach that may aid future researchers and TEA connoisseurs in their journey through this intricate chapter of cultural psychology.

In this concluding chapter, we gather four movements of TEA's future vision: (1) the poetic nature of human development, (2) the methodological renewal of TEA/TEM, (3) the challenges and opportunities brought by AI, and (4) the emerging horizons across domains such as art, sport, and culture.

Poetic Movement

Before we shall explore the notions of TEA let us shift to a yet less scrutinized concept that may be found in this volume, called poetic movement in science. The main portion of this movement dwells in the knowledge that unique resonances of our everyday life are poetically constituted—this is the starting point from which we would like to think further.

The term *poetic movement* refers to the dynamic tension between the *literal* (factual) and the *imagined* domains of human development (Bastos, 2016). To illustrate this more specifically, let us turn to an experiment conducted by Werner and Kaplan (1963):

What could you name this figure (Fig. 1)?

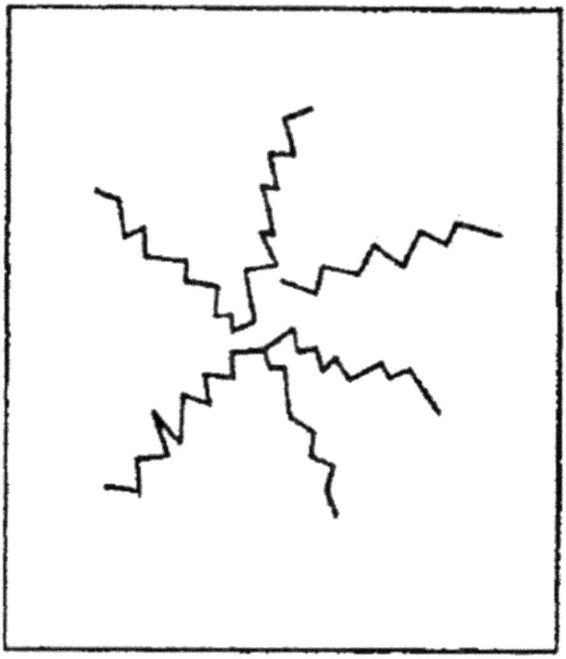

Fig. 1 What could you name this figure? (From Werner & Kaplan, 1963)

Many people would easily respond with names such as "crash" or "broken glass". Yet, there is the possibility for naming it such as "the dance of a caterpillar" or "irregular indentation". Our habitual verbal expressions—which depend on the semiosphere of culture, and our personal, unique feelings that arise from our own body-language relationship—are vaguely but perceptibly distinguishable. However, could one possibly name this figure "the radiance of tomorrow" or "playful water"? Such naming might be logically interpretable, yet to most it would feel strange. This curious feeling originates in the way that individuals connect the literal domain (the form of the figure) with the imagined domain. This connection is not established on entirely "free" properties of the mind. The act of naming an experience (here, seeing or feeling the figure) is at once subjective and inherently social (Fig. 2).

This very process illustrated in Fig. 1 depicts the contingency of life choices—how each trajectory emerges within the interplay between social guidance and poetic movement. In human development, *meaning-making is less logical than poetic*.

The core mission of cultural psychology is to explore how we can richly portray the existential dimension of human life by beginning from this poetic movement—from what is aesthetic in life. Language, while crucial for clarifying meaning, can also frame—and thus dilute—the richness of lived experience. Hence, we must seek ways to describe experience through art, poetry, or performance—forms of expression that are ambiguous yet polysemic. TEM holds significance as a means of exploring the *poetics of life trajectories* through diagrammatic representation.

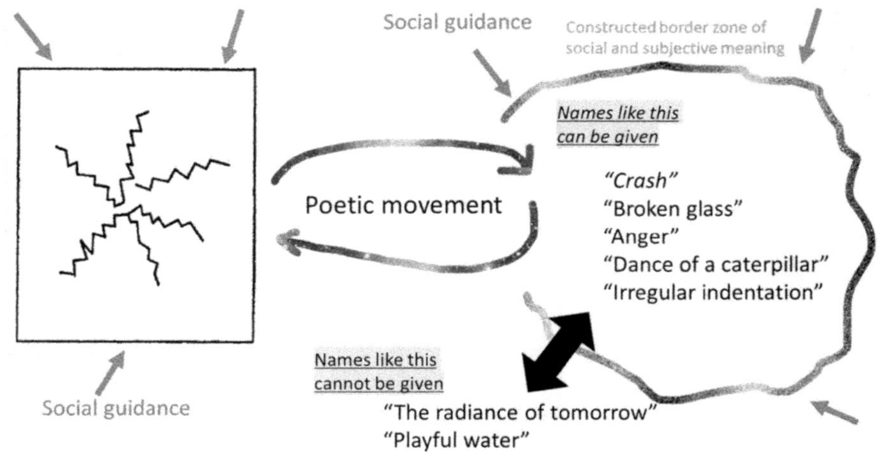

Fig. 2 Social guidance in poetic movement

Having a Cup of Tea

Let us continue now with a simple metaphor that most of us might relate to:

> Imagine a Teabag, let us say a red fruit tea, that glides into a cup of boiling water. Slowly, the water will change, a colorful red will, like branches, grow out of the Teabag and infuse the water. Taking the boiling water along in the ongoing journey that defines the experience of Tea as a concept. It could have been any other mug, any other Teabag, and any other kind of water, but there it is, the unique constellation in front of you. One of many, and still undeniably unique. The insatiable Tea branches, created in the water then slowly disappear due to an overflow of separating and connecting with new, different branches, until the water becomes a consistently red infusion of the fruity Tea that we desired. The taste, nevertheless, might flourish even slower at the time of the transformation from boiling to simply hot water. The connection and diffusion are invisible to us in the already appearing unity of transparent redness. A temporary and still so powerful scenery that emerges in such an insignificant moment of our daily life.

Playground Time

The temporary notion of TEA might be worth highlighting at this moment—after having indulged in a cup of tea. TEA is an approach that lives from its fragility in the irreversible time stream, while the mechanics of phenomena can be approached; meanwhile, the perceived phenomenon of the moment is considered in its instability and uniqueness. Nevertheless, the over-time fading of visibility in the tea metaphor also emphasizes the complexity of phenomena—as the further we shift in the irreversible time, the more options, the more Bifurcation and Equifinality Points appear. So, the visibility and the relatability of the ongoing process become less noticeable.

TEA can be considered as an approach that persists beyond the classical understanding of quality and quantity, as it does not perceive the human as the central subject (objectivation) of mechanics but as the fundamental factor and expert of the phenomenological appearance in its unique Gestalt.

An example of a processual emergence of such a phenomenon might be shown in a simple observation. Here, individuals are expected to join the researcher's observation for a specific timeframe by following the central steps, from initiating the start of a process/goal to experiencing the achievement of that goal. Importantly, participants are not considered as objects but rather as colleagues with expertise in exploring their own life.

Besides the specific role of research participants and their position, it also becomes crucial that time plays a role during an observation in many different ways. It not only functions as a framework to bring the experience in focus, but also the observation and positioning of "when to reflect on the experience". It meaningfully influences how the branches might emerge or fade away. This diversity and fragility of a phenomenon's appearance are both a restriction and an enhancement in contrast to more traditional approaches, as might be found in the TEA — a context in which the factors that support or inhibit the growth of branches are seen as building blocks for new approaches that are shared through transparency toward the own subjective infusions.

Behind and Beyond Classical Generalization: It's TEA

This poetic foundation invites us to reconsider how TEA positions itself in relation to classical notions of generalization. The Trajectory Equifinality Approach (TEA) is unique in its philosophy; meanwhile, it emerges as every invention from the human mind. When it comes to the mind, the infinite and finite nature of meaning-making cannot be called a paradox anymore. The paradox lies purely in our inability to capture meaning beyond the border (rules) that we have embedded ourselves in to preserve. In other words, the aim to overcome borders, like in novelty, is both fiction and reality at once. On one hand, we find the potential to break and reconnect everything that we have seen and experienced, which allows us to continuously perform in novel and unique ways. On the other hand, we have an inability to invent something purely from scratch. While one infinity of potential actions and interpretations is accessed, the other one is much stronger restricted. In other words, the striving for innovation can be extended when we allow other perspectives to be considered besides our cultivated mainstream logic. Nevertheless, the experience of a new variety is fragile, as basic meaning-making structures also underline a certain limitation of the mind. This means that in the most mundane things, we might find an inspiration to think outside our own constructed "box". Nevertheless, that also reminds us that every moment has as much potential to inspire us as to bore us based on how we approach and perceive a moment.

With the TEA, we have a similar phenomenon, while the TEA allows a new approach to a moment by elaborating the shift and potential variation of movements. It also represents a way of generalization. A generalization that is projected differently and is highlighted in its contextualized form, but still represents a modification for simplification. The reason for that is simple: the human mind is bound to the notions of generalization and hyper-generalization, because the essence of generalization is not a process but a sense-making mechanism.

What we call generalization is, in itself, often simply a specific variation of systemic sense-making in which Meta-generalized meaning is cultivated. The alternative term, Meta-generalization, implies here that the generalized meaning is further compressed, for example, through quantitative methodology, in which a previous generalization is used as context to build an even more simplified version of the seen. A system that, from a critical stance, is often compared to linearization. Generalization in itself is neither good nor bad but represents a way through which humans balance the over-complex reality they are embedded in with minimal contextual loss while experiencing a notion of control (a meaningful overview).

The Meta-generalization can be described in the current Westernized globalization as the essence of cultivating classical scientific logic. This is insufficient for the exploration of scientific phenomena that do not fit in purely distorted reality-homunculi. And here we find the starting point for why TEA is a useful tool to extend our horizon by exploring new or different forms of generalization.

Echoes of Meaning in the Ongoing Present

Building on this critique of generalization, we now turn to meaning-making itself, the dynamic semiosis through which trajectories are transformed. As elaborated in the Chapter "*From Vygotsky to TEA: A Semiotic Exploration of Human Action and Purpose*" the cultural-historical semiotics are a crucial concept that can lead to an optimization of using TEA.

To understand a process, we also need to consider the variation of meaning in itself. A sign, and so the meaning-making system behind it, always underlies a duality of being partially shared and personalized. Each experience or goal trajectory has its individual constellation and structure of signs that are cultivated and used to approach the goal in such a way that it feels achieved. The self, the meaning, and even the individual's positioning to needs and goals are not isolated matters, but rather consequently captured in a co-constructed reality in which a multitude of cultivated positionings are colliding. The awareness of trajectories is like the introduction to potential pathways that can support decision-making while also influencing the goal trajectory. It is crucial to understand that the TEM represents a collection of trajectories that might be experienced or had been experienced under certain conditions in a human being. This includes that the pathways need to be included in an evolving process in which the trajectories injected or already persisting are changed by the current interpretations of past and future-related expectations (von Fircks, Chap. 10). The emergence of a trajectory represents the possibility of its experience at a specific moment. Still, it does not mean that this will or has to be perceived by any other participant. It only enhances the possibility that an observer of the contributed TEM might find a hidden trajectory for themself or can retrace their own ongoing paths from a different angle.

How, then, can readers meaningfully encounter this "possibility" within TEM? Autoethnography—or Auto-TEM—offers one compelling pathway (See Campill et al., Chap. 5; Zhang & Kubota, Chap. 12; Koyama & Tsuchimoto, Chap. 13; Fedorova, Chap. 21). By drawing the reader into the unfolding drama of a life trajectory—its ruptures, conflicts, hesitations, and re-orientations—it transforms TEM from a descriptive instrument into a creative aesthetic experience. The potential of TEM lies precisely here: in its capacity to invite the reader's own lived processes to resonate within it.

Of course, any reader who chooses to engage with a text—including those involving TEM—may already approach it with a willingness to empathically enter its world. Yet the diagrammatic form of TEMs often functions less as an invitation to aesthetic delight than as a means to organize experience for analytic purposes. Such clarity has value, but it can also mute the sense of TEM as a project—a performative attempt to explore the existential texture of lived experience.

Here, Bakhtin's notion of addressivity becomes crucial: every voice, he argues, is always directed toward someone (Bakhtin, 1986). If a TEM is a voice, then its task is not merely to display a structure but to reach a reader—to act performatively, poetically, and even radically, as a voice capable of reframing how the world is feelable and thinkable. Enhancing the expressive power of TEM therefore means crafting forms that speak not only *about* realized experience but *to* the reader's own developing experience.

Seen in this light, expanding the expressive possibilities of TEM becomes essential. Visual expressions—such as directional arrows developed within Auto-TEM to render the nuance of decision-making options (Tsuchimoto & Sato, 2024)—suggest this direction. So does the development of hana-TEM, a mode of representation freed from the constraints of formal diagrammatics (Tsuchimoto et al., 2024; Kamikawa et al., Chapter 22). Likewise, Inter-modal Pre-construction Methods (Valsiner et al., 2023), which explore affective feelings across poetry, drawing, annotation, and music, resonate strongly with this movement toward creative openness.

Taken together, these developments suggest that TEM can become far more visual, evocative, and dynamic than the notion of "multi-linearity" typically implies. Accordingly, TEM—as a form of "modeling"—is not merely a representation but an action: a dynamic process continuously renewed through the author's life and, simultaneously, through the reader's ongoing processes[1]. In this sense, a TEM lives not as a static diagram but as an ongoing, co-created movement that reshapes how both author and reader come to inhabit their worlds. After all, possibility is never something that merely inhabits a TEM; it comes into being through the dialogical encounter between author and reader.

[1] For the multilinear nature of reading in autoethnography, see Tsuchimoto (2024).

TEA in the Age of AI: Rethinking Imagination and Nonlinear Futures

Such expressive and semiotic expansions of TEA become particularly urgent in an era in which narratives are increasingly shaped through artificial intelligence—an era in which human imagination meets algorithmic mediation. In the contribution "*Artificial Intelligence (AI) and my future selves: Imagined journeys*" (Verma & Pillai, Chap. 8), the potential of TEA is linked to the current boom in AI research. We have always had an environmental influence impacting our inner narratives as humans, but it has never been as potent as it is at the present time. For the coming generations, AI is a co-actor in their own narrative cultivation. It actively influences the perception of daily life by dynamically framing a virtual environmental context. The multifinal pathways, as visualized by TEA, can be perceived as indicators of a complex, nonlinear reality. The ability to encapsulate such complex dynamics underlines the potential of TEA in an era of emerging AI tools. As the interwoven self-experience between the physical and virtual self emphasizes a change in perception, it remains bound to the same mechanics as before, which can be explored and externalized using TEA. Furthermore, AI's capacity to simulate and rehearse potential future trajectories and pathways allows TEA to evolve into a tool with even greater value for regulating and exploring our potential, as well as past goals and trauma. Here, intense dialogical exchanges between technology and individuals are necessary due to a variety of factors. For instance, AI algorithms represent elements through which the experience of environmental-culture influences our everyday life and, consequently, our meaning mediation. The narrative of the future is a co-authored story, always has been, but the new dialogical partner AI is introducing new structures and rules, which we need to explore and integrate into our methodology, as it simultaneously represents opportunities and constraints for the human being, in their daily life or their position as a professional.

On the other hand, there are aspects of using AI, including in qualitative research, that require careful consideration. Much of the information handled by AI, as well as the mechanisms through which it operates, remains highly black-boxed—with the partial exception of local LLMs, whose processes can be made more transparent—and can be easily reshaped by agents with strong economic or political power. Moreover, its outputs are guided by probabilistic notions of "plausibility." Such issues become clearer when contrasted with the ways in which humans generate narratives and life trajectories.

The model in Fig. 3 is an integrative one that incorporates various concepts related to imagination. Tania Zittoun (Zittoun, 2006; Zittoun & Gillespie, 2016) likens imagination to a "loop," and in this process she points out three important aspects: (1) "triggers" as events that initiate the loop, (2) "(symbolic) resources" as materials that enrich the loop, and (3) "outcomes" as the products generated through the process. If we follow Vygotsky (1930/2002), children's imagination, while poor in symbolic resources, is characterized by a flexibility that is not yet constrained by culture, allowing for the emergence of diverse forms of imagining. Adults, by contrast, are able to engage in imagination on the basis of rich resources, but their

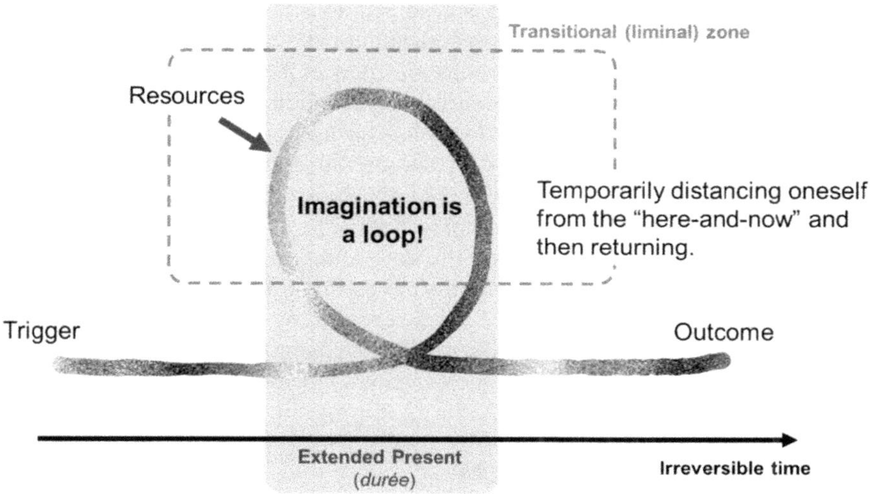

Fig. 3 The imagination loop model (based on Zittoun, 2006, and Zittoun & Gillespie, 2016; incorporating concepts from Valsiner, 2014, and Stenner, 2017).

creativity is often strongly constrained or directed by "logical" or "cultural" guidance. Where, then, should we locate AI?

AI relies on deep learning based on big data, and needless to say, the amount of symbolic resources at its disposal far exceeds what any individual adult could accumulate over a lifetime. Its outputs are generated through probabilistic inference whereas the mechanisms of human imagining cannot be fully reduced to such computational logic. For example, we can associate "TEA" (the Trajectory Equifinality Approach) with "tea," the drink, but AI typically cannot do so in the same poetic, playful way—this is precisely where the magic of poetic movement appears.

So, does AI lack "cultural constraints on creativity"? Of course, AI can generate associations through training or through various forms of customization—ranging from parameter-level fine-tuning to lighter forms of behavioral conditioning such as prompt-based configuration. However, such associative movement is fundamentally probabilistic and differs from the *qualitative leap* supported by human bodily experience and historical becoming. Recognizing this difference makes it clearer how deeply human creativity relies on socially and culturally constituted fields of imagination.

When we compare "adults and AI" in this way, what becomes salient instead are the cultural constraints of human beings. The symbolic resources available to adults are deeply constrained by their personal histories; they are richer than those of children, yet nowhere near the overwhelming quantity available to AI. Nevertheless, the fact that both children and adults are capable of generating magical connections and poetic linkages serves as important evidence that the amount of available information does not linearly determine creativity.

In other words, what truly matters is the miraculous capacity we possess to enact highly complex forms of affective generalization (Valsiner, 2014)—those qualitative leaps through which heterogeneous experiences become meaningfully connected. These leaps do not arise from surveying an infinite space from above; rather, they take shape through the creation of *historical–cultural closures*—forever incomplete—which carve out pockets of finitude within infinity. This dynamic resonates with TEA's orientation toward temporally extending the concept of *Umwelt* (see Miyashita, Chap. 4; Kamikawa et al., Chap. 22).

It is through such closures that new life trajectories, ideas, and artworks become possible. This process—the ceaseless effort to construct finitude out of infinity—is one of the very sources of creativity. Stories generated by AI are likewise ultimately co-created together with a semi-closed world that emerges through the researcher's embodied experience and their dialogical interaction with AI.

The Future Horizons of TEA/TEM

Having explored TEA's poetic, methodological, semiotic, and technological horizons, we conclude with a broader reflection on its future trajectories. Societal development dwells in making the unthinkable thinkable and the impossible possible. In 1903, the New York Times predicted that it would take ten million years for flying aircrafts to be developed (Anslow, 2022). Just a few months later, in 1904 the infamous first flight by the Wright brothers took place, contradicting the estimate made by the New York Times severely. The same was true about a variety of future thoughts and predictions that did or, eventually, did not come to life. AI has been one of them, now expected to become an important part of many social, industrial, and scientific aspects as well as an inseparable aspect of our everyday life. Regardless, human existence and thinking shall hopefully continue and with it, the expansion of variety and possibility for TEA and TEM.

From a theoretical standpoint, more and more interested researchers, professionals, and enthusiasts from around the globe are discovering TEA and its meaningfulness for a variety of spheres. Once an approach almost limited to its country of birth, Japan, TEA is now globally recognized, seen, and used—which could also be proven by the numerous contributions from various fields, perspectives, and countries around the globe. Further popularization might contribute to a wider contextualization as well as the exploration of new trajectories and possibilities for their reconnaissance on both theoretical and empirical levels.

Presently, an important symbiosis of TEA and art was highlighted by multiple research contributions that can be found within this book. No matter if we think of cosplay, opera singing, or other artistic expressions, TEA seems to be a valuable approach for this area. Particularly on the intersection point of psychology and art, TEA offers the opportunity to consider dynamic, temporary, contextual, and cultural matters of art—something that is less prominent in other psychological approaches. By this possibility, deeper analyses as well as the uncovering of aspects so far unseen by psychology may happen, offering many future opportunities for new trajectories.

Beyond art, many more new connections through the use and exploration of TEA can be found. Especially, sport and other active phenomena underline the dynamic notion of TEMs. Sport, as a dynamic nonpareil, was so far observed from reflective or analytical perspectives, not highlighting the aspect of movement and experiencing in ways that are solemnly possible by the creation of customized models—accommodating the dynamic nature of athletic phenomena. Further, the first-hand experience of athletes can be complemented through perceptions and positions of other individuals, who are also actively a part of sports and its communities, such as fans, coaches, etc., as well as it is possible to access the cultural level of such physical striving.

Culture represents a keyword for TEA, as trajectory equifinality bases its foundation on cultural psychology—just as TEA happens to be an inseparable part of cultural psychology and research done in this field. The exchange between TEA and cultural psychological approaches shapes the future of both the discipline and the approach. Either will be pulling the other further and further to new heights and discoveries through their symbiosis and fruitful collaboration in exploration and knowledge-creation.

These expanding applications of TEA also invite us to return briefly to its historical roots. It is essential to recall that contemporary notions of equifinality originate in the philosophy of the organism developed—beyond the boundaries of biology—by Hans Driesch (1908). His work constitutes the intellectual lineage from which the TEA core concept of equifinality first emerged—later receiving different emphases in the general systems theory of von Bertalanffy (1950). The deep analogy between culture and nature that becomes visible here can itself be understood as an equifinality of *Wissenschaft*: diverse scholarly trajectories converging upon shared questions about living systems. At times, we must critically re-examine the disciplined—indeed, disciplined in the sense of trained, educated, and constrained—world of inquiry we inhabit, and seek alternative modes of knowing. TEA offers one such point of departure. Such reflections remind us that TEA's future is grounded not only in methodological innovation but in a long-standing inquiry into what it means to understand living trajectories.

Just like there are multiple trajectories in most finalities, there are infinite future pathways for TEA. Whichever curious researchers decide to take next for their new and exciting ideas, more and more possibilities for this approach can be surfaced and created. Thus, even though we do not exactly know the next pathways, with certainty we know that the future for this aspect of psychology remains bright.

References

Anslow, L. (2022). In 1903, New York times predicted that airplanes would take 10 million years to develop. *Big Think.*. https://bigthink.com

Bakhtin, M. M. (1986). *Speech genres and other late essays*. University of Texas Press.

de Bastos, A. C. (2016). Shadow trajectories: The poetic motion of motherhood meanings through the lens of lived temporality. *Culture & Psychology, 23*(3), 408–422. https://doi.org/10.1177/1354067X16655458

Driesch, H. (1908). *The science and philosophy of the organism: The Gifford lectures delivered before the University of Aberdeen in the year 1907*. Adam and Charles Black.

Stenner, P. (2017). *Liminality and experience: A transdisciplinary approach to the psychosocial*. Palgrave Macmillan.

Tsuchimoto, T. (2024). Multilinearity in 'reading': Bridging cultural psychology and autoethnography. *Possibility Studies & Society, 2*(4), 408–414. https://doi.org/10.1177/27538699241284705

Tsuchimoto, T., & Sato, T. (2024). Career decision-making as dynamic semiosis: Autoethnographic trajectory equifinality modeling. *Culture & Psychology, 30*(1), 48–69.

Tsuchimoto, T., Kamikawa, T., Nakamoto, A., Kato, N., & Nakatsubo, F. (2024). hana-TEM: Drawing my path through art [hana-TEM:アートで描くわたしの径路]. *Qualitative Research and Social Implementation, 1*, 66–77.

Valsiner, J. (2014). *An invitation to cultural psychology*. SAGE.

Valsiner, J., Tsuchimoto, T., Ozawa, I., Chen, X., & Horie, K. (2023). The inter-modal pre-construction method (IMPreC): Exploring hyper-generalization. *Human Arenas, 6*, 580–598.

Von Bertalanffy, L. (1950). The theory of open systems in physics and biology. *Science, 111*(2872), 23–29.

Vygotsky, L. S. (1930). *Воображение и творчество в детском возрасте [imagination and creativity in childhood]*. Gosudarstvennoe Izdatel'stvo. [Japanese translation: 子どもの想像力と創造 (Hirose, N., Trans.; Fukui, K., Notes), Shindokusha, 2002.].

Werner, H., & Kaplan, B. (1963). *Symbol formation: An organismic developmental approach to language and the expression of thought*. Wiley.

Zittoun, T. (2006). *Transitions: Development through symbolic resources*. Information Age Publishing.

Zittoun, T., & Gillespie, A. (2016). *Imagination in human and cultural development*. Routledge.

Index

M. A. Campill et al. (eds.), *New Paths in Trajectory Equifinality Modelling*, Theory and History in the Human and Social Sciences, https://doi.org/10.1007/978-3-032-25855-7

GPSR Compliance
The European Union's (EU) General Product Safety Regulation (GPSR) is a set of rules that requires consumer products to be safe and our obligations to ensure this.

If you have any concerns about our products, you can contact us on

ProductSafety@springernature.com

In case Publisher is established outside the EU, the EU authorized representative is:

Springer Nature Customer Service Center GmbH
Europaplatz 3
69115 Heidelberg, Germany

www.ingramcontent.com/pod-product-compliance
Ingram Content Group UK Ltd.
Pitfield, Milton Keynes, MK11 3LW, UK
UKHW020935180926
475692UK00003B/53

* 9 7 8 3 0 3 2 2 5 8 5 4 0 *